Henri Nissen

Noah's Ark

Ancient Accounts and New Discoveries

Henri Nissen:

Noah's Ark - Ancient Accounts and New Discoveries

Translated from Danish by Tracy Jay Skondin, Bruce Steuer,
Dorthe Orbesen and Irene Kjaedegaard. Edited by Anne Clark.
Cover-design: Ben Alex / Henrik Engedal
Layout: Henri Nissen

Printed in China.
ISBN 9788771320886

Contents:

Chapter 1

An SMS in the Middle of the Night

The journalist Clara Wei got an incredible text message on her cell phone in the middle of the night. It was from the Kurdish monutain guide Parasut.

It was 2:30 am on June 2008 when *Clara Wei* was awakened by the familiar bip-bip of her mobile phone. She wondered who would be texting her in the middle of the night and had to check. It turned out to be a text message from *Ahmet Ertugrul* in Turkey who had apparently forgotten all about the six hour time difference, as it was still daytime in Turkey. When she read the message, she was suddenly wide awake. It said: "We have found Noah's Ark. I am standing right next to it on Mt. Ararat. What are we to do?"

Clara Wei quickly brushed back her long dark hair from her face while reading the message over and over again. She was indeed surprised, but at the same time, she had no doubt that the message should be taken seriously. It was neither April 1 nor New Year's Eve. And "Parasut", as she called him, wouldn't make jokes about something like this. She had met him several times in Turkey, and they had worked together on the project over the last five years. She knew quite well that he had a reputation of sometimes drinking a little too much, but he wouldn't lie about a thing like this.

Ahmet Ertugrul knew how many hours Clara Wei and the others in the Sparkling Sun documentary film company had spent on investigating Noah's Ark.

"Take a lot of photos and stay in touch!" Clara answered. And Parasut did so, but he didn't send any photos. He only hurried down the mountain as it was getting dark in the easternmost part of Turkey.

When Clara got to work the next morning at Sparkling Sun after having spent a restless night, the first thing she did was to tell her boss *Wing Cheung Yeung* about the unbelievable text message she had received. The NAMI team was informed at once to investigate the great news. They did not doubt it either.

"Experts had already confirmed our theory that there would be no kind of human habitation so high up the mountain. So when we found the wood, the only satisfactory explanation was that it must be the Ark of Noah," Clara tells. But the important thing now was to investigate the find and have all details confirmed before releasing the big news to the whole world.

Together with Parasut, Clara Wei was charged with the task of arranging the trip for the Chinese team to travel to Turkey. This took place in late August 2008. Although the weather was bad, the team managed to examine two other locations that might also be connected with the Ark. But the weather situation prevented them from going up to the new place found by Parasut. They had to content themselves with the photos he had taken on the mountain. But could they be trusted? The photos could have been taken somewhere else…

Without getting any proof from visiting the location themselves, the NAMI team eventually had to go back home again. It was very frustrating. All agreed to keep the secret to themselves. They had to know for sure before proclaiming to the whole world that the Ark had been found. Over the years many had claimed to have seen the Ark, but it was usually at a distance or on a satellite photo, and when it came to prove it, their assertions couldn't hold.

This time they had to be sure.

Andrew Yuen got interested in Noah's Ark Ark after reading about it in the news in the 1970's. As an adult he founded Noah's Ark Ministries International (NAMI).

Andrew Yuen – the Driving Force

The Hong Kong Chinese had been making expeditions on Mt. Ararat in Turkey since 2002 due to *Andrew Yuen* (or Man-fai Yuen which is his official name). What first made him interested in the account about Noah's Ark was reading a news article in the 1970's reporting that a satellite photo taken of Mt. Ararat allegedly showed a shadow that could be Noah's Ark. Stories like this have been frequent.

But since then Andrew Yuen has been researching as much information as possible regarding the Ark, and he has climbed Mt. Ararat several times in order to find the Ark that he strongly believes must be there somewhere.

Andrew Yuen is one of the founders of "Noah's Ark Ministries" – or NAMI as the organisation in Hong Kong is called.

NAMI is an international, non-profit organisation comprised of those who have a natural interest in Biblical archaeology. Andrew Yuen is the general secretary. Fiona Leung, the only female participant of the NAMI team on the expedition in 2010, is a fund-raiser for NAMI. The organisation has also been involved in the building of a "Noah's Ark" in Hong Kong, a large centre for schools, organisations and individuals to visit for inspiration. In 2004 NAMI decided that a film should be made to document the search for the mysterious Ark, both NAMI's own expeditions and those carried out by others.

It is a very fascinating story spreading over thousands of years. Therefore, NAMI joined forces with Sparkling Sun, a professional documentary film company on Cheung Shun Street in Hong Kong. The manager, Mr. Wing Cheung Yeung, is a media veteran who has been awarded several prizes for his popular documentary series. He has also participated in NAMI's expeditions. But the big job of researching all about Noah's Ark was left to his creative director, the journalist Clara Wei, who had to travel to Turkey quite a lot of times over the following years. She herself has never climbed the mountain, but has directed the projects from her hotel room in Dogubayazit, the town lying at the foot of the mighty mountain. This is where the ark hunters always stay.

When Wing Cheung Yeung became involved in shooting the film, he found that it was an extremely interesting project. But did he really expect the team to find the Ark?

"Certainly!" he exclaims.

"I was quite sure that it must be there. Therefore, we first did the research work. Afterwards, we searched for the Ark on location."

"But many others have searched for the Ark for hundreds of years without finding it, so why you?" I asked.

"We had noticed that most ark hunters were focusing on research through satellite pictures. Others went to Mt. Ararat for a short period of time to climb the mountain over and over again but with no results."

"But your team got in touch with a Kurdish-Turkish guide...?"

"Yes, we contacted the people living on the mountain. Our guide in Turkey was also working with the rescue team rescuing those who got in danger on the mountain. He was, therefore, very familiar with the mountain. He knew the locations that Westerners had been searching for years, and he also had an extensive knowledge based on what he had heard from locals," Wing Cheung Yeung explained. He himself and two of his camera men were among the six people who climbed the Mt. Ararat in 2009 together with the Turkish guide."

Sparkling Sun produced the documentary The Days of Noah in 2005.

Like in The Days of Noah...

"We produced a documentary of approx. 80 minutes in 2005, "The Days of Noah." In connection with that film, the guide Ahmet Ertugrul led us to a cave which he thought held remnants of Noah's Ark. But as it was filled with ice, we couldn't, at that time, investigate it more closely. The very same year there was an earthquake, so the cave collapsed, and now it was completely impossible to examine it."

"But Ahmet Ertugrul still believes that this location has something to do with the Ark. It is in the same area as the new find. You could see something flat and brownish through the ice...," said Wing Cheung Yeung.

Actually, already several years ago the team found a piece of wood at the top of Mt. Ararat. NAMI even published it at press conferences in Turkey and Hong Kong, but the news never really reached the western media who had heard so many stories over the years of people who thought they had found Noah's Ark.

"It Cannot Be True..."

I myself wrote and published in 2005 a comprehensive book of 320 pages about the long-standing search for Noah's Ark – "Noah's Ark Uncovered" was the English title. Robert Michelson, an American professor at the Technical University of Georgia, who has himself been involved in the search for the Ark, was so kind as to call the book "the most comprehensive book about the Ark search." And, admittedly, it did take me four years to research the material and write the book.

Noahs Ark Uncovered was published i 2005.

The result was a very critical book of those who were searching for the Ark on Mt. Ararat. I tried to demolish the many incredible stories that were rampant. I proclaimed, with the help of a Turkish geologist, that the Ark could *not* be found on Mt. Ararat.

Today I have to realize that, after all, the Ark *could* apparently be found there and that some of the many uncredible clues and eyewitness accounts may have been true.

While researching all possible information about Noah's Ark, I have been diving deeply into so many exciting discoveries that will be thoroughly discussed in the following chapters alternating with eyewitness accounts by those who have **now** found an old, large wooden structure on snow-capped Mt. Ararat.

The Book Is Divided into Three Parts:

1) **A historical part** about Noah, the Great Flood, Mount Ararat and the attempts to find the Ark.

2) **The Kurdish-Chinese breakthrough** for the team in the finding of a large wooden structure.

3) **A part with interesting and provocative background material** providing new knowledge.

The culture-historical material and the many fascinating discoveries will show how important it is if Noah's Ark has really been found.

PART 1
THE STORY

This illustration shows a part of
the 3700 year-old ancient Atrahasis clay tablet
found in Sippar, south-west of Bagdad.
The tablet in cuneiform writing tells about a man
Atra-Hasis ("The Sage")
who survived a mighty flood
due to his construction of a ship.

Accadian was the old Babylonian language in Mesopotamia (Irak),
which was also spoken by the Assyrians.

The tablet is now in the British Museum in London.

Mount Ararat seen from north west

Chapter 2

Everybody Knows Noah's Ark

Any child knows the moving story about Noah who built an ark and thereby saved his family and a pair of all the animals of the world when a flood inundated the earth.

For children it is like a fairytale. Adults perceive the story as ancient tradition, something that supposedly didn't actually happen. Liberal theologians have long since denounced the story from Genesis as a myth.

When the news of the new find on Mt. Ararat was known, I was interviewed by Kristeligt Dagblad (the major Christian daily in Denmark) together with a professor of the theological faculty of Copenhagen, Niels Peter Lemcke. Without so much as having investigated the matter, he categorically rejected that this could be Noah's Ark.

Hearing his argumentation, it was clear to all that he certainly didn't have to look into the matter. From the beginning he stated, "Because it is a myth." The Professor did allow, however, that a boat could have been found on Mt. Ararat, but it simply couldn't be Noah's Ark as this was, according to Mr Lemcke, a myth.

It is certainly a profoundly unscientific approach to let one's preconceptions decide which facts one wants to accept. But like the ark hunter Bill Fry once said during an interview on the Danish TV channel TV2, "There will always be people who reject that this is Noah's Ark – unless a sign saying "Noah's Ark" is found."

And even if such a sign were to be found, there would probably be people who would refuse believing that this is in fact the Ark simply because the house of cards of their preconceptions would fall down, and their outlook on life would fall to pieces. It takes a certain open-mindedness to get wiser.

However, when one looks into the exciting historical and scientific material as I have done for the past ten years, you will find many clues suggesting that the account of Noah's Ark was not another myth but is based on a real event. In the following chapters we shall see many examples of this.

One of the first curious facts that comes to mind is that the account of Noah's Ark doesn't just appear in the Bible. It exists in various forms in all ancient cultures. Obviously it is a common heritage from the earliest times past.

Stories Everywhere

The author Clauss Westermann has gathered 302 flood narratives from around the world. Others estimate that there are around 6,000 different accounts of the Flood in existence. The historian Aaron Smith counted no

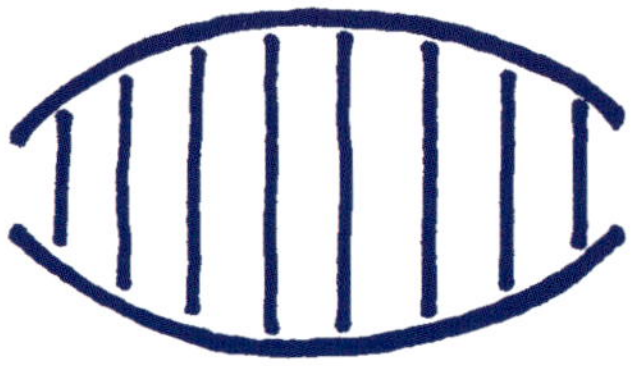

An old Sumerian character describing the earth as boat shaped, and it has eight lines in it which comes from the story of the origin of the Earth after Noah and the ark and "the eight." In stories about the earth's origin in various old civilisations, a "world egg" appears, resembling the boat-shaped object.

less than 80,000 stories in 72 languages that tell of the Flood and about 70,000 of these include a boat.[1]

No matter how many accounts there are, the fact is that stories of the Flood can be found throughout the world in old legends and myths. And most of these include the narrative of people being saved in a boat.

It would be very strange if all of these stories came out of pure imagination, independent of each other. The stories don't have a Christian influence either because many of these primitive peoples didn't have Christian influence until a few hundred years ago. Their accounts are much older. In many cases it has been established that they are 2,000-3,000 years old.

These accounts are, of course, full of local differentiations, but the essence is the same. They all point to the idea that there really was at one time in the history of mankind a great flood.

In the Sumerian account of the Flood, Noah is called Ziusudra (Xisuthros in Greek). In India there is a Noahic account in which Noah is known as Menu.

The Flood According to the Greeks

The Greeks, too, have an account of the Flood in their mythology.

Mesopotamia was conquered by the Greeks around 330 BC. It is not sure if they took the Mesopotamian stories and altered them to fit their own mythology or if they had their own story of the Flood, but we do know that the Greek adapted a large portion of Mesopotamian religion into their own, for example astrology.

The ancient Greek myth of *Deucalion* tells us how this hero brought the population on earth back to normal "after the waters sank."

Deucalion was the son of Prometheus (which means the preconceived or "the extra wise"). According to the myth when Zeus punished mankind by sending a flood, Deucalion and his wife Pyrrha, who sailed in a box for nine days, were left as the only survivors. After the ninth day the box landed on a mountain, Parnassus. The couple then became the generators of the new human family, and their son, Hellen, became the father of the Greeks (the Hellenes).

(The Greek Noah-mountain Parnassus is a mountain chain in mid-Greece with the highest peak reaching 8,061 ft. In ancient Greece it was considered the residence of Apollo and the Muses. The oracular city of Delphi and Castalia can also be found on Parnassus.)

In the Greek account, as in many other older myths, the gods and half-gods play a role in the world of man. Due to that fact, the "enlightened" Western world has considered myths nothing but pure imagination. There is, however, the possibility that real events have been dressed in mythological clothing and changed through the years. Ancestor worship can be found in all ancient cultures and still is practiced in African cultures today. It doesn't take too many years for an ancestor to become a half-god and not much more for him to be given supernatural powers. Thus, a myth is born. This is how it happened with Noah in some of the ancient cultures' stories of the Flood where he is considered a god. The eight that left the Ark have become ancestor "gods" in many of the ancient religions.

The Chinese character for a large ship contains the following three three pieces: vessel, eight, and mouth.
This is a remarkable reference to "the eight" mouths in the Ark. The Japanese and Korean characters also contain pieces pertaining to "the eight."

To Understand the Ancient Sources

In the biblical account, it is maintained that Noah was a normal man that made mistakes like the rest of us. (He got drunk and threw off his clothes; he cursed one of his sons, etc.)

The mistakes of prophets, kings, and other great leaders are told candidly. Therefore, from a journalistic point of view, it is easier to believe the objective, critical story in the Bible than that of the glorified hero and god stories found in other religions and cultures. The Bible is also by far the most well-documented of the ancient writings. Thousands of original copies can be found in many different languages, while most other sources can only be found in limited numbers. Whether seen with religious or worldly eyes, it is in a class of its own. However, the other sources contain accounts of real events, too.

For many years we have had a tendency to assume that the stories from ancient cultures are fallible or fairy tales full of superstition. And we often act as pompous gentlemen based on the value of truth that exists in this era.

For example, every time the supernatural comes into play our scientists give a rational explanation. If a prophet sees something that is to come and it happens hundreds of years later, it is assumed that the prophet must have lived after the fact. The supernatural is shut out because it has no place in modern Western acknowledgement.

If ancient myths are degraded and thrown out in this manner, one misses the possibility of real events being hidden in layers of religion and language.

In this book, we will try to regard the ancient sources with great respect in order to find the answers to the mysteries of pre-historic time.

The Chinese Account of the Flood

Chinese legend asserts that the Chinese are the descendents of Nu-Wah, an ancestor of old whose name bares a striking resemblance to Noah. He survived the Flood together with his three sons and his three daughters-in-law in the exact same way that Noah did. The Chinese character that is used today for the word "ship" comes from a very old character that consisted of a boat and eight mouths.[2]

Among the Miao, or Miautso peoples, these ancient stories especially resemble the first accounts from the Bible. They include the story of Creation, the Flood with Noah and the Ark, and the Tower of Babel. It is quite possible that these narratives have been so well preserved from generation to generation because they are written in a type of rhyme in which accidental changes are not likely.[3]

The Miao people once governed over most of inner China but were driven into the mountains by the Chinese. A missionary, Ernest Truax, spent most of his life among the Miao people up in the mountains. He collected their old accounts and translated them into English.

According to the Miao traditions, it rained for 40 days (the same as the Bible's account), and then 55 days of haze and drizzle caused the waters to rise up over the mountains, and there was no place to go for shelter. The people were overcome with terror. But the patriarch Nu-Wah was righteous. He built a great boat. His entire household came aboard and survived, together with a male and female each kind of animal and birds, two by two. When the time came, God commanded the waters to retreat, and Nu-Wah released a dove (also as in the Bible). The waters receded into lakes and seas. The land was again inhabitable. Fattened animals were offered to the Mighty One, and God gave them his good favor.

The Native American Accounts of the Flood

Among the many tribes there are very different stories.

In the tribal tales of the Cherokee Indians of the southeastern United States, the coming of a flood was told by a dog to his master. "You must build a boat," the dog said, "and put in it all that you would save; for a great rain is coming that will flood the land."[4]

The Tlingit tribe of northwestern Alaska told of a great flood which, driven by wind, covered all dwelling places. The Tlingits saved themselves by tying several boats together to make a great raft. They floated on this, huddling together for warmth under a tent until Anodjium, a magician, ordered the sea to be calm and the flood to recede. [5]

In his book, *Chinigchinich*, Friar Geronimo Boscana wrote, "The Acagchememe Indians, near San Juan Capistrano in Southern California, were not entirely destitute of a knowledge of the universal Deluge, but how, or from whence, they received the same, I could never understand. Some of their songs refer to it; and they have a tradition that a time very remote, the sea began to swell and roll in upon the plains, and fill the valleys, until it had covered the mountains; and thus nearly all the human race and animals were destroyed, except a few, who had resorted to a very high mountain which the waters did not reach."[6]

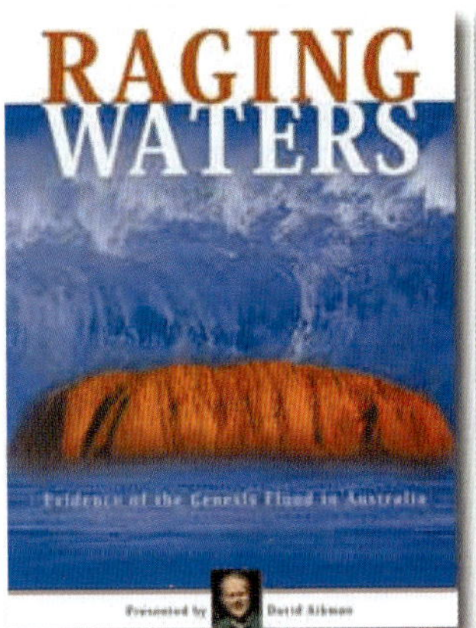

Raging Waters is a documentary video from Keziah Films that shows signs of a flood catastrophe in historical times that transported the mighty but somewhat out of place Ayer's Rock to the middle of Australia's remote desert. Was this Noah's Flood that reached Australia too?

Aboriginals Have an Account of the Flood

The Australian aborigines also had their own story of the Flood long before Christian influence came. George Rosendale, who is himself a part of the Australian aboriginal race, tells[7] that his first time in Sunday school when he heard about the Tower of Babel, he protested wildly, "You whites have misunderstood. The story with the languages didn't happen somewhere in the Middle East but rather up here by Cooktown. My grandma told me our story, and it is just like that there." The grandmother had heard the following story herself as a little girl:

"Our story is that when people broke the laws of the ancestor spirit, He got mad. (The ancestor spirit is the one that created everything and gave life.) He sent a great cyclone that rained and rained until the whole area was flooded except for the top of a hill. The few that made it up there survived, the rest drowned or were eaten by crocodiles when they tried to swim to a safe place."

Many others including the Maori of New Zealand have a story of the Flood from pre-colonization.

Stories of the Flood in All Cultures

John D. Morris and Tim F. LaHaye gathered in their book, *The Ark on Ararat*[8], a list of some of the many accounts of the Flood. The following is the impressive list of over 212 accounts:

MIDDLE EAST AND AFRICA
1. Africa (central)
2. Babylon
3. Bapedi Tribe (S. Africa)
4. Chaldea
5. Egypt (Pharaonic)
6. Egypt (Priestly)
7. Hottentots
8. Jumala Tribe
9. Lower Congo
10. Masai Tribe
11. Otshi Tribe (Kabinda)
12. Persia (Ahriman)
13. Persia (Bundehesch)
14. Persia (Testrya)
15. Persia (Yima)
16. Persia (Zala-Cupha)
17. Syria

PACIFIC ISLANDS
18. Alamblack Tribe (New Guinea)
19. Alfors of Ceram
20. Ami
21. Andaman Islands
22. Australia
23. Bunva
24. Dutch New Guinea (Mombrano River)
25. East Indian Island
26. Engano
27. Falwol Tribe (New Guinea)
28. Fiji
29. Fiji (Rokora)
30. Flores Island
31. Formosa Tribesman
32. Hawaii (Mauna-Kea) Tribesmen
33. Hawaii (Nu-U)
34. Kabidi Tribe (New Guinea)
35. Kurnai Tribe (Australia)
36. Leeward Islands
37. Maori (New Zealand)
38. Melanesia
39. Micronesia
40. Nais
41. New Britain
42. Otheite Island
43. Ot-Danoms
44. Polynesia
45. Queensland
46. Rotti Tribe
47. Samoa
48. Samo-Kubo Tribe (New Guinea)

49. Sea Dyaks (Borneo)
50. Sea Dyaks (Trout)
51. Sea Dyaks (Sarawak)
52. Sumatra
53. Tahiti
54. Toradjas
55. Valman Tribe (New Guinea)

FAR EAST
56. Anals (Assam)
57. Bahnara (China)
58. Bengal Kolhs
59. Benua-Jakun (Malaysia)
60. Bhagavata-Purana
61. China (Fo-hi)
62. China (Joa)
63. China (Tao-tse)
64. China (Upper Burma)
65. India (Rama)
66. Kamars (C. India)
67. Kamchadales (India)
68. Karens (Burma)
69. Lolos (S. China)
70. Mahabharata
71. Matsya-Purana
72. Menangkabans (Sumatra)
73. Satapatha Brahmana
74. Singphos (Burma)
75. Sudan
76. Tartary Mongols

EUROPE & ASIA
77. Celts
78. Druids
79. Finland
80. Iceland
81. Kelts
82. Lapland
83. Lithuania
84. Norway
85. Rumania
86. Russia
87. Siberia
88. Transylvania
89. Wales

HELLENIC
90. Apamea (Cibotos)
91. Apollodorus
92. Aristotle
93. Athenian
94. Cos (Meropes)
95. Crete
96. Diodorus
97. Hellenucus
98. Lucian
99. Megaros
100. Ogyges (Boeotia)
101. Ovid
102. Perirrhoos
103. Pindar
104. Plato
105. Plutarch
106. Rhodes
107. Samothrace
108. Sithnide Nymphs
109. Stephanus
110. Thessalonica

NORTH AMERICA
111. Acagchemens
112. Aleutian Island Indians
113. Algonquins (Manabozho)
114. Appalachian Indians
115. Arapahos
116. Arctic Eskimos
117. Athapascans
118. Blackfoot Indians
119. Caddoques
120. Central Eskimos
121. Cherokee
122. Chippewa
123. Cree
124. Delaware Algonquins
125. Dogribs
126. Eleuts
127. Eskimos (Alaska)
128. Eskimos (Norton Sound)
129. Esquimax
130. Flatheads
131. Greenland
132. Great Lakes Indians
133. Haidas
134. Hareskins
135. Huron Indians
136. Innuit Eskimos
137. Iroquois
138. Kathlamets
139. Knistineaux
140. Kolosh
141. Koloshes
142. Lake Tahoe Indians
143. Lenni Lanape Indians
144. Luisenos
145. Mandans
146. Mantagnais Algonquins
147. Menominees
148. Montagnais
149. Natchez Indians
150. New California Indians
151. Nez Pierces
152. Ojibway
153. Pacullies
154. Papagos
155. Pimas
156. Potawatomi Indians
157. Rio Erevato Indians
158. Salteaux Algonquins
159. Sarcees
160. Smith River Indians
161. Spokanas
162. Thlinkuts
163. Thlinkuts (Yehl)
164. Thompsan Indians
165. Tinneh Indians
166. Twangs
167. Virginia Indians
168. Yakimas

CENTRAL AMERICA
169. Achagnas
170. Antilles

171. Aztecs
172. Aztecs (Coxcoxli)
173. Canaris
174. Cholulans
175. Cholulas
176. Coras (Lowland)
177. Coras (Highland)
178. Cuban Indians
179. Huichals
180. Mexico (Coxcox)
181. Mexico (Mexitli)
182. Michoacans
183. Muratos
184. Nicaraguan Indians
185. Panamanian Indians
186. Rio-Crevato Indians
187. St. Domingo Indians
188. Tlascalans
189. Toltecs

SOUTH AMERICA

190. Abederys
191. Ackwois
192. Araucaians
193. Arawaks
194. Brazilian Mountain Indians
195. Brazilian Sea Coast Indians
196. Caingangs
197. Carayas
198. Chiriguanos
199. Colombian Indians
200. Incas
201. Kataushys
202. Macusis
203. Maypures
204. Orinoco Indians
205. Pamarys
206. Peru (Bomara)
207. Peru (Guancas)
208. Peruvian Indians
209. Rio de Janeiro Indians
210. Tamanacs
211. Terra-Firma Indians
212. Tierra del Fuego Indians

Local Color; The Same Event

Even though the many accounts have local coloring, there is still agreement with the biblical account.

Statistics of Flood stories all over the World

88%	are about a family that is saved; 12% maintain some part of this
70%	tell of a boat that saved the survivors; 30% tell of other types of rescues
95%	only tell of the Flood; 5% also include other causes
66%	blame the catastrophe on mankind's evilness
67%	include animals being saved
73%	include animals in some way
73%	include a worldwide Flood
53%	say that the survivors were rescued from a mountain
35%	include the bird being sent out (like in the Bible)
7%	mention the rainbow
13%	mention an offering afterwards
66%	tell that those saved were forewarned
82%	say it happened locally (often with a local mountain)
9%	specifically mention that 8 people were saved
37%	have coincidental reasons for the catastrophe

A Common Mystical Past

Even though some people lived completely geographically isolated from the Bible's Middle Eastern world, such as the Indians of South America and the Australian Aborigines, they still have their stories of the Flood. Since these stories are placed far back in the history of these cultures, it is obvious that it is not something the whites brought with them.

The most likely explanation is of course that these peoples originally wandered from the same region and took the story with them. The Norwegian explorer Thor Heyrdahl crossed the oceans in a boat made of rush on multiple expeditions from 1947-70 and thus proved that it would have been possible for our "primitive" forefathers – long before Columbus – to cross the Atlantic, Indian, and Pacific Oceans. Since then, many have crossed the Atlantic and the Pacific in very small boats.

Right now new information is being discovered that suggests that the people of the world had connection over the seas by using ocean currents as a means of transport as far back as 3-4,000 years ago. For centuries before our time, people in Mesopotamia were emptying some of America's mines of alluvial natural copper, tin, and silver.[9] They already knew about advanced ball-trigonometry, which calculates distances based on the earth being round. The Sumerians were the first to seperate the circle into 360 degrees. But unfortunately, a lot of this knowledge disappeared under the Roman militant depredation centuries before Christ and was not truly found again until the 17th century by the Europeans.

Our ancient forefathers weren't as stupid and primitive as they are often pictured.

Endnotes

1 According to Werner Keller, *The Bible as History*, Bantam Books, New York, 1980. Sold 10 million copies since 1955.
2 According to Rene Norbergen in *The Ark File*.
3 An English translation can be found at www.icr.org/pubs/imp/imp-214.htm
4 L. Patricia Kite: *Noah's Ark*.
5 L. Patricia Kite: *Noah's Ark*.
6 Boscana, Father Geronimo: *Chinigchinich*, Fine Arts Press, Santa Ana 1933. Ref. CA31291
7 Reproduced in Creation Magazine, see Answers In Genesis.com
8 Morris, John D. & Tim F. LaHaye, *The Ark on Ararat* (New York: Thomas Nelson Inc., 1976), pp. 233-237.
9 James Bailey: *Sailing to Paradise*.

Chapter 3

The Amazing Story

Moses wrote down or collected the material of primordinal time in „Genesis". (See the time table in the chapter: When Did It Happen?). Ill.: José Pérez Montero

Even though the account about Noah's Ark can be found in practically all ancient civilizations, none of the stories are as detailed as the one we find in Genesis. It was probably written by Moses or one of his assistants sapproximately 3650-3550 years ago. He might have had a scroll from which he could collect some information. For example The Old Testament twice refers to The Book of Jasher – *Sephir Ha Yasher* meaning "The Book of the Righteous" (See Joshua 10:13 and Samuel B1:17)[1] It is very likely that The Book of Jasher was a much older scroll than the Pentateuch from which Moses gathered some of his information. Probably Moses also had great knowledge from the Egyptian libraries to which he had free access. At any rate the Jews had an oral tradition.

We Explore the Text

We ark hunters and ark researchers have read the biblical account of Noah's Ark innumerable times and in many translations; we've studied the original Hebrew text word by word in order to attempt to obtain new information about Noah's Ark. Let us mention some of the clues below.

The Ararat Mountains: It doesn't specifically say that the Ark landed on Mt. Ararat but merely on "Ararat's Mountains" – in plural. Because Ararat was a kingdom (Urartu), in principle the Ark could have been stranded anywhere in the Armenian–Kurdish heights. That's why some of us have searched for the Ark on other mountains. The Durupinar Find, the most famous one, was situated on a minor mountain in the vicinity of Mt. Ararat.

The Construction Instructions: "The construction instructions" are also interesting reading material pertaining to the Ark. It is brief. However, the information is very interesting to a ship expert, which we shall see later.

Actually, the Ark has the ideal measure for a ship transporting animal! Incredible! The measure is presented in cubits (1 cubit= 2 feet). However it was probably not the English one. Moses probably used the larger Egyptian Royal Cubit or an even older one. It is worth noting that the cubit measure shrank through the centuries. Why? The explanation may be simple. A cubit is an elbow – a forearm to the finger tips. Certainly, Noah used the cubit of his own time. If the cubit of the present corresponds with an average of 1.85 m, Noah was 2.20 m.

Giants: Giants actually appear in the Bible. The Hebrew word used is "Nephilim." Some believe they were a specific tribe, maybe Cain's branch of the human family. Others imagine they were supermen or demigods. But that is all speculation, which does not correspond with the rest of the Bible. What Moses, in fact, writes is that people in the Pre-Flood era were bigger, and a few bigger people appeared later in the Bible. Later, we hear about human beings of huge sizes, for instance Goliah. The late ark hunter Ron Wyatt claimed having found a human bone (the upper part of a thumb) that was bigger than the equivalent human bone of today. This bone is on view at Wyatt's Museum, Tennessee, USA.

Sons of God: The text mentions "princely sons"" and other translations have "sons of God." Some see here a confirmation of supernatural beings, aliens, and fallen angels.

However, most Bible interpreters believe that "sons of God" in a later era was only the name of the first human generation. The expression "sons and daughters of God" is used elsewhere in the Bible. It can be found in the Book of Isaiah 43,6. *"Bring my sons from afar and my daughters from the ends of the earth everyone who is called by my name, whom I created for my glory, whom I formed and made."* This paragraph obviously refers to humans.

Long Life Span: Other exciting information from the text is Noah's advanced age. At the time before the Flood, human beings obviously lived for hundreds of years. The Sumer table also refers to the pre-Flood kings' long life spans. In an ancient Chinese narrative, one of the characters wails and wonders at the fact that human beings don't live as long as people from the past. So some information indicates that the life span then was longer than today.

One explanation of the long life span could be that people didn't age as quickly because the earth may have been protected from the cosmic rays, which today make human beings age.

According to one theory, there was an ice or steam layer around our planet and either that bubble burst or the ice melted and poured down, thereby creating the Flood.

Afterwards, the rainbow showed, and light and the cosmic rays forced themselves through, thereby making it impossible for human beings to live as long as before the Flood. We shall later return to these exciting theories.

Semitic Storytelling

The Semitic storytelling style found in Genesis actually resembles the journalistic method where the story is often told in two or three circles. The first circle (the title, sub-title, and captions if there are any pictures) is a short summary. The second circle (the introduction) goes back to the beginning and gives a little more information. The third circle (the article itself) goes deeper into detail. If readers don't take this writing style into account, they will misunderstand the text so that they believe the same thing happened 2 or 3 times. There are 3 circles in the story of Creation. The first circle is in Genesis chapter 1, verse 1. The second circle is from chapter 1, verse 2 until chapter 2, verse 3. The final circle is found in chapter 2, verses 4-25.

The circular storytelling also appears when Noah and his family are ordered into the ark. If one doesn't understand Semitic storytelling, Noah will seem to enter and leave the ark several times. But this is how Semitic, circular storytelling works. (Because the verses also have small numbers attached, the words explained in the notes are in **bold**.)

Chapter 6: The Wickedness Spreads

1 When people began to multiply on the face of the ground, and daughters were born to them, 2 **the sons of God**[1]) saw that they were fair; and they took wives for themselves of all that they chose.

3 Then the Lord said, "My **spirit**[2] shall not **abide**[3] in mortals forever, for they are flesh; their days shall be one hundred twenty years."

4 The **Nephilim**[4] were on the earth in those days – and also afterward – when the sons of God went in to the daughters of humans, who bore children to them. These were the heroes that were of old, warriors of renown. 5The Lord saw that the wickedness of humankind was great in the earth, and that every inclination of the thoughts of their hearts was only evil continually.

6 And the Lord was sorry that he had made humankind on the earth, and it grieved him to his heart. 7 So the Lord said, "I will blot out from the earth the human beings I have created – people together with animals and creeping things and birds of the air, for I am sorry that I have made them."

8 But Noah found favor in the sight of the Lord. 9 These are the descendants of Noah. Noah was a righteous man, blameless in his generation; Noah walked with God. 10 And Noah had three sons, Shem, Ham, and Japheth.

11 Now the earth was corrupt in God's sight, and the earth was filled with violence. 12 And God saw that the earth was corrupt; for all flesh had corrupted its ways upon the earth.

13 And God said to Noah, "I have determined to make an end of all flesh, for the earth is filled with violence because of them; now I am going to destroy them along with the earth. 14 Make yourself an ark of cypress wood; make rooms in the ark, and cover it inside and out with pitch. 15 This is how you are to make it: the length of the ark three hundred **cubits**[5] its width fifty cubits, and its height thirty cubits. 16 Make a roof for the ark, and finish it **to a cubit above**;[6] and put the door of the ark in its side; make it with lower, second, and third decks. 17 For my part, I am going to bring a flood of waters on the earth, to destroy from under heaven all flesh in which is the breath of life; everything that is on the earth shall die. 18 But I will establish my covenant with you; and you shall come into the ark, you, your sons, your wife, and your sons' wives with you. 19 And of every living thing, of all flesh, you shall bring two of every kind into the ark, to keep them alive with you; they shall be male and female. 20 Of the birds according to their kinds, and of the

animals according to their kinds, of every creeping thing of the ground according
to its kind, two of every kind shall come in to you, to keep them alive. 21 Also take
with you every kind of food that is eaten, and store it up; and it shall serve as food
for you and for them."
22 Noah did this; he did all that God commanded him.

Chapter 7: The Consequence of the Wickedness

1 Then the Lord said to Noah, "Go into the ark, you and all your household, for
I have seen that you alone are righteous before me in this generation. 2 Take with
you seven pairs of all **clean**[7] animals,[9] the male and its mate; and a pair of the
animals that are not clean, the male and its mate; 3 and seven pairs of the birds of
the air also, male and female, to keep their kind alive on the face of all the earth.
4 For in seven days I will send rain on the earth for forty days and forty nights;
and every living thing that I have made I will blot out from the face of the ground."
5 And Noah did all that the Lord had commanded him. 6 Noah was six hundred
years old when the flood of waters came on the earth. 7 And Noah with his sons and
his wife and his sons' wives went into the ark to escape the waters of the flood. 8 Of
clean animals, and of animals that are not clean, and of birds, and of everything
that creeps on the ground, 9 two and two, male and female, went into the
ark with Noah, as God had commanded Noah. 10 And after seven days
the waters of the flood came on the earth.
11 In the six hundredth year of Noah's life, in the second
month, on the seventeenth day of the month, on that day all the
fountains of the great deep burst forth, and the windows
of the heavens were opened. 12 The rain fell on the earth
forty days and forty nights.
13 On the very same day Noah with his sons, Shem
and Ham and Japheth, and Noah's wife and the
three wives of his sons entered the ark, 14 they and
every wild animal of every kind, and all domestic
animals of every kind, and every creeping
thing that creeps on the earth, and every
bird of every kind – every bird, every
winged creature. 15 They went into the
ark with Noah, two and two of all flesh in
which there was the breath of life. 16 And
those that entered, male and female of
all flesh, went in as God had commanded
him; and the Lord shut him in.
17 The flood continued forty days on
the earth; and the waters increased, and
bore up the ark, and it rose high above
the earth. 18 The waters swelled and
increased greatly on the earth; and the

The Spanish artist José Pérez Montero imagined the scene of animals and birds gathering around the Ark. Did they intuitively sense a catastrophe approaching, like when the animals of the forest flee from a fire, long before human being discover it...? Or had Noah's family been catching the different species overduring several years...?

ark floated on the face of the waters. 19 The waters swelled so mightily on the earth
that all the high mountains under the whole heaven were covered; 20 the waters
swelled above the mountains, covering them fifteen cubits deep.
21 And all flesh died that moved on the earth, birds, domestic animals, wild
animals, all swarming creatures that swarm on the earth, and all human beings;
22 everything on dry land in whose nostrils was the breath of life died. 23 He blotted
out every living thing that was on the face of the ground, human beings and animals
and creeping things and birds of the air; they were blotted out from the earth. Only
Noah was left, and those that were with him in the ark. 24 And the waters swelled
on the earth for one hundred fifty days.

Chapter 8: A New Beginning

1 But God remembered Noah and all the wild animals and all the domestic
animals that were with him in the ark. And God made a wind blow over the earth,
and the waters subsided; 2 the fountains of the deep and the windows of the heavens
were closed, the rain from the heavens was restrained, 3 and the waters gradually
receded from the earth. At the end of one hundred fifty days the waters had abated;
4 and in the seventh month, on the seventeenth day of the month, the ark came
to rest on the mountains of Ararat. 5 The waters continued to abate until the tenth
month; in the tenth month, on the first day of the month, the tops of the mountains
appeared.
6 At the end of forty days Noah opened the window of the ark that he had made 7
and sent out the raven; and it went to and fro until the waters were dried up from
the earth. 8 Then he sent out the dove from him, to see if the waters had subsided
from the face of the ground; 9 but the dove found no place to set its foot, and it
returned to him to the ark, for the waters were still on the face of the whole earth.
So he put out his hand and took it and brought it into the ark with him. 10 He waited
another seven days, and again he sent out the dove from the ark; 11 and the dove
came back to him in the evening, and there in its beak was a freshly plucked olive
leaf; so Noah knew that the waters had subsided from the earth.
12 Then he waited another seven days, and sent out the dove; and it did not return
to him any more.
13 In the six hundred first year, in the first month, on the first day of the month,
the waters were dried up from the earth; and Noah removed the covering of the
ark, and looked, and saw that the face of the ground was drying. 14 In the second
month, on the twenty-seventh day of the month, the earth was dry.
15 Then God said to Noah, 16 "Go out of the ark, you and your wife, and your sons
and your sons' wives with you. 17 Bring out with you every living thing that is with
you of all flesh – birds and animals and every creeping thing that creeps on the
earth – so that they may abound on the earth, and be fruitful and multiply on the
earth." 18 So Noah went out with his sons and his wife and his sons' wives. 19 And
every animal, every creeping thing, and every bird, everything that moves on the
earth, went out of the ark by families.
20 Then Noah built an altar to the Lord, and took of every clean animal and of

every clean bird, and offered burnt offerings on the altar. 21 And when the Lord smelled the pleasing odor, the Lord said in his heart, "I will never again curse the ground because of humankind, for the inclination of the human heart is evil from youth; nor will I ever again destroy every living creature as I have done. 22 As long as the earth endures, seedtime and harvest, cold and heat, summer and winter, day and night, shall not cease."

Chapter 9: God's Covenant with Noah

1 God blessed Noah and his sons, and said to them, "Be fruitful and multiply, and fill the earth. 2 The fear and dread of you shall rest on every animal of the earth, and on every bird of the air, on everything that creeps on the ground, and on all the fish of the sea; into your hand they are delivered. 3 Every moving thing that lives shall be food for you; and just as I gave you the green plants, I give you everything. 4 Only, you shall not eat flesh with its life, that is, its blood. 5 For your own lifeblood I will surely require a reckoning: from every animal I will require it and from human beings, each one for the blood of another, I will require a reckoning for human life. 6 Whoever sheds the blood of a human, by a human shall that person's blood be shed; for in his own image God made humankind. 7 And you, be fruitful and multiply, abound on the earth and multiply in it."

8 Then God said to Noah and to his sons with him, 9 "As for me, I am establishing my covenant with you and your descendants after you, 10 and with every living creature that is with you, the birds, the domestic animals, and every animal of the earth with you, as many as came out of the ark. 11 I establish my covenant with you, that never again shall all flesh be cut off by the waters of a flood, and never again shall there be a flood to destroy the earth."

12 God said, "This is the sign of the covenant that I make between me and you and every living creature that is with you, for all future generations: 13 I have set my bow in the clouds, and it shall be a sign of the covenant between me and the earth. 14 When I bring clouds over the earth and the bow is seen in the clouds, 15 I will remember my covenant that is between me and you and every living creature of all flesh; and the waters shall never again become a flood to destroy all flesh. 16 When the bow is in the clouds, I will see it and remember the everlasting covenant between God and every living creature of all flesh that is on the earth." 17 God said to Noah, "This is the sign of the covenant that I have established between me and all flesh that is on the earth."

Noah's Three Sons

18 The sons of Noah who went out of the ark were Shem, Ham, and Japheth. Ham was the father of Canaan. 19 These three were the sons of Noah; and from these the whole earth was peopled. 20 Noah, a man of the soil, was the first to plant a vineyard. 21 He drank some of the wine and became drunk, and he lay uncovered in his tent. 22 And Ham, the father of Canaan, saw the nakedness of his father, and told his two brothers outside. 23 Then Shem and Japheth took a garment, laid it on both their shoulders, and walked backward and covered the nakedness of their

father; their faces were turned away, and they did not see their father's nakedness.
24 When Noah awoke from his wine and knew what his youngest son had done to
him, 25 he said, "Cursed be **Canaan**;[8] lowest of slaves shall he be to his brothers."
26 He also said, "Blessed by the Lord my God be Shem; and let Canaan be his slave.
27 May God make space for Japheth, and let him live in the tents of Shem; and let
Canaan be his slave." 28 After the flood Noah lived three hundred fifty years. 29 All
the days of Noah were nine hundred fifty years; and he died.

Thus according to Moses in Genesis

So the account of Noah's Ark ends with an embarrassing episode between Noah and his three sons, the fathers of all the world's nations.

In the following chapters of the Bible we are introduced to some of those peoples, who can, to some extent, be identified with peoples of the present.

However, the focus is on one chosen line: namely the line of Moses and the ancestors of the Hebrews.

They are the descendants of Eber (hence the word "Hebrew") Eber was one of Sem's descendants. But Eber's lineage is divided for each generation, when a chosen son – not always the eldest nor the best, passes on the "blessing."

At the time of Abraham, the lineage is divided between the descendants of Isac – and Ishmael – the later Ishmaelites – the Arabs. In the next generation the lineage is divided between Esau, the ancestor of a mountainous people. (The Edomites in the historical Petra in present Jordan) and Jacob, whose 12 sons move to Egypt and become Moses' own people, the Jews, whom he leads out of Egypt and into Israel.

Why This Intense Reaction?

Noah's reaction towards Ham is so intense that there must be more to it than what is mentioned here. A Jewish legend tells that Ham castrated his father while drunk so that his inheritance, one third of the world, would not be split up into smaller bits.

But who says that Noah's reaction was fair? It was, after all, not God who spoke, and Noah was an ordinary human being who could get angry like the rest of us. He had made a fool of himself, and maybe only in anger and in an attempt to pass on his guilt, he hurled his curses at the impudent son like angry fathers have done many times. And have later regretted it.

Whether the curse was fair or not, it looks as if it has turned out to be true since Ham's people the Africans have been victims to slavery more than anyone else – slaves first to the Arabs (Shem) and later to the white people (Japheth).

But Ham's descendants are not *only* Africans but many more peoples – e.g. the original Egyptians before the country was Arabized. Maybe Dravidians and Aboriginals are also of Ham's stock. One of the sons, Cana'an, lent his name to the land of Cana'an – present day Israel and other countries where Abraham went. After the division, it lawfully belonged to Shem and the Semites who according to the Ethiopian *Book of Jubilees*,[9] chapter 8, were given most of Asia while Ham had all Africa and Japheth the North, i.e. Europe.

Endnotes

1 6:2 It is unclear what this text means. "The sons of God" can mean angels, rulers, or men descended from Seth – those that worshipped god according to 4:26. "The daughters of God" could then be everyday women or the women that were descendents of Cain living apart from God. The chosen translation builds on the fact that the word "gods" (elohim) can refer to judges or societal leaders other places in the OT. Lamech from Cain's line was the first to marry multiple wives cf. 4:23.

2 6:3 or possibly "spirits" , or "the breath of life" .

3 6:3 or "continue in" . What this word and verse mean is unsure. The 120 years can either be the normal lifespan of humans from then onwards or the period of time they were given to repent of their evil lifestyles.

4 The word *Nephilim* is often translated intowith giants. Some believe the Nephilims to be a specific race, possibly from Cain. Others suggest something above man or half gods. But this is all speculation that doesn't fit with the rest of the Bible. But what we do see here is very important: Moses tells us that at that time before the Flood and also afterwards in some instances, people were larger! We can also see over-sized men later in the Bible, like Goliath. In the area we think to have found the Ark, oversized human bones have been found. They can be found at Wyatt's Museum in the US States, among other places. centuries BC.

5 6:15 The cubit used here is either the Babylonian, 50.3 cm or 19,6" , the Egyptian, 52.5 cm or 20,5" or the ancient "royal" Hebrew cubit, the breadth of seven hands, or 51.8 cm or 20,2" . Later a shorter Hebrew cubit became the norm. It is 6 handbreadths or 44.5 cm or 17,36" .

6 6:16 Unclear meaning. Most likely it is a cubit's length between the highest side of the Ark and the roof so that light and air could come through a row of windows or openings, cf. 8:6.)

7 7:20 Ritually clean for offerings and food.

8 9:25 Another name for Ham.

9 The Book of Jubilees – one of the earliest Jewish so-called Midrashim, i.e. a free rabbi commentary to the Pentateuch, adding extra details of maybe doubtful character. This commentary is claimed to have been written at the time of Moses. It seeks to draw up a chronological table starting with the creation of Adam in year 1. About the division of the Earth in the days of Peleg (approx. 100 years after the Flood) it says in chapt. 8: „And it came to pass in the beginning of the thirty-third jubilee (1569 a.m.) that they divided the Earth into three parts, for Shem and Ham and Japheth, according to the inheritance of each..."

After that follows a detailed description of the territories as to rivers, oceans, mountains etc. But as mentioned, The Book of Jubilees is not necessarily authentic or as old as what it purports to be. Like other commentaries it may be from the period after the return of the Jews from Babylon, written a few centuries BC.

Chapter 4

The People of the Ararat Mountains

We shall now zoom in on the area where Noah's Ark was stranded after the Great Flood, according to the Bible.

"The waters receded from the earth continually. At the end of a hundred and fifty days the waters had abated; and in the seventh month, on the seventeenth day of the month, the ark came to rest upon the mountains of Ar'arat" (Genesis, chapter 8, verses 3-4).

As we can see, it doesn't say in the Bible that the Ark was stranded on Mount Ararat. It only says "upon the Ararat Mountains."

At Moses' time Ararat was the name of a kingdom up in the mountains. And the tallest mountain in this kingdom was later called Massis by the local Armenian inhabitants. Beside the 5,165 meters tall Massis lies a somewhat smaller mountain of 3,925 meters, which the Armenian called Pokur Massis(Little Ararat) as opposed to Medz Massis (Big Ararat).

In Kurdish the mountain is called Çiyayê Agirî, which means the "fire mountain" (agir = fire, çiya = mountain.)Some Kurds also call the mountain Shaksi Ararat, and the official Turkish name is Büyük or Agri Dagi. Onthe other side of the border in the Iranian language of Farsi, it is called Koh-i-nuh, Noah's Mountain.

It was probably not until the 14th century that the mountain was called Mount Ararat by the European merchants and explorers.

A few kilometres from Mt. Ararat lies a cave fortress that probably originates from Horite times - just a few hundred years after Noah.

The Middle East with the Mountains of Ararat topmost between The Black Sea and The Caspian Sea. Bottom map: The Mountains of Ararat with the Sinear Plaine (Mesopotamia) between the rivers Euphrat and Tigris.

The Twin Mountains of Ararat

From afar Mount Ararat rises majestically all the way up to the clouds. Its snowy peak is only visible in clear weather.

To the northwest it grows into a mountain range, but apart from that it stands almost alone in the landscape as a conical volcano on a plain which only goes 750m to 1,370 m up the mountain. The rest of the mountain is separate.

From the height of about 2,700 m, the mountain gets very steep, in some places there is an ascent of 65 degrees. At 1,335 m the grass disappears and from 4,000 m Big Ararat is always covered by a snow-clad cape. In recent years, however, some of the bottom part of the snow has vanished due to hot summers or global warming. At the height of 3,925m and 5,165 m, the mountain divides into two peaks which in the West are called Little and Big Ararat. Between the two peaks there is an area called The Saddle as it resembles a saddle between two camel humps from a distance. However, there is also another area between the peak of Big Ararat and the so-called "Eastern Summit" which is also called The Saddle.

The circumference of the mountain is enormous. If one plans to go around it, it will be a walk of 80 km.

Not all such mountains are equally impressive but because Mount Ararat stands alone so that one can see its magnificent peak from afar, one cannot help being deeply fascinated by this mighty and beautiful mountain. It is like a two-poled magnet that has attracted travellers and simultaneously repulsed the locals, who know how dangerous the mountain can be if you are caught up in a sudden snowstorm or fall into a glacier. Not to mention all the imaginative stories telling how dangerous or simply impossible it is to climb the "holy" mountain, it is also called The Maternal Mountain, or The Mountain of Pain.

Mt. Ararat – A Hardened Volcano

According to the Bible, the whole planet was flooded for about a year, even the highest mountains were covered by water. However, some of the mountains that we see today could have emerged due to this worldwide disaster. E.g. by the continental plates gliding over each other, raising vast lands, or through the explosions of volcanoes, leaving mountains of lava. A part of Mt. Ararat seems to have formed under water as the mountain partly consists of the so-called "pillow lava." This is lava resembling big sacks, because the lava has been chock cooled. This is known to have happened to the sea volcanoes of Hawaii and Iceland.[1]

According to the Turkish geologist Salih Bavraktutan, who has been the defender of the boat-shaped object of Durupinar, the same fossils of sea animals and plants as were found on the other non-volcanic mountains of the area have not been found here. Therefore, he believes that the upper part of Mt. Ararat wasn't there until after Noah's time due to volcanic eruptions.

That would fit with the recent find of a wooden structure under ice and lava rocks at the height of 4,200 m, which could suggest that the upper part of the volcano came into existence later.

The Kurdish Town

Entering the area, we settled in the town Dogubayazit, which is a Kurdish town like Van, whereas Erzurum is mainly Turkish. Dogubayazit has been the starting point of the most famous ark searches. Here the majority of the well-known ark hunters lived at hotels like Nuh, Ararat, Isfahan, Grand Derya, Tahran, and Ortadogu. This has no doubt influenced the town though these ark hunters were few. A number of Kurdish and Turkish guides, however, have created jobs for themselves by taking ark hunters and tourists into the area. In recent years it has been especially the boat-shaped object that has attracted quite a lot of tourists. As opposed to the possible find on Mt. Ararat, the boat-shaped object can be reached by driving up near it by a steep military road. And there is even a tourist center where the local "ark keeper" Hassan willingly serves tea to visitors – in exchange for a few dollars.

If one visits Dogubayazit in the summer, it can easily be 30-35 degrees C.

In winter, however the temperature can get down to 45-50 degrees below zero. It is a dry cold in this part of Turkey, which has a continental climate. But Dogubayasit has the advantage of being 500 m lower than the towns of Kars and Erzurum, both situated at the windy height of 2,000 m. Also, the volcanoes in the Ararat Mountains make it warmer than it would normally be at this height.

The Borderland of Turkey, Iran, Azerbaijan and Armenia

In fact is most visitors don't come to Dogubayasit because of the Ark but rather because the border of Iran lies only 35 km from the town, and the main road passes by. This creates some business.

This part of Turkey could have even more business if Turkey hadn't closed the border to Armenia and broken off the diplomatic relations to that

From afar one gets a glimpse of Ararat's snow-clad summit from the highway from Erzurum to the Iranian border.

republic, which lies just on the other side of Mt. Ararat. But due to political disagreements (recently after the war between Armenia and Azerbaijan over the enclave Nagorno Karabac) the border has been closed.

This was done in solidarity with the neighboring country of Azerbaijan whose enclave Nakhichevan also borders with Turkey. This enclave is a little stripe of land stuck between Iran and Armenia, whose border with Turkey lies only a few kilometres east of Mt. Ararat.

However, there is quite a deal of business and transport of people via Iran that has been so wise as to keep all borders open, in spite of the quite restrictive rule of Teheran.

Dogubayasit and the two Ararat peaks lie in a remote place as the border to Iran here bows to the east. If the border had continued straight forward, these mountains would have belonged to Iran. The Ararat Mountain has belonged to one country and then to another. E.g. the Russians were here about a century ago.

The Kingdom of Ararat

As shown before the Bible mentions *"The Ararat Mountains."* It was probably Moses who had the Pentateuch written down. Here, the primeval history of man makes up roughly the first eight chapters. Exactly at the time of Moses, there was a kingdom named Ararat. It was also called Urartu. As the Hebrew text has only consonants, it only says RRT. In Hebrew it has been read aRaRaT but uRaRTu in the mountain language.

The next time the Kingdom of Ararat is mentioned in the Bible is in Book of Kings that tells about the Assyrian king who was cut down by his sons while praying in the temple. "...and they escaped to the land of Ararat. And Esarhaddon, his son, succeeded him as king." 2

The Ararat mountains were a good hiding place.

This happens in 681 BC while the Urarturian king Rusa was building a new capital near the Van Lake.

The eastern part of Turkey resembles Iran. Dogubayazit is a completely Kurdish town.

The story is repeated in the book of Isaiah .[3] And in both cases the very same word RRT is used as is also used in the Noah story. However, in many Bible translations The Land of Ararat is translated The Land of Armenia as this land later covered the same territory.

The mighty Kingdom iof Urartu covered present day Eastern Turkey, the northern parts of Iraq and Iran, present day Armenia, Azerbaijan and a part of Georgia. This is a vast mountain area from The Black Sea to the Kaspian Sea. The Kingdom of Urartu existed from 1,300-584 BC, but earlier there were other kingdoms in the Armenian highland.

However, the Urartuans weren't the first.

The Hurrians – The First After Noah

Behind the Castle of Isaac Pasha, which lies on the eastern mountainside opposite Mt. Ararat with a view out over the magnificent valley and the two Ararat mountains, lies an even older castle. It is almost hewn into the rocks and some of us have tried to crawl up the steep steps into the caves.

Caves cut into the sides of rock like this can be found in various other locations in Eastern Turkey where the Hurrians lived at least 4,000 years ago. If we believe the Noahic narrative, that would place them here just after the Ark stranded in these mountains.

The Hurrians are the oldest major people group of whom the archaeologists have found signs up here in the mountains.

Metsamor

Objects have also been found from a very old culture in the Ararat Valley in the Armenian State on the northern side of the Arax River. This is the so-called Metsamor Find, discovered near the nuclear power station bearing the same name which supplies Armenia with approximately 40% of its electricity.

The old Metsamor has been a center of both metal extraction and astronomy. People are supposed to have been living here as far back as 5,000 BC and up to the 17th century.

As early as 2,000 years before the Babylonians, people here had set up a stellar observatory (like Stonehenge in England) allowing them to fix a calendar of 12 months. There are also signs indicating that the zodiac was known here before it turned up in Mesopotamia.

The Hurrians – "The Tall"

The name "Hurrians" can mean the "tall" or "noble." Another meaning of "Hurrians" is "people that live in caves" because of their way of living. The name can also be spelled Khurrians – which leads one to think of the Kurds, who were later found in the area. Maybe they were here all along. The Kurds in Iraq themselves claim to descend from the Khurrians, among others.[4]

The first mention of Hurrian persons and place names is in the end of the third millennium in Mesopotamian accounts – i.e. over 4,000 years ago. It

is evident from these ancient accounts that the Hurrians' homeland was the region east of the Tigris River in the Zagros Mountains.[5] These mountains are just south of Ararat. The kingdom of the Hurrians was called Hurri.

3,000 years before Christ, the Hurrians spread out in the southwest in the area around Lake Van. They also lived in small groups in northern Mesopotamia around the Euphrates River. (As did Noah's descendants according to the Bible.)

Around 1700-1500 BC, they invaded Mesopotamia and Eastern Anatolia in Turkey. From here a number of them continued all the way into modern-day Syria and Israel.

The Hurrians were most likely Indo-Europeans based on the names of their kings and such things as chariots, which were of Indo-European origin.

There are some indications that the Hurrians had connections to the Aryans to the east, in today's Iran and India, as they worshiped gods that are connected to Iran and India (such as Mithra and Varuna). Also with the neighboring Hittites that dwelled further west in Turkey, the Hurrians had much in common. They worshiped some of the same gods, they used some of the same names, and they had some of the same myths. The Hittites were also Indo-Europeans.

The castle Eski Beyazit is built into the Ararat Mountains and originates at least from the Urartu Kingdom (c. 800 BC). It was the forerunner of the town Dogubayazit. In earlier times there was probably an even older cave fortress that might date back to Noah's day. The fortress lies only a few kilometres from Mt. Ararat.

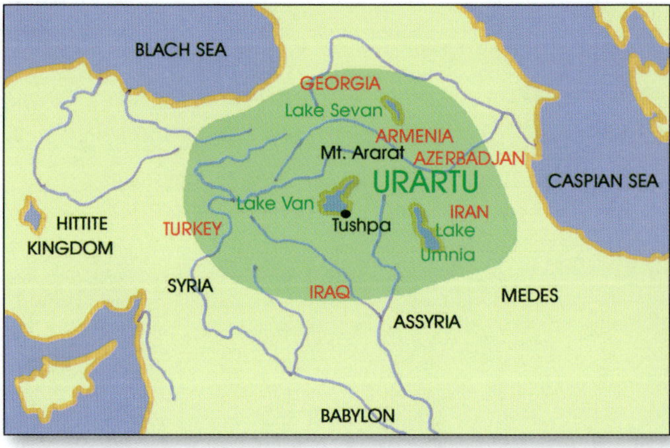

The Urarturian Kingdom existed from ca. 1300 BC until 584 BC. Its primary center was in Tushpa by Lake Van. It covered the Ararat Mountains - but sometimes also the northern part of Iran, present East Turkey and Armenia and parts of Georgia and Azerbadijan.

The Hurrians eventually began to use the Mesopotamian mixed religion and culture, spoke Babylonian, and used the Mesopotamian system of writing when putting their own language down on clay tablets.

But even though many texts written in the Hurrian language have been found, the language has not yet been decoded.

The Hurrians are also in the Bible

Genesis chapter 36 mentions the Horrite, Seir, and his clan called the Horrites (Hurrians). The Mountains of Seir, which are in the harsh mountainous country south of the Dead Sea, were named after him. Esau married Hurrian women and let his daughters marry the sons of the Seir's chieftains.[6] The country in the southern region of present-day Israel and Jordan was later named Edom after Esau. Esau probably lived between 2145-1995 BC.

These Horrites may possibly be some of the same Hurrians that apparently spread out from Ararat and the Zagros Mountains all the way to Syria and Israel.

But Horrit can also mean cave-dweller. Some discern between the biblical Horrites and the Hurrians, but this is probably an artificial discrimination.

The Kingdom of Mitanni

As time went on, the Hurrians became a major power, and around 1550-1250 BC King Sudarna I established the Hurrian Kingdom of Mitanni. The capital was Washukanni on the Khabur River[7], a large tributary of the Euphrates in northern Syria. Eventually, the Hurrians ruled all of upper-Mesopotamia.

But in 1270 the Mirani kingdom was annexed in the Assyrian world empire. Only one little Hurrian stronghold, Hayasha, survived in the Ararat Mountains.

The Hurrians were the first known people in the Ararat Mountains after Noah. They were probably those of his decendants who stayed in the mountains (with Noah) when most of the new generations moved down to the lowlands to the Sinear plains and spread from there.

They Wandered in the East

Most of the ancient, known history of the world comes from Mesopotamia. And according to Moses, this is where people went after the Flood.

They apparently followed the rivers to lower land in the southwest because this is where Genesis, chapter 11 continues after we hear about the Ark.

In most translations chapter 11 reads, "As they migrated eastward, they came upon a plain in the land of Shinar and settled there."(verse 2).

But it is probably a translation mistake that they went "eastward", because otherwise they would not have ended up in Mesopotamia, but in present

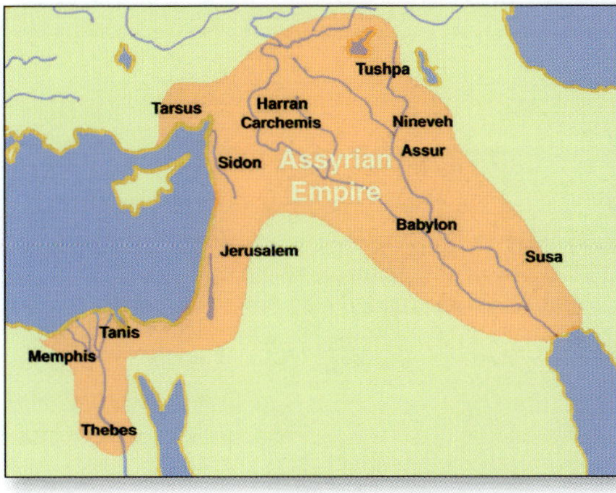

Armenia and Iran. In some translations the text has been adjusted to read "as they migrated from the east" (NRSV) or "as they journeyed east." [8] (ASV).

According to the Book of Daniel, chapter 1, verse 2, the plain of Shinar and the later Babylonia were one and the same. So Shinar was the land between the Euphrates and the Tigris – and it is easy to imagine that Shinar is a Semitic version of the name Sumer.[9]

Sumer is the first "country" known of in the area between the two rivers. Whatever the case, this is one of the first civilizations on earth, from around 3,000 BC. There are also signs of even older settlements like the Ubaid civilization that must have come before the Flood.

Normally, historians place Sumer in the southern most part of Iraq, but originally Sumer (or Shinar) was comprised of the entire span between the two rivers until the new centers of power, Babylon and Akkad, arose. There is actually an area called Cinar (Shinar) that is located all the way up in northern Mesopotamia – in southern Turkey – to which road signs refer even today.

If it is this Shinar that existed, then "eastward" can be read with an understanding that the Euphrates turns eastward just after the river flows down from the mountains. There is also a plain here.

The explanation of the east-west mix-up is that the Hebrew word for east basically means "in front of." This is because at that time the rising of the sun was considered the point from which one differentiated between right and left. The Hebrew text is as such, "And it was as they traveled from "in front." They found a level valley in the land of Shinar. And they lived there."[10] In the Greek version LXX it reads "from the rising."

Mesopotamia

The areas between the Euphrates and the Tigris are called Sumer, Akkad, Babylonia, Chaldea, and Mesopotamia. Between these two rivers, over the next two thousand years after the Flood, bloody wars were fought for reigning power of the Middle East.

According to the Bible, all of these people groups originally came from the Mountains of Ararat. In the beginning they spoke the same language, but in the 5th generation, there was a language confusion and the people split up. This happened in connection with a great tower called the Tower of Babel, which, according to the Bible, was built on the Shinar plain. And that is where remains have been found of multiple large pyramid-like towers, so-called ziggurats. The original Tower of Babel could possibly be the temple-tower in Etemenanki, north of Baghdad. For the latter had also been destroyed, as had apparently The Tower of Babel, and King Nabopolassar and his son Nebuchadnezzar II of Babylonia had to restore it.

However, we return to the Ararat Mountains.

The Assyrian Kingdom was originally (c. 2000 B.C.) just the city state Asshur, named after Shem's son (Genesis 10:22). The Assyrians conquered the Babylonians and became a super power c. 1200 BC. Their capital changed from Asshur to Nineveh (from the Book of Jonah in the Bible) to Kalah to Korsabad (Sargon's Castle). The Assyrians were known for their great administrative skills, great watering systems, and magnificent palaces in the different capitals under the kings Tiglath-Pileser, Sargon, and Sankerib. They kept several Babylonian texts in Assurbanipal's great library in Nineveh. The religion imitated that of the Babylonians, but their main god was Asshur. Noah's grandson. The Assyrians were notorious for their cruelty against the oppressed peoples.
In 671 BC, when they conquered Egypt, they couldn't hold the mighty kingdom together. Shorty after, Egypt seceded, and the oppressed peoples united. In 614 BC, they conquered Asshur, and in 612 BC they conquered Nineveh, which they devastated completely. Henceforward, the Persian empire came to life.

A road sign in southern Turkey shows the way to Cinar (or the biblical Sinear?)

What happened in the Ararat Mountains?

The closest we get to answering who settled in these mountains is the sons of Joktan. What is written about them is that they lived in the Mountains of the East from Mesha to Sephar. According to the Ark hunter and film cartoonist David Deal Mesha is identical with Naxuan (the town of Noah) which appears later in history. Today, there is a big town called Nakhichevan (or Naxcivan) in an enclave of Azerbaijan between Iran and Armenia, approx. 63 miles south east of Mt. Ararat.

The sons of Joktan are the fifth generation after Shem, the oldest of Noah's sons. Joktan's brother is named Peleg because "in his days the earth was divided" (Genesis 10:25) According to the Bible, it is here that people began to wander in different directions – surely a reference to the current events of the Tower of Babel in Mesopotamia.

The World Divided in Three

If we take other less reliable sources into account such as the Book of Jasher[11], then Noah split the world between his three sons in this way:

The descendants of Shem got the Middle East and the East.

Japheth was given Europe and Russia west of the Don River as well as the "distant islands."

Ham got Yemen, Egypt, and the rest of Africa.[12]

There was plenty of room in which to grow. Their descendants could have just gone in three different directions, but instead most of them obviously conglomerated in Mesopotamia and soon began to fight. Ham's son, Canaan, begins with taking the land of Canaan (Lebanon and Israel), which belonged to the sons of Shem. There are also some that travel to Egypt and plant themselves along the Nile, while others go to India and build a civilization around the Indus River. All these civilizations start around 3,000 BC, which almost coincides with the end of the Flood.[13]

The first ruler in Mesopotamia was Ham's grandson, Nimrod.

For centuries his line ravaged alternately with the Assyrians and Babylonians (both of whom were Semitic being of Shem's lineage) and later the Hittites and Hurrians, both Indo-Europeans (Japheth's descendants). Instead of living in each his country, they go back and forth between trying to plunder each other and gain control.

According to the Book of Jasher, Shem remained with Noah. And because

This hill in Cinar (Sinear?) in southern Turkey is considered by some to be related to The Tower of Babel. But most scholars believe that The Tower of Babel lay close to Bagdad.

some of the place names up here are close to the names of Joktan's sons, one could imagine that the Semites were the first to live up in the Mountains of Ararat.

Another theory is that it was some of Japheth's descendants who were the first to live up here. The Armenians, who have been in the area for thousands of years, claim that they are descendants of Haig who was the son of Togarma (Genesis 10:3). He was the son of Gomer, the son of Japheth. And if we look at the first known people that archeologists have connected to this area, we actually hear of an Indo-European people, i.e. the previously mentioned Hurrians.

According to local tradition, Turkey's largest lake, Lake Van, photographed here from NASA's Land Satellite, supposedly encompassed the Garden of Eden.

Lake Van – The Garden of Eden?

If we travel about 125 miles south of Mt. Ararat, following curving mountain roads, we get "down" to Turkey's largest lake, Lake Van which is, however, located at 5,650 ft. Above sea level!

It is an enormous lake that, like Loch Ness, has its own monster as well as a unique breed of white cats, the Turkish Van cat, which is fond of swimming, contrary to most other cats. They are also known for their two different colored eyes.

Lake Van is more than 74 miles (120 km) long and 50 miles (80 km) across at its widest point. It covers an area of 1,434 square miles (3,763 square km) with salt water, for there is no run-off from this high-altitude lake.

According to local folklore, the Garden of Eden can be found on the bottom of Lake Van, but no one is known to have dived there to explore the depths for hidden treasure. Lake Van is probably hiding something, if it is a relic from the Flood. Here is a very exciting challenge for divers.

On the southeast bank of Lake Van lies the provincial capital, Van. Outside of Van lies an ancient castle, hewn into a rock. This originates from the ancient Urartian kingdom that came into being around 1300 BC and continued until 584 where the Medes finally beat the Urartu and destroyed their capital after centuries of Assyrian attempts.

The Urartu were probably descendants of the Hurrians

When the Medes from Iran destroyed the capital of Urartu, the Urartu disappeared out of history as a people. But they may be the ones who were later called the Armenians.

The Urartu Attack Against Nebuchadnezzar

The prophet Jeremiah also names the Urartu (Ararat) when he prophesied around 600 BC that the world power, Babylonia would be destroyed. He names three kingdoms that will attack it: "Ararat, Minni, and Ashkenaz."[14]

The attack came in 539 BC when the Persians gathered an alliance of Medes and other tribes in Iran and eastern Turkey in order to attack Babylonia. Among these tribes were the Urartu, the Minni, i.e. the kingdom of Mannai south of Lake Umnia in Iran, and the Ashkenaz[15], probably a Scythian[16] race from between the Black Sea and the Caspian Sea – that is north of the Ararat area.

This alliance destroyed the new Babylonian Empire, which the Chaldeans had controlled from 612-539 with rulers such as Nebuchadnezzar on the throne. The new Persian regents actually let the Jews who were forced to move to go home from Babylon. So here was a prophecy that came to pass.

The Tragic History of the Armenians

We end our going through the people in the Ararat Mountains with the Armenians who together with the Kurds are people who have lived in the Ararat mountains for the longest time.

Either the Armenians were just the offspring of the Uriartuans, or they were a people emigrated from Iran. At any rate, the Armenians occupied the area until recently but mostly under the rule of others.From 612-559 BC, it wasunder the control of the Medes, and

from 559-331 BC it was in an alliance with the Persians under King Kyros and his successors. King Darius I names Armenia as his 13th satrapy (province) in his writings.

From 331-189 BC, it was under the Greeks and the Seleucid but they were given their own kings.

For a short while Armenia was independent after the fall of the Mesopotamian Empire. Under Tigranes I the Great (c. 95-56 BC), Armenia almost became a world power. But the Romans pushed them back reducing the size of their lands.

In 66 BC Armenia bowed down to this great power and became a Roman colony. However, the Parthians of Iran regularly captured the area from the Romans.

A Christian Nation

After Armenia's conversion to Christianity in the 4th century, the struggle continued between the Christian states of Byzantium and the new Persian Empire, which tried to force the Armenians to convert to Zoroastrianism.

After the Persians, the army of Islam appeared, struggling with the Byzantine over the plagued land. In the 11th century, a great deal of the Armenian people escaped from the perpetual depredation and rooted themselves in Cilicia (the area between the Taurus Mountains and the Mediterranean Sea in present-day southern Turkey). This country, later called Little Armenia, allied with the Crusaders.

But then the Muslim Osmans appeared, conquering Armenia in the 15th century. They have held on to it, vacillating with Persia, until today.

Unsuccessful Alliance with The Russians

In the 19th century the Armenians sought help with the Russians against their Turkish lords. But their rebellion flopede, and they were forced into the north and the south by violent ethnic cleansing. The worst part took place in 1915. The Armenians themselves claim that 1.5 million were killed, and today there are no Armenians left in the mountains of Ararat in eastern Turkey.

The Kurds, who were alreadyin small numbers in the area– took over the area in connection with the ethnic cleansings, more or less with the Turks' knowledge. They took over the property of the Armenians and often gave new names to locations.

In 1920 the Armenians in the northern zone became a part of the Soviet Union which created the Soviet Republic of Armenia in 1936. Today Armenia is an independent state. From the capital Jerevan, the inhabitants can only look across the closed border at the mountain that was always at the centre of Armenian history and which is still on the national coat of arms, but the area including Mt. Ararat became a part of Turkey after World War I.

Yet the strife continues between the Turks and the local Kurds, of which some are fighting for an independent state.

Even though the Ark landed in an area that is considered in the middle of nowhere for many Europeans and Americans, the country has been involved in international conflicts throughout history.

We can conclude that the first known people in the Mountains of Ararat after Noah's time were called Hurrians (the tall and noble cave dwellers). Later, the Kingdom of Urartu (Ararat) arises, and after that, the Armenians appear. Maybe it is just the same people we meet again and again, under different names. Finally the Turks and the Kurds take over the area in 1915 after beingnear the same area for centuries.

Endnotes

1 This theory is stated by Ph. D. Clifford L. Burdick i "Ararat the Mother of Mountains".

2 2 Book of Kings Kongebog 19:37b

3 Isaiah 37:38

4 "The Kurds ... are descendants of two great groups of races: The Pre-Arian peoples like the Gutians, Lulluians, Khurrians, Kassites...etc., and the Indo-Europian peoples which the Medes are the most known ones. The former who spokea hitherto unknown group of languages generally called Asiatic or Caucasian appear from the third millennium BC and remained to the first millennium BC while the immigration of the Medes and other Indo-Europian peoples started from the early second millennium BC."
Ancient History of Kurdistan, Islamic Group in Kurdistan / Iraq – www.komall.org/httpdocs/e/e-kurdistan/e-ancientkurdhist.htm

5 Akhenaten's World – www.geocities.com/Athens/Acropolis/7987/hurria_1.html tells: The first appearance of Hurrian personal and place names comes from Mesopotamian records of the late 3rd millennium. These reveal that the region east of the Tigris River into the Zagros Mountains was the Hurrian homeland.

6 Genesis 36, The Book of Jashar 30:28 and 31:65.
7 The Khabur river is 200 miles long, rising in SE Turkey, and flowing generally south through NE Syria to enter the Euphrates River, near Dayr az Zawr. The Khabur valley, which now has about 4 million acres (1.6 million hectares) of farmland, is Syria's main wheat-producing area. In ancient times the Khabur was known as the Habor; along its banks in Gozan, the Israelite captives from Samaria were settled in the 8th cent. BC. (2 Kings 17.6; 18.11).
http://www.geocities.com/Athens/Acropolis/7987/mitann_1.html
8 Revised Standard Version says "from the east" and Today's English Version has "As they wandered about in the East, they came to a plain in Babylonia and settled there."
9 Aril Edvardsen has the same theory in his 4-volume series about the "Autostrada of the Sun God",Hermon
10 "And-it-was as-they-travelled from-the-east they-found a-level-valley in-the-land-of Shinar. And-they-lived there." (Interlinear Bible af J. P. Green.)
11 A Jewish text found in the Midle Ages of the same name as the book twice referred to in the Bible. It was released in Hebrew in Venice in 1625 (possibly 1613) and then translated and released in smaller editions in Krakow, Prague, Frankfurt, Constantinople (Istanbul), Amsterdam and Calcutta and later in English in 1839 in the USA. It is not sure that this source is authentic.
12 The first king of Egypt, Scorpion, is dated to around 3,100 BC, but the list of kings is built on thin evidence. The Indus civilization is the earliest known civilization in South Asia. It flourished from 2600 – 1800 BC, but signs of older habitations exist – possibly from before the Flood.
13 Traditionally, the Flood is considered to have taken place 2400 BC, but see the alternative chronological table elsewhere in the book.
14 Jeremiah 51:27
15 The Ashkenaz people were named after Japheth's grandson.
16 According to the Jewish historian Josephus, the Scythians were the same people that the Bible calls Magog, normally considered to be the Russians. Josephus writes in Antiquities p. 1,123 that "Magog founded the Magogians, thus named after him, but who were by the Greeks called Scythians."Kapitel 5

Chapter 5

Ararat – the Common Origin of Languages and Genes

The tower of Babel has inspired many painters throughout the ages. Often they have depicted the tower from their European-centered view points.
The real Tower of Babel was probably a kind of pyramid.

A number of things suggest that in antiquity, which we only know from traditions and myths, a lively bit of traffic happened on the world's oceans. And the "original" inhabitants of the Americas, Australia and the Pacific Islands could have arrived from a common starting point, namely the Middle East.[1]

Did they?

If we look at the story in the Bible (and the myths of some other peoples) everyone was spread out from Mesopotamia because they began speaking different languages.

The Tower of Babel

God had,according to Genesis chapter 11,confused the languages in order to stop the building of the Tower of Babel, which evidently expressed human arrogance.

"They said to each other, 'Come, let's make bricks and bake them thoroughly.' They used brick instead of stone, and tar for mortar. Then they said, 'Come, let us build ourselves a city, with a tower that reaches to the heavens, so that we may make a name for ourselves and not be scattered over the face of the whole earth.'"[2]

Some old sources[3] tell that what the tower builders had in mind was to build a tower from where they could storm heaven and capture it from the gods. But as this book builds upon a working theory saying that people of that time were no more stupid, maybe even wiser, than people of today, it seems very unlikely that the reason for building should have been a desire to "crawl into heaven." They knew pretty well that "heaven" wasn't a place situated a few hundred meters above the clouds – they were already at that time familiar with astronomy. Therefore, it is more likely that it has been an attempt to uncover "God's wisdom." People have at all times tried to do so through philosophy, religion and sciencke for example the account about the Serpent in the Garden of Eden tempting man to "be as God" if he ate of the tree of wisdom. And this same story has repeated itself maof times. It is, for instance, worth noticing that one of the computer pioneers (Apple) actually chose a bitten apple as their symbol of the new wisdom that should prove to

NOAH

- **JAPHETH**
  Indo-Europeans
  Gen. 10:6-20
  Europe - Western Asia
  - **Gomer** – Northern tribes – Cimmerians
    - **Ashkenaz** – Allemani tribe – Germany
    - **Togarmah** – Harran - Carchemish – Armenia (Turkey)
    - **Riphath** – Northern Europe
  - **Tubal** – Tbilisi – Georgia
  - **Javan** – Costland tribes – Ionian – Greeks
    - **Elishah** – Hellenic
    - **Tarshish** – Spain
    - **Rodanim** – Rhodos
    - **Kittim** – Cyprus
  - **Tiras** – Thracians – Thor-people
  - **Magog** – Scythians – Tartars
  - **Madai** – Medes – Caspian Sea – Iran
  - **Meschek** – Cappadocians – Muscovites – Russia
- **HAM**
  Egyptians - Africans
  Gen. 10:6-20
  Lybia - Canaan - Ethiopia
  - **Cush** – Cushites
    - **Seba** – Ethiopians
    - **Sabteca** – Ethiopians
    - **Havilah** – Gold Country – Armenia?
    - **Sabtah** – Ethiopians
    - **Raamah** – Ethiopians
    - **Nimrod** – Mesopotamia
  - **Mizhraim** – Egypt
    - **Ludim** – Egyptians
    - **Naphluhim** – Egyptians
    - **Anamim** – Egyptians
    - **Pathrusim** – Patrusians – Philistines
    - **Lehabim** – Egyptians
    - **Casluhim** – Lower Egypt – Philistines
  - **Put** – Africans – Lybia
  - **Canaan** – Jebushites – Amorites – Canaanites
  - **Sidon** – Phoenician
- **SHEM**
  Shemites
  Gen. 10:21-32
  Middle East - Southern Asia
  - **Elam** – Elamites – Persians
  - **Aram** – Assyrians – Syrians
  - **Asshur** – Assyrians – Iraqians
  - **Arpachshad**
    - **Shelah**
      - **Eber** – Hebrews
        - **Peleg**
        - **Joktan**
  - **Lud** – Lydians – Asia Minor

Many people groups can be traced directly back to Noah's descendants by means of sources like Josephus and Homer. This is an attempt to trace some of the nations from the first generations. There are, of course, several theories since most of the original ethnic groups have since then split up or mixed with others.

change the world. From where did they get that idea?

People of the past knew the circumference of the earth and divided up the 24 hours of day and night according to a 6-figure system (4 x 6 hours of each 60 minutes of each 60 seconds). In their constructions they used the figures 1-2-4-8-16 etc. Modern computer technology uses a similar binary numeral system and many believe that they were on the track of a brilliant wisdom that was later lost.[4]

The Tower of Babel was probably a pyramid-shaped building constructed according to some mathematical formulas that are also known from the pyramids in Egypt. In the first decades after the catastrophe of the Flood, men apparently tried to build pyramids all over the world. In fact, ruins of pyramids are found right from China to South America.

The mathematics of the seven storeys of the Tower of Babel seems to refer to specific co-ordinates all around the globe where places of worship or stellar observation were built of big stones, like for instance Stonehenge in England and Metsamor in Armenia.

More than a Myth

This leads to the conclusion that the Tower of Babel was not only a symbolic myth as many theologians today try to interpret as. There really was a Tower of Babel and it may still be there. For instance, ruins of a large pyramid-shaped building have been found in Birs Nimrod about 12 miles from the ancient city of Babylon, 65 miles from Baghdad, Iraq. The tower here was at least 180 feet high (55 mtrs.) and consisted of seven storeys. It could be thebBiblical Tower of Babel. But this is not the only ziggurat (a pyramid-shaped temple tower) that can be found in the area. The largest one is found in Babylon itself. It was over 300 x 300 feet (almost 100 x 100 metts.) at the base and 300 feet high. (According to some ancient sources, only 1/3 of the original huge tower is left behind. The rest either sank into the ground or was destroyed by fire.)[5]

Ararat – the Common Origin of Languages

But if we don't just accept the account of the Bible or that of old myths as truth, is there other evidence suggesting that the people of the world all originated from one region in the world – from Noah's Ark?

Yes, the so-called Indo-European languages can all be traced back to a common Proto-Indo-European language that arose from this region.

The Indo-European languages include many Asian languages such a Bengali, Iranian, Kurdish, Afghan, Nepai , and Romany (the languages of the gipsies of Northern India) in addition to most of the European language families (the Romance, Germanic and Slavic language families). Indo-European is by far the biggest family of languages in the world.[6]

The theory of all languages having a common source was already formed by Sir William Jones in 1786 in Calcutta. Jones found a clear connection between the verb-roots and the grammatical forms in the ancient Indian language of

Noah's Grandchildren

On this map of the Middle East, you can see where the people named after Noah's grandchildren and great-grandchildren supposedly settled (marked in reddish brown). Migration, war, and conquest scattered most tribes all over the world where they split into even more tribes and in some cases united again. Historical sources and archaeological finds confirm where some originally lived while for others it is uncertain. For example, we know with certainty that Javan are the Greeks, but it is unclear whether Tarshish was the present-day Tarsus in Turkey or whether it was Spain. On the Internet you can find many new theories about the history of the various tribes.

Sanskrit and in languages such as Persian, Greek, Latin, Celtic and German which were geographically found very dispersedly. These languages had to have a common starting point.

The linguist Thomas Gamkredlidze from the State University in Tiblisi, Georgia, revised the "language tree" in 1985 and discovered that the trunk – the original Proto-Indo-European language – sprang out of the highlands of Armenia, i.e. the region of the Mountains of Ararat in East Turkey.

The theory, of course, met scepticism from the West which is always the case when research seems to confirm the stories of the Bible. But in 1995 the theory was confirmed with the help of the computer-mathematics of three researchers at the University of Pennsylvania[7] who clearly did not believe in the theory.

So the development of the languages seems to indicate that a very large part of all languages in the world originates from ancient Armenia. And here we must remember that today's Republic of Armenia only forms a small part of the area originally inhabited by the Armenians. This also comprisheEeastern Turkey. In fact, the Armenians had their very centre in the Mountains of Arara– where the Ark was stranded.

So ait can be seenso linguistics also points towards this being the region where it all began.

Artificial Division?

But what about the other language families? Wasn't it only the Indo-European family that originated from Armenia?

According to the Biblical account also the other families of languages came from here and something seems to indicate that the division into different language families is artificial – that all languages had, originally, the same family as a starting point.

The fact is that the theories of language families have changed as the researchers discovered new connections. Like ih other sciences, researchers have tried to harmonize the available facts with the theory that man is supposed to have developed from an inferior ape-stage and that the different races are supposed to have developed independently of each other in different parts of the world. In the 1930's, it was even populin to claim that some races "had not got as far in development" as others. Some evolutionists, for instance, believed that the Africans' shape of their heads was an expression of a lower stage than the shape of the heads of white peop..! But after the Nazis' attempts to make these theories the basis of eugenics and eradicate the "inferior races", these crazy theories were no more heard of, even though, at that time, they were considered reliable science.

According to the Bible, no races are inferior to others. All have Noah and his wife as ancestors.

Some years ago one of my contacts in Ark research, David Allen Deal from the SA, discovered a clear connection in both word and written types between the language that the Maya Indians spoke and wrote in South America and the Semitic language in the Middle East.[8]

And if this close connection between the two languages that supposedly belong each to their own distinct family of languages does exist, then the sharp division into different language families may need a revision.

It is, at any rate, very remarkable that the majority of languages in the world – and with that the majority of people in the world – can be traced back to a common starting point. And that this starting point is lying at the very place from where, according to the Bible, mankind began spreading after the big flood.

Genetic Research also Points back to Noah

In 2009 the University of Leicester in England published a large study of 2,374 European men's genes.[9] The investigation showed that more than 80 percent of the European men, have genes that can be traced back to common ancestors in Anatolia in Turkey. In fact, their original forefather is presumed to come frohe southern Armenia.

According to the Bible, Noah's Ark was stranded at the very same locatiis in the Mountains of Ararat in the easternmost part of Anatolia or Armenia. From here descendants spread souh-weds to Sinerar, the plains between the rivers of Euphratat and Tigris.

The scientist Dr. Patricia Balaresque and her team of researchers reached their results by investigating the commonest European Y-chromosomal lineage, the so-called Haplogroup R1b1b2.

The group is increasing in frequency the further west you go. In Denmark t is found in just under 43 percent of the population and in Ireland in over 85 percent.

Due to this large concentration in the westerly parts of Europe, it has been generally believed up to now that the Europeans descended from hunter-gatherers in Southern Europe in the Palaeolithic period (approx. 40,000 years ago). But Dr. Patricia Balaresque and her colleagues reject this theory. They believe that the geographical distribution of the diversities within this group is best explained by our ancestors spreading from Anatolia in Turkey. The number here is the smallest and the mutations the highest which seems to indicate that the earliest ancestors came from here. (They are, however, not to be confused with the Turks of today as they did not immigrate from the east until around 1071. The ancestors of the Europeans were Indo-Europeans.)

If you try to figure out when the first Indo-European Anatolian ancestors of the Europeans lived, you reach the result that the earliest lived approx. 7,989 years ago whereas the first ancestors spreading toWwestern Europe lived approx. 5,000 years ago. These figures are, however, not exact but simply reached by multiplying the number of generations by an estimated average human life.

The method of calculating the most recent common ancestor, the so-called TMRCA-calculator (The Most Recent Common Ancestor) is not reliable either, as it is based upon a hypothesis of all mutations in the genome occurring at a constant rate which is not quite correct. Therefore, datings exceeding 5,000 years are somewhat unreliable which calls for a certain caution when dealing with the figures.

But genetic research points to being able to trace back the genes of most European men to the area where Noah's Ark was stranded. It is a further indication that the story about the Ark is not a "tall story." It is a story about the very location from where humanity started developing again. According to the Bible, it happened approximatey. 5,000 years ago after the big floong eradicated the earliest people who lived during thx. 2,000 years that passed between Adam and Noah.[10]

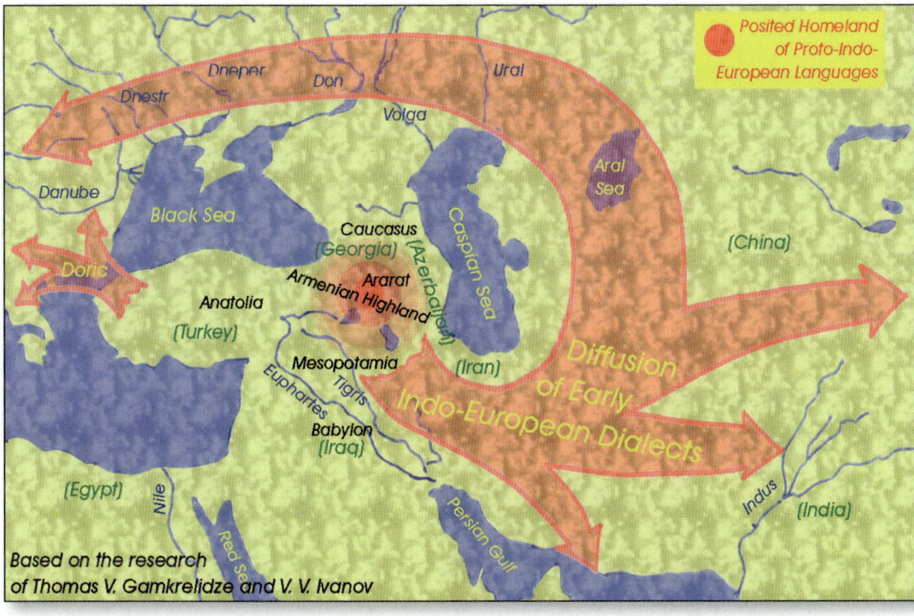

The linguists Thomas V. Gamkrelidze and V.V. Ivanov have researched the development of the Indo-European languages and have concluded that the original Proto-Indo-European language had its starting point right here in the Armenian highlands – also known as Ararat and Urartu – where the Ark was stranded. Other researchers have previously assumed that Europe was the starting point. From the highlands the development of the languages spread to the southeast via Mesopotamia.

Endnotes

1 The Norwegian author Aril Edvardsen has gathered huge amounts of information about this in his major 4-volume work: Solgudens autosrada (The Highway of the Sun God), published by Hermon, Norway

2 Genesis 11: 3-4.

3 Among others the Book of Jasher, chapter 9.

4 Aril Edvardsen: Pyramiden og Orienmysteriet (The Pyramid and the Mystery of Orion), published by Hermon, Norway.

5 The Book of Jasher 9:38 states: "And as to the tower which the sons of men built, the earth opened its mouth and swallowed up one third part thereof, and a fire also descended from heaven and burned another third, and the other third is left to this day, and it is of that part which was aloft, and its circumference is three days' walk."

6 Further, some researchers include the following independent families of languages: the Finnish-Ugrish, the Turkish, the Mongolian, the Tungusic, the Sino-Austrian languages, the Malayo-Polynesian languages and the Dravidian languages as well as Semitic languages, Hamitic language, Sudanese language, Bantu language and several families of languages in America. But these languages all originate from the same primeval language according to the Bible.

7 The researchers were: Donald Ringe, Ann Taylor and Tandy Warrow.

8 Described in "The Nexus – Spoken Language. The Link Between the Mayan and the Semitic During Pre-Columbian Times," Isac Press. Institute for the Study of American Cultures, Columbus, Georgia, 1993.
9 A Predominantly Neolithic Origin for European Paternal Lineages. Dr. Patricia Balaresque, University of Leicester and others. Ref.: www.plosbiology.org/article/info:doi/10.1371/journal.pbio.1000285
10 We also use round approximate figures here as the chronology of the Bible can be calculated in somewhat different ways. See the chapter on chronology.

A map of the world from the 7th century BC describing the Babylonians' understanding of themselves in the world with the two rivers Euphrates and Tigris and oceans surrounding the country in a circle – or the earth as a circular globe?

Chapter 6

Berosus Confirms

There are no pictures of Berosus, but many of Alexander the Great, who conquered the Persian Empire and abducted Berosus to a Greek island.

One of the most exciting of the ancient sources is the Chaldean astrologist Berosus, who lived in Babylon and later moved to Greece. Unfortunately, none of Berosus's original works exist today. His works are only known from quotations and other philosophers' and historians' books.[1] Therefore, one might fear that much has been lost through translation and citation.

When we talk about biblical texts, we have thousands of copies upon which to build our knowledge, and the Babylonian tablets are well kept at the British Museum.

Not so with Berosus. We have to depend on quotes of quotes of quotes.

Berosus's lost works were cited after he died by a Grecian man named Polyhistor (105-35 BC),[2] whose works have unfortunately been lost as well. But his citations of Berosus are quoted again by the Jewish historian Josephus (37-100 AD),[3] a Grecian named Athenaeus (200 AD)[4], the Coptic bishop Clement of Alexandria (150-215 AD),[5] and another Grecian named Abydenus[6] (4th century AD).

Abydenus's manuscript has also been lost, but he is referred to by the Bishop of Caesarea Eusebius (264-338 e. Kr.)[7] and the Byzantine monk and historian Syncellus (9th century AD),[8] who also cites some of the early sources which came after Berosus. It would not be wrong to say that the possibility for mistranslation exists. Despite this fact, Berosus is known as an important historical, though indirectly so, source of prehistory – and Noah's Ark.

The reason that such importance was put on Berosus is that until the clay tablets were found in Mesopotamia in the 19th century, Berosus was almost the only source other than the Bible that we had about life in Babylon.

Alexander the Great is called Alexander the Cruel here. He destroyed, among other things, the famed university of Harran – maybe the first one in the world.

Who Was He?

Berosus lived in Babylon when the Greeks conquered Persia in 330 BC under Alexander the Great. He was probably born around 350 BC.

The Persians had reigned in Babylon for nearly 200 years, from 539-330 BC. The Persian Empire included Egypt, Palestine, and Assyria, as well as other areas. And a great deal of the Empire's knowledge and common history was gathered in Babylon. For a man like Berosus who studied all of this information, it must have been like living in the Library of Congress.

Unfortunately, Alexander the Great destroyed much of the cultural treasures of this society when taking over the Empire.

When in Haran (Rebeccah, Rachel, and Leah's city in southeast Turkey), we saw the ruins of theuniversity, which was destroyed by the Greeks. The university possibly dated back to Abraham's time and is considered the first in the world. Haran plays a role in occult literature.

Berosus Moves to Kos

Berosus left Babylon when the Greeks sacked the city. He was possibly taken there as a prisoner. Back then, the most qualified or best-trained citizens were taken captive and used to work in their captor's capital.

Whether voluntarily or not, Berosus ended up on the Greek island of Kos where he built a school and an observatory for astronomy. Due to his great knowledge, he taught in Athens where a copper statue with a gold-plated tongue, a credit to his speaking abilities, has been erected in his honor.

Berosus wrote three books around 290 BC. Unfortunately, as we mentioned before, the originals have been lost, but they have been cited in so many other books that we know what they were about.

Book 1 described Babylon, the story of Creation, and "the fish man" Oannes, who taught the arts and sciences.

Book 2 and 3 were written about the 10 kings[9] before the Flood, the story of the Great Flood, a list of Chaldean and Arabic kings, and the history of Assyria, Babylon, and Persia.

On top of these, other works describing Berosus have been found. They are often called pseudo-Berosus because experts doubt their authenticity.[10] In these works, details that didn't exist in Berosus's work, such as one of Noah's names being Arsa and cities being named after him, can be found.

The History of the Chaldeans

In his writings, Babylonica describes Berosus's world before and after the Flood based on ancient sources from the Temple of Ball in Babylon.

Berosus's writings of the pre-Flood period also include a number of fairy-tale like stories about a fish-man to whom he gives the Greek name Oanes.

But once in a while, there are interesting coincidences between this account and the one from the Bible. One example is the presence of 10 kings before the Flood is equivalent to the patriarchs of the Bible, of which Noah was number 10. Their names, of course, are different because the names at that time had meaning and therefore changed according to the language one spoke.

Berosus's Noah was named *Ziusudra* (or in Greek *Xi-suthros*) which means "he who found life." Utna-pishtim, the name used for the Noahic figure in Accadian, one of the ancient languages from Mesopotamia, has the same meaning.

The Sumerians and Babylonians called Noah *Atra-hasis*, "the especially wise one."

An ancient Babylonian cylinder depicts the myth of Oanes, a fish god with its legs and human heads, which appears in Berosus' report. In the center is the Tree of Life, also known from the Book of Genesis in the Bible.

Wisdom Is Buried

Even though Berosus follows the story from the clay tablets, he also adds some things that can't be found on the tablets. Namely, the Sumerian Noah, Xisuthros, was told before the Flood to bury his tablets in Sippar, which is located outside of present-day Baghdad. Xisuthros was also raptured to heaven after the Ark was stranded, and he more or less heard a voice from heaven telling him to travel to Babylon and remain there and dig up the tablets.

It is known that a Babylonian dig in Sippar took place under the Aramaic King Nabonid[12] (555 BC) in order to find the ancient writings. Whether they found them or not is unknown.[13]

Berosus also has a set date for the Flood, something that is not found in the ancient tablets, but unfortunately he gives no year.

Berosus's Text: [14]

"Kronos[15] revealed himself to him (Xisuthros) in a dream and said, 'Mankind shall be destroyed by a great flood on the fifteenth day in the month of Daisios.'[16] He (Kronos) commanded that he should bury all of the ancient, middle, and final (that is, all) writings and lay them in the city of Si[s]parenes (=Sippar[17]), the Sun City, and he is to build a ship and go onboard with his relations and close friends. He is to bring food and drink and load it with birds and beasts. And when he had finished this, he was to set sail.

He asked to where he should sail and he (Kronos) answered, 'To the gods to pray that it may be well for mankind.' He obeyed and built a ship five laths long and two laths wide. He did all which he was commanded and brought his wife, children and close friends with him into the ship."

The Birds Are Released

"When the Flood took place and stopped again, Xisuthros released a few birds. They found neither food nor place to rest and thus returned to the ship. After a few days Xisuthros released the birds again; these came back to the ship with food and had clay on them. When he released them for the third time, they did not come back to the ship. Xisuthros understood that the earth was not visible. He loosened a part of the joint of the ship and saw that the ship had landed on a mountain; he along with his wife and daughter and the captain on the ship got out, fell to the ground on their knees, and built an Altar and offered to the gods. Together with those who went out from the ship, he disappeared."

The Bible contains the same elements in Genesis, chapter 8, telling of the release of a bird (verses 6-12), the removing of the roof of the ship (verse 13), and the sacrifice of thanksgiving at the altar (verse 20).

Xisuthros Just Disappears

After this comes Berosus's addition of the disappearance of Xisuthros. This is not in agreement with The Epic Poem of Gilgamesh where Gilgamesh seeks out Xisuthros, who lives together with his wife and looks like a normal man.

"When Xisuthros and his companion did not come back, those that had waited in the ship disembarked in order to look for him and yelled out his name. Xisuthros was nowhere to be seen, but a voice came from the sky commanding them to be god-fearing, for he had been taken away to dwell with the gods and his wife and daughter and the captain of the ship shared in the honor.

And he said they were to go back to Babylon, and he commanded them to take the writings from Sipparos and give them to mankind. He also said that they found themselves in the land of Armenia. When they had heard this, they made offerings to the gods and walked to Babylon."

Where Are We?

It's interesting that Berosus confirms that the Babylonians also came from Armenia, from which they wandered by foot. The people are told that "they found themselves in the land of Armenia," but at the same time we are told that they originally came from Babylon, which they now have to *go back to.*

"The ship landed in the middle of Armenia in the mountains of the Kordyai (Kurds), and some scraped asphalt off of the ship and took it with them to use as amulets."

This "*asphalt*" is the Berossian equivalent of the more precise instructions found in the Bible. There Noah is told to cover both sides of the ship in pitch to make it water-proof.

"After they came to Babylon and unburied the written pieces from Si[s]paros and while they established many cities and built temples, they rebuilt Babylon."

Sippar og Babylon, according to Berosus, had existed before the Flood, and it is from here that the survivors originally came. Berosus does not confirm the modern criticism of the Bible either, which is found in the form of a theory that the Flood was only a local occurrence in which the Euphrates River flooded. If this were the case, the Ark would not have landed in the mountains in Armenia, over a thousand kilometers away.

Astronomical Numbers – or a Mistranslation?

Berosus' numbers are completely exaggerated. If they are true, then there were 432,000 years from Creation to the Flood, but it was a time period in which only 10 kings reigned. There is probably a mistake in the translation, just as when Berosus or the clay tablets give other numbers.

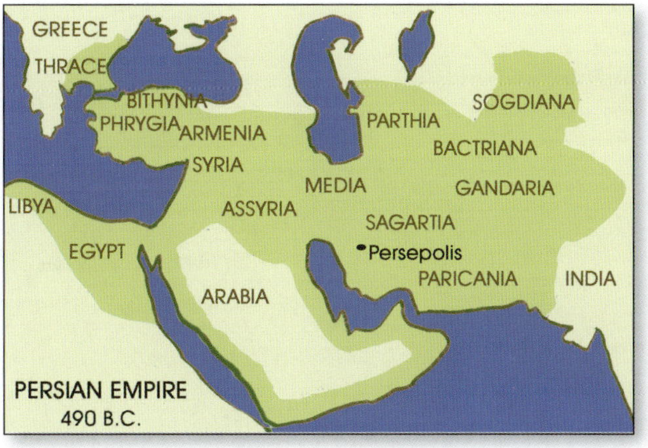

The mighty Persian Empire (c. 490 B.C.) stretched out from Libya to India. Just a few centuries later, at the time of Berosus it was conquered by a new empire, the Greeks.

One of the world's leading experts in clay tablets, Professor Stephanie Dalley of Oxford, England, has looked at the Babylonian numbers, and she thinks that these 432,000 years should be divided by 5. This would give 86,400 weeks, which is precisely the same as the Bible's 1,656 years from Creation to the Flood.[18] (If you reckon with the calculation used in this book, however, there are 2256 years between the two. That means that the Babylonian years must be divided by approximately 3.67)

Berosus's numbers should not be taken at face value when talking about the Ark either. Berosus writes that the Ark was 5 laths long and 2 laths wide. This is the equivalent of 960 x 384 meters (3,150 x 1,260 feet). An American football field is only 360 ft. long (including end zones) and 160 ft. wide. That means that according to Berosus's measurements, there was enough room for almost 70 entire football fields on the deck of the Ark alone! This is about 80 times as big as the statistics Moses and Gilgamesh give.[19]

Was He Telling Where They Were?

David Fasold, one of the pioneers in Ark research, had a background as an officer in the marines and had been a treasure hunter on the bottom of the ocean. Fasold knew that the ancient navigation tool "mr" had been used for navigation and for building the pyramids. The instrument makes a triangle with a right angle (90 degrees) and an acute angle of 36 degrees, the proportion being 5 x 2. Fasold got the idea that Berosus' measurement of 5 x 2 laths was possibly a reference to degrees rather than the size of the Ark. That instead of laths was to be used as a proportion.

David Fasold,art hunter

Fasold unfolded the map and drew an acute angle of 36 degrees based on the meridian in Persepolis, just as the people of Berosus's time would have done when Persepolis was the "Greenwich" meridian.

The Point of Intersection?

Fasold assumed that the Ark lay north of Persepolis because the ancient sources name the Kurdish mountains or Armenia. Therefore, it must lie in the north following the sun westward. But how is one to find the point of

*A Turkish road map of the most eastward, Kurdish dominated Turkey shows Lake Van (Garden of Eden?), the frontiers to Armenia, the enclave Nakhitchevan (Noah's City?), and Iran. Mt. Ararat is here marked with a red circle. According to David Fasolds theory, Berosus was not talking about the size of the ark but giving the coordinates for archaeal location. (44 * 15 east of Greenwich and 39 degrees 26 minutes north of the Equator). The Ark would then be just south of Mt. Ararat, near the Durupinar place, that Fasold was a supporter of.*

intersection between a 36 degree angle and a 90 degree angle?

He guessed that the length of the Ark could be the answer.

If one were to convert the 300 cubits to feet, it would equal 515 feet, provided that the Egyptian cubit was used.[22] If these 515 feet were converted to 515 minutes on a map, they would equal 8 degrees, 35 minutes. (A degree minute is 1/60 of a degree, and we know that the Babylonians used this system. We got it from them.)

If we go 8 degrees, 35 minutes west, where do we end up? **44 degrees, 15 minutes east of Greenwich.** And on which latitude do the two angles cross? The point of intersection is **39 degrees, 26 minutes north of the Equator.**

So where is that? Very close to the "boat-shaped object" that Fasold thought was the remains of the Ark. It is also very close to Mt. Ararat.

There is also another coincidence. Both the Egyptian and the Persian geographic centers lay on the same latitude, 30 degrees north of the Equator. That is exactly 566 minutes south of Ararat, which is the same as the Ark's length 515 feet + height 51 feet = 566 feet.

The Ark was the Navel of the World

One can, of course, accuse Fasold for trying to make things point to "his" Ark (the boat-shaped object). But with little change in the measurement of feet and laths, it would as well point to the nearby Mt. Ararat. And Berosus might well have been misunderstood, or he himself misquoted the old tablets when talking of the *dimension* of the Ark instead of the *distance* to the Ark.

The landing point of the Ark must have been so important for the people after the Flood that the great Egyptians as well as the Persians wanted to place the "center of the world" in relationship to the original "navel" of the new world – the Ark.

We know that they had an advanced knowledge of the circumference of the Earth. They measured this with trigonometry.

Using the stars and the "mr", they could measure exactly where they were on the Earth in degrees from Persepolis or the Great Pyramid. Most of this great knowledge from the first generations after the flood was later lost and then reinvented in Europe in the time of the Middle Ages two or three thousand years later.

Did they carry this knowledge from the Ark – from the time before the deluge? And what other great knowledge did they have in ancient times, which we have not yet reinvented?

Endnotes

1 Berosus is quoted by the following people, among others: Alexander Polyhistor, Josephus, Athenaeus, Clement, Abydenus, Eusebius of Caesarea, Syncellus,

2 **Alexander Polyhistor** (c.105 – 35 f.Kr.) a Greek philosopher, geographer, and historian. Originally he was a slave in Rome, later promoted to citizen. His works have been lost, but he is quoted by Eusebius, Syncellus, Josephus, Atheneus, and Clement of Alexandria.

3 **Flavius Josephus**, a Jewish priest and historian (37-100 AD).

Quoted Alexander Polyhistor.
4 **Athenaeus** (200 AD) Greek grammatician and author.
Quoted Alexander Polyhistor.
5 **Clement** (150 -215 AD) Bishop of Alexandria. Quoted Alexander Polyhistor
6 **Abydenus**, a disciple of Aristotle, the Greek philosopher and scientist who lived in the 4th century. His manuscript has been lost, but he is quoted by Eusebius and Syncellus.
7 Eusebius Pamphilius (264 – 338 AD) Bishop of Caesarea. Quotes Abydenus, Apollodorus, and Alexander Polyhistor.
8 Syncellus (early 9th century AD) Byzantine monk and scribe known as "George Syncellus." Quoted Abydenus, Apollodorus, and Alexander Polyhistor.
9 In Genesis 5 Moses gives us a list of the ten kings – the patriarchs – before the Flood.
10 These were made public in 1498 by a Dominican priest named Giovanni Nanni, from Viterbo, which is north of Rome. He was also known as Annius of Viterbo. He also publicized fragments of Manetho, an Egyptian historian, who was a contemporary of Berossus. His collected works, along with his commentary, was called Antiquities. Six years after Giovanni's death, Petrus Crinitus claimed that they were false. The pope then seized all of the manuscripts and hid them in the Vatican.
11 According to Genesis 10:22–23.
12 According to some of the ancient writings, Nabonid was Babylon's last king and father to Belshazzar, who ruled Babylon together with him in the last part of his reign. This is the same King Belshazzar the Book of Daniel speaks of in chapter 5, explaining how in a drunken orgy he sipped from the holy vessels of gold and silver taken from the temple in Jerusalem. Afterwards he sees a hand write on the wall, "mené, mené, teqél, peres." Daniel interpreted it as such: "mene, God has numbered the days of your kingdom and brought it to an end; tekel, you have been weighed on the scales and found wanting; peres, your kingdom is divided and given to the Medes and Persians." (Dan. 5:26-28). The same evening the Persians came and Belshazzar was killed.
13 According to Komoróczy (1973) pp. 134-….
14 Translated to English from the Danish version by Mogens Weitemeyer, *Herodots og Berossos beskrivelæse af Babylonien*, Published by Museum Tusculanums Forlag, The University of Copenhagen, 1995, ISBN 87 7289 356 7. This version is built on a collection of the safest/earliest sources. The first portion is from Synkellos's Byzantine edition from the 9th century, but in Eusebios's Armenian translations from the 4th century, the measurements of the Ark are given to be the length of 15 shots of an arrow and the width of 2.
15 The Greek name from the Babylonian god Ea, the same as the Sumerian Enki, also known as the Lord of Eridu (Eden).
16 Daisios is a Macedonian month. The date is equivalent with the 11th of either May or June.
17 Ancient city near present day Baghdad.
18 Myths from Mesopotamia: Creation, the Flood, Gilgamesh, and Others (Oxford World's Classics) by Stephanie Dalley. Berossos and Manetho, Introduced and Translated: Native Traditions in Ancient Mesopotamia and Egypt, by Gerald P. Verbrugghe.
19 Gilgamesh speaks of an IKU, which equals the measurements found in the Bible.
20 Most of this information comes from Jonathan Gray's book, The Ark Conspiracy.
21 King Darius (or Dareios) is also mentioned in the Bible, in the Book of Daniel, ch. 6. Daniel, a Jew forced to move, saw the writing on the wall for King Belshazzar. "That same night Belshazzar the Chaldean king was slain. So Darius the Mede received the kingdom at about the age of sixty-two." Dan. 5:30. Daniel became one of the three royal wise men but was thrown in a den of lions because he would not bow down to a statue of Darius. When he survived the den, the king put his faith in the God of Israel and commanded the entire kingdom to "fear and tremble before Daniel's God."
22 Assuming that the Ark's 300 cubits were the same as the Egyptian 20.6 inches, making 515 feet. That is, the exact same as the boat-shaped object in Duripinar.

The Cheops Pyramid at Giza in Cairo was used like the present-day Greenwich Meridian where degrees are calculated.

The Persian Empire confidently moved the meridian to King Darius' mighty monuments in Persepolis. (left)

*Berosus' figures could indicate that the place where the ark was stranded originally was the starting point for degree purposes. The Ark was the common starting point for the great civilizations that arose after the Flood. Ruins of the Tower of Babel are also in the same longitude (44 *) as that of the Ark.*

Kurds around the mountain often live in simple houses built with local materials and grass on the roof. (Photo: Futtrup

Chapter 7

From Josephus to the Middle Ages

Roman bust said to be of Flavius Josephus, the man who at first rose against the Romans and later joined them...

The name **Flavius Josephus** (37 – c.100 AD) often pops up in Ark research due to his book *The Antiquities of the Jews*, which names the Great Flood, the Ark, and Noah.

Josephus fought against the Romans in the Jewish Revolt that led to the destruction of Jerusalem in the year 70 AD He was captured after which he served the Romans. Later he was released, and he settled in Rome. Here he wrote *The Jewish War*, describing the war between the Jews and the Romans, as well as the Jews' own story in *Jewish Antiquity*.

Josephus has been a magnificent non-Christian source from which facts about Jesus and the first Christians can be derived. Thanks to him we have confirmation from an almost enemy source that Jesus, John the Baptist, Pontius Pilate, James, and others indeed lived. He can also confirm other details from the gospels (Matthew, Mark, Luke and John). But the reason that Josephus is such a great source for this information is that the events in question took place in his lifetime or immediately before.

Contrarily, when Josephus writes about the distant past, he has no choice but to depend on the other written authorities such as the Books of the Law (Genesis, Exodus, Leviticus, and Numbers all written by Moses), the works of Berosus or Nic(h)olas of Damascus, or whatever tradition suggests. In superficial articles and books about the Ark, authors often write that "Josephus writes that pitch was scraped off the Ark." But they are forgetting, or don't know, that in this instance Josephus is just quoting Berosus.

Josephus Writes

. . .in process of time they were perverted, and forsook the practices of their forefathers; and did neither pay those honors to God which were appointed them, nor had they any concern to do justice towards men … For many angels of God accompanied with women, and begat sons that proved unjust, and despisers of all that was good, on account of the confidence they had in their own strength; for the tradition is, that these men did what resembled the acts of those whom the Grecians call giants. But Noah was very uneasy at what they did; and being displeased at their conduct, persuaded them to change their dispositions and their acts for the better; but seeing they did not yield to him, but were slaves to their wicked pleasures, he was afraid they would kill him, together with his wife and children, and those they had married; so he departed out of that land.[1]

Josephus the Historian represented here in William Whiston's English translation.

It seems that Josephus either wrote his own continuation to the reference to giants in Genesis, or he supports Jewish legend.

"Now God loved this man for his righteousness, yet he not only condemned those other men for their wickedness, but determined to destroy the whole race of mankind, and to make another race that should be pure from wickedness; and cutting short their lives, and making their years not so many as they formerly lived, but one hundred and twenty only ... God suggested to him the following contrivance and way of escape. He should make an ark of four stories high, three hundred cubits long, fifty cubits broad, and thirty cubits high ... Now this ark had firm walls, and a roof, and was braced with cross beams, so that it could not be any way drowned or overborne by the violence of the water.

This calamity happened in the six hundredth year of Noah's government, ... and this was two thousand six hundred and fifty-six years from Adam..." [2]

Josephus follows Genesis' information very closely here, but interestingly enough he adds an extra story onto the Ark and adds 1,000 years to the biblical chronology, which seems to have 1,656 years from Creation to the Flood according to Bishop Ussher's generally accepted calculations. In Paul L. Maier's translation of Josephus, there are 2,262 years from Creation to the Flood. For more see the chapter "Confused Chronology."

"... the water poured down forty entire days, till it became fifteen cubits higher than the earth. When the rain ceased, the water did but just begin to abate after one hundred and fifty days, (that is, on the seventeenth day of the seventh month,) it then ceasing to subside for a little while. After this, the ark rested on the top of a certain mountain in Armenia; which, when Noah understood, he opened it; and seeing a small piece of land about it, he continued quiet, and conceived some cheerful hopes of deliverance. But a few days afterward, when the water was decreased to a greater degree, he sent out a raven, as desirous to learn whether any other part of the earth were left dry by the water, and whether he might go out of the ark with safety; but the raven, finding all the land still overflowed, returned to Noah again." [3]

Like the Greek version of the Books of the Law in the Septuagint version of the Bible, Josephus, who originally wrote in Aramaic and was later translated to Greek, uses the name Armenia instead of the Hebrew Urartu or Ararat, which originates from a time when this kingdom existed in Armenia. There is no doubt that here Ararat and Armenia are synonyms for the same location. Josephus continues:

"And after seven days he sent out a dove, to know the state of the ground; which came back to him covered with mud, and bringing an olive branch: hereby Noah learned that the earth was become clear of the flood. So after he had staid seven more days, he sent the living creatures out of the ark; and both he and his family went out, when he also sacrificed to God, and feasted with his companions. However, the Armenians call this place, The Place of Descent; for the ark being saved in that place, its remains are shown there by the inhabitants to this day." [4]

Stranded

The William Whiston translation of Josephus from 1737 suggested in a footnote that the Greek name of the location where the Ark was "stranded" or "descended" ("apo bah tay reon" in Greek) was a derivation of the name of an Armenian city, Nachidsheuan, which was supposedly the first city after the Flood. He writes:

"This (apo bah tay reon), or Place of Descent, is the proper rendering of the Armenian name of this very city. It is called in Ptolemy Naxuana, and by Moses Chorenensis, the Armenian historian, Idsheuan; but at the place itself Nachidsheuan, which signifies the first place of descent, and is a lasting monument of the preservation of Noah in the ark, upon the top of that mountain, at whose foot it was built, as the first city or town after the flood. See Antiq. B. XX. ch. 2. sect. 3; and Moses Chorenensis, who also says elsewhere, that another town was related by tradition to have been called Seron, or, The Place of Dispersion, on account of the dispersion of Xisuthrus's or Noah's sons, from thence first made. Whether any remains of this ark be still preserved, as the people of the country suppose, I cannot certainly tell. Mons. Tournefort had, not very long since, a mind to see the place himself, but met with too great dangers and difficulties to venture through them." [5]

Today, a city called *Nakhichevan* (or Naxcivan) exists in an enclave of Azerbaijan between Iran and Armenia about 100 kilometers southeast of Mt. Ararat. There is also a small town north of Igdir on the border with the same name. Linguists cannot agree whether the name comes from the "landing place" or not. And as we shall later see, the original Nachidsheuan or Naxuan has possibly been found much closer.

Josephus continues quoting sources:

Berosus the Chaldean ... when he is describing the circumstances of the flood, he goes on thus:

"It is said there is still some part of this ship in Armenia, at the mountain of the Cordyaeans; and that some people carry off pieces of the bitumen, which they take away, and use chiefly as amulets for the averting of mischiefs."

Hieronymus the Egyptian also, who wrote the Phoenician Antiquities, and Mnaseas, and a great many more, make mention of the same. Nay, Nicolaus of Damascus, in his ninety-sixth book, hath a particular relation about them; where he speaks thus: "There is a great mountain in Armenia, over Minyas, called Baris, upon which it is reported that many who fled at the time of the

Eusebius (264-340) as pictured by André Thevet in Les Vrais Portraits et Vies Hommes Illustrés, 1584.

Deluge were saved; and that one who was carried in an ark came on shore upon the top of it; and that the remains of the timber were a great while preserved. This might be the man about whom Moses the legislator of the Jews wrote." [6]

His Contemporaries

Nicholas of Damascus (born 30 BC) is associated with the Jewish king, Herod the Great, whose biography he wrote. He also wrote about the history of the world. As mentioned above, he wrote about the Ark in the first century, just shortly before Josephus' time.

It's very interesting that Nicholas writes about the timber using the past tense. It was "long preserved," but now it is obviously gone or hidden.

We also notice that the writer doesn't keep to the biblical account. Here it is not only Noah and his family that are saved, but "many fugitives" crawl up this awesome mountain even though the Bible tells that even the tops of the mountains were flooded and everyone perished.

This is worth noting because Nicholas writes in a Jewish context, whereas the Biblical account must have been common knowledge. But it was well known that Herod was not especially God-fearing, and the people with whom he kept company were not either.

When Nicholas refers to Noah landing on Baris (which is probably the same as Marris, the Armenian name for Mt. Ararat), it's not a fact from the Bible either, but rather it tells that Baris is obviously the highest mountain at this time.

The First Christian Sources

With the onset of Christianity, a new interest in Noah's Ark came about. Many from the Church wrote about the Ark.

Bishop Theophilus of Antioch in northern Syria (180 AD) restates the biblical facts but also adds,[8] "And of the Ark, the remains are to this day to be seen in the Arabian mountains..." Is it plausible that the Kurdish Mountains were also called the Arabian Mountains? Or does this Theophilus have his own theory?

٤٤- وَقِيلَ يَٰٓأَرۡضُ ٱبۡلَعِي
مَآءَكِ وَيَٰسَمَآءُ
أَقۡلِعِي وَغِيضَ ٱلۡمَآءُ وَقُضِيَ ٱلۡأَمۡرُ
وَٱسۡتَوَتۡ عَلَى ٱلۡجُودِيِّۖ
وَقِيلَ بُعۡدٗا لِّلۡقَوۡمِ ٱلظَّٰلِمِينَ ۝

The Church Father **Eusebius** was bishop in Cesarea and as the author of ***Chronicals*** was also the first ***church historian.*** He wrote in the 3rd century that *a small part of the Ark* could still be seen in the "Gordian Mountains." Again, we are in the Kurdish Mountains, but he is probably quoting Berosus.

The historian, **Faustus of Byzantium** (4th century), who was a Greek and wrote about Armenian history, also placed the Ark in the Gordian (Kurdish) Mountains in the Canton of

Gordukh. He does this in connection with the tellings of St. James (Bishop of Nisibis, now Nusaybin c. 100 km from Cudi Dagh in Syria). Legend has it that St. James tried in vain to find the Ark but was instead awarded a piece of it by an angel. Later retellings locate the occurrence on Mt. Ararat, but James was a bishop in Syria.

Bishop Ephiphianus of Salamis[9] (4th century) also states that the Ark landed in the Gordian Mountains. He also asserts that the remains can still be found, and if one searches well, one can also see the altar that Noah built to thank God for his salvation. In 380 Ad., he argues the truth of Christianity and writes, "Do you seriously suppose that we are unable to prove our point, when even to this day the remains of Noah's ark are shown in the country of the Kurds?" [10]

Or course, this could also just be empty rhetoric, but this Greek bishop also states as late as 380 AD that the Ark "even to this day" is shown in the land of the Kurds. Since the Kurds have never had their own country, he must be referring to the areas where the Kurds traditionally lived.

Isidore of Seville (560-636) from southern Spain also places the Ark in the Kurdish Mountains but adds without any explanation that, *"Ararat is a mountain* in Armenia, where the historians testify that the Ark came to rest after the Flood. So even to this day, wood remains of it are to be seen there."[11]

We know that there was no mountain in Armenia called Mount Ararat at that point. The Armenians, Kurds, and Turks all have their own names for the largest of their mountains. But in Europe, the largest mountain, from this point on, came to be called Mt. Ararat.

We only know Isidore's writings from a quote in the 16th century, so a later rewriting of names is also possible.

Muslim Understanding

The Qur'an, the holy book of the Muslims, was written after the 7th century.

Here Noah is considered one of the prophets, and it is written, "The Ark came to rest upon Al-Judi" (Houd 11:44).

According to Muslim tradition, multiple Al-Judi mountains exist. One of them is Cudi Dagh, or Jabal Judi, on the border between Syria and Iraq. Cudi is pronounced Yudi, with a soft j or y sound. This mountain has been connected with Noah's mountain. Place names all over the mountain also refer to Noah and the Ark.

Another possible location is the Judi Mountains in Saudi Arabia, which are geographically closer to Islam's two holy cities, Mecca and Medina.

The third Al-Judi Mountain is precisely the same place where the boat-shaped object has been found – on the border of Iran.

Mohammed was very interested in both Judaism and Christianity, and some experts believe that he was a member of a Jewish-Christian monotheistic

sect in Saudi-Arabia before he began a new religion.

Many biblical stories can also be found in the Qur'an, but the stories have been given their own character. The account of Noah in the Qur'an, for example, is about evil people refusing to worship only *one* God. This was the exact same problem Mohammad had with the heathens in Saudi Arabia. He had stopped serving many gods and argued, like the other *hanifs* (monotheists = Jews and Christians), that there was only one God.

Confusion About Where the Ark Is

Bishop Eutychius was the bishop in Alexandria in the ninth century, and he says, "The Ark landed on the mountains of Ararat;" as it says in the Bible, but he also adds that, "It is Jabal Judi near Mosul." This city is all the way down by Nineveh, over 150 miles south of Mount Cudi Dagh, the other Al Judi. I feel obliged to point out on his behalf that he lived in Egypt.

Al Masudi, a well-known geographer and historian in the 10th century, constitutes that the Ark landed on "Jabal Judi" and in addition adds that it is about 25-30 miles from the Tigris River. This description fits Mount Cudi in Syria.

Ibn Haukal, a Muslim geographer, who in the10th century also calls Noah's mountain Al-Judi (as does Muhammed in the Quran) but puts its location around Nesbin (today Nusaybin in Syria) where Noah supposedly built a city at the foot of the mountain.

In the 12th century, **Benjamin of Tudela,** a Jewish explorer, writes that a certain Omar Ben al-Khatab removed the Ark from the twin peaks and re-established it on an island in the Tigris known as Jizireh Ben Omar. He writes, too, that the aforementioned lies at the foot of Mt. Ararat, but it lies at the foot of Cudi Dagh. So the conclusion must be that he either didn't know what he was talking about or that at this time some people called Mount Cudi Mt. Ararat. Due to a lack of information, the confusion multiplies.

The Dominican monk Vincent of Beauvais mentioned "the first city Noah built" by the name of Laudume, and it was supposed to lie at the foot of the mountain. (Painting from Il Capitolo del Domenicani.)

Was the Ark Hidden by a Volcanic Eruption?

We know that at some point a great volcanic eruption threw a sixth of Mount Ararat in the air leaving a gorge, Ahora Gorge, on the northeast side of the mountain. We're not talking about the 1840 earthquake that annihilated the village and monastery there. No, this was a much greater explosion that happened maybe even thousands of years ago.

Along with such an amazing act of God, ash, lava, stone, and earth were spread over a very large area. The explosion of Mt. St. Helens in Washington State in 1980 is comparable in strength.

This great explosion on Mt. Ararat could have obliterated or hidden the Ark

From the harem the women could overlook the beautiful landscape and imagine themselves far, far away.

The Isaac Pasha Castle is in the middle in front of the old cave castle in the mountains, which is all a few miles behind Dogubayazit. The original city, Beyazit, lay just below the castle according to old pictures. (Photo: Futtrup)

under ash, earth, and lava while at the same time making the surrounding area uninhabitable and killing the population so that no one after this time could tell exactly where the Ark lay.

We also know that there was a mega volcano on the other side of the border in Iran and that there are regular earthquakes in the vicinity.

If these volcanoes exploded around Jesus' time or before, that would explain why no one knows, based on early sources, where the Ark lies, but insecurity has set in because the Ark has actually disappeared.

Of course, our ancestors knew that the Ark was located in Ararat – but they didn't know exactly where.

The Silk Road to the East

One day we were standing together with Dr. Salih Bayraktutan, the geologist studying one of these so-called "anchor stones" on a little mountain around the Valley of the Eight.

Just below us WAS a small road ran which reminded me of the narrow roads that run between the fields in Denmark. It twisted and turned up through the mountains until it disappeared.

It was the ancient Silk Road. By means of this road, **Marco Polo** (1254-1325) and the other adventurers and travelers had journeyed by foot, horse, or camel on their way to the Far East in search of silk, spices, and other rare goods in order to bring them to the West and sell them for large sums.

The Isaac Pasha Castle

These travelers also had to pass the local kings' castles. One of these castles was the Isaac Pasha Castle, which is located with a view over the valley. It is only 400 years old, but before this castle was built, another castle existed, chiseled into the face of the mountain just behind the Isaac Pasha castle. The caves here date back to the Urartu (1300 BC) and probably even the Hurrians (c. 2000 BC), who were also called cave dwellers.

The traders most likely paid a polite visit to the castle on their way. For the most part, they were welcomed with great hospitality, invited into the beautifully decorated guest hall at Isaac Pasha's castle, and given food and drink while they told of news from distant lands through which they had traversed. They may also have traded with these kings, but gifts were definitely bestowed upon them.

From the dining room stretched a corridor to the master's harem where the most beautiful women, often from far-away lands, spent their lives behind high walls. From the harem's quarters, a staircase led to a small, enclosed garden where the women could enjoy the rays of the sun up in these somewhat cold heights. They never came outside of the castle walls, but they could always look out over the majestic landscape and dream themselves away. They surely were not allowed to speak freely with the travelers. Women and men were kept at a distance, but through the eunuchs the women may still have heard news from the lands where they once lived before they were given away as gifts.

Ararat Could Not Be Overseen

The travelers from Europe had to come through this exact valley where the impressive Mt. Ararat with a snow-dressed Ataturk top towers with its 16,945 feet. They surely thought about the biblical account of Noah's Ark. And if it didn't land on the highest mountain, then where did it land?

Many travelers told of the mammoth Mount Ararat "where Noah's Ark landed," but besides this cheap assumption, there were no serious studies. Comments like "people say it's still up there" continually arose, but there wasn't any fast evidence among these thin claims.

Let's meet some of the traders that took the Silk Road past this spot. Even if they can't tell us much about the Ark besides that "people say it's still up there," they can tell us something about the setting and environment.

William of Rubruck (1255), a Franciscan monk, was sent by King Louis IX of France to the Mongolian emperor. He writes that, "Near this city (Naxua) there is a mountain of which is said, 'Here lies Noah's Ark.' The one (is) larger than the other, and Araxes (River) flows at the foot of them; there is a city they call Cemanum, which, when translated, means 'eight', and they say that it is named after the eight people that came out of the Ark and who built it on the great mountain. Many have tried to climb it but have not been able to."

And then he retells the story, with a bishop as the source, about the pious monk who tried in vain to climb the mountain and was finally stopped by an angel who gave him a piece of the Ark that is now kept in the Etchmiadzin monastery in Dadjivan.

William ploddingly adds, "The mountain doesn't seem so high to me that men shouldn't be able to climb it." But he finds an explanation in the local mythology.

"An old man gave me a good reason why not to try climbing it. The mountain is called Massis, which is (the) feminine (form) in their language. 'No one' he said, 'should climb the mountain. It is the mother of the earth.'" (Now we know that the word Massis is not feminine. That type of word doesn't have a specific gender in Armenian, but the mountain could have been understood as a mother anyway.)[12]

William naming "The City of the Eight," as he calls Cemanum, makes this story about the Ark particularly interesting.

At this time the area was still inhabited by Christian Armenians, even though they had fallen under Turkish rule. They *could* have shown him The Valley of the Eight with its ancient monuments as well as the village that is now called Arzep, which we visited to see the so-called anchor stones. But we cannot know if it is the city that he calls "The City of the Eight."

Vincent of Beauvais writes in the 13th century, "In Armenia there is a noble city called Ani where a thousand churches and a hundred thousand families or households are to be found. The Tartars captured this city in twelve days. Near it is Mount Ararat where Noah's Ark rests, and at the foot of that mountain is the first city Noah built, called Laudume. Closer by the city flows the river *Ararthosi*, which traverses the plain of Mongan where the Tartars winter, and it then empties into the Caspian Sea..."

Adam Olearius mentioned that the Ark might be petrified.

That city Noah supposedly built, *Laudume*, could possibly be the same city William of Rubruck calls Cemanum – "The City of the Eight." It could also be the city Rubruck calls Naxua. We will come back to that later.

But the big city with the thousand churches is hard to find. Today Ani is a ghost town 45 km east of Kras. The city still has a one-kilometer long wall and many ruins. It was partially destroyed by an earthquake in 1319, and the Silk Road took another route, causing the city to lose its significance. But according to the *Lonely Planet* guide for Turkey, Ani should have had almost 100,000 inhabitants.[13]

Odoric of Pordenone (1286-1331), a Franciscan monk from northern Italy, also visited this area and wanted to climb the mountain. He doesn't call it Ararat, but Sarbiscalo, which is most likely the same mountain, and he also states that the local people believed that no one would ever be able to climb this mountain because it doesn't please "the highest one" (God).

There is also **Jordanus**, a French Dominican friar and missionary to India, who around 1330 describes the mountain, supposedly inhabited by great snakes and wild animals. He doesn't scale the mountain either but believes he has been to the location where Noah planted his vineyard.

The last part is very interesting because there actually is a place in The Valley of the Eight which some connect with Noah and his vineyard because of its ancient stone walls.

Marco Polo, the famous explorer, who adorns the Italian bank notes, also passed Mt. Ararat – but he didn't explore it more closely.

Marco Polo is often named in association with travels past Mount Ararat in the 14th century, but even this great adventurer does nothing more than retell local legends about the mountain.

He writes, "In the central part of Armenia stands an exceedingly large and high mountain upon which it is said that the Ark of Noah rested." And he mentions that the upper regions of the mountain never thaw (*The Travels of Marco Polo*, New York, Crown Publishers, 1958).

Sir John Mandeville, who from 1322-1356 traveled around the world, and Jean de Barbe or Jean de Bourgogne from Liège in France, are possibly one and the same man. He tells that people went from Erzerum (a college town today) to a mountain he called Sabissocolle. This name sounds very familiar when considering Odoric's city name, Sarbiscalo. But John Mandeville continues:

"...and there beside is another mountain called Ararat, but the Jews call it Taneez, where Noah's ship rested, and still is upon that mountain; and men may see it afar in clear weather. That mountain is a full seven miles high; and some men say that they have seen and touched the ship, and put their fingers in the parts where the devil went out, when Noah said "Benedicte" (*blessed).* But they that say so speak without knowledge; for no one can go up the mountain for the great abundance of snow which is always on the mountain, both summer and winter, so that no man ever went up since the time of Noah, except a monk, who, by God's grace, brought one of the planks down, which is yet in the monastery at the foot of the mountain. And beside is the city of Dayne, which was founded by Noah, near which is the city of Any, in which were one thousand churches." [14]

John Mandeville is most likely referring to Vincent of Beauvais' account. But that he writes this after the earthquake of 1319 without pointing out its effect on the city makes a man question how much research he did.

The Spaniard **Gonzales de Clavijo** (1415) also describes the mountain and mentions that there is a city at its foot, a city that Noah supposedly built but has since been deserted. It may be *Laudume* or *Cemanum*.

Otherwise he has no new information about the Ark.

Adam Olearius was a German envoy to the court of the Shah of Persia. He had changed his family name from Olschlager into Latin. In his book from 1647, he describes the great Ararat Mountain and states "The Armenians, and the Persians themselves, are of opinion, that there are still upon the said Mountain some remainders of the Ark, but that Time hath so hardened them, that they seem absolutely petrify'd." Then he mentions a wooden cross that was supposedly made of wood from the Ark.[15]

A contemporary of Olearius, the French traveler **Boulé Legouze,** drew sketches of both Big and Little Ararat in 1647, but they were unfortunately completely unrealistic views made in accordance with the style of the time. Besides placing the Ark at its peak and pointing out St. James and the small mountains, the sketches tell us nothing of interest.

The Englishman **Sir John Chardin** made a woodcut in 1711 of Ararat seen from Echmiadzin that is more realistic than Legouze's. It shows the Ark in an almost legendary way on the mountain's peak. You can also see that it was made before the earthquake of 1840 when the Ahora Gorge grew in breadth.

People Say...

Thus far we have the statement of many travellers quoting people who say "It (the Ark) is up there on Mount Ararat." Sometimes a black spot on one of the sides of the mountain was pointed out and was said to be the Ark. But it later turned out to be a projection of rocks.

However, we can conclude that the knowledge of the position of the Ark gradually disappeared. This probably happened after the gigantic volcanic eruption which, at the time of Jesus or during the centuries after, blasted one side of Mount Ararat and devastated the whole area.

The local people dared not climb the mountain because local rumor said that those who entered the Ark died. Was this just common superstition? Or did someone experience what Panda Lee and the first team did when they opened the hollow and entered the wooden construction? Namely that they got very sick?

Now we shall meet a Dutch traveler, **Jan Janszoon Struys**, who in 1694 almost against his will was taken up on the mountain. Here he encountered a sick monk who told him that he had been inside the Ark! [17]

Endnotes

1 *Antiquities of the Jews* - Book I, Ch. 3.1. Translated by William Whiston. Irrelevant sentences have been removed and marked with ellipses (...).

2 *Antiquities of the Jews* - Book I, Ch. 3.2-3. Translated by William Whiston.

3 *Antiquities of the Jews* - Book I, Ch. 3.5.

4 *Antiquities of the Jews* - Book I, Ch. 3.5.

5 Note 18 Antiquities of the Jews.

6 *Antiquities of the Jews* - Book I, Ch. 3.6.

8 Marcus Dod's translation of Ante-Nicene Fathers, II, 117.

9 Cyprus

10 Quoted from Jonathan Gray's *The Ark Conspiracy* p. 10.

11 Isidore of Seville, Etymologies, in *Scriptorium Classicorum Bibliotheca Oxoniensis*, (1911), XIV,8,5, trans. Montgomery, p. 80.

12 John Montgomery: *The Quest for Noah's Ark*, 2nd Edition, 1974.

13 *Lonely Planet: Turkey* pp. 623-624.

14 John Montgomery: *The Quest for Noah's Ark*, 2nd Edition, 1974.

15 Tim La Haye and John Morris: *The Ark on Ararat*, Thomas Nelson Publishers 1976.

16 This location was later examined by Navarra, among others, and it was established to be nothing more than a rock projection.

17 Research of Mount St. Helens' eruption – which was very similar to Mt. Ararat's – shows that everything was destroyed within a 45-mile radius, but the vegetation came back at an amazing pace after the catastrophe.

Chapter 8

A Monk Knew About the Ark

A Dutch globetrotter came to the city of Erevan in Armenia on June 30, 1670. Erevan – or Yerevan – is now the capital of the republic of Armenia, which is situated on the northeastern side of Mt. Ararat.

The Dutchman's name was Jan Janszoon Struys. He had travelled many countries in Europe and Asia from 1647 to 1672. He was probably some kind of pirate, and he had at this time been captured and sold as a slave to a Persian master. Later he was freed by a Georgian ambassador to the king of Poland.

He tells about all this in his memories published in 1677 in Holland. They were also published in French in 1681.[1] Struys was a man without formal education but more experienced than many European scholars.

Of course, one can doubt the truth of what Struys tells. For instance, he quotes the monk as saying that the weather on Ararat would be milder the higher you get. This is not true. Jan Janszoon Stryus claims to have met this sick hermit monk at Mt. Ararat. And this monk claims that he had been into the Ark, and he gave Jan a cross that he had cut out of the old ark wood and wrote a document to verify it.

Let Jan Janszoon Struys explain:

On the 30th of June, 1670 we arrived at Vruvan or Erivan. This city is situated at the foot of Mt. Ararat.... My master intended to sell me at Erivan, but the local inhabitants expressed no desire to buy me. When he had given up hope of a sale, two Carmelite monks asked if I were not a surgeon. They assured me that had I any skill along that line they would give me a case for which I would be very well paid if I succeeded. I answered that I was no surgeon and had never practiced the art.

Those good men did not believe me; after they had conferred together for some time, I clearly observed from their expressions that they took me for a competent surgeon but one who dared not admit it in his master's presence. So they took my master aside... Said one of them, "My brother is suffering from hernia and if your slave can cure him I shall make you a present of fifty crowns." My master replied, "Let me see to it." ... To me he said, "Are you aware that this gives you the chance to recover your freedom? If you're smart, you will take the opportunity, for you may never be afforded another so attractive or certain." ...

The proposal troubled me deeply. I knew my master to be the most grasping and avaricious man imaginable, and he was being tempted by a sure thing – an opportunity that would knock but once. Then there was the matter of the promise of my freedom, but I feared the blows of the rod, which I would be incapable of fleeing if the operation did not succeed to his liking. But after thinking it over a bit, I resolved to do everything my master wished me to do.

He praised my decision, ran to the monastery and promised them a miracle. The monk and he came to terms on the price and the following morning we left to find the patient, who lived as a hermit on Mount Ararat.

His hermitage was so far from the foot of the mountain that it took us seven days to reach it, and every day we covered five miles.[2] Every night we found a hut where we could sleep and each morning the hermit who occupied it would secure a donkey and a peasant for us - the peasant to guide us and the donkey to carry our provisions and wood. Without the latter, you cannot survive on this uninhabitable mountain. The cold is so intense that a horseman can go at full gallop on the ice for three hours without danger. The only means of warming oneself is the wood one carries, for there are no bushes or tries, not even thickets or brambles, and on the entire mountain not a bit of topsoil exists.

The first clouds through which we passed were dark and thick. The others were extremely cold and full of snow, though at a little lower altitude the temperature was high and the grapes and other fruit had fully ripened. When we experienced our third cloud-layer, we thought we would die from cold; we were at the end of the line, nothing could warm us up, and if that icy interval had continued another quarter of an hour, I believe that we would have died right there. But when we could proceed no farther, we providentially came upon one of the hermitages I mentioned previously. There a great fire was built for us, but it took me more than an hour before I felt it. From that day on, the farther we climbed, the more temperate the air we breathed and this mildness continued right to the cell of our patient. We arrived there the 7th of July.

The cell is large and well-hewn in rock, and the good hermit told me that he never felt more heat or more cold than he did just then, and neither was in evidence. He added that during the twenty-five years he had lived here he had experienced not a single gust of wind or drop of rainfall. And, said he, on the summit of the mountain, the climate is even more tranquil, for nothing ever changes there; it is for this reason that the Ark does not deteriorate and has remained for so many centuries in as pristine a state as on the first day it landed there.[3]

While my patient was talking, I was carefully observing him. When he had finished, I made him lie down, took his pulse, and examined the area in question. I found that he was suffering from a rupture, and that the hernial swelling resembled a large hen's egg.

"How long have you had to put up with this discomfort?" I asked him. "Only a month," he replied. "Good!" said I. "The cure does not come too late: I bring you a successful remedy."

I touched the ruptured spot again and told my patient with a laugh that in a week or two he would be as well as I.

The good monk was so overjoyed that he embraced me and said a hundred complimentary things, including the fact that I was quite obviously a true expert in my profession and that he was privileged to have fallen into my hands. Since his belief was important to my task, far from disillusioning him by sham modesty, I reinforced his conviction by relating numerous instances of high success in much more difficult cases. I put him in such a good frame of mind that he was half cured before I had even begun my operation! ...

The brave hermit thanked me so profusely that I was embarrassed. He added that his sacred vows prevented him from giving me rich presents and that he had nothing more precious than a cross attached to a little silver chain. He removed it from his neck and gave it to me. It consisted of a little fragment of reddish-brown wood, and with it he gave me a piece of the rock on which the Ark came to rest. Such a high value did he attribute to these pieces of wood and rock that, in his judgment, I would be too rich if I retained them. If, on the other hand, I was willing to take them to St. Peter's Church in Rome, he assured me a recompense that would make my fortune.

He had been born at Rome, and he said that his name was Domingo Alessandro, and he was the son of one of the richest and most influential families of Rome...

When I was ready to depart, I thought that it might not be a bad idea to obtain from him an attestation as to my experience on Mt. Ararat. He willingly gave it to me in the following terms: [4]

> I have thought it unreasonable to refuse the request of Jan Janszoon (Struys) who besought me to testify in writing that he was in my cell on the holy Mt. Ararat, subsequent to his climb of some thirty-five miles. This man cured me of a serious hernia, and I am therefore greatly in his debt for the conscientious treatment he gave me. In return for his benevolence, I have presented to him a cross made of a piece of wood from the true Ark of Noah. I myself entered that Ark and with my own hands cut from the wood of one of its compartments the fragment from which that cross is made. I informed the same Jan Janszoon in considerable detail as to the actual construction of the Ark and also gave him a piece of stone which I had personally chipped from the rock on which the Ark rests. All this I testify to be true – as true as I am in fact, alive here in my sacred hermitage.
>
> *Dated the 22nd of July, 1670, on Mt. Ararat.*
> *Domingo Alessandro of Rome*

Carrying these holy relics, whose possession fulfilled all my desires, and proud of the fine success of my first operation, I descended the mountain with my donkey and my guide. I followed the same route as before, but I experienced far more difficulty than the first time, particularly while the ice-laden clouds hung over a path so rough, slippery, and steep that at each step we ran the risk of going head over heels. Toward the foot of the mountain, the wind, the rain, and the even more treacherous pathway made me almost despair of getting back at all. I did arrive – but not without vowing never to return there in all my life. Neither the Ark nor the rock which cradles it (as my hermit's testimony asserts) would have an attraction sufficient to draw me there again.

Thus I saw the famous Mt. Ararat, and my experience goes to prove that, although the climb is difficult, the mountain is not inaccessible as many claim.

Endnotes

1 Struys' report on Ararat is in chapter 18 in his book "Les Voyages ... a Moscovie, a Tartarie, a Perse, aux RE & a plusieurs autres pays Étrangers" (trips to Russia, the Tatars, to Persia, India & to several other foreign countries).

2 The distance of 35 miles may represent the entire journey from Erevan in Armenia to the hermits cottage on the mountain. (60 km. or 35 miles). Struys states that Erevan is situated at the foot of the mountain, and it looks like that because the mountain is so big. But the distance is still some 35 miles.

3 Struys might have misunderstood the monk. Neither the temperature nor wind or weather is milder at the summit.

4 The attestation is recorded in Latin and is followed by a translation into French.

Small horses and donkeys dragging climbers' baggage as far up the mountain as there are passable trails.

Chapter 9

The Return of Pharaoh's Curse

Ricky Aalten and her husband Gerrit have seen all of the Chinese film footage of the find.

According to **Jan Janszoon Struys**, a hermit had actually entered into some remainder of the Ark in 1694. The man grew ill as he apparently suffered from a hernia. However, Struys wasn't medically trained and probably didn't speak the monk's language. Could it be that the monk didn't only suffer from a hernia but had grown ill from staying in the millenia old Ark?

This happened to the whole Chinese team when they entered into the old wooden construction, which has probably been hidden under the ice and rocks for some millennia.

When the archaeologist Howard Carter and his team in 1922 opened Tutankhamun's grave, they all got ill. After 6 years, 11 of the participants of the expedition had died. Besides the more mysterious explanations, there are various medical theories as to what might have happened. According to one theory, they inhaled poisonous molds. Archeologists have actually found poisonous fungal spores in samples from Egyptian graves and 40 mummies.[1]

Howard Carter died from lymphoma in 1939, but this wasn't until 16 years after having opened the grave.

The Whole Team Grew Sick

Ricky Aalten has assisted her husband Gerrit in his life-long ark research, especially for the last eight years. They have spent much of their leisure time studying books. And rather than going on beach holidays, they have gone to Istanbul or Dogubayazit. She has even been part of the way up Mt. Ararat but "only as far as a donkey can climb" she notes. Ricky and Gerrit have had the opportunity to study the Chinese team's imagery in detail and also the "secret" recordings that haven't been published lest they should disclose the location.

"What makes you believe that the Ark has now been discovered?"

"For the first time in history they came up with a lot of evidence not just six eyewitness accounts. But apart from that, they come up with photos, and they have wood dated. It has been filmed, and officially all the little pieces of material that are in the media is not all. They have 20 hours of film. They have all the proofs for entering and for coming out. So the location can of course not be shown in the media," Ricky explained.

"Why not?"

"Because there would not be any ark left once everybody knows."

"Another thing is that it matches all the eyewitness accounts from the past. Even going back to 1670, there was an eyewitness account from someone. Since 1670 there has been an eyewitness account from a well-traveled Dutchman. And so many eyewitness accounts have popped up. And they just matched this find."

"But some of the people who said that they saw something and found something weren't telling the truth?"

"You can always see *something* if you look at Mt. Ararat. I have looked at close-up photos, and because it's volcanic, it has many shapes. And from a distance, you may think you see the ark at different place."

"What do you see in the video?"

"There are more rooms, but they also have different sizes."

"Like if you want to build one for a human being, you wouldn't build one about six meters high; that is not necessary. Other rooms are too small to live in, and it's the same with the width. Some rooms are only 8 meters wide, and others are only 1.5 meters wide. And the doors they are very small, almost like the threshold starts above the knee so you have to step into the doors."

"Why do you think that it was made like that?"

"I think that the only explanation that I can think of is that so the animals would not walk out. I mean it's logical. In Holland we have these doorswhere we keep horses, and half of the door is open, and the other half stays shut."

"Are there other signs that there were animals in this place?"

"We have pottery but very large pottery lying on the floor, very flat. When we have animals at home, we use that kind of thing for feeding them."

"If you look at the eyewitness accounts, they all speak about the same color, red brown or dark brown. They also say that it has been broken off, and it has a hole into which you can enter; this matches. Also, some people mention that there is something in there like a virus that can kill you. Many people don't know, but our hole team went into hospital three weeks after the find because they had problems with their inhalation system. Panda Lee became very ill with cancer. He has got it in all his body. And the doctor said it could have been from a virus or radiation. It is strange since also people have written in the past warning others not to go into the ark because it can kill you."

"Why did they become ill?"

"It's like the curse of the Pharaoh. When you enter rooms that haven't been entered for centuries and finding something in there that can kill you."

"We have something that we call septic. It's a disease that comes from animal droppings that have turned into dust over many years, and there are even viruses in it, and if you breathe it, you can die within a fortnight. It's very dangerous. They did want to take precautions, but we are all amateurs. That's why there are now scientists to come along and help."

"Do you know if this cave was closed when they found it?"

"Yes, it was shut down after it had been entered. Not all the rooms had been entered before, but the first room has been entered before. Because there is hay and straw in there. We know that the first room has been visited in the past. But in the other rooms they had to knock holes in them in order to get in. There are even more rooms to enter into, but some spaces are simply too dangerous to enter. They think that they may collapse."

"The hay that they found, do you think that's from a more recent time?"

"Yes, because I don't think that it would keep for about 4,500 years. Another reason is there is also some pottery in the room which is more recent."

"Is it true that some walls are rounded?"

"Some of them are. The top of the ceilings are not straight but curved, and the wood itself was shaped by a different kind of technique used on the inner walls than on the outer walls. And the staircase they found is a beam with cuts just like a round tree. Only human beings can go up there, not animals, except a monkey maybe."

"So perhaps it was frozen for about 4000 years. Right?"

"Yes, some of the spaces they entered are quite recently defrosted. And some of the spaces are sort of rotting. That means they have been exposed to air for a longer time."

Radon Radiation

The cause of Panda Lee's illness may also be *radon.* This is an element with radiation number 86, and the symbol Rn. Radon is created from the decay of radium and is usually in the form of a gas. The health authorities in most countries warn against possible radiation from radon. In the official building regulations, there are now rules about how to build new houses in a way that protects people against this form of radiation as the alpha radiation may damage living cells.

Radon in the air we breathe increases the risk of developing lung cancer. According to the World Health Organization (WHO), radon is the second-most important contributor to lung cancer (after active smoking).

The risks of radon is about 25 times greater for smokers than for people who have never smoked, but the risk is also significant for non-smokers.

The concentration of radon in the subsoil under buildings is usually thousands of times greater than in the home in general. It is therefore important to insulate the home against irradiation. Rocks and clay in the subsoil increases the risk of exposure.

This might be the explanation of Panda Lee's sudden illness.

Endnotes

1 Illustreret Videnskab (Science Illustrated) no. 1/2000 page 14

Although many explorers in the Middle Ages described the mountain and the local people's observations, it was only a few who climbed the "painful mountain" like these modern mountaineers. (Photo: Frede Donskov)

Chapter 10

Several People Claim to Have Seen the Ark

The Estonian doctor and professor of physics, Dr. Johann Jakob Friedrich Parrot, climbed Mt. Ararat with an expedition as early as 1829.

The fact that the locals themselves were afraid of scaling Mt. Ararat is repeated again and again in the accounts from the first explorers. Here, we also learn that the Estonian doctor and professor at the university in Dorpat, **Dr. J. J. Friedrich Parrot**, together with an expedition of five people climbed Mr. Ararat in 1829 as many as three times.

The local people seemed to have formed a superstition saying that nobody who climbed the mountain to see the Ark would live to tell about it. But Parrot defied their belief by climbing to the summit and placing a cross there.

Afterwards Parrot wrote the book *Journey to Ararat*. But he did not *see* the Ark even though it is inferred in such films as David Balsinger's *The Incredible Discovery of Noah's Ark*. A film that didn't always stick to the facts.

However, Parrot was the last Westerner who managed to see St. James' Monastery before it was wiped out by a large earthquake in 1840. The monastery was situated 6,394 feet up the mountain and also bore the name of Araxilvank after the Arax river.

Parrot tells in his book, "The Monks showed me a piece of timber, manuscripts, and artifacts, which they claimed came from the ark."

Parrot started a comprehensive mapping of the mountain which other mountain climbers continued to work on, among these the German Dr. Herman von Abich who in 1845 named a large glacier at the north side of Mt. Ararat after him: *The Parrot Glacier.*

In regards to the possibility of finding Noah's Ark, Parrot writes in his book:

"Should any one now inquire respecting the possibility of remains of the Ark still existing on Ararat, it may be replied that there is nothing in that possibility incompatible with the laws of nature, if it only be assumed that immediately after the Flood the summit of that mountain began to be covered with perpetual ice and snow, an assumption which cannot be reasonably objected to; and when it is considered that on great mountains accumulated coverings of ice and snow exceeding 100 feet in thickness are by no means unusual, it is obvious that on the top of Ararat there may be easily a sufficient depth of ice to cover the Ark, which was only thirty ells high" (30 ells = 15 meter = 45 feet).

So as indicated above, Parrot makes it clear that the Ark may easily be found in a frozen state under the snow if we assume that immediately after the Flood the summit was covered with a perpetually growing layer of ice. The depth of the snow has afterwards been measured to 300 feet so this would make ample room for a 45 feet high Ark to hide.

Did They See the Ark As Far Back As 1833?

A wandering tale says a shepherd from the village of Bayazid (now Dogubayazit) saw a large wooden ship on the mountain in the early eighteen hundreds.

In 1833, only a few years after Parrot's expedition, a **Turkish expedition** apparently confirmed the shepherd's story. Allegedly, they found "a wooden hull, sticking out of the southern glacier in the summer time." And an expedition in 1840 revealed the same discovery.

However, this information has not been further verified.

Kozmo Fyodorovich Spassky-Avtonomov, a Russian scientist who moved to Baku, climbed both mountain tops in August 1834 with an Armenian guide – not with the purpose, however, of finding the Ark but to observe the stars. Maybe this was only the official reason.

In 1835 the German-born **Carl Behrens** climbed to the top and testified that Parrot's cross was still there, but he himself did not see the Ark or parts of it. It may seem strange as his expedition is taking place in the interval between the expeditions in 1833 and 1840 which both claim to have seen the Ark. The snow may, however, have covered the place for Carl Behrens. And don't forget that the mountain has a circumference of 50 miles and that the trackless and impassable ground is rather difficult to survey.

The Earthquake That Demolished the Monastery

In 1840 a violent earthquake took place in the Ahora Gorge at Mt. Ararat, killing about 2,000 people. It was in connection with this earthquake that an expedition was checking the rumors of the Ark being seen on the mountain.

The earthquake of June 20th hit in the evening and destroyed the 200 or so houses that made up the village built around the 800 year old St. James' Monastery. Apparently, all of the victims were killed within moments of the quake whose underground roar sent rocks from the skies raining down over the village, the monastery, and the Kurdish shepherds alike.[1]

In 1845 the German-born **Dr. Herman von Abich** arrived and also mastered the mountain. The eastern tip of two glaciers have his namesake, Abich I and Abich II. Apparently, this German doctor had no interest in finding the Ark. Like Spassky-Avtonomov he officially wanted to see whether one could see the stars better if one came to a sufficient altitude as not to be blinded by the surrounding light.

The next year in 1846, the British scientist **Henry Danby Seymour** climbed Mt. Ararat together with two Armenians and a Cossack officer. He returned again in 1856.

After von Abich came the Russian **Colonel Khodzko** who took on Mt. Ararat in 1850 with a team in order to systematically comb the mountain to find the Ark. Unfortunately, he found no such thing, but he spent five days at the top of Mt. Ararat which is in itself quite an achievement. No fewer than 60 persons were involved in the expedition which left behind a snow pyramid with a bronze plate saying that the expedition had taken place from August 6-18, 1850, under the Russian Tsar Nicholas.

Also, a British major, **Robert Stuart**, and his team climbed the mountain in 1856. They described their experiences in the *Royal Geographic Society*, "Additional Notices" (1876-1877, pp. 77-92).

Stuart and his men found Abich's oak cross from the expedition in 1845. The cross, however, was not standing at the top, but 1200 feet further down.

In a location north of the Ahora Gorge, you find hundreds of volcanic stones probably dating back to the first huge eruption several thousands of years ago when 1/6 of Mt. Ararat was blown away leaving the Ahora Gorge behind.
2.000 people were killed by the 1840 earthquake.

Also in 1856 the English clergyman, **Charles Hudson**, made the attempt.

In 1866 German mountain climbers set up a cross on the mountain, but their names are unknown. In 1868 *The Alpine Journal* tells of an expedition led by the Englishman **Douglas W. Freshfield**, and in 1871 **Radde** and **Siewerss** of unknown nationality climbed the mountain. None of them, unfortunately, found the Ark again.

The Unbelievable Story

Haji Yearam, or Jeremiah Pilgrim as he was called after being in Jerusalem, claimed that his father had been on Mt. Ararat as a guide for three Western, atheist scientists. They wanted to prove that the Ark did not exist, but when they got up the mountain, they saw it.

Tim LaHaye and John Morris tell in their book *The Ark on Ararat*, 1976:

"They went inside the Ark and did considerable exploring. It was divided up into many floors and stages and compartments and had bars like animal cages of today. The whole structure was covered with a varnish or lacquer that was very thick and strong, both outside and inside the ship. The ship was built more like a great and mighty house on the hull of a ship, but without any windows. There was a great doorway of immense size, but the door was missing. The scientists were appalled and dumbfounded and went into a Satanic rage at finding what they hoped to prove nonexistent. They were so angry and mad that they said they would destroy the ship, but the wood was more like stone than any wood we have now. They did not have tools or means to wreck so mighty a ship and had to give up. They did tear out some timbers and tried to burn the wood, but it was so hard it was almost impossible to burn it.

They held a council, and then took a solemn and fearful death oath. Any man present who would ever breathe a word about what they had found would be tortured and murdered.

In 1915, just before Haji died at 75 years old, he told his story. In 1918 on his death bed, one of the three atheists told his story which matched in every detail." [2]

Haji was an adventist. His spiritual leader *Reverend Williams* from Brocton, Massachusetts, claims that Haji's incredible story was confirmed by one of the three scientists, who on his deathbed in London confessed everything. This is supposed to have been printed in a newspaper article in 1918 in either Brocton or Boston. Haji died in 1920.

Despite strenuous searching, this article was never found. But a liberal (atheist) scientist from The Royal Geographic Society in London, *Henry Danby Seymour,* actually climbed Ararat in 1845-46 and again in 1856. He might have been in a debate about Noah's Ark with the scientist and politician *James Bryce* who himself climbed the mountain 20 years later in 1876. So the story may not be totally plucked out of the air.

English Politician Found Wood

The above mentioned **James Bryce** (1838-1922) was a recognized English viscount, parliamentarian, and author, who through intense studies was convinced that the Bible's historical accounts were true.

Bryce climbed Ararat in 1876 where he was forced to trek the last leg alone after his guides had given up at the snow line. But before they left him, he actually found a 4-foot long and 5-inch thick piece of formed wood in the snow at a height of over 13,000 feet – more likely at a height of 13,500 feet. This is almost at the same height, at which the wooden structure has now been found!

At that time it was not possible to date wood and it is uncertain what Bryce did with it. In his comprehensive dissertation, he writes that he cut off a piece of the wood and brought it with him. But today we do not know where this piece of wood is kept. It cannot be excluded that the wood may have been from one of the wooden crosses that Parrot, Abich, and Khodzko had set on Ararat's summit some years before. Neither does Bryce claim it to be from the Ark. His exposition is a typically English understatement, only mentioning that everybody is free to look further into the matter.

The same year, 1876, Englishmen **Telfer** and **John Evans** climbed the mountain. In 1878 Englishman **G. Percival Baker** was on the mountain, and on September 7th he also reported to have found wood which he tells of in the *Alpine Journal* 1879 – possibly the same wood as Bryce left behind.

And three years later in 1882, the Russian **Sivaloboff** climbed the mountain. So, indeed, there is a lot of activity and interest in the matter in those years. And then something unexpected happened.

The Ahora Gorge arose from a series of amazing earthquakes. In 1840 a village and a monastery beneath the gorge were destroyed. The pictures here were taken in June 2004 when we followed the road north of the mountain into the Turkish corridor between Armenia and Iran into Nachevan. You can catch a glimpse of the gorge (left) and the close-up details (above) where so many have searched in vain for the remains of the Ark.

A New Earthquake In 1883

On May 2, 1883, the Ararat region was again shaken by a powerful earthquake. A village was buried under rock and ice. The Turkish government sent authorities to assess the damages, and along with them came the British colonel Gascoyne who was an attaché with the embassy.

Tim La Haye writes in his and John Morris' book, "At last they were rewarded by the sight of a huge dark mass, protruding twenty or thirty feet from the glacier, on the left side of the ravine. ...It was in a good state of preservation, being painted on the outside with a dark brown pigment, and constructed of great strength. ...the explorers found it filled for the greater part with ice, the interior being partitioned off into compartments about twelve or fifteen feet high..."[3]

In my first book about the Ark, I wrote that it has not been possible to find the original press release. The closest thing to it was an article printed in the British religious magazine, *Prophetic Messenger*.[4] But the Dutch Ark researcher Gerrit Aalten has traced the find of the Turks and Gascoyne to be mentioned in a number of newspapers all over the world. One of them was the *New York Times* which on August 10, 1883, carried an article from the *Pall Mall Gazette* (an English evening paper that later merged with the *Evening Standard*). Here is the article.

Noah's Ark Discovered

From the *Pall Mall Gazette*:

There is one cheering item of news from the East at the present moment which will do much to divert people's minds from dwelling on the subject of cholera, the Suez Canal, and other pleasant subjects of that sort.

A Constantinople contemporary announces the discovery of Noah's Ark. It appears that some Turkish Commissioners appointed to investigate the question of avalanches on Mount Ararat suddenly came upon a gigantic structure of very dark wood protruding from a glacier.

They made inquiries of the inhabitants, (Q. 1,725 in their report.) These had seen it for six years, but had been afraid to approach it because a spirit of fierce aspect had been seen looking out of the upper window. Turkish Commissioners, however, are bold men, not deterred by such trifles, and they determined to reach it. Situated as it was among the fastnesses of one of the glens of Mount Ararat, it was a work of enormous difficulty, and it was only after incredible hardships that they succeeded. The ark, one will be glad to hear, was in a good state of preservation, although the angles – observe not the bow or stern – had been a good deal broken in its descent. They recognized it at once.

There was an Englishman among them who had presumably read his Bible, and he saw it was made of the ancient gopher wood of the Scripture, which, as every one knows, only grows on the plains of the Euphrates.

Effecting an entrance into the structure, which was painted brown, they found that the Admiralty requirements for the conveyance of horses had been carried out, and the interior was divided into partitions 15 feet high. Into three of these only could they get, the others being full of ice, and how far the ark extended into the glacier they could not tell. If, however, on being uncovered it turns out to be 300 cubits long it will go hard with disbelievers in the book or Genesis.

Needless to say, an American was soon on the spot and negotiations have been entered into with the local Pasha for its speedy transfer to the United States. The State of Armenia, however, which is at present much disturbed, has happily hitherto prevented this act of vandalism."

Even though the article is written in a somewhat annoyingly superficial and curious language often used by journalists for the sake of entertainment and we are uncertain of facts, there are, after all, some quite interesting details in the article especially compared with the new Kurdish-Chinese find:

1 The wooden structure was only partially covered by ice.

2 The color of the wood was said to be dark brown.

3 The wooden structure had partitions – three that you could get into and others that were full of ice (cf. the latest Kurdish-Chinese find).

4 The partitions were as high as 15 feet – also analogous with the latest discoveries.

5 The locals had known of the structure being there for six years, i.e. about the same time as Bryce and Baker found wood.

6 The locals were obviously permanently afraid of climbing the mountain.

It could be interesting to find the original description from "a Constantinople contemporary" which this superficial article is built upon.

During my research I came across a newspaper in New Zealand, the *Evening Post*, which in 1883 actually denied the story. According to this newspaper, it was said to have been invented by a prankster in Auckland, and the editor of the original source, the *Levant Herald*, was said to be in prison in Turkey and his paper was suppressed for a year or two.[5]

NOAH'S ARK DISCOVERED.

From the Pall Mall Gazette

There is one cheering item of news from the East at the present moment which will do much to divert people's minds from dwelling on the subject of cholera, the Suez Canal, and other pleasant subjects of that sort. A Constantinople contemporary announces the discovery of Noah's Ark. It appears that some Turkish Commissioners appointed to investigate the question of avalanches on Mount Ararat suddenly came upon a gigantic structure of very dark wood protruding from a glacier. They made inquiries of the inhabitants, (Q. 1,725 in their report.) These had seen it for six years, but had been afraid to approach it because a spirit of fierce aspect had been seen looking out of the upper window. Turkish Commissioners, however, are bold men, not deterred by such trifles, and they determined to reach it. Situated as it was among the fastnesses of one of the glens of Mount Ararat, it was a work of enormous difficulty, and it was only after incredible hardships that they succeeded. The ark, one will be glad to hear, was in a good state of preservation, although the angles—observe not the bow or stern—had been a good deal broken in its descent. They recognized it at once. There was an Englishman among them who had presumably read his Bible, and he saw it was made of the ancient gopher wood of the Scripture, which, as every one knows, only grows on the plains of the Euphrates. Effecting an entrance into the structure, which was painted brown, they found that the Admiralty requirements for the conveyance of horses had been carried out, and the interior was divided into partitions 15 feet high. Into three of these only could they get, the others being full of ice, and how far the ark extended into the glacier they could not tell. If, however, on being uncovered it turns out to be 300 cubits long it will go hard with disbelivers in the book of Genesis. Needless to say, an American was soon on the spot, and negotiations have been entered into with the local Pasha for its speedy transfer to the United States. The State of Armenia, however, which is at present much disturbed, has happily hitherto prevented this act of vandalism.

The New York Times

Published: August 10, 1883

The news of the discovery of Noah's Ark in 1883 was published in major world newspapers, as here in the New York Times.

But the retraction is probably not the whole truth, either. As a journalist I must, to my shame, admit that you cannot always take newspaper articles as the most reliable source of truth. When reading the denial, you sense a certain gloating towards the local church people who have naively jumped to accept the good news of Noah's Ark. Now the newspaper is able to take it all to pieces. We journalists love to do that. But the retraction is just as unreliable as the original article is said to be. As we can read, the local paper is referring to a local prankster in Auckland. But after all, the news had been printed in other papers all over the world who had received the information not from the *Auckland Herald*, but from the *Levant Herald*.

THE CENSOR ON DUTY.

Drawing from Mark Twain's report of the problems of the Levant Herald with censorship in the Sultan's Istanbul. The name of the newspaper had to be changed several times - when censorship authorities closed the magazine.

Some months ago a story went the round of the New Zealand, and Australian, and English, and American papers to the effect that a gigantic structure of dark wood had been discovered in a glacier at the bottom of a deep ravine of Mount Ararat, by "Captain Gascoyne, the well-known scientific investigator", that its dimensions and arrangements agreed with those Scripturally attributed to the "Ark in which Noah and his family navigated the waters of the Deluge"; that the Trebizonde correspondent of the Levant Herald had reported this discovery; and that at the instance of the German Ambassador the Sultan had taken steps for the preservation of the Ark, defeating the designs of an astute American who had endeavoured to purchase it from the local Pasha for exhibition. This story excited extraordinary interest all over the world. It was implicitly accepted by many people, and, we fear, formed the subject of many sermons, as an evidence of the truth of Holy Writ. The Pall Mall Gazette, the Daily News, the Daily Telegraph, and other London papers—even The Times itself—published this story with various comments. In the religious world of New Zealand it created much excitement. We ourselves have received earnest requests from three different clergymen that we should publish this most interesting and valuable intelligence. But we were compelled to confess that we felt exceedingly sceptical as to the truth of the story, and we preferred to wait for some confirmation. Confirmation has come at last, but—we grieve to say—of our disbelief and not of the story. The report was commonly quoted as from the Levant Herald, but that paper had been suppressed for a year or two and its editor in a Turkish prison. Nothing could be learned about the celebrated "Captain Gascoyne." Not a syllable could be found as to the alleged discovery in any paper of earlier date than the eve of last All Fools' Day, on which date the full story appeared in the Auckland Herald. And now the sinful author of this wicked hoax—a contributor to that journal, who writes under the *nom de plume* of "Pollex"—openly confesses that he concocted the whole affair as a piece of "humbug," for which proceeding he now expresses the most profound contrition. Well he may! We fear he will not be easily forgiven by the host of worthy and credulous people whom he has ruthlessly hoaxed.

Above the lenient retraction from the Australian newspaper.

Reputable Newspaper and Editor

The *Levant Herald* was actually the oldest and most reputable newspaper in Constantinople (Istanbul). It was published in French and English and was often quoted along with other internationally reputable papers. In spite of censorship, it continued appearing with 12-16 pages every Wednesday night. It described the situation in Turkey and the Middle East (the Levant) from 1856 up to 1915 when the violent Turkish encounters with Armenians and Greeks put an end to the paper. For instance, the newspaper described the revolution in Turkey in 1908. In his book *Innocents Abroad* the well-known author Mark Twain actually mentions how difficult it was for the *Levant Herald* to live with the censorship of the sultanate. He mentions that newspapers are frequently closed down by the censorship in Istanbul. Thus the *Levant Herald* had to change its name to The Eastern Express and later to the *Levant Times and Shipping Gazette* in order to continue being published.[6] The editor was Dr. Lewis Francis Mizzi[7] who had a doctorate in law (LL.D.). He could speak 25 languages and seemed to know how to get on in many of them. He was also president of the International Association of Lawyers for Consular Courts. As a Maltese he was honoured in 1928 with the prestigious Order of St. Michael and St. George.[8]

This type of editor would hardly print something that was pure nonsense in his otherwise serious newspaper.

Dubious Bishop

In 1887 the Nestorian Archbishop of Jerusalem and Babylon, **Dr. Nourri**, according to what he said, led an exploration to the sources of the Euphrates River. He went up Ararat and reportedly saw a hull through the eternal snow and commented,"The only things accessible were the ship's bow and stern. The middle part was covered in ice. The Ark is made out of dark red planks of a very thick wood."

But later Nourri, who was also said to be an Iranian prince, could not prove his fine titles, and his explanations were not convincing in that he boasted of specific details, but had only seen the Ark "from a rifle shot's distance."[9]

So this more or less takes away credibility from Nourri's explanations.

Wood Again

But in these very years, we see a renewed activity among mountain climbers on Mt. Ararat.

In 1888 **Yevgeniy Markov** finds wood as he climbs the mountain together with Ivan Kovalewski and a young Miss Mosokevich. Markov was a member of the Imperial Russian Geographic Society. The wood was found above the timber line close to 14,000 feet. But the wood bore the initials C.B. matching two earlier Russian mountain climbers. Maybe they had carved their initials in the wooden cross planted by Parrot.

The year after, in 1889, we hear about another two Russian expeditions, led by **Semenoff** and **Rapholovich**.

In 1890 the French **Julies Leclerq** takes on the mountain, publishing a few years later a book about his *"Voyage au Mont Ararat."* However, it does not appear clearly whether he has been on the mountain himself. This also goes for another Frenchman that same year, **Chautre**.[10]

In 1891 the first Americans, **Thomas Gaskell Allen Jr.** and **William Lewis Sachtleben** climbed the mountain. Many of their fellow-countrymen were to follow during the next century.

In 1892 came **T.J. Allen, Wantner** and **G. Merzbacker**. In 1893 the Englishman **Lynch** and the Russian lieutenant **P. Postukhov**. Lynch was an author, a geographer and a member of Parliament. He has written an account of his experiences.

In 1894 **M. Zimmer** and **Posharski**.

In 1897 the Swiss **A. Oswald** described his ascent of the mountain. And in 1900 we read about the Russian **Poggenpohl**, a member of the *Russian Geographic Society*, who was escorted by a number of Russian soldiers.

So the list of mountain climbers in the eighteen hundreds is very long. And allegedly, some of them find wood.

In 1902 and 1910 we meet another couple of Russian mountaineers, **Ivangouloff** and **Seylaz**. And in 1912 the two Americans, **Edgar J. Banks** and **Dr. Gibson** participated in the last expedition while Ararat was still under Russian/Armenian control. After that the Turks captured the territory. The Armenians were chased out or killed in fightings with the Turks and the Kurds.

Later on, in 1916, the territory around Ararat was again taken by the Russians for a few years until the revolution in Russia put an end to the period where Mt. Ararat was under the control of a culturally Christian country. From that time on, Noah's mountain has been situated in the Muslim camp.

James Bryce (1838-1922), English politician and author, climbed Mt. Ararat in 1876 and found a 4-foot-long piece of processed wood (125 x 13 cm) in the snow above the 13,000 ft. mark (3.962 meter).

Armenian Shepherds

Since the Armenians inhabited the territory until they were finally driven out in 1915 after years of ethnic purging, Armenian refugees are often consulted by Ark hunters who want to know whether they might be able to remember something.

The Armenian Arthur Churchian, born in 1915, lived all his life in the U.S. In 1975 he told that his father, **Jakob Churchian**, saw the Ark in about 1890, i.e. in the years when the world-wide interest in finding the Ark on Mt. Ararat was extremely intense. Arthur Churchian's description of the Ark is so detailed that one would think he had been there himself. But as the very same person who told to the newsletter "Ararat Report" (edited by the Ark researcher Bill Crouse) that he also believes there are small beings living in the earth and that this is being kept secret by the authorities, it is rather difficult to have confidence to what he is telling.

We will come back later to another Armenian, George Hagopian, who told in great detail about the Ark which he remembered from his childhood during these very same years.

Wrong Mountain

After World War II, a small group of five Turkish soldiers claimed to have seen Noah's Ark on their way home from World War I. They were illiterate, but once they found out that Americans were interested in Noah's Ark, they got a friend who could write to send a letter to the American Embassy in Turkey in 1946 to offer their services as guides for Americans that wanted to search for the Ark. The route from Baghdad described by these soldiers is, however, more reminiscent of the road to Mt. Cudi, in the southern part of Turkey, which they would pass by when following the Tigris river.

As far as is known, no soldiers were requested as guides for Americans. And since then these soldiers have not shown their faces.

The Russian Version

In August 1916, when Ararat was again Russian territory, a Russian pilot, **Vladimir Roskovitsky**, claimed that on a reconnaissance flight he saw an ice-covered lake where the one end included a gigantic hull breaking out of the ice. One fourth of the wreck was covered in ice. One side was torn up, and the other side had a large door with two stories, but the one was missing. Roskovitsky's superior apparently flew over the area afterwards and confirmed the existence of the wreck.

After this sighting, **Tsar Nicholas II** sent out an expedition led by a Mr. Pastounow, and 150 soldiers worked on the mountain for a month. A scientific expedition measured the Ark and took some photos as well as samples of the woodwork. But everything disappeared in the revolution.

This incredible story of the Ark has come into Violet Cummings' book, *Noah's Ark: Fable or Fact* along with many sources.

Some years ago, however, this story was taken somewhat apart. But still, some facts are mixed in with it.

The first time the story came out was in an American religious magazine, *New Eden*, in 1939. Author **Floyd M. Gurley** has confessed – unfortunately not until 1986 – that the details of the story were the work of imagination.[11] But he told Ark hunter Eryl Cummings that he had received some of the information from a Russian immigrant. Cummings also says that he has knowledge of a British copy of a religious publication that Floyd M. Gurley copied almost word for word.[12]

Benjamin Franklin Allen, a retired officer, constituted after the article that Gurley had uncontrollably added on to certain facts that he knew to be true, namely that two Russian soldiers had told about a pilot having seen something that could have looked like a ship, after which infantry was sent out. They concluded that it must be Noah's Ark.

The last Russian tsar, Tsar Nicholas II, is said to have sent an expedition of 150 soldiers to Ararat to measure the Ark.

But Was There More Behind It?

Alexander Koor, a Russian colonel, had actually written a similar anonymous account of the Ark that was much more detailed then Gurley's version. It was published in the Belarusian newspaper, *Rosseya*, in 1945. He claimed that he didn't know of Gurley's story which was printed five years previously. (Author and journalist Rene Noorbergen doubts this statement and believes that Koor actually used Gurley's account but just added more detail.)

Koor (who died in 1971) had been stationed in the Ararat region during the Great War where he pointed out 20 historical sites that should be looked into more deeply. Many things were found, among these was a Sumerian inscription (from a period shortly after Noah's time) in Karada near Ararat that read: "God sowed the word's seed in the water … the water filled the earth, it came down from above...his children landed on the mountain."

In a statement[13] he explains that a Russian lieutenant named **Zabolotsky** probably saw something from his aircraft in 1916 that could resemble Noah's Ark. Koor later hears in 1921 second and third-hand accounts of the follow-up that took place in 1916 and 1917 where some believed the Ark to be found in the "saddle" between Big and Little Ararat.

Violet Cummings has a vivid and detailed description of how the Ark supposedly looked with many rooms, etc., that it measured 500 x 50 feet, and that it was covered in a dark brown wax-like material both in and outside. The wood was well-kept except for a hole in the bow and the entryway in the side where it was a bit deteriorated and crumbled at the touch. The wood was supposedly cedar or larch wood. The Ark also supposedly lay with one side in the ice.

In the surrounding area, burned wood was found and something that could have been a stone altar, which, naturally, could lead one's thoughts to Noah's sacrifice after the Flood.

All of this information, with photographs and drawings, was supposedly sent via courier to the commander-in-chief by order of the tsar.[14]

But the tsar regime was ended in 1917, and most of the tsar's family and many leaders were murdered under the Bolshevik Communist Revolution. Along with the royal family, this evidence also disappeared – that is, if it ever existed at all.

Stories About Russian Photos

There is also an instance about a document that three Russian pilots, who were on the expedition, were supposed to have given to a Mr. Evans along with their names and rank confirming that the Ark was "as good as new" and that they had measured it and performed other tests. The door was gone and they took pictures and film, which were sent to the Russian government. Evans' daughter, Mrs. **Gladys Evans** gives this account. But unfortunately the document "disappeared while cleaning."

A Mr. **Alvin Holdenbecker** from Minnesota tells that his aunt Eva had a father that was a medic for the Russian Ark expedition. Aunt Eva at 19 helped out in the house of the tsar's family, and her father, who was a good friend of the family, showed her the pictures.

She claims that the Bolsheviks killed as many of the expedition members as they could find and that they confiscated all of the photos and reports and that she was the only survivor because she was sent to the court of Keiser Wilhelm in Germany.

She has described the Ark in the pictures as three stories tall with an eave on the top that had openings for light and ventilation.

But her word is the only evidence we have. Or more correctly – her nephew's word.

Research hasn't been able to confirm the Russian expedition either. The previous head of the KGB denied the existence of an "Ark file" to Armet Arslan, an Armenian Ark hunter.

Kurdish sheep shearer at the warm sulfurous sources in Diyadin.

But a Sunday-school teacher, Sister **Bertha Davis** of Hotville, California, is said to have shown photos of the Ark in 1935-41 that could have resembled the Russian claims. Three people say that they saw these photos: Joe Bosse, Walter Hefner, and his sister Maurine.[15]

Two American soldiers from World War II, **Dale Nice** and **Roy Tibbetts**, gave a taped interview in New Mexico in 1977 where they tell that they both saw similar photos that an Australian soldier, **R. Taylor**, showed them. He claimed that he had taken the pictures himself.

Not to be mistaken for **Hardwicke Knight**, a well-known photographer from New Zealand, who professedly in 1936 climbed the mountain and found wood in a frozen lake but took it for some balks left behind by the military.

Filmed?

The Russian expedition continues to haunt us. **Ray Lubeck**, an American machine worker on Midway Island during WWII, claims that in 1942 he, along with about 30 others, saw a black and white film of approximately 50 Russian soldiers marching past "Noah's Ark" near the top of Mt. Ararat. The approximately 30-second long silent clip had an American commentator who said that the Russian soldiers were on their way to attack the Turkish soldiers. But Lubeck believes that the soldiers were from WWI based on their olive green-grayish uniforms. How in the world, though, did he see this on a black and white film?

Lubeck describes the Ark as 75 feet wide by 50 feet tall and hundreds of feet long. He says it was completely intact, lying out in the open in an area without any snow.

Lubeck didn't publicly disclose his story until after he had been to a seminar with painter Elfred Lee in the 1980's. Despite multiple attempts, no such film clip could be found in the archives in Washington, and likewise Lubeck has been unable to find any of his 30 buddies that supposedly saw that same film.

So too, this clue leaves us at ground zero…

Endnotes

1 Described by James Bryce in the book *Transcaucasia and Ararat*

2 LaHaye, 46-47

3 "At last they were rewarded by the sight of a huge dark mass, protruding twenty or thirty feet from the glacier, on the left side of the ravine. ... It was in a good state of preservation, being painted on the outside with a dark brown pigment, and constructed of great strength. ... the explorers found it filled for the greater part with ice, the interior being partitioned off into compartments about twelve or fifteen feet high..." – LaHaye p. 57.

4 Violet Cummings, *Noah's Ark: Fable or Fact?,* Spire Books 1975.

5 "The report was commonly quoted as from the *Levant Herald,* but that paper had been suppressed for a year or two and its editor was in a Turkish prison. Nothing could be learned

about the celebrated Captain Gascoyne. Not a syllable could be found as to the alleged discovery in any paper of earlier date than the eve of last All Fools' Day, on which date the full story appeared in the *Auckland Herald*. And now the infill author of this wicked hoax — a contributor to that journal, who writes under the nom de plume of Pollex,openly confesses that he concocted the whole affair as a piece of "humbugr," for which proceeding he now expresses the most profound contrition. We fear he will not be easily forgiven by the host of worthy and credulous people whom he has ruthlessly hoaxed." The *Evening Post*, New Zealand.
6 British Library Newspapers, Colindale
7 Partial Listing of Levantine published newspapers of Turkey
http://levantineheritage.com/newsp2.htm
8 The International Bar Of Consular Courts – www.maltamigration.com/about/foma/convention2000/full/topic1f.shtml
9 According to Lloyd Bailey: Noah, University of South Carolina, 1989
10 According to Bulletin Soc. Geogr. Marseille, 1890
11 "I have a letter from Floyd Gurley, with Floyd Gurley's personal letterhead on top center in blue that he sent me from Hawaii to San Diego. When I tried to reply I was told he had died. I sent for a copy of his death certificate and also have that. In this letter he confessed to me that the Roskovitsky story was a total fabrication for his magazine. Even the name was his friend who drove a street car in San Francisco. He said that he "hangs his head in shame" for all the problems caused by publishing the story." (David Fasold in a letter to Mathew Kneisler, February 20, 1998, published on Kneislers website.)
12 B.J. Corbin, *The Explorers of Ararat*, (Gci Books, 1999), 376.
13 Bright: *The Ark, A Reality?* Guilderland NY, 1989, 45.
14 Violet M. Cummings: *Noah's Ark: Fable or Fact*, 57-58.
15 B.J. Corbin, *The Explorers of Ararat*, 38.

A Kurdish woman boils water for the family picnic.

Chapter 11

The Ark Was Discovered in 1883

During the last 35 years, the Dutchman **Gerrit Aalten** has tried to find material about Noah's Ark. Journalist Clara Wei got acquainted with Gerrit Aalten in her research, and when NAMI presented the spectacular find, Gerrit Aalten helped to present it at the press conferences in Hong Kong and Holland. It was also Gerrit Aalten who pointed to his Dutch compatriot, Jan *Janszoon Struys*, who in 1694 was very close to the secret of the Ark – without ever having searched for it.

I asked, *"Gerrit Alten, when did you get involved in the Ark search?"*

"About 35 years ago. The first illustration of the Ark that I saw, was when I was 8 years old. And from then on I got interested. When I was about 23 years I started to collect information. My main purpose was to gather as much information about the Ark as possible without going onto the mountain myself. That was my first intention because many people had already been on the mountains. There were a lot of expeditions."

"Many people claim they saw the Ark..."

"Yes. I myself studied about 30 objects. 30 look-alike arks, but they were not the Ark."

"But you still believed it was there?"

"Yes, because there were constantly new stories to examine."

"Did you go up the mountains yourself?"

"Yes, in 2006 I went to a location called Angel's Rock. It was promising, but the Ark wasn't there."

"How did you get involved with the Hong Kong Team?"

"I was asked whether I could verify some of the things they had found, accounts in books, eye witnesses' stories. A lot of details agreed with what has now been found."

"What makes you believe that the Ark has now been found?"

"They have found the same structure that was found in 1883, when some Turkish emissaries climbed the mountain. They also found strong planks, and there are some details that confirm this find. They found a room which they describe as 4.50 meters high, like the one that has now been found."

"But if the Ark was found as long ago as 1883, why wasn't it believed?"

The Dutch Ark Researcher Gerrit Aalten (right) along with Parasut (left) attended the press conferences in Hong Kong and Holland in May 2010.

"It was believed. It was mentioned in all the major newspapers in the world, but people forgot about it again. There were no follow-ups or investigations."

He shows a photo copy of the article from the *New York Times* from the 10th of August 1883.

Wars Made People Forget About the Ark

During the years following the find there was great political unrest in eastern Turkey and in the world. The countries fought about Armenia right up to World War I, when a large ethnic showdown displaced the Armenians from the area. The world was preoccupied with the war and with licking its wounds. In Russia the revolution broke out, and the communists took power. And in Turkey the mighty Ottoman Empire collapsed and was replaced by Ataturk's modern Turkey, which fought wars with the Greeks. In short, the world was preoccupied with "more important things" than to find a prehistoric relic.

"Even the place was forgotten?"

"Yes."

"Do you think that some of the accounts since then, about people claiming that they found the ark, actually could be true?"

"Yes. I believe that it could have been the same place."

"So the people who claimed to have found the Ark weren't all liars?"

"No."

"Which significant information seems to indicate that the Ark has now been found?"

"First and foremost, the location. It is very high up where no one would settle. It is close to an area with waterfalls. It is in a place where no one would build a house. It is cold; there is ice and volcanic rocks. Because of the height, it is difficult to breathe there."

"You have watched the videos that were recorded up there also, those that haven't been published. What do they tell you?"

"That they are old ancient remains. The Ararat is known from the Bible as the place where the Ark was stranded. And there should be some remains up there."

"Couldn't it have been a monastery up there?"

"No, people couldn't have lived at that altitude."

"What indicates that this is the remais of a boat and not a house?"

"The rooms are very irregular. It is not a human habitation. There are small doors, 1 x ½ meter, not suited for humans but rather for animals."

"Did they find anything else other than wood?"

"Yes, remains of feed and pottery which is also interesting. There were eight rafters in a little room of 2 x 2 meters, ideal for animals."

"They found some wooden pegs. Are they of a recent date?"

"No, everything indicates that these are ancient."

"How could they make such fine crafts 4000-5000 years ago? Could they build such a large ship?"

"Yes. For instance the Bible tells us that they knew how to make iron at that time, and we know that people lived much longer then. So it was possible for them to learn from experience. I believe that they knew more than we know now, in some respects."

"Are the people of the Hong Kong NAMI team serious?"

"Yes, the guide tells me that these Chinese were the only people who showed the right respectful attitude towards the mountain and the inhabitants of the region. They prayed before climbing the mountain. They endured many hardships, and they kept coming back to gather more information."

"Will others be able to see the place later?"

"Yes, I think so."

"Will you go there yourself?"

"No. I have no need to go there. But I would be happy to assist."

"What do you think this breakthrough in the Ark research should tell people of today?"

"We do not need an Ark in order to believe in God and his word. But it will prove many things from the Bible. For instance, that there was a Flood. Jesus also speaks about the Ark – and I do not think he would lie. He speaks of it as a warning in "the last days" and urges us to find the living water and the eternal life."

"So you think that the Ark may be a sign to the modern world from God?"

"Yes, I think so."

Gerrit Aalten believes that the Ark was already found in 1883 - but lost again.

Chapter 12

Navarra: I Found the Ark

The Frenchman Fernand Navarra was the catalyst for the growing Ark interest leading several explorers to climb Mt. Ararat in the latter half of the 20th century. The title of his book *I found Noah's Ark* created wide spread sensation. And his vivid accounts led many to believe that the Ark had finally been found – even if it might lie under the ice.

In 1939 Navarra was serving in the French Army in the Middle East, and in his spare time he would climb mountains with an Armenian refugee, Alim. Once, when they were on the mountain of Hermon, Alim told him of the holy mountain of his native country.

Another man had told Alim that the Ark was up there. So for the next 15 years, Navarra collected all available material on the Ark, the Deluge and the countries neighboring Ararat.

Navarra in 1952 drew across Europe to Turkey and onward to the Iranian border 1,000 km away. At that time it was much more difficult to travel than now.

When he reached the easternmost part of Turkey accompanied by locals and Turkish soldiers, he succeded in climbing to the top of the mountain, a height of 5,137 meters.

A Myth Destroyed

Afterwards, they attempted to reach the place on the western side that the local monks would always point out from the ground as the little black shadow where the Ark supposedly projected from the ice. Obviously, none of the locals had made the effort to go there to see for themselves. When Navarra arrived fairly close, the "Half Ark" sticking out disappointingly turned out to be a rock projection. So at least now that legend was destroyed.

However, Navarra was familiar with the diverse accounts of the Ark lying in a lake. Therefore, they also attempted to reach the Kop Lake, which is at 4,000 meters. Here his followers left him, shaking with cold, according to Navarra's accounts.

He continued on his own, which was perilous, higher up to the Parrot Glacier. At this very spot, Navarra, alone, at 2 o'clock p.m. on the 17th of August 1992, makes his incredible discovery. He writes the following:

Fernand Navarra, Harry Bud Crawford, and Hugo Neuberg climbing the Parrot Glacier in their attempt to find the Ark in 1969. (Photo: Elfred Lee)

"These Are the Remains of the Ark"

"I am alone on the glacier that is lying shiningly clear and naked. I am so excited that I don't feel the fatigue. In the sky an eagle hovers in regular circles, carried by the wind.

I pass a glacier arm and climb a moraine. At one side I can see a mass of ice streaked with crevasses, at the other side a steep rock wall, and at the bottom a dark mass.

In fact, it stands out. There are curves and straight lines encountering each other. The object is a hundred and twenty meters long in all, and the shape looks by and large like the rail of a ship.

I have never had visions. I am a matter-of-fact man and pin my faith on the faculty that does not necessarily characterize the visionary, namely common sense.

What can it be? At this height, in the middle of the glacier and the great waste. Maybe the ruins of a structure? A church, a refuge, a house that has never been mentioned in any account or tradition, and was never discovered by people coming to these parts. Or the wreck of an airplane? Even in the history of the heroes of the air balks of this size were never used to build an airplane.

We have got to face it: these are the remains of the Ark. It simply cannot be anything else. This is probably what is left of the flat bottom of the biblical ship after the disruption of the upper construction. Doesn't Berosus tell us that the people of the Ararat region in his days would break pieces of the Ark to scrape off the pitch covering?

The balks they left alone have remained untouched through the ages, protected by Nature. And protected they are indeed today. Opposite the steep rock wall are enormous blocks worked loose and covering the dark contours.

The Ark is there, but one cannot reach it. Even though I had the necessary equipment and could get down there, these blocks would certainly crush me.

All that I can do today is to fix the place in my head as precisely as possible and then return to my companions. But I solemnly declare that I will return." [1]

New Mountaineering in 1953

Loyal to his promise, Navarra returns in 1953. However, he suddenly feels violently indisposed – maybe due to the height, and he has to give up. He believes that he was only a hundred meters from the Ark.

The year after, there is an American, **John Libby**, claiming he has been only 30 km from the object believed to be the Ark. This makes Navarra decide to go there in 1955 for the third time.

This time he brings his wife and three sons in order to make them appear like a tourist family lest they should attract too much attention. Together with his eldest son, just eleven years old, he again climbs Ararat from the west side. On the second day at approximately seven o'clock a.m., they reach the Kop Lake. They continue to the glacier where Navarra thought he saw the shadow of the Ark under the ice. They are exhausted and put up the tent.

Again Navarra gets seized with inexplicable anxiety, and while Raphael sleeps, he takes some of the cocaine he brought with him.

During the night a storm comes on, and blocks of lava tumble down around them. The day after they both fall down, experiencing showers of hail, etc. But eventually they reach a deep crevice in the ice where Navarra rediscovers one of the wooden balks he saw a few years back.

"It had to be the Ark," he concludes a little too optimisticly. It turns out to be just moraine clay.

Afterwards, they are at the point of freezing to death in a snow storm that lasts for 13 hours. However, they later succed in excavating a real balk from the ice.

In spite of everything, they manage to get safely down again, and later Navarra visits experts in Bordeaux, Cairo, and Madrid . These experts study cellular changes, formation of lignite, quantity of fossilization, cambia, etc.

Navarra's book is published and is a great hit.

The Frenchman Fernand Navarra with the shaped piece of wood that he believed was from Noah's Ark because he found it high up on Mt. Ararat. The first examinations actually indicated that the wood was some 5,000 years old, but two carbon-14 tests showed that it was only between 1300 and 1900 years old. But the carbon-14 tests might have been wrong.

Doubts About Credibility

Then attacks start coming. Navarra's companion Alain Seeker denies being on the expedition with Navarra in 1952-53. He may have his personal reasons for this, since he left the expedition because of the cold, according to Navarra.

Navarra's son Raphael, who was with him in 1955 when the balk was found, has since refused to make a statement on the find.

Furthermore, Navarra's follower and friend from the first expedition, *J. A. de Riquier*, later made a serious accusation against him of having tried to obtain a piece of wood from an ancient construction in a village below the mountain with the intention to "find" it on the mountain.

A Turkish lieutenant *Sahap Atalay*, who claimed to have climbed the mountain in 1952 with Navarra, made a public charge against him much later. This was in 1969 in connection with Navarra's last expedition with SEARCH. This was a charge that Navarra had brought up wood with him onto the mountain in order to earn money on the sale of photos and books. Indeed, Navarra never mentioned having brought Sahap Atalay with him in 1952.

And last but not least, a Carbon-14 test of the wood shows that it can only be between 1300 and 1900 years old, so it is much too young to originate from Noah's Ark. However, this comes to light much later as the leader of the SEARCH organization, created to explore Navarra's discoveries, didn't want to make it public. He had problems with alcohol abuse and was killed in a rather mysterious car accident in the middle of the night.

Interest Aroused in America

However, due to Navarra's discoveries, particularly the Americans' interest in finding Noah's Ark on Mt. Ararat flourished immensely.

Various organizations were formed to equip expeditions for the Ark hunting on Mt. Ararat. The organization playing the most important role at first was SEARCH that was lead by the former Adventist Pastor Robert (Bud) Crawford.

SEARCH sent an expedition to Turkey in 1969, and Navarra was the pathfinder.

The painter and photographer Elfred Lee, the oldest living ark hunter veteran from the SEARCH era, joined this expedition. He has played a central role in the resent ark hunting as I documented from my interview with him. He described the many attempts by SEARCH to follow up on Navarra's discoveries.

He was able to reject most of the claims against Navarra, but he reaffirmed that the Carbon-14 test had proved that the wood was too young to originate from the Ark, though it had first been put to another test claiming it was 5000 years old.

Help from National Geographic

We started getting great assistance from the Smithsonian Institute and from National Geographic. I got to know the editor. And we were told that white oak was frequently used for ocean ships as it is very well suited for this purpose.

Whether gopher wood was white oak is unknown. What gopher wood is, nobody knows. However, the ark hunter Don Shokey believes it to be wood produced through a process, a lamination of wood with bitumen resin between the wooden layers. And there was bitumen resin in the wood that we found.

The wood was fully saturated and hard as stone. It was fossilized, very compact, and black; the cambia were barely visible. This also renders the theories of the Flood concerning the hydrosphere even more probable. Furthermore, Dr. Wilbur Libby, the inventor of the date system of the Carbon 14 Test, told us that this date theory involves certain problems as to reliability. The wood that we found was influenced by carbon from melt-water that had run through it for over hundreds of years. "So things were not so simple as they might seem," Elfred Lee explained.

Dr. Libby said, "We have a problem with your wood tests. This piece of wood is not as dry as a piece that was hidden in a earthen jar in a New Mexican cave. This is wood that lay in melt-water at a high altitude and was bombarded with carbon again later. This wood is polluted with newer material. Besides, there are sheep and goats up there, and plants grow there but not trees. There is organic material in this water, which has contaminated the wood and makes it seem very young in a Carbon-14 Test."

Fernand Navarra, in the foreground, resting on Parrot Glacier where he led the SEARCH expedition in 1969 with team members such as Harry "Bud" Crawford and Hugo Neuberg, seen in the background. Elfred Lee took the photo.

Same Place – Same Wood?

Now that wood has been found in the ice again of the right age according to the tests, the question is whether Navarra's wood originated from this find but showed the wrong age according to tests. The Carbon-14 Test is not a hundred percent reliable. But normally the error will be just 500 years at the most.

If, however, a disaster like the Flood occurred with totally different climates before and after, it would inevitably influence results of carbon 14 tests made on wood from that period, especially as this wood was afterwards encapsulated in ice for thousands of years.

As a measure of precaution till now, the Kurdish Chinese team has refused to say whether their wooden construction was found in the same area on Mount Ararat where Navarra maintained having found his piece of wood. They fear that the find would be plundered before they can examine the site.

Endnotes

1 Fernand Navarras: *I found Noah's Ark*, 101-102

2 B.J. Corbin: *The explorers of Ararat*, (California, 1999).

3 Henri Nissen: *Noahs Ark – Uncovered*. Scandinavia 2005, 157-170.

Besides being an ark hunter, Elfred Lee is also a reputable artist who has painted quite a number of well-known persons. Here is a somewhat humorous painting of president Ronald Reagan – as a "barbarian."

Chapter 13

An Interview with Elfred Lee

The artist Elfred Lee played a key role in the new interest in Noah's Ark, which arose in the wake of Fernand Navarra's finds. Usually it was not Lee, who went public in the mMedia, but he was the one who researched and documented, being a photographer and painter.

He is the only living participant from the Navarra / SEARCH expeditions, and he has personally spoken to many of the so-called eyewitnesses – that is, people who said they have seen the Ark or parts of it.

Unfortunately, the leader of the SEARCH organization, whom Lee worked for, turned out to have both personality and alcohol problems. This resulted in many problems, which Lee frankly told us about when we interviewed him in 2004.

- Elfred Lee, you have played a key role in the search for Noah's Ark. When did you get involved in the search?

"In 1968-69 right after I came back from Vietnam, I was contacted by the SEARCH Foundation, and they needed somebody with my skills. There had been other groups that were looking for the Ark, but we wanted to add scientific research and credibility to the search. So I moved to Washington D.C. and lived there for many years," explains Elfred Lee.

As a missionary child born in Korea in 1940, he went through World War II as a child in a prison camp in the Philippines for three years. He personally experienced starvation, and witnessed torture, and was saved from execution by American paratroopers in 1945. Five years later, he was once again rescued by American troops from the Communist invasion in Korea.

Because of these experiences, he volunteered in Vietnam as a photographer and an illustrator for the U.S. Army and was shot down in a helicopter while taking movie footage for the Pentagon. After Vietnam he worked in Silicon Valley illustrating space shuttles among other things.

- Were you employed by SEARCH?

"Well, when they had money, I was given a little… I was a member of the board and one of the early pioneers. The work was based on information from the Frenchman Ferdnand Navarra from Bordeaux. He wrote his book *I Found Noah's Ark*. He made a lot of claims, and we wanted to prove them and to verify his fin. My job was to document it," said Lee.

- You went on an expedition with Navarra in 1969 and 1970?

"Yes, in 1969 we had a very good expedition with Navarra and his son Coco, who spoke English. We had a scientist from the Arctic Institute of North America and a British scientist who had worked at the South Pole. There were Ralph Lenton, Hugo Neuburg, Ross Arnold, John Bradley, and the Crawfords. These men were very strong physically and scientifically, and they brought equipment. Queen Elisabeth had even honored one of them for heroic work in the Arctic. They were good with ice, and we needed people who could see what was inside the ice. They brought coring augers and depth-sounding electronic equipment. I was the photographer, and I recorded the movie that has been shown on television over and over."

Wood from the Ark?

- *When you went up the mountain with Navarra, he found wood again?*

"Yes, more pieces of wood, and exactly in the right place where he said he had seen it earlier in 1955. Even Hugo Neubergen, the worst critic that was with us, accepted this. He and Navarra didn't get along too well. Hugo was very well educated and could speak German, and Russian and more languages, and he was built like Rambo or Arnold Schwarzenegger... Navarra hated him from the very beginning and called him a boy scout and a cowboy.

- *When Navarra and SEARCH had found this wood, you called a press conference in Istanbul. Why?*

"I did not. It was Navarra and Ralph Crawford, the president, who wanted this. Crawford had some personal problems with money and drinking and... He had his own agenda. I honor him for the hard work he did. But I do not like the way he wanted publicity. I cautioned saying, 'Please gentlemen, let us not have a press conference here in Istanbul. Let's get back to the States and have the wood dated first by scientists and others.'

"But I was very young, 29, and they owerruled me. Crawford and Navarra were two of the same kind. They loved publicity. So we had our 15 minutes of fame. We had found Noah's Ark, and our photos and names went all over the world. Now when I look back, I see it was ridiculous, but I do admit I was caught up in the excitement."

- *Yes of course. But then you had the wood tested....*

"Yes, then the men went traveling through Europe, and I brought the wood back home. I had carried it down the mountain every day in my backpack. I went directly to the University of Pennsylvania that had the finest carbon dating lab at that time. I turned it over to them, but I did something that nobody knew about. I was testing Navarra. I had been to his home, and he had given me some wood from his discovery in 1955. Even though I trusted him, I wanted someone smarter than me to verify it. So I marked two samples of wood: 'N' for Navarra's wood and 'O' for ours.

Nobody knew. They were all in Europe."

- *What did the test reveal?*

"Everything came out exactly the same. It showed that Navarra found his wood on the same spot as we did. That is very important because some of the critics that were with him in the first place said he had planted it. They were also charismatic prima donnas who envied him and his fame."

- *Do you think they criticized him because of that?*

"That was part of it. We need critics. That is why I'm talking to you, provided you will publish this. I want to clear the record. I want honesty, and if I'm lying, please tell me."

- *Okay, I will.*

"The wood had been soaked in the same melting water, the test showed. It could not have been taken from a village nearby as some implied. When the men came home from Europe, they also had the Forestry Department test the wood, and both of them said the wood was a species of white oak."

- *But the wood was too young to be from Noah's Ark....*

"Yes, the test showed that it was between 1700 and 1900 years old."

The Facts Were Hidden

- *What happened when you showed the result to Crawford?*

"Crawford had been talking too much in public about Gopher wood that was "5,000 years old." When I showed him the reports, he immediately said, "Hide the report! Don't publicize the reports. They will use it against us. There is something wrong." So we put it in a file."

The American SEARCH organisation persuaded Fernand Navarra (in the middle) to lead an expedition to the place where he had found wood on Mt. Ararat in 1955. In 1968 the expedition had to be cancelled due to his sprained foot. But in 1969 these five men went to Turkey. Here are Hugo Neuberg, Ralph Lenton, Navarra Harry Crawford, and Elfred Lee in Dulles Airport. (Photo: Elfred Lee)

- How did you feel about that?
"I felt bad."

- Later you got a letter?
"Then Jean A. de Riquier (who was Navarra's climbing partner in 1952) wrote a letter accusing Navarra of attempting to purchase a piece of timber from an ancient structure in a nearby city. I went to the president and showed him the letter. Hugo Neuburg was in the office that day and translated it from French. And immediately Crawford said, "'Destroy that letter. It's wrong, something is wrong. Don't say anything about this letter.'"

I felt bad about that too. In my heart I thought, what is the truth then? I wasn't ready to give up, but I would not go on TV or publicly tell falsehoods.

My attitude was that all the report was still not in, and we needed to look at it all and make a report.

Then Rene Noorbergen came along. He was a good author and had already written a best selling book, and he and I became good friends. I saw his family and so on. He had also been through World War II as I had been.

He, of course, was very critical.

Then Navarra turned over to us his test that had been made in Bordeaux, Cairo, and Madrid. These people did not use carbon dating. But they were very good at ancient dating – especially in Cairo. They studied the cell modification from Navarra's wood. And this is why I'm so thankful I also sent in a piece of the Navarra wood and knew there was a connection. Any studies on Navarra's wood applied to ours and vice versa. These people were very good at studying ancient material with lignite formation, cell modification, the amount of fossilization, growth rings, etc. They concluded that this wood was 5,000 years old. So Crawford was happy again."

The SEARCH team in 1969 photographed in the base camp. From the left Fernand Navarra Jr., son of the French explorer Fernand Navarra, then Harry "Bud" Crawford, who was general secretary of SEARCH, Fernand Navarra himself, Elfred Lee, and in front the two scientists Hugo Neuberg and Ralph Lenton. (Photo: Elfred Lee)

Political Problems…

- *Then the mountain was closed. Why?*

"There was an uprising in Turkey at the universities at that time, and Turkey and Greece had their problems with Cyprus, and as usual there were anti-American demonstrations because we tried to be friends with both the Greeks and the Turks….

Anyway, Crawford went to Greece, which wasn't very wise at that time, and he even boasted that he was working for the CIA. That of course spoiled everything. Now it came out in the news that we were illegal scientists working on Mt. Ararat. So the expedition in 1970 was called off, and the mountain (Mt. Ararat) was closed for 12 years.

So Crawford was sent back to Denver, Colorado, and he was later killed in a tragic and mysterious car accident in the middle of the desert at two o'clock in the morning. It's suspicious. He talked too much."

Jim Irwin Gets Involved

When Jim Irwin, the astronaut, got involved, he managed through his political connections to get permission. He had planted a Turkish flag on the moon. He was the one driving around in a moon-car, and he also discovered the "Genesis stone" on the moon, which showed that elements were created, not evolved. He was converted on the moon. He came back as a Christian and wanted to get involved in the search for the Ark. And that was when I got involved again.

- *What did you do in the meantime during these 12 years?*

"In the meantime I was also involved with answering questions, helping people with information and the next thing I knew, they were on TV or making films, and I was here in debt. But that's okay – it's not my project. I just happened to be involved longer than any other living person now and happen to know more about the location of Noah's Ark than anybody else we know. If anybody knows more, stand up. I was there at the right time, and I had the skill and education and training needed. I have a Master's degree and a Doctorate in archaeological illustration.

While we were waiting to get permission, we raised money – probably over a million dollars. We hired fundraising firm, and there was a Korean firm that specialized in raising money from Christians. So we paid Colonel Pak $37,000 for a mailing list. Later we found out that he was using our money to raise money for Sun Myung Moon to support the Moonies."

Ed Davis claimed to have seen a large ship with multiple decks broken in two lying in a deep gorge on Mt. Ararat. Here we see Elfred Lee's painting according to Ed Davis's description. The two pieces of the Ark are seen lying at the top of each side of the gorge.

Chapter 14

Hagopian's Story

Elfred Lee spent days with George Hagopian hearing his story about the Ark, which Hagopian claimed to have seen as a child in Armenia.

The year after Navarra and SEARCH had found "wood from the Ark" on Mt. Ararat and before it had been confirmed, so-called eyewitnesses showed up claiming to have seen the Ark! One had even been in it. His name was George Hagopian, who in 1970 at the age of 72, told his unbelievable story to painter Elfred Lee.

Hagopian's Story

As a ten-year-old, George Hagopian followed his grandfather on an 8-day trip to the top of Mt. Ararat in 1912. On this trip, claimed Hagopian, they both saw the Ark.

Even as an old man after living most of his life in the US, Hagopian could obviously remember in detail what the Ark looked like. He was helped along, however, by Elfred Lee, who painted the Ark according to Hagopian's description. Lee tells, "We got a letter from a lady, Mrs. Mary Board, in Maryland, who knew George Hagopian. She wrote that he was from Armenia and as a child he and his father had been on Mt. Ararat with their sheep every summer."

"He lived alone in his garage next to his too big house. He was broken hearted, old, sick, and lonesome, and she wanted us to get his information. Other expeditions had also received letters from her, but they had not followed up."

"So I went out to Maryland to talk with him. He was about 72 at that time. He had a very heavy Armenian accent, and it was very difficult to understand him at times, but because of my foreign background from Korea, I understood him. I interviewed him for hours. I made sketches from all that he explained from the mountain. At that time the border was on the other side, and he had to go into Russia to go up Mt. Ararat," Elfred Lee explains.[1]

It May Be True

In my first book I tried to prove that Hagopian's story was unreliable. I was prejudiced as I assumed that it could not be true. Today, I have to admit that even though his story sounds a bit fantastic, it may be true – apart from a few inexactitudes.

He says that he went with his uncle to find grass after four years of drought. And there were actually four years of drought from 1901-04, but born as he was in 1898, he was only six years old in the fourth year of drought. He says that he was 8-10 years old. He also says that two years later he went up at the age of 12. This is not enough to exclude the story.

Even though Hagopian was only about 5' 5", he claims that later he was one of the Sultan's body guards. As he was Armenian, this sounds unlikely. We know for sure that the Sultan assisted in exiling and oppressing Armenians. But Lee explains that Hagopian was a strong wrestler and hid his nationality. Hagopian claims to have attended three of the Sultan's "murders", where Hagopian says a stand-in was hit. It is hard to believe, but it was a turbulent period. The party of the Young Turks started a revolution in 1908, the Sultan tried to set up a counter-revolution in April of the next year upon which the Young Turks took over again, leading to the removal of the Sultan and the inauguration of his brother as Sultan.

Hagopian claims that he fled when the Turks were eradicating the Armenians in 1915, but was caught on the Russian border with a false passport and sent to work in the coal mines in Siberia for 18 months. When he came out he only weighed 97 pounds and lived off of selling warm water and bread in Yerevan, the capital of Armenia. From this he earned enough money to travel to the US.

When in his seventies, Armenian George Hagopian told that he had seen the Ark on Mt. Ararat as a child, and that it looked like the one in the picture as he "dictated" to artist and Ark hunter Elfred Lee. In Hagopian's memory the Ark is nearly square with only slightly rounded edges, looks as if it were assembled in the middle, and includes a box with a row of windows set on top. The dimensions were bigger than those in the Bible as well.

He claims that in 1922 he was threatened by American government officials in uniform and representatives of the Turkish Embassy at the Mayflower Hotel to keep quiet about the Turkish assault on the Armenians. This is the reason he gives as to why he had not told about seeing the Ark until now as an old man.

Ed Davis discussing his eyewitness account with the Armenian Ahmet Arslan at a secret meeting in 1987. Photo: Elfred Lee.

Hagopian estimates the Ark he saw to be about 1,000 feet long and 600 feet wide, about double the length and seven times the breadth of the Biblical measurements of the Ark (517 ft. x 86 ft).[2]

Hagopian also says that the Ark was whole and he was even inside of it.

In light of the new find of the wooden structure, Hagopian's story doesn't seem so unlikely any more. He and his relatives may, in fact, have been "inside the Ark" or at any rate inside the wooden structure that has now been found.

But due to the long time span between Hagopian experiencing it at the age of 6-10 and his telling it at the age of 72, there is a great risk that he is not remembering all details correctly.

Other Eyewitnesses

Retired sergeant Ed Davis is, next to Hagopian, the Ark hunter that has been taken most seriously. Ed Davis claims that while he was stationed in Iran during the Second World War he saw the Ark "broken in two" on Ararat.

I have to admit that much in Ed Davis' personality and narrative style gets my alarms going even though he apparently passed a lie detector test with an okay score. This has all been thoroughly explained in my first book. At best, I think he is confusing truth with lies. Some of his details simply cannot be correct. But here is a short summary of what he claims to have seen.

Davis and the three Kurds come to a protruding rock. The weather is gray and foggy, but suddenly the sun shines through the mist, and the Muslims point to a specific spot and say, "That is Noah's Ark." Davis can't see it at first, but then he does. It's "a huge, rectangular, man-made structure partly covered by a talus of ice and rock, lying on its side. At least a hundred feet are clearly visible. I can even see inside it, into the end where it's been broken off, timbers are sticking out, kind of twisted and gnarled, water's cascading out from under it," reports Davis.[3]

His companion, Abas, now points another direction where the other half of the Ark is lying a bit further down. And the Kurds say that the Ark is broken into multiple pieces.

Davis contends that he can see "at least three stories" in this end of the Ark, and Abas says there are 48 compartments in the top. Davis also believes he can see passageways inside the Ark. But they must wait until the next day to crawl down there with ropes Abas tells them. And the next morning it snowed. So there were no further explorations, according to Davis.

The new thing is that the Ark has broken into two halfs since Hagopian's eyewitness account. That water was cascading from under it, and that it was lying clearly visible. If so, it must later have been covered with ice and rock, but this could, theoretically, have happened in connection with the frequent earthquakes.

Was Davis on Another Mountain?

The question is, did Davis ever see the Ark other than on the painting Elfred Lee made for him in 1987 based on his descriptions. There were windows here that didn't exist in his first description from 1986, Ark hunter Doris Bowers pointed out. Another Ark hunter, Bill Crouse, was also skeptical. He noted 6 discrepancies in Davis's explanations[4], which are abbreviated here:

1. Davis has explained that he was in Harmadan, Iran, and could see Mt. Ararat. But the distance from here is over 400 miles. The curvature of the earth would make this impossible.
2. Davis claims to have driven from Harmadan to Abas's village below the mountain in just one half of a day. This would also be impossible on such poor roads in 1943.
3. It appears[5] that he traveled with Kurds. But Davis said that Abas was Lourd, which is the people group from around Harmadan. A Lourd would not be a village chief on Ararat, which is surrounded by Kurds.
4. If the Ark were there where Davis alleges (about 13,000 feet above sea level), it would be visible in the summertime.
5. Davis tells us that Abas and his people had previously found honey still in the jars on the Ark as well as feathers in cages, fish bones, and beans that could still be eaten.
6. Davis also claims to have seen the Garden of Eden. Exactly 50 miles from Harmadan, there is a mountain called "Kuh e Alvand" which is also traditionally the landing place of Noah's Ark[6] as well as the Garden of Eden. It is 11,700 feet high and only covered in snow part of the year. Many things suggest that if he was anywhere, it was here. Davis died in 1998.

Boasters and Conmen

In 1973 the American Ed Behling was stationed in Diyabakir, Turkey, in the Air Force. One day after church back home in the States, Behling told how he had seen the Ark. He didn't know that an Ark hunter was there that day – Bob Stuplich, who had sedulously tried to find the Ark.

Behling was now brought forth in the news as a new eyewitness that confirmed the Ark's placement on Ararat.

In a radio interview in 1982 with Prophecy in the News in Oklahoma, he said that he and some Kurds conquered Mt. Ararat in 1973 and saw Noah's Ark there. But a number of his explanations don't fit in the puzzle. He estimated the distance to Mt. Ararat to be around 100 miles, while the real distance is 249 miles. The Ark hunter Pat Frost, who has been up the mountain nine times, believes that his description of the area is a copy of Lee's drawings from Hagopian's story. After the interview and the attention it created, Behling has withdrawn and refuses to answer any more detailed questions from other Ark hunters.

The most likely explanation is that this man's mouth was too big. One lie covered another and the snowball effect started and ended with Behling in a trap.

An Incorrigible Liar

Another boaster was Donald M. Liedmann, whom Violet Cumming wrote about in her book *Noah's Ark: Fable or Fact?*

In 1969 he made himself out to be a neurologist from the University of Uppsala in Sweden with a Ph.D. from another university. He also told of photographs he had seen from the Russian expedition to Mt. Ararat which Ark hunters believe to have taken place during the First World War.

According to Liedmann, he had been a squadron leader for the Royal Air Force and was shot down two times in six months and miraculously survived. Actually, he kept up this deceit from 1969-1978.

But when Liedmann attended Trinity Church in Lubbock, Texas, for a short period in the 1970's, he used another name, Jakob Liedmann. Again, he shared unbelievable stories that impressed people. However, a pilot from the church took this Royal Air Force "veteran" up flying, and here he was uncovered as a fraud, not knowing the simplest aviation terms.

After confessing his sin face to face with the whole congregation, the poor liar was given counseling and pastoral care for three months after which he disappeared yet again.

Deliberate Atheist Sabotage

It was even worse when in 1985 actor George Jammal claimed to have seen the Ark on Ararat. It was planned sabotage. His deceit continued for eight years, and he was even filmed as an eyewitness on *The Incredible Discovery of Noah's Ark* which was aired on CBS on February 20, 1993.

The program was produced by Sun International Pictures and was largely based on the film *In Search of Noah's Ark,* which was produced by the same company in 1976.

In June of 1993, *The Skeptics' Society* was able to reveal that its counselor, Gerald Larue, together with Jammal stood behind this practical joke. The *Associated Press* and *TIME* magazine printed the revelation that reached the entire globe and did great damage to the reliability of the Christians – as planned by the skeptics.

The Ark film that was the basis for much of the CBS program, "In Search of Noah's Ark", was also aired on NBC on May 2 and December 24, 1977.

Besides so-called eyewitnesses, some Hollywood tricks were used to manipulate the viewers.

This film, unfortunately, gave the search for Noah's Ark a touch of unreliability that has haunted serious Ark hunters ever since. The false stories and much too smart assertations without evidence to support them have had the same effect as in the fairytale where a child teases the grown-ups by shouting over and over that there is a wolf. When the wolf suddenly appears, nobody believes the child.

The same has happened to the Ark. Too many have claimed to have seen it in order to win their fifteen minutes of fame. Now the Kurdish-Chinese team has found a wooden structure surpassing even the wildest expectations. And yet it is very difficult to be taken seriously by the media. The world hardly reacts when hearing that the biggest find in history may have been made. But there are also other reasons for that, especially the many atheist attempts to exclude religion from the public space.

Endnotes

1 In an interview with the author of this book.

2 Notice that these measurements are based on the Egyptian cubit, not the later English one. If you compare them with the English, then Hagopian's measurements are even more exaggerated.

3 From his eyewitness account at the Ark-a-thon meeting in Farmingdale, USA, 1986, restated in The Explorers of Ararat, 1999.

4 In "The Ararat Report"

5 From his account in Don Shockey's book, The Painful Mountain, Pioneer Pub. Co., 1986.

6 In Dr. John Montgomery's book The Quest for Noah's Ark 2nd ed. Dimension Books, 1974, he presents a French map from a 1730 lexicon of the Bible (Dictionnaire historique de la Bible, Calmet) drawn by Pierre Daniel Huet. Here the "Arche de Noe" is on a mountain that – with a bit of good will – could be Kuh e Alvand or Alvand Kuh-Mountain in Iran. But Mount Ararat lies right next to it. The map is not a precise map either, but rather a fabled map of "earthly paradise" including The Garden of Eden marked to lie in southern Iraq.

Chapter 15

Ark Fever

James Irwin was not only interested in the moonwalking. He attempted to find Noah's Ark on Mt. Ararat eight times. When he fell into a deep gorge in 1982, he nearly died. Nevertheless, Irwin came back again in 1985, '86, and '87.

After Navarra's incredible discovery of wood on Mt. Ararat that unfortunately didn't have the right age, the real hunt began. Numerous expeditions, organizations, and private persons followed the SEARCH expedition.

It was probably more than religious convictions that caused Americans, in particular, to climb up Mt. Ararat. It was also adventurism. Most of these mountain adventurers were men, but also a few tough women made the effort.

For some it became an entire obsession. The Ark *had to be up there*. They were taken by Ark Fever and came back time and time again. They put themselves in danger, and some met a fatal end like the 28-year-old Paul Jernæs of Drammen, Norway. In September 1986, presumably killed in the mountains, Jernæs tried to reach the top and disappeared. He was never seen again, and his body has never been found.

James Irwin, who was the 8th astronaut to walk on the moon, fell from a cliff when he tried to find the Ark in 1982. According to the leader of the group, Bob Stuplich, Irwin had four teeth knocked out, four gashes in his head, and his hands were torn and swollen to double their normal size.[1] After a month in the USA to regain his strength, he went back to Mt. Ararat again and again in 1985 and '86 and '87.

You have to admire these Ark hunters' courage and stamina.

But now and then, some of them behaved rather badly and unprofessionally. Bud Crawford, the leader of SEARCH, not only concealed the information of the age of Navarra's findings, he also went to Greece at a very unfortunate time with unrest between Greece and Turkey concerning Cyprus. And as if this wasn't enough, he kept boasting that he was working for the CIA. When this came to the ears of the Turkish authorities, they cancelled the next SEARCH expedition in 1970 and closed down Mt. Ararat for expeditions the next 12 years.

Finally a Systematitian

One of the Ark hunters who has most systematically researched the supposed Ark findings is an American, Dr. Charles Willis. He is a neurologist, has a degree in religion, and has been interested in archaeology for many years.

In 1973 an expedition, which his son John accompanied, revealed with new photographs that the rock at 12,000 feet thought to be the Ark, or at least a man-made object, was only a rock. Willis believes that this misunderstanding could have been the source of many false allegations including those of George Greene, Ed Davis, Ed Behling, and George Hagopian – some of the more dubious "eyewitnesses."

Willis studied the uppermost part of Ahora Gorge where many Ark hunters continually return in belief that the Ark must be hidden here. Willis didn't find it here either. Afterwards, he said he believes it may lie so deep in the ice that it wouldn't have been destroyed by the glacial movements. In 1983 he explored the eastern plateau. In 1986 he tried again. Based on a new theory by Guy Leduc that the Ark was also built with iron and bronze, the whole group combed the eastern plateau with metal detectors. This too gave negative results.

But Willis was systematic. In 1988 he returned with an expedition probing the eastern plateau with radar, which revealed the ice to be 80 feet deep, but there was no trace of an Ark. They tried again further and further west on the top of Ararat where the ice was 95 feet deep. Again the radar returned with no signs of the Ark.

Finally, they drilled holes to a depth of 40 feet, which showed nothing but ice.

"The Ark Isn't Here"

After all of these grueling expeditions, Willis and his team, which consisted of only committed Christians, concluded that the Ark was not to be found on Mount Ararat and that the *assumed* findings were of little or no value.[2]

After that Willis instead concentrated his interest on Mt. Cudi, which lies much further south, on the Iraqi border.

Dr. Charles Willis near the top of Mt. Ararat where he conducted expeditions in 1983, 1984, 1986, and 1988. On the last trip his team investigated the east plateau with radar and drilled holes in the ice. Dr. Willis's conclusion was that the Ark could not possibly be located on Mt. Ararat. Instead he has started looking on Mt. Cudy near the Iranian border. (Photo: Charles Willis, www.ancientworldfoundation.org)

When the Americans finally gave up looking for the Ark, the search was continued by the Italian mountain climber Angelo Palego, who has been on Mt. Ararat almost every year since 1990. He confidently claims that he has found Noah's Ark at a height of 14,000 feet and shows photographs in newspapers and on his website of the alleged find which he sets to be 39° 43' 0,08" N and 44° 16' 51,5" E.

Not many of the other Ararat Ark hunters support Palego's find. They believe that it is just another rock or a basalt cliff that has previously been mistaken for the Ark in aerial photographs.

The Long List of Expeditions

The following list of post-Navarra Ararat expeditions is not exhaustive. In addition to these expeditions, many others were planned and fell through because they were not given the necessary authorization or because of Kurdish terrorism. Most of the expeditions in the following list were carried out in full.

John Libi, USA, conquered Mt. Ararat eight times from 1954-69. The closest he came to a find was his discovery of some stone walls which could have been used as a stall for animals.

Secret expeditions by the **National Geographic Society**, the Smithsonian Institute, and David Duckworth in 1958, 1964, and 1968 are not officially confirmed but based on the evidence from multiple sources[33] most likely took place. The expeditions were kept a secret because the prestigious institutions did not want to put their reputations on the line claiming to search for Noah's Ark, which was considered a myth. The guard, Duckworth, believes to have seen a pieced together picture of a ship.

Search Foundation led expeditions in 1968 and 1969. They were American financed with explorer Fernand Navarra as the main detective, Elfred Lee as the drawer, and others. The first expedition had to be cancelled when at the last moment Navarra sprained his foot. On the next trip in 1969, pieces of wood were found – wood which Navarra was later accused of having laid one day when he separated himself from the group.[4] The wooden pieces were at first evidence estimated at being approx. 5,000 years old, but later studies based on the Carbon-14 method showed that the wood was only 1300-1900 years old.

In 1972 Dr. **John Morris** together with John Bultema, Bill Ellison, Roger Losier, and John Seiter ascended Mt. Ararat and examined Ahora George, Cehennem Dere, and Parrot Glacier. Here John Morris was hit by lightning while he stood on Zap Rock and thanked God for his protection... (Talk about an electrifying experience!) Despite the paralysis and a snowstorm, they all made it down alive.

In **1973 John Willis**, Dr. Lawrence Hewitt, Eryl Cummings, Ray Anderson,

Jerry Williams, Geoff McMahon, and Jack Darnell took on *Cehennem Dere* (Hell's Canyon) and revealed that an object at 12,000 feet was only a rock.

In **1974 Bob Stuplich** and Dr. John Warwick Montgomery together with others climbed Mt. Ararat and saw a black spot in the ice on the upper part of the Parrot Glacier and the Abich I area.

In **1975 Bob Stuplich** climbed the Parrot Glacier on Mt. Ararat.

From **1976** until **1993 Ray Anderson** and others were on Ararat five times.

In **1978 John McIntosh** went up Mt. Ararat on his own, and in 1982 he went with Jim Irwin, among others. He went in 1984 with Rick Hatch and Doris Bowers, in 1985 with Bill Crouse and others, and in 1986 he was in Turkey to research Ed Davis's claims but had to give up any hope of climbing the mountain due to Kurdish terrorist activity. In 1987 he and Dick Bright also had to give up. In 1988 he went along on Al Jenny and Chuck Aaron's aerial photography trip. In 1989 other Ark hunters asked him to stay home because of a book Dick Bright had recently published including a picture of John McIntosh baptizing a young man in the Euphrates River. They feared he would be arrested. He was in Turkey again in 1993 but in vain and in 1996, 1997, and 1998 where again they were not allowed to climb the mountain but instead looked at anchor stones and other things.

In **1982** the astronaut **James (Jim) Irwin**, who walked on the moon in 1971, climbed Ararat. At one point he left the group and fell. He survived but broke his leg and had his face all scratched up. All together he took part in six different expeditions to Mt. Ararat. The others were in 1983, 1984, 1985, 1986, and 1987. He died in 1991.

In **1983 Bob Stuplich**, Jim Kunes, and Bill Spear took on the mountain and photographed it from a small plane. The same year Dr. Charles Willis and a team climbed the eastern plateau.

John Morris, Ahmet Arslan, Brian Bartlet, Ed Crawford, and Donald Barber were also on the mountain.

In **1984 Don Shockey** took on Ararat, the first of nine trips. The same year **Bill Crouse** was also there. **John Morris** from the Institute for Creation Research was there with his group. **Marvin Steffens** came with a group from International Expeditions, and **Jim Irwin** came with his High Flight Foundation group together with John Christianson, Dick Bright, and Ron Wyatt. On this trip Jim Irwin visited the boat-shaped formation on a close-by mountain together with Wyatt and was very taken by the site, but he continued looking on Mt. Ararat.

Elfred Lee on horseback on the SEARCH expedition in 1969 before climbing Mt. Ararat. (Photo: Elfred Lee)

In **1985 Bill Crouse** was in charge of the Probe-expedition on Mt. Ararat, where Elfred Lee, John McIntosh, Bob Garbe, Ken Alexander, Jim Willis, and others also took part.

The same year **Jim Irwin**, Bob Stuplich, and Dick Bright reached the top from the south side but were called back by the authorities via radio.

The Institute for Creation Research sponsored a trip with only Turkish members to avoid problems getting authorized.

In **1986** Norwegian **Paul Olav Jernæs** disappeared and probably died on an illegal attempt to climb the mountain when it was closed.

The same year **Jim Irwin** and Bob Stuplich were arrested for alleged espionage but were quickly released.

On the other hand Dr. **Charles Willis** and his Snow Tiger Team managed to find themselves on the mountain's eastern plateau for eight days. This huge team included Steve Connelly, Guy Leduc, Pat Frost, Bob Garbe, Carl Nestor, Richard Froiland, Deborah Redmer, James Willis, and Charles Willis himself.

Dick Bright, Ron Lane, and Ahmet Arslan climbed with their Summit Expedition Team. Dr. **Ole Honningdalsnes** should have been on this expedition, but he disappeared.

In **1987 Bob Stuplich** and Jim Irwin again took pictures of the west side from a helicopter, and Dutch Jon van den Boesch from Evangelische Omroep

The Snow Tiger Team in 1988 on Mt. Ararat's southern face at an elevation of 12,000 feet. The participants were Robert Baker, B.J. Corbin, Donald Davis Jr., Guy Leduc, Scott Little, Larry Mast, Ross Mehan, Willis Newton Jr. and Willis Newton III, Deborah Redmer, Robert, Margaret and Christopher Roningen, James Willis and finally Charles Willis who can be seen in the center behind the Turkish flag.

filmed for a series about the creation of the world.

This same year **John Morris** represented ICR on the mountain with an expedition.

In **1988 Al Jenny**, Chuck Aaron, and John McIntosh took more helicopter photos of the mountain.

And also in 1988, Dr. Charles Willis (as mentioned above) and Snow Tiger Team held an expedition with radar and ice drilling on the eastern plateau at about 16,500 feet. The team was large and comprised of Robert Baker, B.J. Corbin, Donald Davis Jr., Guy Leduc, Scott Little, Larry Mast, Ross Mehan, Willis Newton Jr. and Willis Newton III, Deborah Redmer, Robert, Margaret and Christopher Roningen, James Willis, and Charles Willis.

In **1989 Chuck Aaron**, Bob Garbe, and B.J. Corbin climbed for an "Emmanuel Expedition" with underground radar testing on the western plateau. Other members of the team included David Montgomery, Kathy Montgomery, Paul Schiemer, Chuck Aron Jr., John Wanvig, and Debbie Redmer.

In October of that same year **John Morris**, Bob van Kampen, Grant Richards, and Henry Morris III were there on an ICR expedition.

In **1990 Robin Simmons**, Don Shockey, Chuck Aaron, George Adams, Ahmet Arslan, Carl Baugh, B.J. Corbin, and others were in charge of the "Ararat 8 Team" filming and taking videos from a helicopter as well as doing mountainside research.

Also in 1990 Italian **Angelo Palego** climbed Mt. Ararat. He claims to have seen an outline of the Ark in three pieces under the ice near the places where Navarra claimed to have found sub-glacial shadows of the Ark – around Upper

Parrot Glacier west of Abich I.

In **1993 Dick Bright** and John McIntosh went to Turkey to land on the mountain by helicopter. They didn't get further than Kars where their authorization was terminated because of terrorism in the Ararat area. But the Italian explorer, Palego, was allowed.

In **1994, '95, '96, '97, '98**, and **'99** multiple Ark hunters were in Turkey, but none of them were given permission to climb Mt. Ararat. **Dave Larsen** of the USA is on the list from 1999. In 1999 and 2000 a group of earlier Ark hunters from the USA BASE Institute (Bob Cornuke, David Faltot, Bob Stuplich, Larry Williams, and Dick Bright) climbed the Sabalan Mountain in Iran instead.

In **2000** the only things that took place were meetings at Ataturk University with Jim Hall, Rex Geissler, John Bradley, Peter Aletter, Michael Holt, and Yavuz Konca. But Palego climbed the mountain.

In **2001** there was an international peace climb on Mt. Ararat.

In **2002** the mountain swarmed with Ark hunters due to the attention an (unsuccessful) satellite picture of Mt. Ararat created. According to local guides, over 100 people were on the mountain this year, and there are now plans of opening a café and building more easily accessible paths. Tourism has taken over.

After the end of the tourist season, **Palego** was up the mountain again in December.

In August **2004 Daniel P. McGivern** from Hawaii planned to invest $900,000 in investigating the "Ararat Anomaly" on the north-western corner of the western plateau with Ahmet Ali Arslan, professor at Seljuk University in Turkey, as guide. The interest was due to the *Washington Post Insight* magazine having published secret CIA photos. The paper paid for new satellite photos – in vain.

In **2005 John McIntosh** led an expedition with Dow Pursley and Matthew Kneisler. However, John McIntosh slipped on the ice and fell, breaking an ankle and several ribs. He had to be rescued from the mountain by Turkish military.

In recent years Mt. Ararat has been open for tourist climbing. For $1,500-$2,000 you can now spend just under a week on Mt. Ararat. Here you stay in a so-called basecamp under primitive conditions at a height of approximately 10,000 feet making daily hikes and mountain climbs from the camp. The final goal is getting to the top of the mountain.

But these climbs are not actual Ark expeditions. The tourists follow marked paths to make sure they are not injured. In return, the chances of accidentally coming across the Ark are small.

2004-2011: With only a few in the West knowing, the Hong Kong Chinese group from Noah's Ark Ministries has made several expeditions together with the Kurdish-Turkish guide Ahmet Ertugrul, colloquially called Parachute. After a preliminary research trip in **2003**, they made their first expedition onto Mt. Ararat in **2004** and have returned since then once a year, some years several times. It was these expeditions that led to the discovery of a big wooden structure hidden under ice and rock at a height of approximately 13,700 feet.

Endnotes

1 Bob Stuplich from *The Explorers of Ararat*, p. 100.

2 Charles Willis in *The Explorers of Ararat*, p. 124

3 Rene Noorbergen's interview with a past employee, David Duckworth, letter from army chaplain Clair Shaffer to Dr. Willis about a group from The National Geographic Society that spent the night in Trabzon, Turkey, on their way back from Ararat, and shortly discussed in *The Explorers of Ararat* pp. 430-35

4 This is suggested by many including Bud Crawford, who was a part of the expedition in 1969.

From the time when nothing tangible had yet been found. - Ed Davis coaching Elfred Lee in drawing the Ark so that it matched his account. The picture is from the 1986 Ark-a-thon, an Ark-hunter convention, where Ed Davis turned up and impressed the audience with his story. The question is whether it was true or not…

Chapter 16

The Boat-Shaped Object

One day in 1948, a young Kurdish man of 22 came running, yelling at the villagers in Nazar, "Noah's ship has been found!" This young man was a shepherd named Reshit. The village of Nazar, which was renamed Uzengeli after this happening, lies about 13 miles south of Mt. Ararat, according to the maps, on the opposite side of the valley.

An earthquake in the spring of 1948 had shaken the area causing a mighty mudslide that rushed from the top of the mountain down its slope.

From this mass of mud emerged an oval-shaped object, reminiscent of a colossal boat...

The Story Hits the World Press

One day a prosperous 69-year-old farmer, Shukra Asena, brought the story all the way to Ankara where he found an *Associated Press* correspondent, Edwin B. Greenwald.

The Turkish papers brought forth the news on November 13, 1948. Foreign papers followed suit by reproducing the AP story soon afterwards.

Unfortunately, certain misunderstandings weaseled their way into the story as it was retold. The story now told about a man named Reshit that had seen the remains of an object he claimed to be a boat high up on Mt. Ararat for it was there the Western world assumed the Ark rested.

This new story included the expected addition of Mt. Ararat's description, of course with an unfathomable height and terrific glacial masses. The Ark had immersed due to an unusually warm summer with large run-off from the ice. AP also amends the story by Reshit seeing the Ark in a fissure from his field, which is about 2/3 of the way up the mountain. (This is quite an awkward place to have a field!) Reshit, according to the AP version, "climbed down to it and with his dagger tried to break off a piece of the bow. It was so hard it would not break. It was blackened with age. Reshit insisted it was not a simple rock formation. 'I know a ship when I see one,' he said."[1]

But it really wasn't on Mt. Ararat that Reshit had seen the curious object.

Author Violet Cummings includes this mystical Reshit, whom no Americans had spoken with at this point, as one of her "eyewitnesses" in her book[2] about the Ark and sets the whole event on Mt. Ararat.

It wasn't until Reshit was an old man that now-deceased naval officer David Fasold found him and got the true story – some 40 years after the fact.

A Pilot Pictures It from the Air

In 1959 a Turkish pilot named Sevkut Kurtius was photographing the border area in Eastern Turkey in accordance with NATO's wish for a new and better map. This corner of Turkey lies adjacent to the former Soviet republic of Armenia, thus by heredity, the arch-enemy of the Soviet Union.

When Captain Ilhan Durupinar, who was both a captain in the Turkish Air Force as well as a cartographer, reviewed the pictures, he noticed this object and reported it to his superiors. Could it be a Russian missile?

The photographs were sent to an expert in photogrammetry, Dr. Arthur Brandenburger from Ohio State University in Columbus, Ohio. Dr. Brandenburger has since then helped to find Russian missiles on Cuba, which marked the beginning of the Cuban Missile Crisis putting the world on the verge of nuclear war.

Brandenburger immediately saw that this was a boat-shaped object and not a missile. But a boat up in the mountains was strange.

It couldn't be Noah's Ark, could it?

The First Expedition

Journalist Rene Noorbergen, who has worked as a war correspondent and is now very interested in finding the Ark, tried to get an expedition in the works. Later, Noorbergen wrote the book *The Ark Files* in 1974.

In June of 1960, an expedition traveled to Turkey.

They were given military assistance and due to the lack of suitable roads were forced to travel on horseback. When they finally got to the site, the only thing they saw was mud. They used dynamite to see if there was anything interesting under the mud, but the only thing they found were some strange quadratic stones. They stayed at the site for only two days, after which they concluded that this was just a natural formation.

Pictures of the find were published in the Australian magazine *PIX* in July and later in *LIFE* magazine on September 5, 1960, with the following text:

NOAH'S ARK?
Boatlike form is seen near Ararat

While routinely examining aerial photos of his country, a Turkish army captain suddenly gaped at the picture shown above. There, on a mountain 20 miles south of Mt. Ararat, the biblical landfall of Noah's Ark, was a boat-shaped form about 500 feet long. The captain passed on the word. Soon an expedition including American scientists set out for the site.

At 7,000 feet, in the midst of crevasses and landslide debris, the explorers found a clear, grassy area shaped like a ship and rimmed with steep, packed-earth sides. Its dimensions are close to those given in Genesis: "The length of the ark shall be 300 cubits, the breadth of it 50 cubits, and the height of it 30 cubits," that is, 450x75x45 feet. A quick two-day survey revealed no sign that the object was man made. Yet a scientist in the group says nothing in nature could create such a symmetrical shape. A thorough excavation may be made another year to solve the mystery.

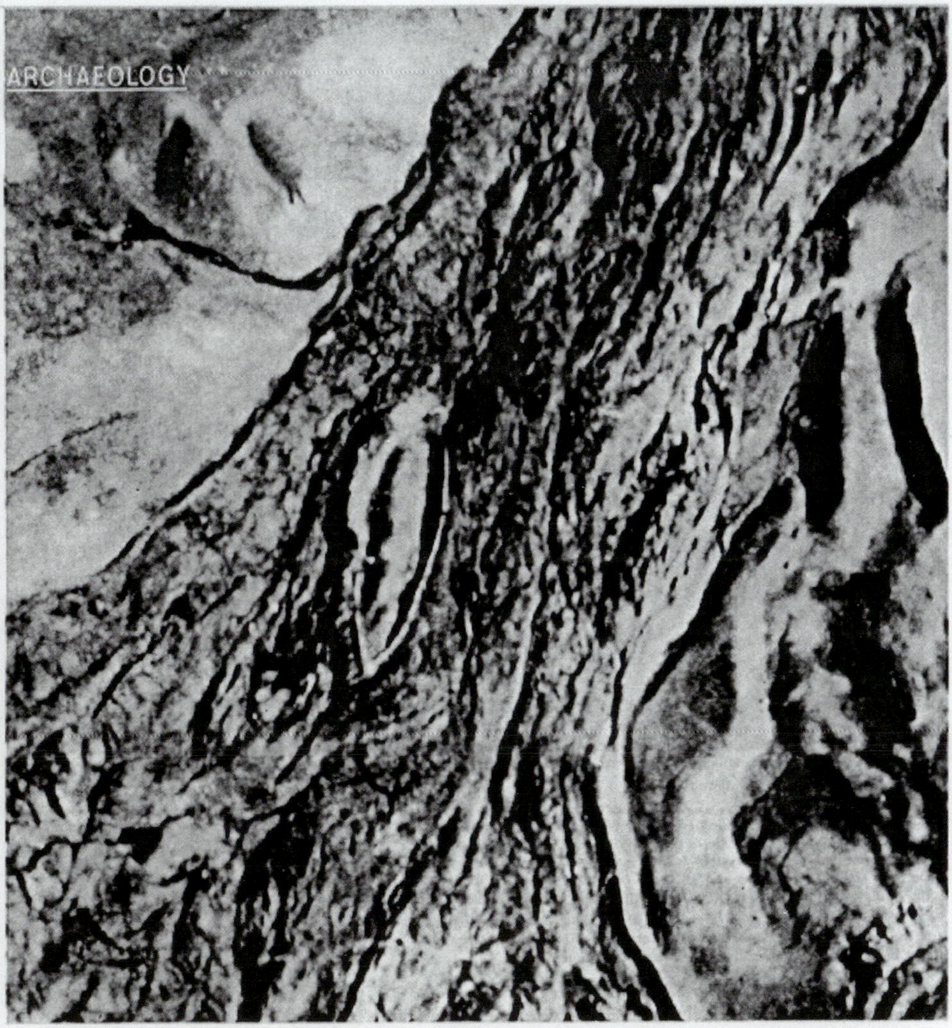

FROM THE AIR the ship-shaped outline lies in the center of a landslide on the slope of a mountain that is only 25 miles from the Russian border. The landslides are of recent origin, may have packed thick mud and stones around the strange form. The photo was shot by a Turkish aerial survey plane from 10,000 feet.

NOAH'S ARK?

Boatlike form is seen near Ararat

The September 5, 1960, article printed in LIFE magazine including an aerial photograph of the area surrounding the boat-shaped object sparked new interest in finding the Ark.

Ron Wyatt spend most of his life investigating the boat shaped object and other spectacular findings. Ron Wyatt died in 1999.
Photo: Viveka Pontén

For 27-year-old Ron Wyatt, the picture in *LIFE* magazine was decisive. He dedicated himself to the Ark and other controversial archeological discoveries that the Ark led him to until his death in 1999.

The Real Dimensions

Ron had noticed that the boat-shaped object didn't have the same dimensions as was normally expected of the Ark. It was more than 500 feet long, while the Bible cites the Ark to be only 450 feet long.

But it turned out that Moses, who saw to it that the story of the flood was written down, could have used an Egyptian cubit of 20.6 inches, while an English cubit is only approximately 18 inches long. The English cubit comes from what would later be Mesopotamia.

That made the boat-shaped object of 515 feet fit with the 300 cubits of the Ark, although it was somewhat broader. But this could have been due to the sides of the boat having collapsed a bit.

The Anchor Stones Are Found

When Ron Wyatt went to Turkey for the first time together with his two sons, they discovered the so-called "anchor stones" in a valley below Mt. Ararat. And Wyatt evolved many theories of how Noah had lived there together with

This clip from Wyatt's amateur film is the only known photo containing two stones; one of them is overturned. Unfortunately we cannot see the engravings because of the lighting. Here we have inserted engravings based on a sketch made by Mrs. Wyatt. The stones were later stolen and are yet to have appeared. But various people have seen them, including Dr. Bayraktutan. You could see the rainbow, the ship riding on the waves, eight people where two were larger than the others.

his family. He also found an old stone house, some graves, and some stones with engravings of a boat, eight people, and a large wave. On a mountain close to the boat-shaped object, Wyatt discovered an old stele engraved with a boat.

The astronaut James Irwin (on right) was quite occupied with finding Noah's Ark. Here he is with Ron Wyatt in 1984 in Turkey.

No to Archaelogical Digs

Wyatt did not obtain permission to excavate the mysterious boat-shaped object. In return, an earthquake in 1978 freed the formation from its surroundings.

The locals called the earthquake an unusual earthquake, a miracle that made Noah's boat rise from its grave. And the area was called Mashur – which means risen.

Ron brought some samples of the curious, quadrangular "stone" found in the middle of the formation back with him and had them tested. The tests showed that it was petrified wood.

Jim Irwin Gets Interested

In 1983 Ron Wyatt contacted astronaut James Irwin, who in Ankara arranged for Ron to be introduced to influential people[3] with contacts in the Turkish government so that Ron could obtain permission to scan the area

The find of the large stones in The Valley of the Eight convinced Ron Wyatt that he was on the right track of the Ark. David Fasold thought they were anchor stones (sea anchors) from the Ark. Here is another ark hunter, Flemming Andersen, along with local Kurds.

with two metal detectors. James Irwin and others from his group went out to see the object and witnessed its scanning. To their surprise, the signals from the scanning showed the presence of metal at regular intervals in straight lines down the ship. There were also signals recognizing metal on the outer sides at 9-foot intervals.

On a video filmed by Ron Wyatt, Jim Irwin said, "Yeah, we got some real positive readings, didn't we, as we went up and down the long direction of the formation ... The spacing (between positive readings) made it appear like, very much like it was, you know, a man-made object."[4]

As for Irwin, he himself continued searching on Mt. Ararat. Gradually the relations between Wyatt and the other Ark hunters on Mt. Ararat grew very tense. And it only made things worse that Wyatt was a rather complex personality, sometimes proposing theories that did not always seem to hold water. Some of the incredible finds he made, disappeared or simply could not be found later on. Some of the people who joined Wyatt's wing – e.g. David Fasold, Jonathan Gray and David Deal – had their own galloping theories that contributed to confusing the issue, too.

In 1985 multiple extensive examinations were taken of the boat-shaped object with three different types of scanners. Tape was laid out to mark where positive results – and thus signs of an underground structure – were found. It is still a mystery what it is ...

Enter Baumgardner

In 1982 John Baumgardner, a geophysicist from the Los Alamos Laboratories, examined the boat-shaped object with three different scanners. Every time the machine gave a positive reading, they laid a stone down and marked it with yellow tape.

They went back to the boat-shaped object in August of 1985 to take up their work again. But as they were also bringing a film crew to record the event for ABC's 20/20, local nationalists took advantage of the media coverage to call attention to their freedom fight. They attacked. The military hit hard and killed many Kurds while others fled. Afterwards, the entire area was declared to be in a state of emergency.

Geophysicist John Baumgardner was very interested and traveled to Turkey eight times.

Baumgardner was more and more convinced that this could be Noah's Ark. In all, he visited the site eight times between 1985 –1988. He participated in two large investigations together with Dr. Salih Bayraktutan in 1987 and 1988. In 1987 they used radar technology and scanned the boat-shaped object 72 times at 2 meter intervals. They took 1200 magnetometer readings in a detailed analysis. They also took multiple measurements with a seismograph. In 1988 they drilled four holes and performed yet another seismographic scanning.

But after having examined the area systematically, Baumgardner declared himself convinced that the boat-shaped object could NOT be Noah's Ark.[5]

In a letter he wrote in 1996 that can be found on the Internet, he rejects categorically that the boat-shaped object could be the remains of the Ark.

> The footage of me in the video that has been shown several times on U.S. and British television during the last three years reflects my early enthusiasm about the possibility of a connection of the site with Noah's Ark, but it does not accurately represent my very firm conclusions reached after the extensive geophysical investigations we conducted at the site in 1987 and 1988.
>
> I am convinced the remains of the Ark must be somewhere else and that such remains are emphatically not associated with this boat-shaped formation. The central claims Wyatt and Fasold have been making about the site are bogus.[6]

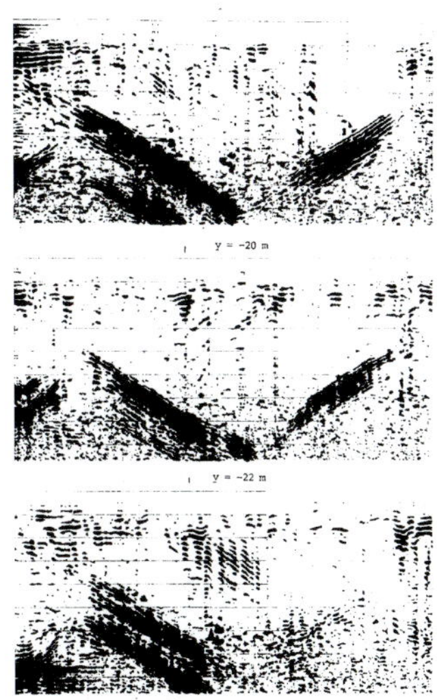

The results from the scannings showed a mysterious V shape, like the keel of the ship.

Ron Wyatt suggested that Dr. Baumgardner had taken another stand because he was afraid of losing his job.

I interviewed Dr. Baumgardner in connection with my previous book and here is what he says in regards to Wyatt's comment.

"Ron's assertion that I take the position I do because I am afraid I will lose my job is just not true. I am very bold in my creationist convictions here. For example, in February I presented a public lecture entitled "Exposing Evolution as Intellectual Fraud" in our community center. This has since been aired several times on our local cable television station."

The radar apparatus had to be pulled up over the eminence where Baumgardner believes the V to have occurred.

"I am convinced that all of this data, including the seismic measurements we obtained in 1987, are internally consistent and point to the very firm conclusion that the shape and stability of the site are due to a buried rocky ridge. Mud from one or several mudslides flowed around this crest-like obstacle, producing the very symmetrical almond-like shape," Baumgardner states.

The radar measurements revealed a V shape under the boat-shaped object that could be taken as a keel. But Baumgardner says that the V shape is due to the large variations in the surface topography.

Baumgardner continues, "In 1988 we drilled four holes in order to collect samples to determine the composition of the subsurface material. This drilling revealed a large, mostly subsurface, ridge of rock below the centre line of the site. As a matter of fact, this rock body is actually exposed at the surface for approximately one third of the full length of the object – from just above the middle to near the lower end."

"In the drill cores it was rather easy to distinguish the material associated with the mudslide from the underlying rocky ground because of the presence or absence of pea-sized gravel. This gravel was ample in the mud, but totally absent in the underlying rock body."

"The V shape we found in 1987 matches the location of the ridge we identified in connection with our drilling in 1988. The V shape in the radar reflection profiles actually represents a horizontal layer several meters below the ground surface. As we crossed the site dragging the radar antenna over the ground surface, we first climbed several meters vertically to the top of the crest and then descended an equal vertical distance on the other side."

"The V shape in the radar profile was the result of the greater vertical distance to the horizontal reflecting layer of rock when we were at the top of the crest compared with when we were in the depressions on either side of the crest. In other words, the V shape was due to the large variations in the surface topography."

"The drilling cores gave us actual samples of the material below the surface and enabled us to interpret the radar measurements with a high degree of certainty."[7]

In the interview, Baumgardner rejects most of the evidence, or indications, put forward by Ron Wyatt, David Fasold,[8] and Jonathan Gray[9] as imagination and overinterpretations. And he doesn't hide that he thinks Wyatt deliberately twisted facts, saying, "The reason I disassociated myself from Ron in 1986 was my conclusion that he could not be trusted, that he was given to lying as part of a deeper psychological problem," Baumgardner says point-blank.

Wyatt, however, continued his scannings and investigations and got more and more convinced of the opposite. According to him the scannings showed that there were compartments and passages under the surface of the earth. But the scannings gave no immediate basis for proving that.

Removed by Terrorists

Wyatt always seemed to be the magnet of drama. In September 1991 Wyatt and his traveling companions Richard Rives, Marv Wilson, and Dr. Alan Roberts were removed by Kurdish PKK terrorists and had to hike through the mountains for three weeks before they were free to go.

The purpose of the terrorists was to call attention to the Kurds' fight for freedom. But their action also called attention to Wyatt's work so that more people began getting interested in the curious boat-shaped object.

I visited the boat-shaped object three times myself and worked together with Dr. Salih Bayraktutan, a Turkish geologist. As we saw it, there were so many extraordinary things about the place that we were rather convinced that it could actually be the remains of the old ship. At that time we couldn't imagine that Wyatt and Fasold were merely lying or having a lively imagination. But we were pretty aware that quite often they jumped to conclusions. A critic once remarked playfully that Wyatt got his exercise by "jumping to conclusions."

In September 2002 I spoke with Dr. Bayraktutan about the problem of Wyatt's and Fasold's many assertions and Dr. Baumgardner's total rejection. He didn't understand his old friend Baumgardner's point of view, but he added with a reference to Wyatt:

> We don't have to exaggerate or conclude something that isn't sure yet. Facts speak for themselves. We have a boat-shaped object at an elevation of 2,000 meters that did not occur naturally. We haven't found anything that refutes the possibility of this being Noah's Ark. We can see signs of specific structures in our scannings that are not naturally occurring. The way in which the object is thought to have traveled down the mountain in a mudslide is very interesting. We have now found signs of an early civilization up on this mountain, etc, etc, etc.
>
> All of this requires continuing the investigations.

Dr. Salih Bayraktutan has taught as a professor of geology at the University of Erzerum.

Even though the outline of the boat-shaped object was easy to see from the air, before the 1978 earthquake, it was difficult to differentiate between the surrounding dirt mounds close up. After the earthquake the sides were freed of multiple yards of mud causing it to stand out clearly as you can see in this picture taken by Dr. John Baumgardner's research team during the 1987 exploration.

Despite the many investigations, it remains, however, a big mystery what the curious boat-shaped object in Durupinar actually is.

If the new find at Mt. Ararat proves to be the real Noah's Ark, the boat-shaped object cannot be the Ark, too. But what is it then? Some believe that it is a prehistoric fort in the shape of a boat. Much seems to show, in any case, that it is man-made.

But now the boat-shaped object has suddenly become of no immediate interest due to the new, great find at Mt. Ararat.

Endnotes

1 The article from Associated Press Istanbul, Nov. 13

2 Violet Cummings, *Has Anybody Seen Noah's Ark?* 1982 Creation Life 0-89051-086-5. Until recently Reshit was entered in the list of eyewitnesses on the most official Mt. Ararat website: http://www.noahsarksearch.com/Eyewitnesses.htm

3 E.g. Dr. Gulek who had functioned as a minister in the government of Ataturk

4 "Yeah, we got some real positive readings, didn't we, as we went up and down the long direction of the formation....The spacing made it appear like, very much like it was, you know, a man-made object." (Video interview documentary: "Discovered – Noah's Ark")

5 Creation Magazine, year 14, No. 4

6 www.tentmaker.org/WAR/BaumgardnerLetter.html (by Gary Amiraoult)

7 Dr. John Baumgardner in an e-mail to the author from October 2001 to March 2003 – which he allowed us to publish.

8 David Fasold, *The Ark of Noah*, Knightsbridge Publishing Comp., New York / 1988 Wynwood Press * 0-922066-10-8.

9 Jonathan Gray in *Discoveries: Questions Answered*, p. 56, Adelaide, Australien, 1999

Chapter 17

Photographs and New Technology

Is this the Ark or just a 620-ft. lava rock? - This picture is an enlargement of the so-called "Ararat Anomaly" from what was until recently a classified CIA photo from 1949 which can be seen at the bottom of the page.
This photograph has been popping up among Ark-hunters for many years for the simple reason that it was top secret.
New satellite photos seem to show that the anomaly has slid down the mountain. But it is still not known whether this is anything more than a lava rock.

From 1953-1955 an American military photographer **William Todd** from Yuma, Arizona, was involved in taking photos of Turkey in its entirety to use for new topographical maps. During a shoot William Todd saw something he believed to be abnormal jutting out of the ice around Ahora Gorge on Mt. Ararat at about 14,500-16,000 feet. The plane was about 2,000 feet above an object everyone in the plane believed to be Noah's Ark.

Even though Todd developed the negatives himself and dealt 4-5 pictures to each of the crew members, they all disappeared! He gave his own pictures (according to himself) to a Baptist preacher who died. After his death the pictures were not to be found again. Todd has since then lost contact with his military buddies, and The Naval Photografic Science Center Archives in Washington, D.C. who should have the negatives can't find them.

George Greene took pictures from a helicopter at almost the same time in 1953 of a boat-like object on Ararat but couldn't raise the funds for an expediton. He was murdered in 1962, and his snapshots disappeared. About 30 people have affirmed that they too have seen his photos.[1] But in the 1970's, **Tom Crotser** from Holy Ground Mission established the object he photographed to be a large rock formation.

The rock is located at a height of 12,000 feet on the eastern edge of Ahora Gorge, and it is most likely the same rock Todd saw. Again this same formation was studied by **Bob Stuplich**, who in 1983 performed an extensive photographing of Mt. Ararat via helicopter.

Also jet fighter **Gregor Schwinghammer,** USA, recounts that he saw something that could have looked like an Ark from his F-100 when he flew over it in 1959. From the pictures he took, no one could figure out what it was. Since then the pictures have been made public in a newspaper without Schwinghammer's blessing.[2]

Pilot **Gus Pipkin**, California, also believes to have seen a ship on Ararat from his DC-4 in good weather when he was flying from Erzurum to Diyarbakir in 1963.

Air captain **Walther D. Hunter** claims to have seen two snapshots taken from a U2 plane in 1969-

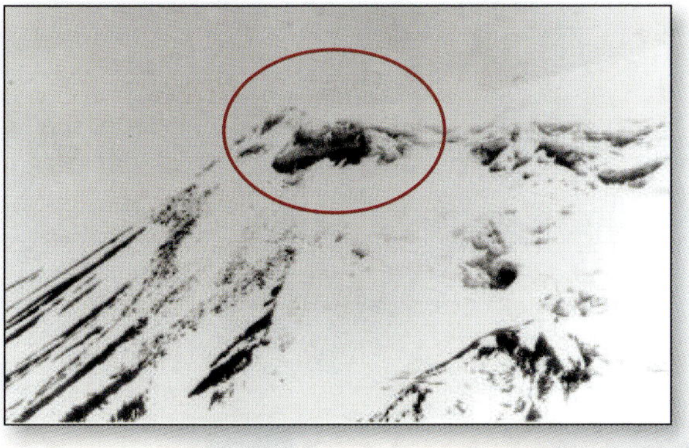

70 containing an object resembling a ship. It had pointed ends, just like the photographs an employee at the Smithsonian Institute believes to have seen.[3] What Hunter saw could possibly have been the pictures of the boat-shaped object the Turkish pilot Durupinar took in 1959. An object that was not on Ararat.

US Navy Lieutenant **Al Shappell** says that he saw a "boatlike structure" when he flew over Mt. Ararat in 1974 on a top-secret mission to photograph the object as it was thought to have possibly been a Soviet radar station. He estimates the object to have been 300 feet long x 200 feet wide and 30-50 feet high, about 2/3 of the Ark's measurements according to the Bible. It was rectangular like a box and was close to the top of the mountain.

US Air Force General **Ralph Haven**, who was stationed in Ankara, Turkey, testified to Elfred Lee in 1985 that he had seen the object that Lee had told him about and of which he had shown pictures. The general confirmed that the Air Force had pictures of the object and that he had even seen two slides of it at Fort Leavenworth, Kansas, in a presentation for some people who were going to Turkey. But when he looked into it again, the slides were missing from the presentation.[4]

Satellite Pictures

Ed Crawford, a Canadian Presbyterian minister from Edmonton, claimed in 1987 to have seen the Ark on a satellite picture. The picture he referred to was taken in 1973 by a land-based satellite and can be found on the internet.[5] It is probably the same formation that Bob Stuplich reported in 1974 as a "black spot." Land-based technology wasn't so advanced that it could give all of the information Crawford claimed to have.

Crawford had also climbed Mt. Ararat in 1983, 1987, and again in 1990, and on his last trip he made it to said object and marked it. The find is located at lattitude 39° 42' 59,7" N and longitude 44° 17' 29,3" E.

Edward Crawford also believes that he found a proto-Sumerian inscription in the Ahora Gorge on Mt. Ararat in 1983.[6] The text, or proto-Sumerian signs, read according to his interpretation; "God's sacrifical covenant of the sky-brought bow (rainbow), go forth, procreate, and be fruitful."

Scott van Dyke from the Mount Ararat Research Foundation in Texas in 1989 got a Turkish firm to map out 50 square miles of the border of Mt. Ararat at over 10,000 feet. They used a high resolution Zeiss camera with four different types of film, including infrared, and took 910 overlapping photographs in stereo pairs (displaced to show depth).

At least it could now be maintained that the Ark was nowhere to be found under the snow line. If it was on the mountain, it had to be up in the icy parts (unless it was buried deep under the lava).[7]

George Stephen III, who is a remote sensing specialist trained by the military, can evaluate pictures taken at great distances such as from satellites and airplanes. He believes that in 1989 he spotted two manmade objects near the top with an estimated distance of 1200 feet between them. He says that from time to time they are covered with 30-70 feet of ice. The area he is referring to is the same area that Ark hunters Shockey, Simmons, Adams, and Arslan had looked at earlier.

The same Stephen has previously worked on establishing the location of the Israelites' crossing of The Red Sea[8] based on similar distance photography. There were plans to photograph the area above the ice line with both a hyperspectral camera (HSI) and a thermal IR-camera. The latter can measure temperature differences, and the hope was that a possible Ark will give off a different temperature than stone. Finally, a Synthetic Aperture Radar (SAR) that can "see" through the ice was also to be used.

New Satellites with Better Resolution

On October 18, 2001, earthwatch in London sent a new global observation satellite, the Quick Bird 2, into orbit from Vandenberg Space Center. This satellite can take pictures with a resolution down to one half meter (1.5 feet) which makes it the best commercial global observation satellite in the world.

Professor Porcher Taylor from Richmond University is a prominent member of the American think tank Center for Strategic and International Studies (CSIS) in Washington.

Since 1993 he has been gathering information about an abnormality on Mt. Ararat found on topsecret military pictures and photos taken by the CIA.

But until 2002 the CIA denied the exsistence of any such pictures as the CIA has a policy to destroy any photos after the information has been taken. However, the Defence Intelligence Agency (DIA) made six such pictures public in 1995. These pictures can still be seen on DIA's website.[9]

In 2001 Taylor got the *Washington Post's* magazine *Insight* to pay for a private satellite to take pictures of Mt. Ararat's northwest side. The pictures, taken from 15,000 feet, are of the side opposite Ahora George, where many mountain climbers up until this point have searched – despite the fact that the Ark can hardly be in this crater that originates from a huge volcanic eruption. The pictures of the abnormality were given to experts. Four of these said it was a manmade formation, two believed it to be a rock, and one considered it undeterminable based on the pictures given. The abnormality is thought to be more than 600 feet long, and one expert in historical nautical vessels believes he can identify the remains of the hull of a ship sticking out of the glacier.

The CIA had Pictures

In 2002 Porcher Taylor and the *Washington Post* magazine *Insight* succeeded in having top secret CIA pictures from 1949 handed out by using the law on openness in administration. Porcher Taylor found that the CIA had

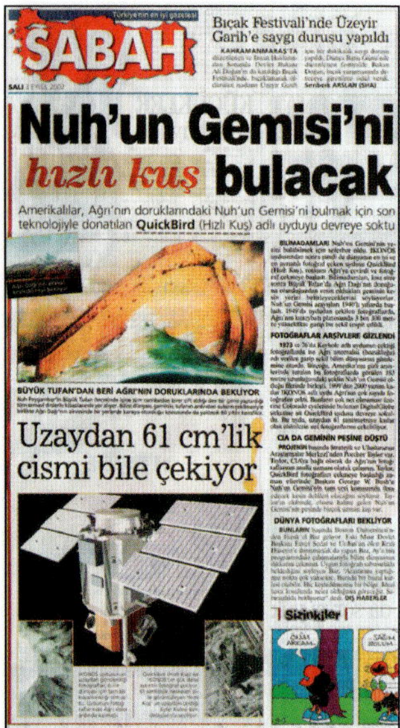
SABAH

Bıçak Festivali'nde Üzeyir Garih'e saygı duruşu yapıldı

Nuh'un Gemisi'ni hızlı kuş bulacak

Amerikalılar, Ağrı'nın doruklarındaki Nuh'un Gemisi'ni bulmak için son teknolojiyle donatılan QuickBird (Hızlı Kuş) adlı uyduyu devreye soktu

BÜYÜK TUFAN'DAN BERİ AĞRI'NIN DORUKLARINDA BEKLİYOR

Uzaydan 61 cm'lik cismi bile çekiyor

The large Turkish newspaper SABAH reports a new attempt to find Noah's Ark by means of a satellite known as Quick Bird. The article is dated September 3, 2002.

also in 1956 taken photos in high resolution from U2 planes and in 1973 by using remote-sensing from a KH-9 satellite and even more sophisticated photos in 1976, 1990, and 1992 from an advanced KH-11 satellite. But it is the 1949 photo that most clearly shows something 'abnormal.'

From October 1999 to the summer of 2000, a different satellite, Space Imaging's private Ikonos-2, took four pictures of this location without bringing the Ark to light. But a team of analysts composing of seven scientists and picture experts couldn't come to an agreement about what was in these pictures. Some believed the object to have moved since 1949 which could mean that it isn't even a part of the mountain.

The pictures from Ikonos can only show objects that are one meter or more in size, but the team still believed the pictures to show an object broken in multiple places whose color makes it stand out against the surrounding volcanic rock. The surface of the object also looks smoother than the circumjacent sharp rock formations, they believe.

In September 2002 there was yet another attempt to reveal the Ark at Mt. Ararat from the satellite Quick Bird.

However, none of the photos taken from airplanes or satellites which have attracted so much attention have led to actual discoveries.

Today, everyone interested in the Ark can log onto the electronic map program Google Earth and examine Mt. Ararat from above.

Endnotes

1 According to Violet M. Cummings, *Noah's Ark: Fable or Fact?*", p. 144

2 Interviews with Schwinghammer in *Ararat Report*.

3 Rene Noorbergen interview with ex-employee David Duckworth, letter from Army Chaplain Clair Shaffer to Dr. Willis about a group from the National Geographic Soc. staying overnight in Trabzon, Turkey, on their way from Ararat. See *The Explorers of Ararat*, p. 430-435.

4 *The Explorers of Ararat*, p. 458-459.

5 www.vonbora.com

6 "Field Notes" section of Research & Exploration, a Scholarly Publication of the National Geographic Society, Autumn 1944.

7 Mt. Ararat is a volcanic mountain which has grown over a period of at least three eruptions. The last one is probably after the Flood.

8 Mentioned in the book *The Gold of Exodus*.

9 Reported in *The Explorers of Ararat* p. 466.

船

挪亞方舟

PART 2
THE GREAT DISCOVERY

The darker illustration above shows the old
Chinese characters for a large ship.
It consists of three characters:
Symbol for boat (left), the number 8 (top), and the symbol for mouths.
An ancient reference to the ark with eight people.
The smaller, lighter symbols below
are the modern Chinese
characters for "Noah's ark."

The dramatic cover of the Chinese documentary film from 2005.

Chapter 18

The Chinese Conquer the Mountain

For centuries and even for millennia, there have been accounts of people searching for and claiming to see parts of the Ark on the mysterious Mt Ararat. But not all accounts were credible, as we shall see later. However, some stories might be true, but people wouldn't believe them anyway.

At any rate, a lot of things indicate that several people were on the site where the Kurdish-Chinese group has now found tangible remains of a big wooden structure that may very well be Noah's Ark. So even if skeptical Westerners, such as myself, have quickly rejected these "eye-witness stories" as lies or imagination, the stories may have been true.

Later we shall look at some of the people who stated that the Ark was still there, hidden under the ice, on Mt Ararat. Some of them lived more than 2000 years ago, but most of them pop out in the 1800s and the 1900s. Especially after the Second World War, there was a rise of interest in the Ark.

However, in 1990 the Turkish authorities closed the mountain since some Kurdish separatists had taken advantage of the Ark search to draw attention to their struggle by burning the tents and equipment of one expedition, threatening to execute the Ark hunters, and in another case they kidnapped the Ark hunters.

But in 2000 the authorities decided again to allow Ark hunters and tourists climb Mt. Ararat.

Although at that time, many American Ark hunters had lost some of their enthusiasm after all the disappointment.

Just as the American expeditions to Mt. Ararat began to fade out, and more and more people started getting interested in other mountains that might be potential sites to look for finds, such as Durupinar, Mt. Cudi, etc., the Chinese team from Hong Kong appeared in Turkey.

They were in an organization with the Chinese name 挪亞方舟國際事工 – or in English, Noah's Ark Ministries International, NAMI, established by Andrew Man-fai Yuen.

Noah's Ark Ministries International (NAMI)

An international organization comprised of ark researchers, scientists, and Bible scholars, NAMI seeks the truth of the Ark from a faith-based yet objective, scientific perspective. In the future, it will continue to invite academia to participate in historically, culturally, geologically, and archeologically informed scientific research of the Ark.

After a preliminary study trip in 2003, they made their first actual expedition on Mt. Ararat in 2004 after which they returned at least once a year.

The Chinese approached the Ark hunt in a different way from the earlier Ark hunters.

1. HUMILITY: They started humbly examining what the Kurds, who had lived there for many generations, already knew. In this way they bonded closely with the guide Parasut, who knew much more than he would normally tell tourists.
2. RESPECT: They showed respect for the locals, their culture and religion. From the very start, they worked on having close cooperation with the Turkish authorities in the Agri province,and they hired Turkish experts.
3. INTEGRITY: They didn't conceal that they were Christians and even brought a pastor with them to exorcise the demons that the Kurds feared, and they asked God to help them find the Ark. This didn't cause problems in their relationship with the Kurds; on the contrary, it caused mutual respect. Parasut later expressed his wish for such people to find the Ark, namely people who showed respect for God, the people, and the culture.
4. ENDURANCE: Even though some expeditions had to be cancelled, the Chinese patiently returned year after year – some years more than once. They sacrificed vast sums of money on the exploration that was collected privately or procured through the production and sales of a documentary.

The Hottest Summer in 500 years

In just the first year, they observed and filmed a "broken opening" at an altitude of 4,200 meters, which they believed could contain the remains of the Ark. Considering how many Ark hunters have searched Mt. Ararat for years under many personal hardships without finding even a shred of proof, it is extremely fortunate that the Chinese group found something on their *first* expedition.

Could it be due to the fact that the Chinese came in a period when global warming had made an impact so that sites which had been hidden were now revealed by the melting ice? In April 2004 NAMI happened to discover a weather report from an American satellite predicting that in that year Turkey would experience the hottest summer in 500 years.

Actually the biggest find up to this point was discovered by Frenchman Ferdinand Navarra, who found a big wooden balk during an extra hot summer in 1955. The year was called "Observation Year" as it was the hottest year during a number of hot years.

Navarra found his balk at the same altitude, 4,200 m, at the site where the Kurdish-Chinese team in 2004 found the "opening" of a cave in the snow.

McGiven Must Give Up

A businessman from Hawaii, Daniel McGiven, planned to send an expedition to find the Ark by means of photos taken from the Early Bird Satellite. By a certainty of 90%, Mc Given's team believed they could localize the site. However, McGiven didn't get the opportunity to accomplish his prestigious expedition. For some obscure political reason, the Turkish authorities refused to give American Ark hunters admission to Mt. Ararat from April to August.

Problems with Spirits?

The leader of NAMI, Andrew Man-fai Yuen, had traced the Ark from another angle – a spiritual one. He wondered why the Kurds who had lived near the mountain for all those years hadn't found the Ark themselves. They must know something, he thought. And by and by he found out that some Kurds actually knew something but considered it to be a taboo.

In the middle of August, Andrew Man-fai Yuen received a video cassette from the Kurdish guide *Ahmet Ertugrul* (Parasut) which contained a strange discovery.

"I saw the footage of Mt. Ararat devoid of snow. In the midst of the mud and the rocks you could see an object like a pillar. They said that it was the remains of Noah's Ark, and that it could be entered. But the Ark's entrance was not on the video, because it couldn't be filmed," explains Andrew Man-fai Yuen.[1]

I asked, "How come? Is it so scary that you're unable to film it?"

He said that there were magical powers in that place. It was very unique, very occult. If your camera was rolling, it would suddenly stop or start playing up.

The Kurds also said that watches would suddenly stand still as if time had stopped. Andrew was doubtful and asked many questions. He wanted to see the place but the Kurd answered that he could only get military permission for two foreigners to climb the mountain.

Andrew thought that if there really were problems with spirits, the best person to bring was pastor Lee Chi Kwong, for he had dealt with exorcism before. He immediately accepted.

"I believed that even if we met something strange, we could drive away evil spirits by simply calling out the name of Jesus Christ," he explains, on the video film which the Chinese later produced.

On the 12th of October 2004, Andrew and Lee travelled to Turkey daring to enter the militarily surveyed and perhaps even demon-possessed area together with their Kurdish friends.

On the 18th the Kurds took the Chinese up the mountain. All in all, they were an expedition of 12 people. They stayed overnight in a base camp at an altitude of 3,000 m before they travelled the remaining distance on foot. On the video taken, the Muslim Kurds and the Christian Chinese stood shoulder to shoulder, gathered in prayer around the fire while Pastor Lee Chi prayed in a loud voice and with great conviction, praying for protection and praying that they would find the Ark. The team leader Parasut remarked that it was cloudy and that the climb the next day would depend on whether "your God will grant you a miracle." And then Andrew sent an sms to Hong Kong to mobilize the Christian friends to pray for good weather the next day from 5 am to 8 pm.

A Known Phenomenon?

The next morning there was lovely sunshine and clear weather, and they climbed into the Valley of The Ghost, a smaller valley on the mountain at an altitude of 4,200 m and a place where nobody will search for animals gone astray. The place was said to be taboo. Way back in history, locals have claimed that there were spirits on the mountain.

Sir John Mandeville, an English knight, wrote an account of his travels between 1322 and 1356. In *The Travels*, chapter 13, he writes, "That mountain is a full seven miles high; and some men say that they have seen and touched the ship, and put their fingers in the parts where the devil went out, when Noah said "Benedicte."("Blest")

And when the Turkish expedition in 1883 apparently found remains of the Ark, they questioned the locals. According to the article that was spread all over the world, the local inhabitants have known of the appearance of the Ark for six years. But due to the fear of spirits, they didn't want to approach the Ark. It is taboo. Det er tabu.

On the 10th of August 1883, the *Chicago Tribune* printed the following:

> "A paper at Constantinople announces the discovery of Noah's Ark. It appears that some Turkish commissioners appointed to investigate the avalanches on Mt. Ararat suddenly came on a gigantic structure of very dark wood, protruding from the glacier. They made inquiries of the local folk. These had seen it for six years, but had been afraid to approach it, because a spirit of fierce aspect had been seen looking out of the upper windows. The Turkish Commissioners, however, are bold men, not deterred by such trifles, and they determined to reach it."

When the Chinese and the Kurds arrived at the rock cave whose opening had become visible, the opening of the cave absolutely resembled a devil face with two horns. That the Kurds are really fearful of the place can be observed from the video. Parasut went ahead, and in his peculiar English uttered some confused words that "if God is with us, if Noah wants us….Otherwise we will be back…"

Technical Problems

While the Kurds slowly and fearfully dared to approach the opening, the camera man tried to film, but the camera didn't work properly. The picture became fuzzy every time that the camera was directed towards the opening.

Pastor Kwong and Andrew Yuen, head of Nami, shows the entrance to the cave after the Kurds had broken the horns of the devil's mask, and a distorted face seems to emerge. The picture is from the Chinese DVD documentary The Days of Noah. Here with more contrast and a white ring added.

It was as if the camera was subjected to technical disturbances. When the camera was turned in another direction, the picture was fine. After three trials the camera stopped working all together and a reserve camera had to be put to work.

A Face Appears

The Kurds now started to throw big rocks at the "mask" until the horns were broken off.

"I thought that a face appeared on the wall when the Kurds broke the horns of the mask and kind of removed the mask," says Andrew.

And strangely enough the two cameras worked again, and the team could also film into the opening where the Chinese thought they could see dark wood under the ice and a wooden wall.

They felt like crawling inside. But Parasut holds them back because the cave is full of water and the ice isn't thick enough, only three centimeters thick it turned out when Parasut cut into it with his ice axe. So they might have fallen into the ice-cold water on the freezing cold mountain.

Having promised the Kurds and the military that they would just film and not bring anything down with them, they contented themselves with throwing rocks into the cave. From the noise, they reckon that the cave must be big.

The Christian Chinese had conquered not only the physical mountain but also a spiritual one, namely the fear from which the Kurds had suffered for generations. And in a spiritual manner, the way was prepared for their finding the remains of Noah's Ark later on.

When the Chinese returned in 2006 to examine the cave, it turns out that an earthquake had destroyed it.

However, the Chinese and the Kurds found a thread which they followed, and in 2008 they made the great find nearby. Maybe it is the same find with another entrance. The site is yet a secret in order to protect it from grave robbers.

Great News Ignored

After returning to Hong Kong, the Chinese held a press conference in November of the same year to tell about their find.

Apparently the news was reported in many media sources already in 2004, but even though I have been following the search for the Ark with intense interest for years, I have never heard or read about the discovery made by the Hong Kong Chinese. I think the news was spread mostly in Asia, whereas the European and American media weeded out this "curious piece of news" in their usual arrogance towards religious matters.

Documentary

The Chinese, however, were not easily stopped. Already in 2005, NAMI released, in cooperation with the documentary film company Sparkling Sun, a documentary, *The Days of Noah*, which was shown in cinemas in Asia. The film was about the search for the Ark, and it created great interest in some areas of the world.

In the film they tell about the local Kurds' discovery of the fact that reddish snow falls on Mt. Ararat approximately every twenty years. This inexplicable phenomenon is followed by several years of an extra fine harvest. The last time that reddish snow fell on Mt. Ararat was in 1998 the Kurds say. But, in contrast to earlier times, the good harvest failed to come. And the Kurds wondered about the reason why. Was it significant?

As opposed to irreligious Westerners who would just dismiss it as a chance natural phenomenon, the Christian Chinese listened with interest. They knew by experience that there is "more between heaven and earth" than meets the eye.

Parasut's Secret

When the leader of NAMI, Andrew Man-fai Yuen, visited the Kurdish guide Parasut, he noticed that the Kurd had several fine ancient pieces of pottery. One of the earthen jars was more than three feet tall. And Parasut told him that similar objects were in use at the time of Noah. He didn't say that they originated from the Ark or from where he had gotten them. But gradually they discovered that Parasut, who grew up on Mt. Ararat, had a family secret.

Endnotes

1 Andrew Man-fai Yuen In the film *The days of Noah*, The Media Evangelism Ltd. 2005.

Chapter 19

Parasut Discovers Wood at 13,100 Feet

Some of the petrified wood found by the guide Parasut in 2006 was examined at the University of Hong Kong.

In August 2006 NAMI's regular Kurdish guide *Ahmet Ertugrul* (Parasut) found a wooden structure on Mt. Ararat at an altitude of 13,100 feet (4,000 meters). To find wood that far up was incredible. People have never lived above the altitude of 3000 meters on Mt. Ararat. Furthermore, at the altitude of 4000 meters there is always snow and ice, at least on the northern side of the mountain where Parasut probably found his piece of wood. On the southern side of the mountain, the ice can melt up to 500 meters below the summit – as it did in 2010 after a series of warmer than usual summers.

Parasut contacted the Chinese team in Hong Kong that was planning to pursue the discovery and make a film.

Even though they were convinced that they had been very close to discovering the Ark in 2004, they knew they needed tangible proof if they were to convince the world that the millenarian ship from the Holy Bible was real.

Now Parasut found something that resembled proof. The team asked him to send a piece of the wood in order to have it examined at a laboratory in Hong Kong. *The Applied Geoscience Centre of the Department of Earth Science* at the University of Hong Kong confirmed that the sample was a piece of wood which had been petrified.

How Old?

It is generally claimed that fossilization takes place over thousands of years, namely because the geological conditions are always explained by mainstream evolutionary theories. World disasters, such as the Flood, are not taken into account, despite the fact that more and more signs show that there actually

A fossilised trunk (left) and a fossilised stump of a tree, which was found in Léré in Tchad. Both have a look of having been sawn by man – and therefore are not many millions of years old…

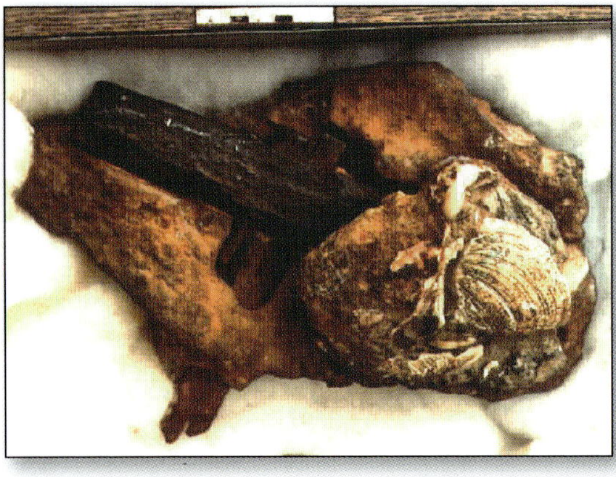

The London hammer is fossilized in sandstone and should therefore, according to evolutionary theory, be millions of years old.

was a flood disaster about 5,000-6,000 years ago, as explained in this book.

In reality, however, there are many examples of fossils that contain articles from recent times, such as a hammer, and therefore, these fossils aren't necessarily extremely old. Under special conditions, for example, wood can go through a process which makes it hard as stone. (I myself have found fossilized tree trunks in Chad, Africa, near the town Lere close to the Cameroon frontier. The tree trunks looked as if they had been chopped or sawn by humans.)

The London Hammer

Perhaps the clearest example that the theories about the millions of years cannot be correct, however, is the London hammer, which was found in June 1936 in Red Creek near the small town of London in Texas. Due to the hammer being encapsulated or at least being encircled with sandstone it should normally be from a geological period of 360-460 million years ago, according to these theories. (Some scientists have argued for the material surrounding it being only about 110-120 million years old, but that off course does not make out a significant difference.) Probably the hammer can be dated only a few hundred years back or at least no more than a few thousand years.

Loophole

Obviously the theory about petrifaction in the geological layers can't be correct. But of course the adherents to this theory have a loophole explanation for this. "Minerals in solution can harden around an intrusive object dropped in a crack or simply left on the ground if the source rock (in this case, reportedly Ordovician) is chemically soluble." (Cole, 1985)[1]

The geologist Stromberg has proven that petrifaction can happen over a period of a few hundred years – even in a few decades. But still some scientists maintain their millions of years explanation.

In any case Parasut's find of wood might actually originate from the Ark of Noah in spite of it being petrified.

But let's remember that the wooden structure from the great 2008 discovery was NOT fossilized and not destroyed either. Probably because it was hidden in ice over thousands of years and not exposed to wind and weather.

The Ark-interested Chinese at once contacted Turkish archaeologists, geologists, and climbing experts before they sent a team in February 2007 of 10 persons on an expedition up Mt. Ararat for the second time.

Their destination was the cave at the height of 13,776 feet found already in 2004, as well as, the other cave at 13,100 feet where Parasut had found petrified wood.

Earthquake

After having struggled their way up the mountain, they were faced with great disappointment. The cave they had seen in "The Valley of the Ghost" at 13,776 feet up the mountain had collapsed completely due to an earthquake. It was impossible to investigate the cave. Due to bad weather conditions, the team had to make several attempts during that year in order to accomplish what they had come for, the goal of the expedition.

Great New Find

In August 2007 the team finally succeeded in uncovering a large, petrified wooden structure and carried new samples down from the mountain. On that occasion they measured the wooden structure they had found to be no less than 38 feet long (11.5 mtrs.) and 8.5 feet tall (2.6 mtrs.)! Now their research really began to pay off. Such a big wooden structure had never before been discovered on the mountain. In any case, there had been no proof so far that it existed even though "eyewitnesses " over the years had told about similar discoveries. But now the team could video the location and document their find.

The team, however, had to first remove all the volcanic ash covering the place. They already knew that there was something valuable under the ashes, and they were right. Once the ashes were removed, the woody surface structure appeared.

After this remarkable find in August, the Chinese held a press conference in October in Hong Kong where they invited Turkish representatives.

Besides the mountain climber and guide Parasut, the prominent experts who had been on the team participated: Dr. Ahmet Ozbek, geologist at the Kahramanmaras Sutcu Iman University in Turkey; Dr. Özlem Cevik, archaeologist at the Trakya University; Professor Otkay Belli, Director of the Institute of Eurasian Archaeology at the University of Istanbul, and Dr. Selim Pullu from the Afyonkarahisar Kocatepe University. E. Mushin Bulut, Director of the Ministry of Cultural Affairs in the Agri Province, who represented the Turkish state at the press conference in Hong Kong.

Nothing New from the East in the Western Media

The interest of the press and others was considerable, both in Turkey, Hong Kong, and other parts of Asia. But again, the news didn't really register in the West. Nobody in the old "Christian world" apparently seemed to realize that the polite Chinese and their Turkish friends had made the most significant and remarkable discovery so far in the search for the Ark. No matter what they had actually discovered, no wooden object that big had ever been found so high up on Mt. Ararat.

Six months later in January 2008, the Noah's Ark Ministries held another press conference, this time in Dogubeyazit itself, the town situated at the very foot of Mt. Ararat, which has been the starting point for most of the Ark expeditions. At this press conference, NAMI published plans of future cooperation with the Turkish authorities and experts.

Officials from the town government of Dogubeyazit and the Province of Agri signed agreements of cooperation concerning the exploration of Noah's Ark. This is also a new approach as compared to all previous expeditions, some of which have been made without the permission of the authorities, resulting in many cancellations and misunderstandings. But the Chinese secured cooperation with the local authorities and inhabitants at an early stage.

The Incredible Text Message

Suddenly the Kurdish guide, Parasut, got a secret tip about where to find the Ark. Up to this point, Parasut had not wanted to or had not been able to tell from where he got the tip. But one day in June 2008, he found the opening through which he could get "into the Ark" – that is into the wooden structure of which they had come across but had never succeeded to get inside. This day in June, however, Parasut sent a text message to Clara Wei, his closest contact person in Hong Kong.

The message read: "We have found Noah's Ark. I am standing right beside it now on Mt. Ararat. What are we to do?"

It is after this text message that Clara received in the middle of the night due to the time difference that NAMI decided to act quickly. Even though Clara had asked Parasut to send some pictures of his discovery, he hadn't yet done so. But NAMI couldn't risk wasting time.

Failed Expedition

Together with Parasut, Clara Wei was assigned to organize a new Chinese expedition in Turkey. This was done at the end of August 2008.

In spite of very bad weather, it was possible for the team to investigate two other sites that also could have a connection with the Ark. But due to bad weather they were unable to reach the new site Parasut had talked about. They had to be content seeing the photos he had taken at the summit of the mountain. But could they be trusted...? The pictures could have been taken somewhere else.

Without getting proof from visiting the alleged location themselves, the NAMI team finally had to return home again. It was very frustrating. They all agreed to keep the secret to themselves. They had to be sure before they proclaimed the news all over the world that the Ark had been found.

Many had claimed to have seen the Ark, but it was usually at a distance or on a satellite photo, and those allegations couldn't be verified when examined more closely.

This time they had to be sure.

Endnotes

1 http://paleo.cc/paluxy/hammer.htm
http://www.creationevidence.org

Chapter 20

Exit Randall Price

The American Bible archaeologist Randall Price was close to joining the Nami team. But the Kurd Parasut protested.

While doing research for the documentary, Clara Wei had come across the American research author and professor, Dr. Randall Price. He seemed to be an obvious candidate for the team that was to investigate the new discovery made by Parasut.

He had a Masters of Theology from Dallas Theological Seminary and a Ph.D. in Middle Eastern Studies from the University of Texas at Austin. He had also studied at the Hebrew University of Jerusalem and was fielding excavations in Israel together with the University of Texas where he taught Biblical archaeology and history. He has been in charge of a number of excavations on the Qumran Plateau in Israel from 2002 to 2008.

Furthermore, he was Executive Director and Distinguished Research Professor of Judaic Studies at Liberty University in Lynchburg, Virginia, USA. And Dr. Price also had his own "World of the Bible Ministries," an information service and a website specializing in Biblical archaeology and Biblical prophecies relating to the Middle East.

Clara Wei contacted the American professor and invited him to attend the press conference in Turkey which NAMI held in 2008 in the small town of Dogubayazit after their find of wood on Mt. Ararat. He brought along Dr. Don Patton and David McQueen.

Earlier that same year, the geologist Dr. Don Patton and the Ark search veteran Dr. Don Shockey went to Hong Kong in order to personally hand over and explain their geological analysis of the wood that Parasut had found. In their opinion the petrified wood was a piece of volcanic tuff (rock). However, according to Dr. Randall Price,[1] they agreed to share information including Dr. Price's satellite photos and to make a joint expedition that summer.

Initiated in the Secret

As Dr. Price was now a sort of partner, he also received the unbelievable message from Parasut that he had located Noah's Ark or, in any case, a wooden structure on Mt. Ararat – and had been inside it.

So the American team members were, according to Dr. Price, contacted by Clara Wei and invited to come over immediately so that they could see "the Ark." Price assumed that Parasut's discovery was based on the satellite photos he had shared with the Chinese. Nevertheless, the Americans had to pay 17,000 Euro for eight of Parasut's photos to be emailed to them only showing pottery vessels in a dark room. Parasut didn't want to send the more exciting photos for fear that they would be hacked by others, but he promised to show photos of the wooden structure when they arrived in the city of Van, about 95 miles south of Mt. Ararat, where they had arranged to meet. And

Clara Wei, who had seen the pictures, was able to explain to the Americans that they showed a cave and a wooden structure with a door.

Parasut also demanded 120,000 Euro upfront to buy equipment and permits before the expedition could take place. After consulting the Chinese, the Americans accepted to pay their half of the advance payment, 60,000 Euro. Anxious to be led up to the Ark site, the Americans joined the Hong Kong team in Istanbul in August, and together they traveled to Van where they met Parasut.

Fateful Meeting

"That night Parasut showed us the same photos described to us by Clara. However, the cave in the photos had a tree and other foliage in front and the wooden structure with a door was a rock-cut tomb! Parasut was upset that the Americans questioned his photos (the Chinese did not) and would not speak to us directly after this. He told the Chinese that he wouldn't show any other photos because he said the Americans had GPS capability and would know exactly where the Ark was located! Despite this outright deception, the Chinese asked us to continue to trust Parasut and be patient," the American professor explained.[2]

Price was hardly fully aware of how deeply he had offended the honor of the Kurdish man by questioning his reliability in public.

Things didn't look any better in September when Parasut was training some local people for the ascent to the site, while at the same time refusing to train the American group even though he had said that they had to be tested before he could take them up. All the Americans were experienced mountain climbers so Parasut's "test" was an insult to them as well.

Dr. Price and his colleagues now wanted to leave and asked for their money back, but the Chinese tried to resolve the conflict and offered to send their young, well-trained videographer to film the site of the Ark and then afterwards show the footage to the Americans so that they could see for themselves that the site was real enough. But when the cameraman later told them that he had not been allowed to come near the cave, the Americans angrily left the place.

Wing-Cheung Yeung.

The documentary filmmaker Wing-Cheung Yeung explained what happened.

"The major problem was that the weather was very bad. Parasut told us that the weather would make the climbing difficult. It was very dangerous to climb. He suggested that we relinquish our plans to climb the mountain. We waited for a period of time," Yeung said.

During this period Dr. Price and the Turkish expedition team leader had a discussion regarding the issue of whether or not to climb Mt. Ararat. They were not in agreement and it ended with Price no longer trusting the local expedition team. As a result, their joint efforts were brought to an end. The Hong Kong team served as mediator. "We tried to reconcile them so that our cooperation could continue. We tried many things in an attempt to resolve the conflict between them. Yet, we did not succeed due to differences in cultural background and in opinion," explained Yeung.[3]

While the Chinese went back home, the American group stayed in Turkey and met shortly after in late September 2008 with Dr. Richard Bright who has climbed Mt. Ararat about 30 times, including several times with Jim Irwin, the U.S. astronaut. He took them in early October up the mountain to a height of 13,000 feet (3,963 meters). Upon their return from the mountain, they were told that Parasut was very angry that they had chosen a rival Kurdish guide. And the relationship was now – if not before – irreparably broken.

Before the Americans went home, Dr. Don Patton and Dr. Randall Price participated in a Noah's Ark and Mt. Ararat Research Symposium in Dogubayazit. After the symposium Clara Wei made a final attempt on behalf of the Chinese to persuade the Americans to continue their joint efforts. Parasut had now handed over the pictures to the Chinese which she gave to the Americans together with a promise of refunding their share of the expenses for the mountain climbing.

Randall Price has published numerous books, DVDs and other material about biblical archeology in the world, offered on his website www.worldofthebible.com

Differences in Cultural Background

All through the course of events, you sense an enormous clash of cultures between the very self-assured, no-nonsense, American approach and the eastern, Kurdish approach where issues like honor and shame are extremely important. And between them you have the reserved and polite Chinese who came to realize that they couldn't deal with both groups at once.

The relationship was further damaged when Dr. Price on September 30 wrote a very direct letter to Andrew, the leader of the Chinese team, accusing him, point-blank, of having broken his word and of not behaving as a good Christian merely because Andrew had chosen to say goodbye to Dr. Price and his group and follow Parasut. On May 7, 2009, this letter was put on Dr. Price's website and this action was, of course, very defamatory to the Chinese leader of NAMI.

Incidentally, Dr. Price returned to Mt. Ararat the year after in the summer of 2009, and he participated in a new expedition to the summit of Mt. Ararat with Dr. Richard Bright. Here they learned that the Chinese team was preparing a new expedition in October with Parasut. As it still wasn't possible for the Chinese to persuade Parasut to allow the American group to participate, the partnership was finally brought to an end by Clara Wei's returning two-thirds of the money on behalf of NAMI, keeping one-third for expenses already incurred during the unsuccessful attempt to reach the ark.

Tit for Tat...

When the news about the discoveries made by Parasut and the Chinese was published in May 2010, Dr. Randall Price was one of the first to express his critical opinion to the press. He vigorously hinted that the Chinese had been cheated by the Kurdish guide whom he accused of being an alcoholic, and he quoted another Kurdish guide for saying that Parasut himself had arranged for wood to be carried up the mountain – that is to say, it was all sheer humbug.

The Chinese were appalled by Dr. Price's accusations. Such statements, of course, gave rise to a lot of scepticism in the U.S. – especially in biblical archaeological circles where Dr. Price was considered a reliable expert. These circles had always shown an enormous interest in finding the Ark, and it was to the very same circles that the Chinese Christians had been looking for sympathy and understanding for the project. They had expected Dr. Price to stand up for the find. But now he did just the opposite. They saw it as an act of revenge rooted in personal disagreements between two strong-minded men who were unable to reconcile.

NAMI at once issued a statement from the press conference in the Netherlands on Randall Price's released document "The Alleged Discovery of a Wooden Structure on Mt. Ararat by a Chinese-Turkish Expedition That is Claimed to be the Remains of Noah's Ark." The following is NAMI's answer:

In response to the recent reporting on the doubts of the discovery of the wooden structure on Mount Ararat by Noah's Ark Ministries International (NAMI) and the Turkish research team, based on the personal opinion and letter released by Randall Price, NAMI would like to clarify our standpoint on the matter.

1. NAMI worked with Randall Price for a short period of about 2 weeks in 2008 in Turkey, but we have never climbed the mountain together with him. His letter mentioned that he has "difficulties with a number of issues related to the evidence at hand." We are not sure about what kind of evidence he is referring to since he has never been at the location of the wooden structure we identified. We had terminated cooperation with him in early October 2008. Furthermore, he never received an update on Panda's expedition in late October 2008 nor any of our expeditions since then. This we regret because Dr. Price is an archaeologist and would most certainly have been able to help the team in interpreting the find.

2. Everyone who has ever climbed Mount Ararat knows that the terrain above 3,800 meters is so rugged that you cannot carry anything more than a backpack. We have contacted Mr. Muhsin Bulut, the Director of Cultural Ministries, Agri Province, where Mount Ararat is located and sought his opinion about the possibility of transporting large quantities of timber and constructing a large wooden structure at an altitude of 4,000 meters. He assured us that the mountain is a restricted area and strictly monitored; therefore, such activity is impossible.

3. So far we have received a lot of feedback and many e-mails from various Ark researchers. Some of them we know and some we don't. Most of them have shown a lot of positive interest for this discovery.

We welcome alternative opinions on the search for Noah's Ark. To provide a means for the general public to get to a more complete picture of the discovery and the stories behind the discovery, our official website www.noahsarksearch.net will feature interviews with members of our research team and experts from various fields to share their viewpoints and to provide the latest information on the search for Noah's ark.

Noah's Ark Ministries International April 30, 2010

P.S. We would also like to make it clear that NAMI has not officially invited another scientist John Morris as the consultant for the ark search even though we did meet with him once in 2005.

John Morris Is Not a Consultant

The P.S. refers to the statements for which Dr. John Morris is quoted in *Catholic News Agency* on May 5, 2010, and in other media. Here you can read that Dr. Morris has been a consultant for the Chinese team since 2005 but that he declined to be at the NAMI press conference in Hongkong on April 25 on the following grounds, "I'm a scientist. I need to have good evidence. As of right now, there is none." Although he doubts that Kurdish workers would have been able to haul the wood to the site, he said the evidence remains inconclusive.[5]

Dr. John Morris is president of Dallas' Institute for Creation Research, a private organization specializing in research and information concerning the theories of creation as opposed to the theory of evolution. Dr. Morris himself has also climbed Mt. Ararat several times. On one occasion he was unluckily struck by lightning when a thunder storm suddenly appeared. He lost consciousness and was thrown down a slope but wasn't seriously injured by the event. Dr. Morris has no doubts that the Ark exists and also believes that it can be found on Mt. Ararat. But like many others in the American creationist circles, he has chosen to keep a sceptical distance to the Chinese NAMI. So therefore, NAMI keeps their distance from him as well. They make it very clear that he has not been NAMI's consultant.

Was It Possible?

When the Turkish-Chinese team and the authorities categorically exclude the possibility of Parasut being able to construct the wooden structure on the mountain, Dr. Price describes on his website how this could have been done:

In the summer of 2009, our team's Kurdish workers transported by hand a 1,000-pound generator to 3,963 meters (13,000 feet), a 400-pound generator to 5,183 meters (17,000 feet), and at the same elevation, we built a house out of steel and plastic that held seven people. This was done in only a matter of a few weeks. We also observed Kurds carrying wood up the mountain to be used for fuel as well as observed the remains of large wood fires at various elevations. According to my sources, Parasut and his workers transported the wood from Erzurum and carried the wood to the cave over the last year and a half. This does not prove that this happened, but it shows that it could happen.[6]

Seen from a bird's eye view, Erzurum lies more than 150 miles (250 km) from Mt. Ararat, so why should Parasut go that far for wood as claimed by his rival guides? And after having "proven" that it could be done, Dr. Price actually adds in a more conciliatory tone:

> If the structure "discovered" by NAMI's guide Parasut is confirmed by independent, qualified scientific investigation (at the site) to be Noah's Ark, then I join in praising God and congratulating NAMI for the greatest discovery of all time. However, until this is confirmed in this manner, I have reservations based on my professional training as an archaeologist, my experience with Parasut and NAMI, and my acquaintance with locals in Dogubayazit who have professed personal knowledge of a hoax by Parasut.[7]

Another Mentality

One would think that it should be taken very seriously when locals accuse Parasut outright of swindle and claim that he himself has carried the wood up the mountain. In Europe and the U.S., it is rather unusual to get away with making direct accusations of humbug without risking a libel case where the accused is either convicted or the accuser found guilty of defamation.

But after having been in contact with guides and local people in and around Dogubayazit myself during the past ten years, I have come across many incidents of people accusing each other of serious crimes such as burglary, robbery, lies, and even murder.

- I think it is irresponsible behaviour, says Wing-Cheung Yeung.

When the new find became known, I received two emails shortly thereafter: one from a local guide and one from a Turkish university lecturer both clearly asserting that it was a clear case of fraud. I would probably have taken their accusations more seriously had I not been aware that they both had a vested interest in throwing suspicion on the find made by their "rival." I would probably also have been more willing to believe them had I not previously been confronted with the local mentality where the air is often thick with accusations and where old grudges can lead to never-ending conflicts, occasionally with a tragic outcome.

There is no doubt that Dr. Price has heard the rumours he refers to. But isn't it a cheap shot to refer to "anonymous locals" in Dogubayazit who have "professed personal knowledge of a hoax by Parasut" – especially since these locals aren't mentioned by name?

Wing-Cheung Yeung, member of the Hong Kong team, puts it like this:

I personally think that it was not scientific enough for a scientist to make such a declaration. He just heard it. Does he have any solid evidence to base his accusations on – such as photos or videos to prove that the location is bogus? Just because he's heard "something," he makes a declaration. I think that this is irresponsible behavior, which is disheartening for me. [8]

Muhsin Bulut, Director of the Ministry of Culture in the Agri province, reacted strongly to Randall Price's criticism of the Kurdish guide.

Consequences

The Turkish people's anger at Dr. Price's questioning the reliability of the Turkish-Chinese find strongly expressed itself through the statement made by Muhsin Bulut, Director of the Turkish Cultural Ministry in the Agri Province, at the press conference in Holland:

"In response to the statement by Mr. X, I have to say that I don't know who he is. I don't know what his idea is. He climbed Mt. Ararat in 2009 but without a proper permit for Ark Search. In his public statement, he totally discredits our people. However, I know NAMI and I believe they are trustworthy."

But he added:

"As usual, Mt. Ararat welcomes Ark Search activities, of which permits will be issued by the Cultural Minister in Ankara. All applications should be addressed to the Cultural Minister. This discovery is very important and special. Turkish Academic and Cultural Ministry will be glad to cooperate with search teams for future studies."[9]

A possible interpretation of the last "kind" comment could be that people, who publicly discredit and throw suspicion on a project given the green light by the authorities, cannot be sure to be permitted to climb the mountains in the future.

Parasut fights back

In a video spot with Panda Lee from Holland, Parasut gives an answer to the accusations made by Price shortly after the announcement of the discovery. Sometimes Parasut expresses himself in a cryptic manor because of language difficulties. Therefore some words have been added to explain what he probably means to say:

We have done all the work. We have found it (the ark). And we believe it (is the ark).

Dr. Price is coming like a sickness (like something very bad). Why is he jealous of us? Noah's Ark belongs to all people. The professors and the scientists, they can come and they can work. And they can do a good deed for their religion as well.

Of course the Turkish government knows that you (the Chinese team) are Christians. And they mention it in Turkish news. "The Christians found the ark with the Turkish team, "they say And it means in my idea, that if they are real Christians, they can work on this project (even if they are not Muslims as most Turks). They don't cut it out (in the news, that you are Christians).

They (Price and others) don't have to make a fight with us. Turkish professors say about Price that his original location is in Israel. He knows Israel in a better way. He can go and he can do his own work there.

When a person comes to Mt. Ararat, he can't say, "I'm the first – the number one to be here. He (Price) came as a visitor, but we were born here. Last year (2009) he came and worked in the ice as a scientific researcher, but what scientific research? We know everything. He digs one meter in the ice and he'll come back next year and dig five meters more. But next year the snows have covered the hole.

We don't speak about some factory or economy, but about religion. And everybody has to respect each other. Men from the Turkish government come and speak about the Bible and the Koran, the holy books. And you can't tell them a lie.

We are just mountain climbers and we are enjoying our work. It (the criticism) can't stop us. He (Price) just wanted to recognize his name in there (as someone who found the ark). They say he has local people in my city and everything. If he is a human, does he speak like this? He can come with his local information (that the wood was carried up the mountain) and his friends also. We can sit in front of this man and we can speak face to face. Who is a liar, who is? We can do it not (only) in Turkey but in his country, in America or somewhere else. And he who gets ashamed must leave the table.

The ark is found already. Don't damage yourself (by harming others). Don't make damage or trouble for the people. We are just very friendly."

Oriental Communication

Parasut's statements make a good lesson in Asian communication.

One never says anything directly to the other person's face. One beats around the bush. Without mentioning the core of the matter, one manages to suggest some hints to which the other person can respond.

One doesn't articulate the hard facts but rather speaks about honor and shame. What Price has actually done is not the issue here but rather the way he said or did things. That he comes as a stranger and tells Parasut to his face simply that he questions his local information is something that can't possibly end well.

Endnotes

1 Randal Price, editor on his homepage:Worldofthebible.com/news.htm

2 Worldofthebible.com/news.htm

3 Video item on www.noahsarksearch.net/eng/ -Query 1: Are rumors more scientific...

4 www.noahsarksearch.net/eng/randall.php Statement of NAMI April 30,2010.

5 Boston, Mass., May 5, 2010 / 02:56 am (CNA/EWTN News)

6 www.worldofthebible.com/news.html

7 www.worldofthebible.com/news.html

8 Video clip on www.noahsarksearch.net/eng/ -Query 1: Are rumors more scientific...

9 Statement by Mr. Muhsin Bulut, Director of the Turkish Cultural Ministry in Agri Province

Chapter 21

Interview With Panda Lee

When in September 2008 the Chinese had to return home without seeing the cave that Parasut told about, the leader Andrew Man-Fai Yuen decided to act quickly to clarify the issue. He found a credible Christian coach in Hong Kong, Panda Lee, who was physically fit and had knowledge of climbing mountains.

After a short introduction, Panda Lee was sent directly to Turkey where Clara reported that the weather was good for climbing. Panda himself knew virtually nothing about the whole project.

Panda states, "I knew nothing about the project when people from NAMI called me. The Secretary General only spoke with me for two hours, and the next day I headed for Turkey!"

"We kept it very secret. My wife did not know what I was up to and neither did I," Panda told us when we meet him in the Dutch city of Zeist after the news was presented at a press conference. Local people had arranged for lodging at the distinguished hotel Figi & Slot in Zeist.

The stones Rolled towards Us

Panda: When I went up the mountain in October 2008, it was the first time I'd been there in Turkey. I followed the Turkish team up to over 4000 meters height. When I arrived there, the first thing I saw was the wood frame, a wood structure. At times it was very steep; there was a 70-80 degree angle. The volcanic rocks were very loose and fell down. The slope was about 70-80 degrees, very steep.

– *But you couldn't just go all the way up at once?*

Panda: No. I had to go up to the base camp and settle there for the night. And then next morning, early morning I went to the location.

– *Was it difficult to climb the mountain?*

Panda: Yes, later. First we were hit from a strong wind and there was snow overall. The first night it snowed all the night. The next morning when I started until I went back it was not snowing and that was amazing. Thanks to God.

– *Are you used to climbing mountains?*

Panda: Yes. I brought all my climbing equipment from Hong Kong. I'm a climbing instructor as well.

– *But this was the most interesting experience that you had yet...?*

Panda: Yes there is a big difference from the climbs I did in the past. Normally we go up the mountain following the track. But this time there was no track. But the Turkish guide knew about where it was.

The first day we came up to the base camp late in the afternoon, about 8-9 pm at night. The next morning I went to the top, but I could only stay there for 2 hours before the sun rose. It's very dangerous because the sun is melting

ıe snow and the volcanic rocks get very loose at this time.

When we went up to the place, every 2-3 minutes stones fell down towards s. The guide needed to have someone observe the stones falling down towards s when I followed the guide and the camera man to the location.

– Was it like a hole you could crawl into?

Panda: Yes. Before I came, the Turkish team had already used a month to emove the ice and ashes.

We didn't have much time there – a quick up and a quick back.

– But you went into this hole? Can you describe what you see?

Panda: Yes. I saw wood, a structure, old wood, quite nice. I couldn't see any ıetal nails used to make the structure. They had used tenons in the left side.

– What color did the wood have?

Panda: Dark brown, but some of it was a little yellow, some was more dark ed.

– Do you know that kind of wood? Have you seen it before?

Panda: Yes, in my country China there are some very old buildings of wood, hich are like this.

– Could you enter into another room also?

Panda: No, no. My observation wasn't a room but a structure. I went to four laces, but not to start with. In 2008 I saw only two places, but in 2009 I went ack and saw two more.

ood Craftsmanship

– How did you feel when you came into this wooden structure and knew at it could actually be the Ark of Noah?

Panda: Wow that was amazing… But I needed to observe as my mission as to confirm if it was a wooden structure. But then I thought wow that's mazing if that structure is about 5000 years old. The technique used to uild it is very good.

– The people who built this ship must have been very clever?

Panda: Yes, very clever. If you see some real ships made of wood, then you now that the shipbuilders are very clever, because the wood is curved and ıey have to use equipment to cut the wood into curves so that each piece of ood has the same size.

– Couldn't the wood have been brought up by somebody?

Panda: No, no, no. This is impossible on this mountain because of the very teep slope and the area is volcanic.

– But if we imagine that somebody tried to carry it up. Would it be npossible?

Panda: How? It's a very big structure. It would be a big operation to do it. It

anda Lee photographed in October 2008 at one of the descents to the Ark ind. Note the many stones that were buried under wooden construction. (Press photo released by Nami.)

took us a year to get into it. All the structure is under the glacier and frozen and on the top are tons of volcanic rock.

It's impossible.

A sign?

– You are a Christian? What was your religious feeling about this?

Panda: The first thing I did when I was at the location was to pray. I praised God. It's amazing if this ship is 5,000 years old. Also, the world is quite bad no matter if you look at the people or environment. If we think about the world at the time of Noah and today, it's somehow similar.

– Do you think that it's a kind of sign from God that you found the Ark now?

Panda: Yes.

– A sign for humanity to turn to belief in God again?

Panda: Yes. I believe in God – no matter if I discovered the Ark or not. I think God proves he is here and he is in control.

– So many people have been searching for this Ark through centuries, and then you suddenly get into the project, and you are one of the first persons to see the ark. Why you?

Panda: This is the interesting point, but I didn't want to discover the Ark. I just received a phone call from a pastor, that he needed a man for a project. Then I meet the chairman of NAMI, and he used two hours to present it to me. Next day, I flew from Hong Kong to Turkey.

– Next day?

Panda: That's it. There I needed to wait for the weather to be better, before I could climb the mountain. My goal at that moment was to confirm if it was a wood structure. I don't know why it was me.

– You didn't want to be famous yourself?

Panda: No, no. I'm only a little part in this project.

Hit by Blood Cancer...

– You are married. What did your wife say to all this publicity?

Panda: The first time she didn't know what happened. Me as well.

But the next time I was a little bit worried. After the project, I had a change in my body. I got cancer, lymphoma, blood cancer. All the doctors, the experts they told me that I am in the last stages.

But, thanks to God, I can still help the people and share my experience with different kinds of people, the youth, and do some coaching.

– Did you get this sickness after your climb in October 2008?

Panda: I got the report in January 2009.

– Does it mean that you can't climb anymore?

Panda: I suppose I can't, because I lost my blood. I only have 40% because of the cancer.

I need to stay at home, and to stop all my activities. But until now God

The picture of the otherwise unknown carpenter and climber, Panda Lee from Hong Kong, went around the world and was printed in many newspapers for publication. The image is here made brighter so that the wooden planks stand out more clearly. (Press photo provided by NAMI).

continues to give me the energy to go hiking. My professional job is to help people, bring them to the mountain, and to let them experience, and give them a message. I can continue to work, I don't know why. All the doctors said that it's amazing. It's a miracle, they say, even though only one of them is a Christian. They haven't faced such a case before.

Thanks to God.

Planks 20 Meters Long

At the press confernce at Kasteel Vanenburg in Putten, Holland, in May 2010, Panda Lee testified, that he had seen the wooden structure:

In October 2008, I climbed the mountain with the Turkish team. At an elevation of more than 4,000 meters, I saw a structure built with plank-like timber. Each plank was about 8 inches wide. I could see tenons, proof of ancient construction predating the use of metal nails. We walked about 100 meters to another site. I could see broken wood fragments embedded in a glacier, and some 20 meters long. I surveyed the landscape and found tha the wooden structure was permanently covered by ice and volcanic rocks Prior to my expedition, the Turkish team had excavated the site to expos the structure. [1]

Endnotes

1 Panda Lee at press conference May 11, 2010, in Putten, Kasteel Vanenburg, Holland.

Panda Lee being interviewed in the Netherlands by the author of this book.

Chapter 22

The Secret Tip

Ahmet Ertugrul found the big wooden structure - but he got a secret tip...

Ahmet Ertugrul is Parasut's real name. He is the guide who led the Chinese to the site of the big wooden structure. He and the NAMI group are 99% sure that this is in fact the Ark.

At the press conferences, Parasut only revealed a hint of the way he discovered the Ark.

He said, "I got the secret information about the mountain site in June 2008."

Where this secret information came from, he doesn't say. But he states how he knows about the many natural caves on the mountain.

"I'm the rescue chief in Dogubayazit in Eastern Anatolia. As such we check out how many caves we have on the mountains in case of rescuing, so that people can wait in a cave for us. How many hours they can stay there, etc. are things we always check out," he explains.

"In past time – from 1884 and up till now – many ark searchers have come, and we work for them. I'm also a mountain guide. And we found out this location in June 2008. I took my team there and then we found some wood, and we discovered that there was a wooden structure. And I took some photos there," Parasut explains.

But why didn't he go public with his find?

Parasut says, "I only thought about sharing these photos with NAMI (Noah's Ark Ministries) because I had been working with them for many years. We just sent the photos to the NAMI and then they sent their own person to investigate, for they just had to be sure. They sent Panda Lee, and I took him to the mountain site – and then we just left the site because we didn't have enough equipment to investigate. We didn't want to destroy anything."

Mutual Respect

As we have already mentioned, Parasut had worked closely with the Chinese in NAMI for several years, and a close and respectful cooperation had come about, as opposed to the cultural clash that emerged when the American Price Group entered the cooperation for a short while.

The Chinese in NAMI are born-again Christians, while Parasut is a Muslim. So there could have been many things they would disagree about, but instead they showed respect for that which was important to the other party. And the Chinese manifested a humble attitude as to the Kurd's great knowledge of the mountain. This respect was rewarded by Parasut.

When the Chinese produced their documentary of approximatey 80 minutes in 2005 called *The Days of Noah*, it wasn't just to tell about well-known explorers coming here from abroad to find the Ark but also to tell about the locals and the local culture at the Noah Mountain.

In the film the guide Parasut first leads the film crew to the cave where he thought parts of Noah's Ark could be found. However, it was filled with ice, so it was not possible to examine it in detail. In that same year there was an earthquake so that the cave collapsed, making it impossible to examine it. Something flat and brown was visible through the ice. It was also in this area that Parasut found a fossilized piece of wood, which was only volcanic tuff stone according to his counterpart Randall Price. Was the tip a satellite photo?

Price has suggested that Parasut could have found the wooden structure from the satellite photos that Price shared with the Chinese and Parasut during their brief cooperation. Without answering directly, Parasut mentions that he knows all the caves on the mountain and that he lives here, so there is no need to dig into the snow. A stranger who visits the area cannot teach him anything.

We may never know which hint Parasut had that led him to the right opening. It does sound a little optimistic that it would be a satellite photo, taking into account that these renowned photos previously had never led to any discovery. And if so, Price himself could have visited the site when he climbed the mountains twice with the very experienced ark hunter Richard Bright.

But if it wasn't the photo, what "secret tip" could it then be?

Was it a tip from an old ark hunter who wasn't able to climb the mountain any longer? When I for instance interviewed the very experienced ark hunter Elfred Lee for my last book, he told me that he believed he knew where the Ark was. Lee was born in Asia – in Korea. He also participated in the NAMI film as one of the sources.

Was it a tip from an Armenian who was unable to come and climb the mountain due to the hostility between Armenia and Turkey? As it is known, the Armenians inhabited the area until approximately a hundred years ago. Several of the accounts of eye witnesses in fact originate from Armenians who had climbed the mountain as children or who had heard stories from parents and grandparents. Today the Diaspora Armenians mainly live in the USA, Canada, Russia and in Lebanon. I, myself, have been approached by a Russian Armenian woman who might know something but a planned meeting didn't come about.

Was it a dream, a revelation, which Parasut saw in a vision? Muslims often experience such supernatural incidents. Or was it the Christian group in Hong Kong who had a prophetic word, which they passed on to Parasut?

Was it a tradition handed down in the Kurdish community? Maybe a written message found in a jar in an estate of a deceased person? Or the last words of a dying person. "If you go 75 steps to the left at the triangular rock and climb the slope, halfway between ......you will find..." Well, this may sound a bit too dramatic, but in my interview with the film man Wing Cheung Yeung in another chapter of this book, he suggests this possibility saying, "In the past many people have been on the mountain, and maybe some of them entered the cave. They told the secret to their son and grandchild, and they handed it down. So maybe the information originates here. Some families may have had such a secret, but the grandchild or the great great grandchild wasn't there himself."

Reality Surpasses...

In fact it was an elderly Kurdish relative who told Parasut about the cave in The Valley of The Spirits with the mysterious face at the entrance. This appears from a video recording with Parasut in *The Days of Noah*, where he admits to having kept a secret for many years. A family secret that was handed down for four generations. Parasut always expresses himself very mysteriously in English, but rewritten in fluent sentences, this is what he says:

"There was this old man.... I know him, because he was really a writer and he had a feeling for history. I always liked these kind of people. And he gave me information for my search for Noah's ark.

We made a promise to each other. This old man never wanted to give the information to people from outside. Many tried to get his information. But he decided to find the right people to pass it on to."

The old man's name was Ali Kaderi Sunay. He was the uncle of Parasut's mother. In 2004 when Parasut spoke of him, he was 82 years old. Parasut met him in the 1980s and Kaderi believed that Parasut could find the Ark. So he passed the ark secrets on to him.

His story goes like this:

A 300 Year-old Secret

About 300 years ago, the shepherd Abbas was tending his sheep as usual on the mountain Ararat.

Because the soil was barren, he led his sheep higher and higher up the mountain until he discovered a new place. It was a strange and mysterious place. Abbas went inside this place. He discovered that inside it was like a huge wooden building with partitions and even wheat!

Abbas didn't have time to investigate, but he took a small bag of wheat with him back to his place.

He also tried to protect the location. He took some of the wood and closed the entrance. He thought he would come back later and look for it.

The wheat he brought down from the mountain was brought to Iran, now on the other side of the border, and there they tried to sow and grow it. But it was too dry after all those thousands of years.

Abbas kept thinking about this place. He believed that the building he had entered was actually the legendary Ark of Noah. He wanted to go back and search for the Ark again, but sadly, he died before he could fulfil his dream.

But his story about the Ark was handed down for generations – and finally to his great-great-grandson, Kaderi. And he as well kept the secret for 70 years.

During the earthquake in 1840 and a volcanic eruption, the Ark was apparently moved. The descendants of Abbas were now unable to find it.

When Kaderi was young, he also wanted to find the hidden Ark. But after

The Kurd Kaderi passed the secret story of the Ark on to his relative ...

World War I, there were a string of battles and border disputes in the area, and there was no time to search for the Ark. Sometimes Ararat belonged to Iran, sometimes to Russia, and finally Turkey kept the mountain until today.

Kaderi believed that the Ark always has been protected by some mysterious power. "Perhaps it was God protecting it for the right people to find it," Parasut imagines. Or was it another mysterious power? . . .

Actually some odd phenomenons were taking place when the Kurdish-Chinese team went up to the place in 2004. And they were probably the last to see the mysterious face or mask at the entrance before it was destroyed by an earthquake.

It all sounds like an adventure. Except that Parasut actually found the place. And from there he was led on to the great discovery some years later.

A New Hint from a Secret Source

Four years later Parasut received new information from a secret source! He explained at the press conferences:

> I got to know the secret location in June 2008. The source told me that this is Noah's Ark. I took a team there to search the area and found a wooden structure. I took some photographs of the interior structure. Since I have worked closely with NAMI for some years, I informed them of the discovery.

Only Parasut knows who his "secret source" was. And he won't tell.

Chapter 23

The Final Breakthrough

After Panda's visit that confirmed Parasut's information, the Chinese were anxious to examine the cave first hand and returned in February 2009. That wasn't the best season to climb the mountain, and during the risky climb, the Chinese team experienced a violent snow storm.

Simultaneously, the tense relations between Turks and Kurds were politically explosive because of Kurdish separatists' acts of terrorism. A Turkish military operation was on-going at the same time, and so the search had to be abandoned for the second time. The Chinese had to return to Hong Kong without having seen the great find. Very great sums of money had already been spent, but they had to continue the search until they succeeded.

The Six from Hong Kong

Finally in October 2009, the team succeeded in returning to climb the awe-inspiring mountain, which this time showed its gentler nature though it also was snowing this time around.

Six Chinese participated in this expedition along with the guide Parasut and his Kurdish assistants.

The leader of the team was **Andrew Yuen** (or Man–fai Yuen). He is the General Secretary of NAMI, which he himself helped found.

Fiona Leung participated as the only female member. As fund raiser in the NAMI project, she offered to take part in the expedition in the summer of 2008. After several attempts she finally succeeded in arriving at the finding place and went into the Ark – or at least into the wooden construction that was found at the peak of Mt Ararat.

From the film company Sparkling Sun, Director, **Wing Cheung Yeung,** also participated. He is a media veteran and has been awarded prizes for several popular documentaries. He was involved in the Ark search in 2004 when his company was asked to produce a documentary. Two anonymous camera men joined Yeung in the expedition, documenting the team's visit into the wooden structure.

Panda Lee, who had been on the site to verify Parasut's information in October 2008, again joined the expedition – in spite of his serious leukemia, which was discovered after his first visit.

There were also two cameramen on the expedition in 2009. Yeung had brought them to document everything. Their names have not been published, but they'll probably show up at the end of their film.

At the hotel in Dogubayazit, the ever-present Coordinator, Clara Wei, brought together all the threads.

Fundraiser Fiona Leung tells about the tough climb at the press conference.

A Hard Climb

The fundraiser Fiona Leung, who amongst others has been responsible for collecting money for the many expeditions, joined the historical expedition as the only female member. Though she was relatively fit, she admitted that it wasn't a very pleasant climb:

> The expedition was difficult. We stayed a few days in base camp at 2,800 meters above sea level in order to acclimate. All of us suffered various symptoms of mountain sickness. The weather on Mount Ararat was unpredictable. Fine sunny weather would be overwhelmed by heavy fog in an instant. The difference in day and night temperatures was as much as 30 degrees Celsius. At night, temperatures dropped below minus 20 degrees C and one night it even snowed. The last section of the route leading to the site was very rugged. We negotiated steep terrain of 60 degrees and could see rock basalts rolling towards us as the sunshine caused melting snow to loosen, which rolled down. Some of the rock basalts were as large as a head and could seriously have injured anyone.

In the next chapter, one of the members accounts for this epoch-making expedition.

Chapter 24

Interview with the Film Director

The following is an interview with Wing Cheung Yeung from Sparkling Sun, a documentary film company in Hong Kong that has won awards for its documentaries.

Yeung: I got involved in the NAMI project in 2003. The NAMI group employed us to do research and produce a documentary on the quest for Noah's Ark. Sometimes we sent a team to Dogubayazit in Turkey to talk to the locals; at times we sent people to meet the ark hunters. We checked the internet and books.

– Did you yourself believe it was possible to find the Ark?

Yeung: Yes, I believed it would be there. That's why we first did our research and then we searched for the Ark on the site.

– But many people have searched in vain for the Ark for centuries. Why should you find it?

Yeung: We noticed that most ark hunters were focusing on research through satellite pictures. Others went to Mt. Ararat for a short while to climb the mountain again and again with no results. The search in the past was very difficult. For some it was ok because they had their licences and could stay for a longer period. But most of the people couldn't stay for any longer than 2 weeks or 1 month every year. The next year they would come back.

– Are there special months when you cannot go up the mountain because of the weather?

Yeung: Yes, the weather is very difficult. But the matter is also politically sensitive.

– But your team got in touch with a Kurdish-Turkish guide?

Yeung: Yes, we contacted the people living on the mountain. Our guide in Turkey also worked in the rescue team that rescues the endangered on the mountain. So he had a very thorough knowledge of the mountains that was based on many years of experience. He knew the sites that Westerners had already searched through the years, and he had some knowledge from the local people.

(The guide took Yeung and two camera men in the six person group up the mountain in 2009. Even if Yeung says that he believed it was possible to find the Ark, the purpose of his company's research was not in fact to find the Ark but to make a film on the quest for the Ark on Mt. Ararat. Among other things the film was to procure money for a Noah's Ark Park that NAMI was constructing in Hong Kong.)

Yeung: The four of us went into the ark with one of the camera men and the other one was outside to film there.

– So it was you and Fiona and Andrew?

Yeung: Yes, Fiona and Andrew. He is the leader of the team and the general secretary of NAMI, and the fourth person was Panda. Panda had been at the site in 2008, and in 2009 I went there with the team.

– *What did you see when your team arrived at the site?*

Yeung: Actually I went into two locations. The first place was a hole, which I entered, and then there was about 2 meters down to a wooden staircase.

A staircase?

Yeung: Yes, an old staircase of wood, and inside we saw some old beams of wood at the top. And at the top of the beam there were some wooden nails. The locals said they were used to tie up the animals. And under the ice there was a wall – actually two walls. The wall was about 5 meters high, and there were also wooden beams at the top. For the height is a huge structure, but not very wide, only about 2 meters.

– *You went into this room, and could you from there continue into another room?*

Yeung: Actually the room was tilted. The local guide wouldn't let us go in there. It's very dangerous. Also some rocks fell down. At the end there was a wooden room.

– *Through a door?*

Yeung: No, not a door, but at the end there was a big room we couldn't enter, but then Panda crawled inside. Because my job was shooting and video filming, I went outside. But Panda went in at the same location. Because of some hesitation on the part of the cameraman, Panda slid down. After he slid down, the local guide tried to rescue him and take him out of the location.

– *He fell down?*

Yeung: Yes, and then Panda had the chance to see another huge structure.

– *When you say a structure, was it a room?*

Yeung: It's not a room. We called it a space. It has a huge wooden wall, but it's very narrow. We couldn't see the top.

– *You say that there was a wooden floor, wooden walls, and a wooden ceiling? Could it be a house built up on the mountain if somebody wanted to rest there?*

Yeung: Actually we called the structure a vessel. Because it's level. . .But not exactly a room that people can live in. I think it would be difficult for people to live there but more suited for animals because the structure is not very regular.

– *If it's not regular, what is it then?*

Yeung: There were these big walls, and then we went deeper into the spaces which were triangular. A room to live in wouldn't be triangular. It's obvious. Therefore, we called it a vessel.

– *Do you think it's because it was a ship at some time?*

Yeung: Maybe. Maybe it's a kind of corridor from a ship. I don't know.

– *How long was the longest piece of wood?*

Yeung: I think it's over 10 meters.

– Dids it look very old?

Yeung: Very old because of the tenons. It's quite special in such a room. And also by the wooden beam we could clearly see the wooden structure. But the others parts were under the ice. Therefore it's difficult to test how old it could be. But from the wooden beam and tenons you could see that it was old.

– What is the significance of the find? What will it mean to the world?

Yueng: Many people, local archaeologists and local ark researchers, will research this place. They will examine the place. In the past they found nothing. From the historical accounts, we can see that some people went inside and saw the structure and wrote in the papers. This time it's quite crucial and important that we can find some wood there at this altitude – then it's properly the Ark.

– Now you found some parts of the Ark, do you think that there is something more in there or is it split into more parts?

Yeung: We can't just go from one space to another because there are small doors or hatches and some team members couldn't open them for it's very dangerous. The oxygen level is very low, so we can't breathe. But I think that we will eventually be able to move from one space to another.

– You told me earlier that this wood structure is buried under ice and lava stones?

Yeung: Yes, and some of these stones are volcanic stones at the top. It is 4 to 7 meters under the ground. Ice and stone cover the wooden structure. You can't see it from the outside.

– Is it broken?

Yeung: I think some parts are broken. Some beams are broken, but some rooms are fine and in good condition.

– But this team went into 7 different spaces? So you know there are at least 7 spaces.

Yeung: But not only the 7 spaces which we have on video. But some rooms are broken.

– But you can't go in because it's broken?

Yeung: Someone might can go in, but not this time. Maybe later on.

– But how do you protect it from grave robbers, who will try to take it and sell it?

Yeung: It's difficult, but we haven't shown the entrance from outside. All is on our video. We asked for protection from the government. The most important is that the local government protects it. I think many from Dogubayazit now want to search for the space or some researchers from the outside will try to hire a local guide to bring them to the location.

– But is it so that there are places where tourists are allowed to go, and then there are these places outside where tourists are not allowed?

Yeung: Actually, this place is not allowed for tourists to go there. So it's difficult to find. But because it's becoming big news, many want to find it

– In the presentation you mentioned that this Turkish man Ahmet Er-

tugrul went up there first since he got some clues from other people. Who where these people that mentioned that he could find it there? Did anyone go there before him?

Yeung: We call it a secret source, news from other people. But he won't tell us. He got the secret news, and then he went there, I think to verify, so he went there first. After he went there, he called us. He was very excited because he was on the mountains for many years, and he hadn't seen such a structure before.

– *But this secret source who told him that he might find it, why didn't he come forward before?*

Yeung: I don't know, maybe he trusts us. In the past many mountain people went to the top. And some of the searchers went inside and told the news. They told the secret to their sons and maybe grandchildren and other generations. Maybe the news originates from this. Some families might have such a secret, but the son or grandson hasn't gone there yet.

– *And the guide, is he Turkish or Kurdish?*

Yeung: He is Kurdish.

– *So the secret could have been handed down within this group of people through centuries?*

Yeung: Yes, maybe.

The film director Wing Cheung Yeung being interviewed for this book by Henri Nissen.

Chapter 25

The 7 Spaces

Panda Lee in room no. 2. The picture is enlarged elsewhere.

Wing Cheung Yeung explained at the press conference that the so-called wooden structure (or the Ark) is broken. However, the team members were able to enter the structure through various openings. The team discovered seven spaces.

1 One of the spaces discovered is frozen in ice. Under the ice is wood with a wooden beam protruding out of the ice. There is also tenon construction on the wall, and it is obviously an artificial or man-made structure. (Pictures of this space have not yet been published.)

2 The space seen by Panda Lee is L-shaped. This is the first space that was discovered. It's L-shaped and its features match well with some spaces discovered later, containing similar tenon construction. We concluded that it was originally a box-shaped room and had heavily decomposed, Yeung explanes.

Panda Lee examines the planks in room no. 2.

Room no. 2 is buried under ice and volcanic rocks and decomposed by the surroundings. In the middle of the picture wood is seen.

All photos are made freely available to the press by Noah's Ark Ministries International (NAMI) in Hong Kong.

3 This room is more than 5 meters high. Team members had to be lowered down through a broken opening to get inside. All the walls are made of wood, and the space is not box-shaped. Strictly speaking, the walls are not vertical but rather curved and inclined. The small door on one side, with the dimensions of one meter high and half a meter wide, presumably leads to another space, but our team did not risk going further due to the lack of oxygen.

An unknown form of crystal was found in room 3.

Unknown white marbles covered the floor in room 3.

In room 4 there is a balk with wooden nails - to tie the animals by?

4 This room is box-shaped having a dimension of more than two meters in height, width and length. There is a wooden beam with wooden nails on one side of the wall. It is believed that a rope was hooked on these nails to keep animals in place. On another wall, there are racks.

The entrance to room 4 is very narrow. One must go through a hatch.
On one wall in the room, there are more than 2 x 2 metres.

5 A very small tunnel-like space connects two spaces.

The wood in the small room no. 5 is clearly damaged and is disintegrating, as seen in the pictures.

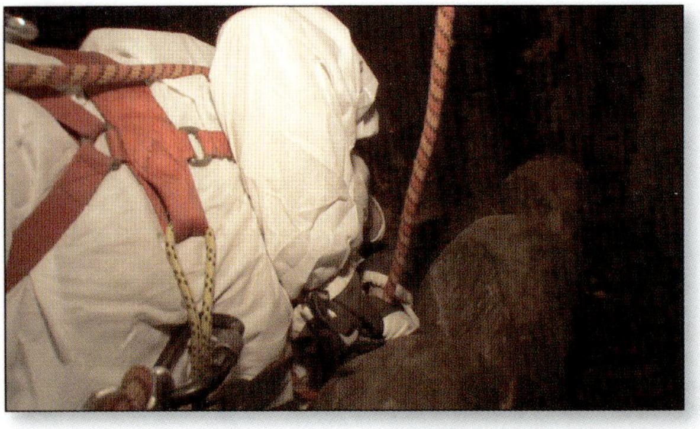

6 A few wooden staircases were found inside the structure, which seemingly were carved out of tree logs. Our team climbed one and found a door in the ceiling and concluded that the wooden structure has more than one floor. We tried to open it but failed. Since we did not want to destroy the structure, we will try again with appropriate equipment in the future.

A hatch in the ceiling of room 6 suggests that the wooden construction has several floors. According to the Bible, the Ark had three decks.

7 The team has not entered this space. They viewed and took pictures from a small opening above. The height and width are estimated to be 5 meters and 12 meters respectively.

The team on its first expedition was unable to get into this seventh space, which is the largest of the found rooms. The picture was taken through an opening. The floor appears to be covered by a form of marbles, maybe the same as were found in room 3.

It was difficult for the team to reach the various rooms. As shown in the picture here, the rooms are partly covered by ice. A cameraman slipped at one point down a corridor and a new room was discovered.

This is all according to the filmmaker *Wing Cheung Yeung.*

Below, Yeungs grafic of the size and relations between the seven spaces are shown.

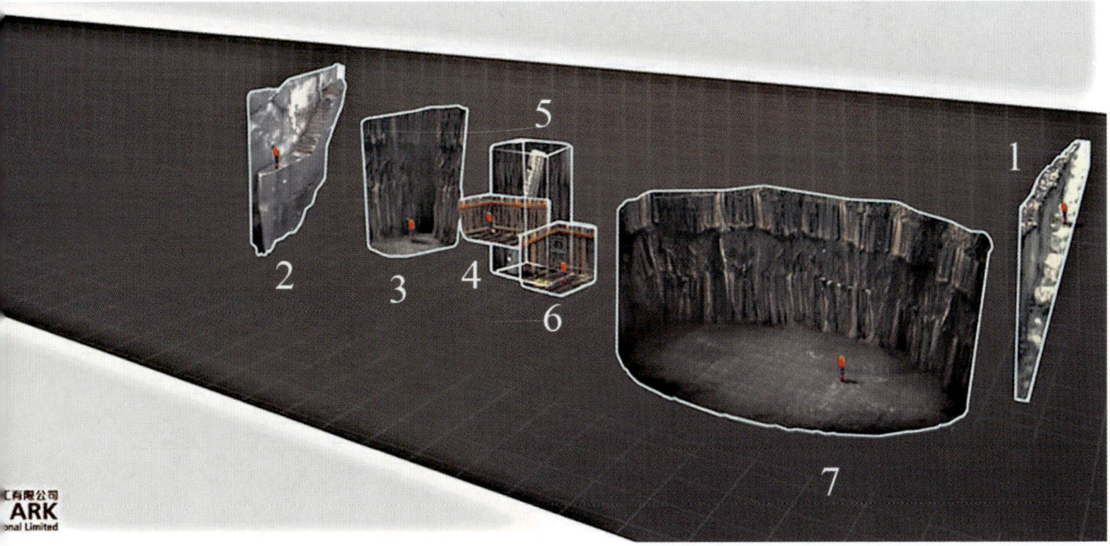

Bottom: (from left) Panda Lee, Ricky Aalten, Wing Cheung Yeung and Gerrit Aalten in conversation with the author of this book. At the presentation of the major finds, the Chinese team stayed at Hotel Figi in Zeist in Holland.

Chapter 26

A Huge Secret Made Public

It would take almost two years from when Parasut made his discovery until the important news was finally released at press conferences in April and May 2010. The time was used for examining the wood further, taking new expeditions, and shooting a documentary. The first press conference was held in Hong Kong; then there was one in Beijing. The final one in Holland for the European and American press.

"How could you keep a huge secret like that to yourselves for so long?" I asked Clara Wei when I met her in Zeist, Holland, where she was coordinating the visit of the NAMI team.

"It was, I admit, very difficult to keep it secret, but the reason why we succeeded, I think, was because the members of the NAMI team are Christians. They took it very seriously," Clara says. Clara is not a believing Christian herself although her family background is Catholic.

"I have no religion," Clara says with a smile, having spent half her working time over the last few years researching the Bible on Noah's Ark.

She has had contact with, and personally met, many of the well-known Ark hunters all over the world. None of them have had the good fortune to find the much coveted old ship even though they have suffered great hardships in their precarious attempts. A couple of them actually died while searching, and one was kidnapped. And now it ended up being a Turkish-Chinese team making the great discovery.

"How have you been able to finance all this research?" I asked.

"NAMI has raised the money. They are Christian, and they believe that if it is God's will, He will also help find the resources. So whenever we have felt lost, we have pulled through due to their belief and spirit of self-sacrifice. We have always received the money just as we needed it," Clara says with a smile.

NAMI is not a church but a non-profit organisation involving people from different churches.

The dynamo behind NAMI is Andrew Yuen. It was a newspaper article back in the 1970's that first aroused his interest in Noah's Ark. The article was about a satellite photo taken over Mt. Ararat, and the picture allegedly showed a shadow that could be Noah's Ark. There have been a great many of that kind of story, and they have always turned out to lead nowhere. But this story aroused Andrew's interest.

Since then, Andrew has been investigating all that he could find out about the Ark, and he has climbed Mt. Ararat several times in search of it as he was fully convinced that it was there, somewhere deep below the ice at an altitude of 4,000 meters. And one day in October 2009, Andrew finally suc-

進一步確定挪亞方舟遺骸
港探索員獲土國頒榮譽市民

梁藝齡尋挪亞方舟獲表揚

港探索隊 方舟再發現

Have Hong Kong evangelists found the biblical Noah's ark?

港探索隊揭秘 方舟遺骸曝光

由香港人和土耳其人組成的方舟探索隊，於土耳其東部的亞拉臘山尋找挪亞方舟遺骸時，在高於海拔四千米的冰川發現有四千八百年歷史的木結構，土耳其政府更擬將發現申請列入聯合國世界文化遺產。

探索疑似方舟遺址 4港人獲土國嘉許

Noah's Ark found on Turkish mountain?

ceeded in reaching the goal of his desires. At the press conferences in Hong Kong, Holland – and especially the one in Beijing – he proudly told about the great, Chinese find, not in English, but in Chinese, his mother tongue (translated below):

ABC News

'Noah's Ark' discovered on Turkish mountain

- We call it a breakthrough in the search because the search team and I personally entered a wooden structure high on the mountain. The structure is partitioned into different spaces. We believe that the wooden structure we entered is the same structure recorded in historical accounts and the same ancient boat indicated by the locals, Andrew Yuen said.

Noah's Ark remains found?

The press conference in the Chinese capital of Beijing took place on the 28th April 2010 and attracted tremendous attention from the media.[1] It was held at the Beijing International Convention Center. The Turkish Embassy in China was represented by Mrs. Liknur Yigit who is the Counselor of Culture and Information. The attending journalists asked a lot of questions. Sohu, one of the biggest search engines in Mainland China, launched a special coverage of the find including interviews with expedition members.[2]

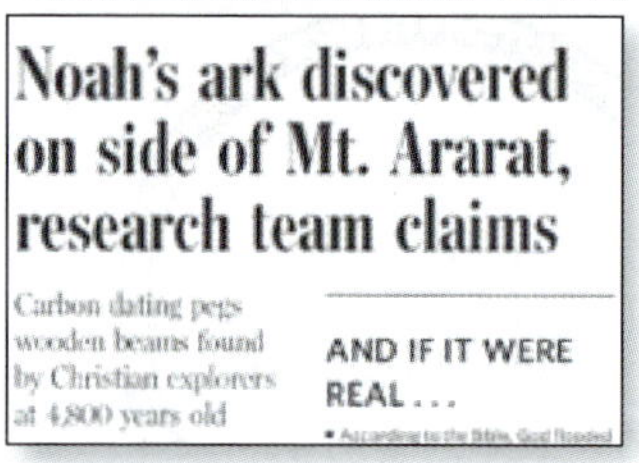

Noah's ark discovered on side of Mt. Ararat, research team claims

Carbon dating pegs wooden beams found by Christian explorers at 4,800 years old

AND IF IT WERE REAL . . .

Official Support

At the press conferences, not only the Chinese team and the Kurdish guide stood forward, but also representatives from the Turkish government and the Ministry of Culture. They announced that they would apply for the find to be included in the UNESCO World Heritage List, a list of historic buildings worthy of preservation and of great value to all mankind.

Together the Turks and the Chinese signed a joint agreement of cooperation regarding the exploration of the find. In the agreement it says:

"We agree to collaborate on scientific search and study related to Noah's Ark on Mt. Ararat. The results are of significance to the whole world in that humankind should cherish its common beliefs and origins. We believe that the discovery of Noah's Ark will resolve centuries of national ideological conflict. We are dedicated to working towards a better, peaceful world."

The Turkish archaeologist, Professor Oktay Belli (left), did not hesitate to call the find "History's greatest discovery." Here he is at the press conference together with NAMIs leader Andrew Yuen Man-fai.

On this occasion the governor of the Agri Province in Turkey, *Murat Güven*, appointed four members of the Hong Kong team honorary citizens of the Agri Province.

The press in Beijing: *The Chinese press was very interested when on April 28, 2010, the NAMI team from Hong Kong visited them. The team held a press conference in Beijing International Convention Center. Media coverage of Noah's Ark in Communist China was huge ...*

Turkish honorary citizens: *In recognition of the Hong Kong team's commitment and contribution to the exploration of the Ark on Mount Ararat and its subsequent discovery, Deputy Governor Murat Guven (center) on behalf of the Agri province, made four expedition members honorary citizens. are the first foreigners to be granted this status. From left: Fiona Leung, Panda Lee, Deputy Governor Murat Guven, Andre Andrew and Wing Cheung Yeung.*

TURKEY

Explorers claim to have found the ark

Hong Kong A group of evangelical explorers yesterday said they believe they

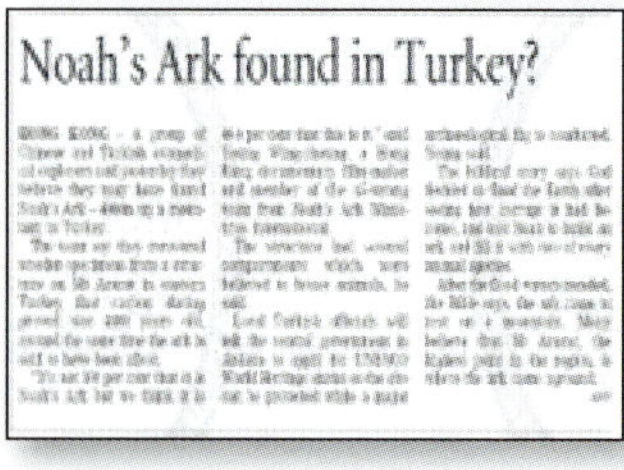
Noah's Ark found in Turkey?

Is this a glimpse inside Noah's Ark?

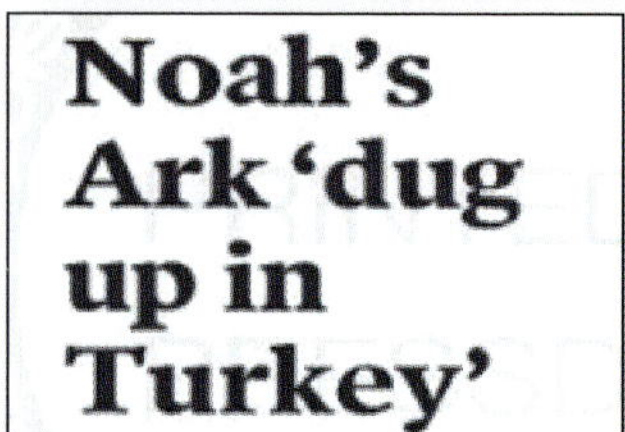
Noah's Ark 'dug up in Turkey'

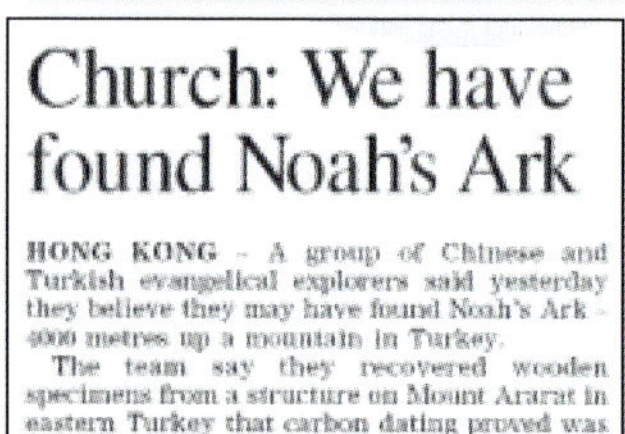
Church: We have found Noah's Ark

HONG KONG – A group of Chinese and Turkish evangelical explorers said yesterday they believe they may have found Noah's Ark – 4000 metres up a mountain in Turkey.

The team say they recovered wooden specimens from a structure on Mount Ararat in eastern Turkey that carbon dating proved was

Explorers 'discover' Noah's Ark in Turkey

ANKARA – A group of Chinese and Turkish explorers said on Monday they believe they may have found Noah's Ark, wire services reported.

The team say they recovered wooden remnants some 4000 metres

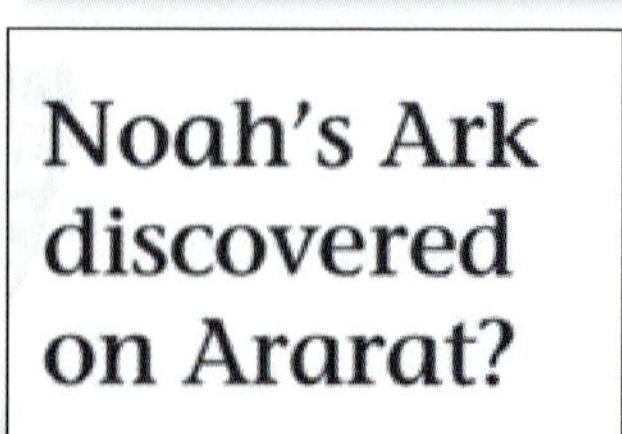
Noah's Ark discovered on Ararat?

"Shocking News"

Muhsin Bulut, Director of the Ministry of Culture in Agri Province, called it "shocking news for the whole world" that the Ark had been found.

He said, "For more than 2,000 years, historical and eyewitness accounts tell us that there is an ancient boat on Mt. Ararat that survived a great flood and landed on the mountain. People believed that it is Noah's Ark. I believe the team has finally located this ancient boat and I believe it is Noah's Ark."

The next to speak was *Ibrahim Sahin* who is district secretary of the town of Dogubayazit where they had planned a big civic festival in June this year to celebrate the find. However, due to political disturbances in the area, the festival was postponed several times in June and July and finally, late in July, postponed for an indefinite period. The reason for this last indefinite postponement was the explosion of a bomb in Dogubayazit in connection with demonstrations staged by Kurdish separatists against the conduct of the military towards the separatists resulting in two Kurds being killed. The authorities feared that the separatists would use the celebration along with the visit of people from abroad to cause disturbances and gain press coverage. As previous riots have led to both killings and kidnappings, the authorities were afraid to take the responsibility for protection of the guests during the conference and the festival.

At the presentation in Holland, *Mehmet Raif Karaca*, the Turkish consul general, was also on the panel, as well as a member of the Turkish parliament, Mehmet Hanifi Alir, who gave his support to continuing the exploration and further stated:

> The story of Noah and Noah's Ark is mentioned in all Sacred Books, such as Zend Avesta and Abrahamic religious books, Old Testament, New Testament and Quran. According to Judaism, Christianity and Islam, Noah's Ark rested on Agri Dagi, which is named Ararat, Cudi, Cebel Haris, etc. The discovery is very important to humanity. Very serious scientific studies should be done as soon as possible. As the local authority, we, the government, ministries and parliament, will provide all necessary assistance and help to cooperate with all scientific search teams for future exploration.

Greatest Discovery in History!

In addition, a Turkish geologist and a Turkish archaeologist were present.

The archaeologist, Professor *Oktay Belli,* said among other things, "The search team has made the greatest discovery in history. This finding is very important and the greatest up to now. On Mount Ararat, human settlement has never reached up to 3,500 meters. Mount Ararat is a holy place and has rich historical accounts about Noah's Ark on the mountain. Many people have searched the mountain for the holy Ark. This discovery is the first serious team search that found a wooden structure under the ice."

And the geologist *Dr. Ahmet Özbek* explained how the conditions at the location of the find had helped preserve the structure for thousands of years without decaying or petrifying. He said, "In present days, the permanent snow line on Mt. Ararat is 3,900 meters. The wood structure was found higher than 4,000 meters."

The low temperature and environmental condition of glacier deposits and volcanic material helped the preservation. He also explained that the proportion by weight of wood material was able to carry loads up to 5 times its weight. So this structure can bear heavy weight without breaking into pieces.

Dr. Tom Zoutewelle, as seen here between Andrew Yuen and John McIntosh, has a doctorate in biology and geology, specifically in palaeo botany and sedimentology, from the University of Ulrecht. He is chairman of the Dutch Creation Fund, a researcher at Loma Linda University, and a member of Earth History Research Center in the U.S. and the Fachgruppe Geology Studiengemeinschaft Wort und Wissen, Germany.

American Backing

Another well-known figure in Ark circles, the experienced American Ark hunter *John McIntosh,* was also present in Holland. He has climbed Mt. Ararat quite a number of times and has been director of the SEARCH Foundation that was established after Fernand Navarra made his first find in 1955.

In 1985, John McIntosh along with John Irwin, the astronaut, and others were victims of a violent attack by Kurdish PKK separatists[3] while participating in the Probe expedition to Mt. Ararat. The militant people of PKK took the equipment they could use and set the rest afire. Then they lined up the Ark hunters while bringing their guns to shoulder level and aiming at the Ark hunters like a firing squad. But instead of killing them, they sent them quickly down the mountain so that they could tell the entire world about the attack. PKK's motive for the attack was to attract attention to the more than 20 million Kurds who have been unable to establish themselves as an autonomous nation – apart from having obtained partial autonomy in Northern Iraq after the removal of Saddam. Most Kurds still live in Turkey. It is, however, only a minority of the Kurds that support the violent actions staged by PKK which have so far cost the lives of approximately 10,000 Kurds and Turks.

Now it is actually a *Kurdish* guide who, along with the Chinese, found the Ark, and John McIntosh, a veteran in Ark searching, had to admit that this could very well be the remains of the Ark. He did his best to avoid saying anything negative about his American fellow countryman Dr. Price, but he also made it clear that more investigations were needed:

> Besides large wooden beams, one can also see large, flat wooden areas of wall, some of which are covered in ice. Presently, to me, it seems nearly impossible that the large wall areas of wood and very large timbers could have been placed there as has been suggested by some of the local people living near the mountain. The compartments are located at such

an inaccessible and difficult location, with different levels evident, that it seems to me that it is highly unlikely that they are related to any explainable normal mountain construction such as for shelter or animals… This site might indeed be some of the remains of Noah's Ark, but further exploration and research needs to be done to be certain of what is here.

How Do We Preserve It?

The Dutch geologist, R. Tom Zoutewelle, expressed concern as to conservation of the find now that it has been laid open:

> What I saw on the video, the wooden structure joined together with rocks and the ice, looks promising to me. My personal fear and my question, is it possible to conserve the structure for a long time? The environment is hostile. There is a volcano. There is an ice sheet moving downwards, so it must be a special location to preserve the structure. From what I've seen in the video, I see some elements that could explain the conservation. I am very glad. I think it will turn out to be the Ark. Everyone on the earth will know Noah's Ark is there. Everyone has to know that Noah's Ark is a historical fact, I think it is important.

Conformity with Early Eyewitness Accounts

The Ark researcher Gerrit Aalten from Holland emphasized the importance of the find saying, "For the first time in history, the discovery of Noah's Ark is well documented and revealed to the worldwide community." With more than 30 years experience in collecting information, Mr. Aalten believes that detailed eyewitness accounts make the Ark puzzle complete because all of them mentioned the same significant details that exactly match this astonishing find on the mountain.

He continued, "Just a few of the many details that are matching this find are the height it's found on, which is **above "the 4000 meters level"**; another detail is, the way the Ark is situated on the mountain which is **"slightly tilted"**; it has a **"reddish/brown wood appearance,"** the end of the Ark **"is decayed and broken and has a hole" through which one can enter;** most of it is **"embedded in the ice and rock debris"**; the Ark is **"very solid and of high quality"** and **"very dark, long and rectangular."**

In conclusion, Mr. Aalten said, "There's a tremendous amount of solid evidence that the structure found on Mount Ararat in Eastern Turkey is the legendary Ark of Noah."

Endnotes

1 Beijing Press Conference: http://it.sohu.com/s2010/noah/

2 Item from the press conference: http://it.sohu.com/s2010/noah/

3 The Kurdistan's Workers Party (Partiya Karkaren Kurditan), a North Kurdish left wing party, better known under its Turkish acronym PKK. The party was established in 1978 by approx. 50 people and gradually grew stronger through its armed fight against the Turkish "oppression of the Kurds."

Chapter 27

Where Is It?

To not attract grave diggers, the Kurdish guide and the Chinese NAMI team have kept it a secret where they found the large wooden structure. The Turkish authorities in the Agri province have, however, been informed about the place.

In October 2010, NAMI officially cancelled an expedition lest they should attract public attention. This and other expeditions have been carried out secretly at different times, according to my information.

From the different pieces of information that have emerged, one guess could be that the discovery was made at the lowest part of the Parrot Glacier on the north-western side of Mount Ararat.

That was my guess when a Danish mountaineer asked me about the location in September 2010. Erik Futtrup from Aarhus climbed the mountain with two other Danes and a German group. The aim wasn't to find the Ark but to climb the snow-clad top just as Erik has climbed other "holy" mountains.

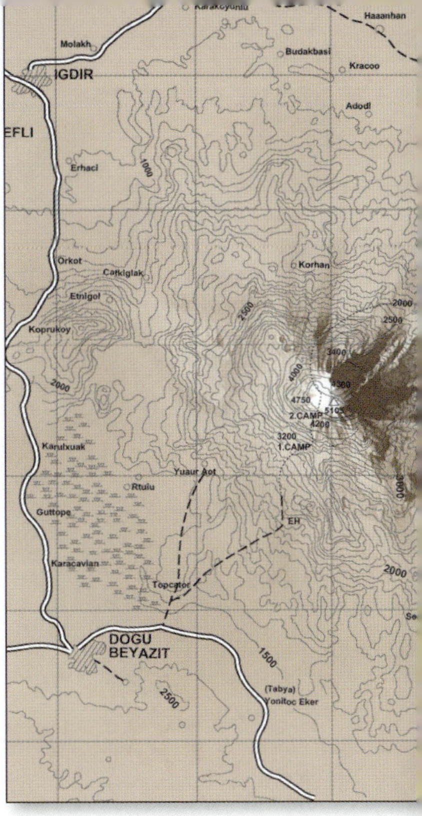

To climb Mt. Ararat is an amazing experience.

"Some think that it sounds like a cliché that one can have religious experiences wandering in nature, but both my wife, Birgitte, and I feel that we in this way meet God. It is great for us to encounter creation in this way," Erik Futtrup explains. "Mount Ararat has long been on my to-do list, and with a colleague I arranged it just before the end of the trekking season. The weather can be tricky at this time of the year, but on our climb it was really fine and cloudless at the peak."

"Mount Ararat is, indeed, a fantastic mountain – iconically beautiful and on par with some other free-standing mountains like Mt. Fuji and Mt. Kilimanjaro," affirms Erik, who is a member of The Globetrotters' Club.

"One rejoices almost continuously on the entire route because it is so beautiful and compelling. It is quite special. For even if the area around the mountain is fertile, the mountain itself is rather barren. There are rocks, a bit of grass at the bottom, and apart from that one can only hear a couple of birds occasionally sing," related Eric to me on his smart phone while descending from the mountain.

Climbers must camp on the rocky surface before they cover the last distance from Camp 2. In winter snow provides a softer surface ...

Very Tough

– Was it tough?

Eric: Yes! We were really well prepared, and I believe that most people will

be able to reach Camp 2 that lies at 4,150 meters. But from there everything must go perfectly.

One mustn't be sick; the weather must be good; one mustn't have gotten injured en route; one must have sufficient strength left. That's why one normally walks quietly during the first days, and then the great goal is to climb the last large hurdle, which is 4 hours of tough climbing on some really unpleasant terrain like gravel that slips under your feet.

Many were nearly worn out before we got through it, but then one gets to the ice cap covering the peak; one can see the goal, and then strength and willpower return. At the peak it is windy, and it is extremely cold. I don't know precisely how cold.

– *How was it then, finally having reached the top?*

Eric: One gets addicted... Last year I climbed a "real" mountain peak at the same altitude, and one wants to do it again, even though it is very demanding. I thought about an old Shu-bi-dua song "Standing on an Alp Top" (A popular Danish song). But it is incredibly beautiful and wild.

It's a great feeling when after 2-3 days of climbing, one is finally standing on top of Ararat in the 5,137 metres - or 5,165 metres? Both figures are mentioned. Eric checked the height on his GPS: 5.140m (+/- 5 meters).

Close to Noah's Ark

– *Did you consider that Noah's Ark was probably stranded here?*

Eric: I pondered quite a lot the fact that the Chinese find was probably

somewhere near the glacier and in fact most likely within a few hundred meters from where I was. Besides this I thought a lot about the whole area being the cradle of civilization.

Before Erik Futtrup travelled to easternmost Turkey, we joined forces and attempted to guess the site of the Ark on the mountain.

We guessed, as before-mentioned, that the find was at the bottom of the Parrot Glacier on the northern side.

The illustration below shows Mt. Ararat's upper ice-clad part seen from the northwest to the southeast of the three mountain peaks on top and the great glaciers sliding down the mountain in different directions. Left: the Ahora Gorge.

Survey of the Mountain

First, one must pass or climb the mountains lying adjacent to the mother mountain. There is only a passable road up the hill to approximately an altitude of 8,050 feet if you ascend from the southeast. After that, you can only pass by foot – possibly with the help of donkeys to carry the baggage for yet another while. But the last part even donkeys cannot go without breaking their legs on the many volcanic rocks or in the snow that covers the stones in the winter. But where do you search for the Ark?

Ark hunters have tried to find the ark in many different places. They have supposed that the Ark is perched far up since first, it is said to be stranded on the "mountains of Ararat," and second, it would have been discovered by shepherds should it have slid below the hillside. So it is usually up near the ice cap, in the upper-most area, that people have searched for the Ark.

Several Peaks

The mountain actually consists of two mountains and in antiquity was called **Twin Mountain** (notably in the poem Gilgamesh). It consists of two peaks.

But only a few ark hunters have been interested in the smaller of the two mountain tops, Little Mt. Ararat (in Turkish Kucuk Agri), located northeast of Great Mt. Ararat (Buyuk Agri in Turkish) towards the Iranian border.

Little Mt. Ararat is, after all, 13,000 feet. Had it lain by itself, it would have been considered as a mighty mountain, and it would have attracted more interest. But now it is literally in the shadow of Big Mt. Ararat.

The highest peak of Great Ararat is called **Ataturk** and is located in the southwestern part of the ice cap. Only a few hundred meters away is the **Eastern Summit**, the eastern mountain peak is called **Cacmac** and is only slightly lower than the mountain peak at 16,800 feet.

Moreover, a third peak is called **Nonu** at approx. 16,000 feet.

The Saddle

The area between the two highest mountain peaks on the Great Ararat (Ataturk and Cacmac) is called the **Saddle**. It was here that the Russian Colonel Koor claimed that the Ark was located, just below the saddle on the northeast side. He examined carefully the mountain in the period when Russia ruled over the area.

The Abich Glaciers

Between the two mountain peaks on the northeastern part stem two major glaciers, **Abich I** and **Abich II,** which from here slip into the Ahora Gorge. The two glaciers are named after Herman von Abich who ascended the mountain in 1845. As the glacier ice penetrates through the ice gorge, ice is stained dark. Therefore, the lower part is called **Black Glacier** or **Araxes Glacier**.

This side of the mountain turns over against the Republic of Armenia. From here one can see the capital Yerevan.

The Ahora Gorge

The mighty **Ahora Gorge** on the northeast side of the mountain was caused by a huge volcanic eruption perhaps thousands of years ago (according to the geologist Salih Bayraktutan). There has been an outbreak the size of the one on *Mount St. Helens* in the United States for a very large part of the mountain is simply blown away. But under the lee of this new divide around 1,000 years ago, a convent, **St. Jacob Monastery**, was founded, and a town

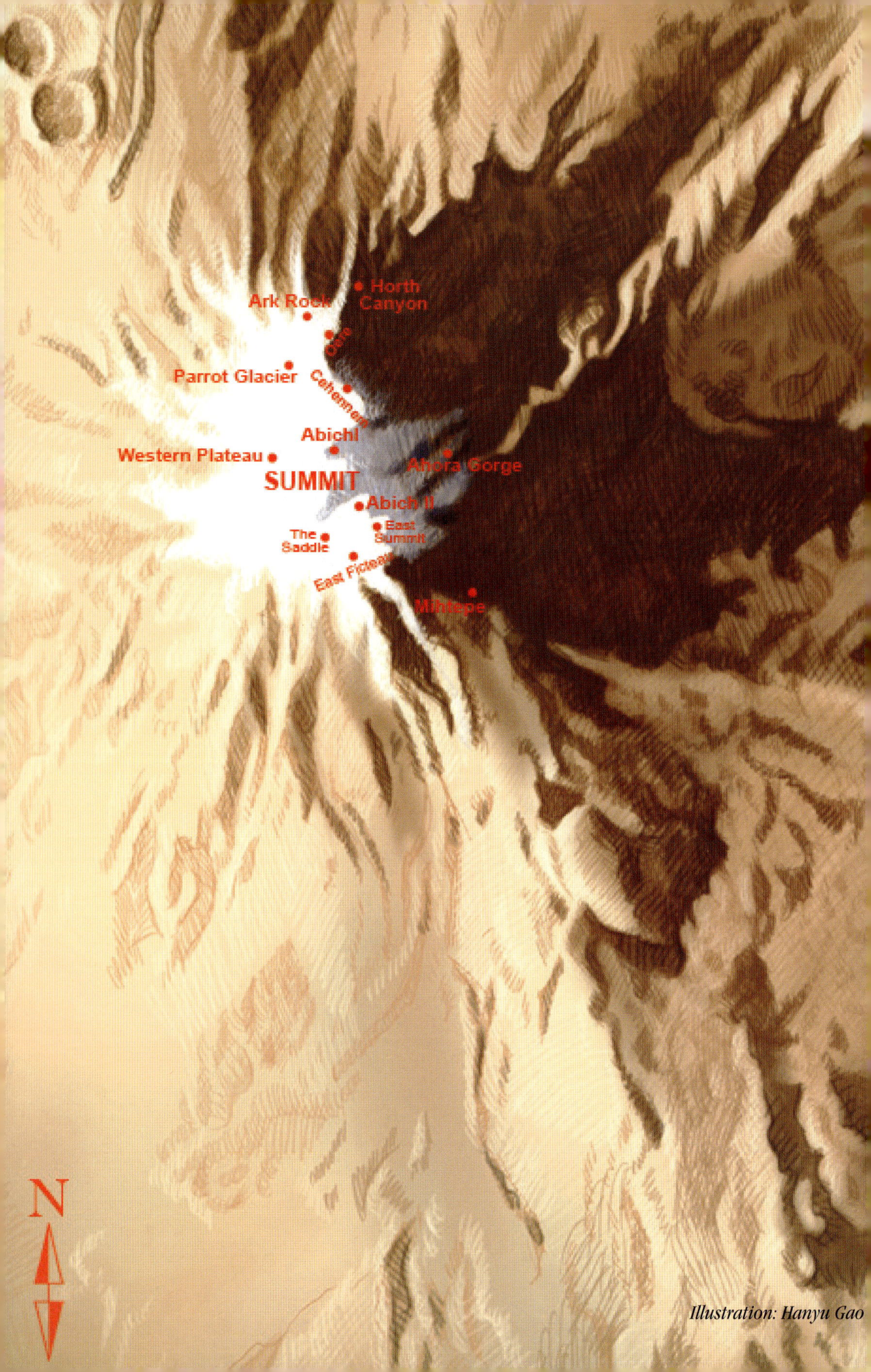

Illustration: Hanyu Gao

grew around the monastery where, according to foreign visitors (eg. Parrot in 1829), there were relics – that is, parts from the sacred Ark, which were stored in the convent. The monastery was located at 6,394 feet (1949 m) and was also called Araxilvank the **Aras** River.

But in 1840 there was again a major earthquake in the gorge, which blew the gap larger and completely wiped out the approx. 200 houses and 2000 people in an instant. At the bottom of the canyon is a place called **Jacob's well**.

In 1955-53 an American military photographer from his plane saw something unusual sticking out of the gorge at approx. 14500-16000 feet (4.5 to 5 km). Consequently, many arkhunters searched the upper part of the Ahora Gorge.

Later, a large rock formation was discovered ca. 12,000 feet (3,657 m) at the eastern edge of the gorge, so it's probably the cliff which the military photographer saw and considered to be the Ark.

Hell Divide and Doom Top

In the **northwestern** side of the Ahora Gorge is a V-shaped area which has the uninviting name of *"Hell Divide"* – in Turkish **Cehennem Dere** or *"Valley of Hell."* Moreover, there is a pointed hill in the foreground of the V valley, called "Doomsday Peak."

It was here in **Northern Canyon** that *John Morris* in 1972 was hit by lightning and crashed into a cliff but survived. And here the astronaut *James Irwin* later fell and broke his arms and legs. Here, *Hardwicke Knight* supposedly found dark, soft timber just below the ice when he was kidnapped in 1936 on Mt. Ararat, but later released.

Parrot Glacier

If one moves from the mountain peak to the northwest, one gets to the big **Parrot Glacier** that flows down over the northwest side of the mountain. Since sunrays do not reach this side before the evening, the snow here is not thawed in the same way as is done on the east and south side. Hence, the Parrot Glacier continues for one kilometer down the steep mountainside. The Parrot Glacier is named after the Estonian physician and professor at the University of Dorpat, *Dr. J. J. Friedrich Parrot*, who climbed the mountain three times in 1829 and later described it in a book.

Parrot Glacier has interested many ark hunters.

It was here that *Ferdinand Navarra* sought and found wood (1953-1955) and later the U.S. SEARCH Team searched (1968-1969).

There is also a formation called **Ark Rock** which has been taken for the Ark, but it is only a rock that may, however, have moved.

At the top of the glacier the Italian *Palego* claims to have found one of his finds, but there has not been the greatest confidence in his claims because he works entirely on his own.

Below one of the Parrot Glacier "fingers" at 11,800 feet is the only lake on the mountain, **Lake Kop** (or Kip). Here climbers often camp, and the Kurds wash sheep fur in the icy water.

East Glacier is another great glacier, which flows from East Summit down over the mountain's east side, east of the Ahora Gorge. It was nearby that the British politician *James Bryce* in 1876 found a piece of processed wood.

Plateau on Top

On top of the mountain on the west side is a flat area, the **Western Plateau.**It is believed that there was once a volcanic mountain here which has sunk, leaving a hole. The ice thickness here was measured in 1989 with GPR radar to ca. 250 feet.

The plateau leads to the western mountain side where the **Ararat Anomaly** exists. It is an ark-like rock that has been studied closely on satellite photos.

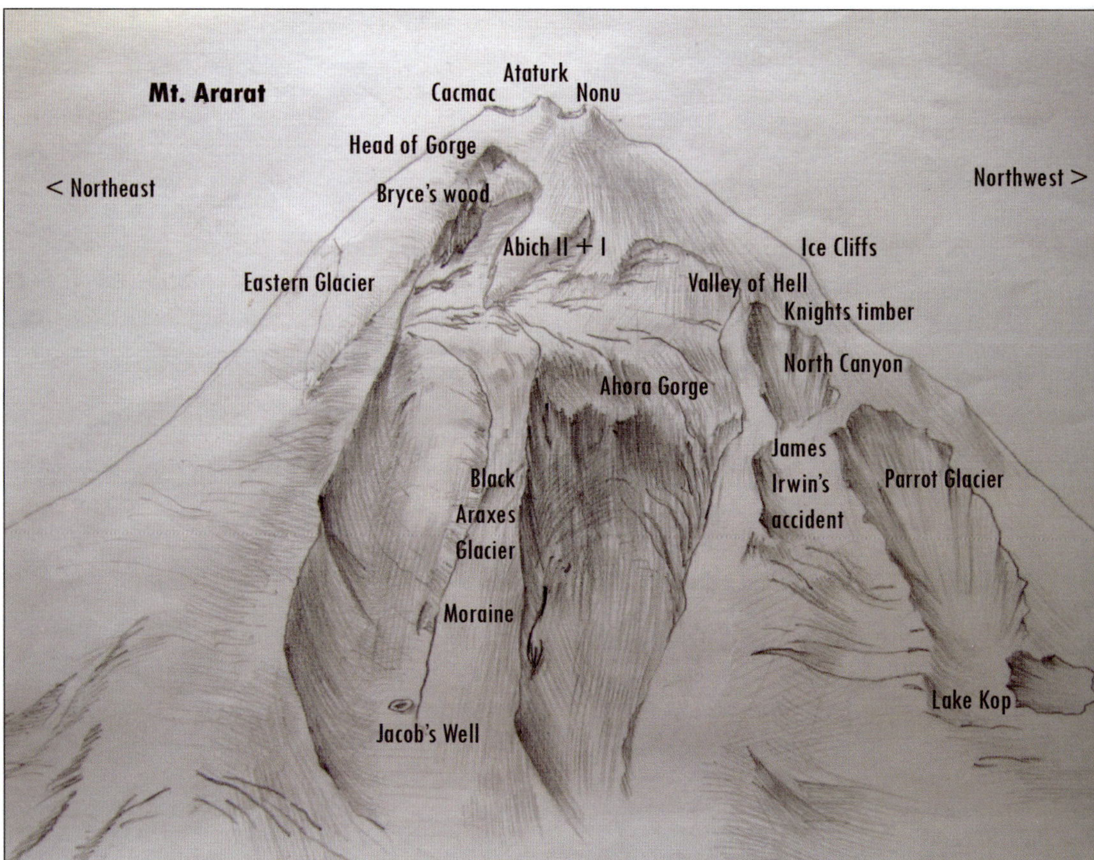

Drawing of Mt. Ararat as seen from the north where many expeditions have explored the mountain. In the foreground is the mighty Ahora Gorge where once stood a monastery and a town at the bottom. To the right is Parrot Glacier. (Illustration by Hanyu Gao.)

Further down the **western** side of the mountain, the local people from the lowlands sighted a **black stain** that could resemble a protrusion. The locals said it was the Ark which protruded.

The Frenchman Fernand Navarra therefore climbed up near the spot in 1953. He could apparently not get quite close to the black spot but could still determine that this was merely a rock.

There is also a cave of ice, the **Ice Cave**.

The Sunny Side

On the **southern** side towards the town of Dogubayazit and Iran is also a dark area in the ice for approx. 4,420 m (14,500 feet), which is particularly visible when snow covers the mountain. The stain has also been selected to be the Ark protruding from the ice. But it has proven to be only a hollow in the ice, now called the **Eye of the Bird**.

On the south side also runs a **Southern Glacier**. Here, a shepherd in early 1800 claimed to have found something of the Ark, and a Turkish commission in 1833 described "a wreck of wood that in summer protrudes from the southern glacier." But it might be the "Bird's Eye."

Close to The Valley of the Ghost

The reason we believe it to be so is due to the fact that the Chinese in 2004 found and filmed a cave in "the Valley of The Ghost," which lies here at the altitude of 4,000 meters. An earthquake in 2004 made the cave collapse. But the Chinese and Parasut kept on searching the area, and in 2006 Parasut found a fossilized piece of wood, and this was probably near by. The Chinese have stated that the great discovery that Parasut and they made in 2008 at 4,200 meters was only a hundred meters away from Parasut's first find. So everything seems to indicate that the finds were all made close to "The Valley of The Ghost."

This seems to fit with the find lying outside the paths that mountain climbers usually take. They usually climb to the top by hiking up from the southeastern side facing the Iranian border. The advantage of climbing from here is that the snow melts in the summer so that the ice cap in warm seasons retreats up the mountain and only covers the last 500 meters of the summit. It is also only the last 4-6 hours of hiking that are really steep and where the lack of oxygen makes it difficult to continue.

On the north side, it is generally more rugged, which fits with the find having been made on a 65 degree incline, and here the ice cap extends down to 4,000 meters above sea level most of the year.

The Parrot Glacier is named after the German doctor and mountaineer Friedrich Parrot, who in 1829 climbed to the summit of the mountain and left two crosses. The Parrot Glacier was also the place where the French ark hunter *Fernand Navarra* found a wooden beam in 1955.

In the following years, the SEARCH Organisation with Navarra attempted to

The site is kept a secret by the Kurdish-Chinese team to avoid grave robbers. But it's probably somewhere in the drawn area - namely the lower steepest part of the Parrot Glacier on the northwest side of Mt. Ararat towards Armenia.

find the Ark in the same area. Later, in 1989, the Italian ark hunter *Angelo Palego* claimed to have found the Ark at respectively 4,800 meters on the western plateau and other parts further down at 4,300 meters and at 4,065 meters – that last place being exactly at the Parrot Glacier.

Finally, it is mentioned that the find lies near a waterfall, and it is very natural that there are streams and waterfalls below the glacier.

So the fact that it was here that Parasut and the Chinese finally found the large wooden structure fits very well with the previous claims of having found parts of the Ark nearby.

The Guides' Confirmation

According to our agreement, Erik Futtrup asked his Turkish guides whether they knew where the Chinese had discovered a find. The guides confirmed that it was in the lowest part of the Parrot Glacier.

– *Did you happen to come across the Ark?* I jestingly asked Erik when he had safely returned from the mountains.

"No. Actually, I didn't see the least stick or branch – the mountain is practically barren," Erik responded. "The Ark and the whole story is extremely interesting, but one knows for sure that it doesn't just float somewhere on top of the mountain."

After his climb Erik continued around the great mountain in order to get to *Nachichevan*, the little Azerbadjanian enclave between Iran and Armenia. Possibly the name means something like Noah's Zion (Noah's City). It was probably the first city after the Flood and the place where Noah lived.

The tomb monument for "The prophet Noah" in Nakhichevan city in an Azerbaijani enclave east of Mt. Ararat. The grave is located, and next to a ruined castle on a hill in the oldest part of the town. From a painting from the 19th century, the grave was located and a monument was erected. The guide mentioned that a film crew from Hong Kong almost succeeded in getting permission to have the grave opened a few years ago.

View from the summit of Big Mount Ararat down to Little Mount Ararat that is approximately 1000 meters lower.
(Photo: Frede Donskov)

Chapter 28

Doubt about Genuineness

In 2010 and 2011, Dr. Randall Price and his associate Dr. Don Patton continued to question Parasut's find that they considered a cunning hoax. And the tone of these attacks was very sharp and personal. Patton referred to the ark hunters as fraudsters by name and with photos.

Since both Dr. Price and Dr. Don Patton are highly respected in the creationist circles in the U.S., many Christians interested in the ark have published Price's and Patton's explanations on other websites, warning of this 'fraud' and these fraudsters. And the atheists have clapped their hands for yet another 'religious swindle' being exposed. But is it a swindle?

As previously mentioned, the attitude among ark hunters in the U.S. has often been rather uncompromising. If someone, for instance, makes a mistake, is unreliable, or is of another opinion as to the location of the ark, others will immediately throw themselves on him in a very condemning way. That is what happened to Ron Wyatt, and it is now happening again with the Chinese.

Wyatt may have been wrong about the boat-shaped object. And he may have imagined more than the instances showed. But he himself believed in what he said, and his imagination doesn't make him a criminal. Nevertheless, he was exposed as a 'fraudster'.

And when the Chinese appeared on the scene with their great find, the same happened again. Opponents were quick to decide that the find wasn't genuine, and they are, consequently, referred to as fraudsters.

As we shall see from this chapter, part of the Chinese's released findings can justly be questioned. And in regards to the persons involved, you will always be able to find personal weaknesses that may put them in an unfavorable light. (Even Jesus was accused by the orthodox Pharisees of being a drunk and surrounding himself with the wrong people.)

The Silent Chinese

The Chinese are convinced that they have found the ark, and who wouldn't after finding a large wood structure on Mount Ararat at an elevation of 4,200 meters? It is quite possible that they may later turn out to be mistaken, that they were deluded by a guide who couldn't be trusted. Unfortunately, Parasut also has his personal weaknesses and comes up with unfortunate and self-contradictory statements. I myself have not been able to get an interview with him even though I went to both Istanbul and Dogubayazit to meet him in 2010. Again and again, he eluded me with weird explanations.

But at the end of the day, the decision of the genuineness of the find is not to be based on whether or not the involved persons can pass the personality test of the opponents but is based on the find actually being the Ark or not.

Illustration from Dr. Don Patton's website (www.Noahs-ark.tv). He's claiming that the famous photo of Panda Lee is taken from a film scene built by Parasut in the crevasse shown to the right. A board is found floating at the bottom of a crevasse.

The Chinese have chosen to keep silent and are convinced that, little by little, their find will show its credibility. Then the bragging opponents will be left ashamed. But let us have a look at the criticism.

Patton's Disclosure

Dr. Don Patton claims to have found NAMI's location of the Ark at Mount Ararat. This has actually been kept secret in order to prevent unauthorized persons from looting it, and the army guards the place. A Scottish ark hunter trying to find the site without permission has even been reported missing.

A local guide (from Murat Camping, a competitor of Parasut's firm) took Don Patton to a crevasse which held some wood deep down that looked like the room where the Chinese *Panda Lee* is photographed.

Patton maintains that it is the remains of a film scene built by Parasut from old planks from Trabzon on the Black Sea. This allegation is based upon statements from an anonymous local person who is said to have taken part in building the film scenery.

In video and photos, Patton is showing a board that, according to what he says, had been found floating at the bottom of a crevasse.

The board is blackened by soot or ashes to make it look old, but when sawn through, it appears to be light on the inside and evidently not very old.

To Patton this proves that the wood from the find is not from Noah's Ark but from a more recent date. And like Price, he accused Parasut of having cheated the Chinese. Also, the Chinese journalist and film producer *Clara Wei*, hired by NAMI to document the find, is accused of being part of the fraud. She is called a "NAMI fraudster."

Planted Evidence and Counterevidence

Clara Wei was infuriated by these accusations and responded by implying that Don Patton isn't a proper scientist since his doctorate degree wasn't obtained from a recognized university.

She is convinced that the find is genuine. In regards to the board shown by Patton together with Salih Bayraktutan on a video, she says, "That board must have been planted by Patton or others to throw suspicion on our find. When looking at the surroundings in Patton's pictures, I can see that he is somewhere else other than where we have been."

Don Patton also maintains that the picture referred to by the Chinese as "Space 7" in the schematic survey of the find is the same picture that he and Price got from Parasut in 2008 to prove that Parasut had found wood. This was a year and a half before NAMI published their find so Patton sees this as fraud.

However, Parasut's discovery of the wood structure was made about two years before the release in May 2010 which means that Parasut may have taken this photo from the site without revealing to the Americans that it came from the big find, which they didn't learn about till later.

However, Patton was told that the photo showed Parasut's minor find of wood, whereas Space 7 is said to be a big room of 5 x 12 meters.

Furthermore, Patton points out that the photo seems to be manipulated. It is a photo showing Parasut's first find of "petrified" wood, but according to Patton, it is only volcanic rock. (Patton hired a petrologist, David McQueen, who made a report concluding that it was not petrified wood.) The color of the photo has been changed, appearing now in dark brown unlike the original photo which was in grey and didn't look like wood. The film crew in Hong Kong has, obviously, been a little too creative with the illustrations.

Later on, however, *Fiona Leung* from the NAMI expedition shows a piece of wood in which case there is no doubt about it being real wood. But Patton claims that the examples of wood found by NAMI at the site were planted by Parasut.[1]

Dr. Don Patton (third from the left) boldly names filmmaker Clara Wei a "non-NAMI fraudster" on this picture on his website.

On the table is seen Parasut's disputed "petrified wood" that Patton claims is only volcanic rock.

Two Turkish brothers, Davut and Erkan Gimrin, deny having written the letter on Dr. Price's website accusing Parasut of fraud.

False Letter Revealed

In January 2010, Dr. Randall Price published a letter from two Turkish brothers, *Davut and Erkan Gimrin.* In the letter they claim to have taken part in building the wooden structure up on the mountain for Parasut. This letter was so incriminating that the Chinese had to deviate from their plan of waiting patiently for the truth to prevail. Now, even friends began to question their find. I also wrote Clara myself confronting her about the clear indications of the find being a fraud.

But Clara Wei managed to track down the two brothers as they are the only ones in the neighborhood with these names. In a video put on the Internet by Clara Wei, the brothers maintain that they *never* wrote the said letter! And they insist that the contents of the letter aren't true either. They show their passports and write their signatures which clearly show that their signatures in the letter have been forged.

After the Chinese threatened Randall Price with legal action, he withdrew the false letter. But he still insists that the ark find is false.

The Printing Postponed for a Year

I wish I could have included more proof of the find in this book. But the Chinese keep their cards close to their chests. And the scientific examinations that were expected to be quick have made slow progress.

Although I tried quite a lot of times, I was never allowed to visit the site of the find which is known to only the NAMI team, the Kurdish guide Parasut, and very few others.

I also didn't get documentation of the carbon-14 test stating that it was 4,800 years old. This test is the strongest evidence that it was the ark that they found. But the pictures and the videos are, on their own merits, impressive as well.

The Chinese have published a new film in Chinese about the find. The

English version is said to be in the pipeline. It is apparently being changed continuously in order to weed out errors.

This means that I have had to delay the publication of this book in English for more than a year.

But at long last there has now been a development in the story. An American archaeologist has been admitted to the site. He makes clear that, whether or not this is Noah's Ark, it is definitely a genuine archaeological find.

"These sites are extremely important for archaeologists and conservators," states Dr. Joel Klenck, an archaeologist from Harvard University.

The Find Is Genuine

Dr. Joel Klenck is an archaeologist from Harvard University and is head of the *Paleontological Research Corporation*, an organization established by him in 2007 that "provides comprehensive worldwide archaeological and paleontological services including surveys, excavations and research."

Dr. Klenck has examined the site, analyzed the archaeological remains, and completed a comparative examination.

"The site is remarkable," states Klenck, "and comprises a large all-wood structure with an archaeological assemblage that appears to be mostly from the late *Epipaleolithic*[2] Period." (These assemblages at other sites in the Near East have calibrated radiocarbon dates between 13,100 and 9,600 BC)

The site is wonderfully preserved and exhibits a wide array of plant materials including structures made of cypress and one room with a floor covered by chickpea seeds."[3]

Klenck additionally notes, "I was most impressed by the artifact assemblage, particularly the basalt bowls, stone cores, and debitage."

So based upon the objects found at the site, Klenck suggests that it dates back to an earlier period more than the 4,800 years that the radiocarbon dating of the Chinese allegedly showed. But other finds are, however, of a more recent date.

"Two small ceramic bowls from the *Chalcolithic Age*[4] (5,800-3,000 BC) and *Bronze Age* (3,000-1,200 BC) were placed in one of the rooms of the structure."

If it is the ark, the earlier objects could have been brought along before the Flood and the new ones could have been added after the Flood.

121.1 Meters Long and 23.8 Meters in Wide

Klenck reports, "The surface scatter of the wood above the large structure is 121.1 meters in length and 23.8 meters in width. The construction is at least 5.2 meters deep, and several measurements of the exterior walls exhibit angles moving inward toward the base of the edifice. Also, there are stair-like features that descend through the middle of the multi-storied structure, and there is mortise-and-tendon construction."

He remarks, "That this large wood structure is located on Mount Ararat with what appears to be a mostly Epipaleolithic assemblage is noteworthy."

"The site is no hoax," Klenck states, "and the size and excellent preservation of the edifice will enable it to be studied by numerous scholars."

He notes, "The large wood structure is buried under tons of stones and ice, and most of the edifice remains unexplored."

Unprofessional Handling

When it comes to NAMI's radiocarbon dating of the site to be approximately 4,800 BC, Klenck considers that some errors have been made since the initial discovery team was comprised of people with limited archaeological experience.

He remarks, "Instead of obtaining samples from cores and unexposed locales and wrapping them in tin-foil, surface samples were retrieved with bare hands or cotton gloves. The date most likely reflects a sample that was contaminated by ancient visitors or modern explorers to the site. Most of the assemblage portrays a much earlier period."

He suggests that all future radiocarbon samples should be delivered to archaeology departments at Istanbul University that will date the artifacts or send the samples to archaeometry facilities at the University of Berlin.

The Cave Nearby

Klenck also notes that a nearby cave exhibits artifacts similar to those in the large wooden structure. The cave site possesses botanical remains of chickpeas, flax fibers and rope, pieces of fabric, bone artifacts, and vessels made of an organic material.

He adds, "In both the large wooden structure and cave, most of the bowls are made of an *organic* material, perhaps animal stomachs, and the flaps are folded over wood or bone collars. Several of these bowls resemble early ceramic types from the subsequent *Pottery Neolithic Period* (6,400-5,800 BC)."

Important for Archaeologists

"These sites are extremely important for archaeologists and conservators," states Klenck, "particularly with regard to the preservation of wood and plant materials and the examination of architectural features." He is emphatic that the Antiquities Authority of Turkey needs to protect the research area and allow only approved archaeologists and conservators to visit the sites.

"These precautions must be completed," remarks Klenck, "to prevent adventurers and local mountain guides from breaking off pieces of wood and removing artifacts from the research area."

Klenck is confident that the skepticism among archaeologists as to the genuineness of the site will disappear little by little as more researchers and conservators complete their analyses and publish reports in scientific journals. Klenck adds, "The evidence is wide-ranging. On the other hand, only a little of the construction has been examined, and much of the area is inaccessible since it is covered by ice."

A Flood Or a Long, Cold, Dry Winter?

Klenck points out that archaeologists and others are discussing how the transition from the so-called *Pleistocene* and *Holocene*[5] epochs (10,900 – 9,500 BC) and to the beginning of the *Pre-Pottery Neolithic* stage around 9,600 BC took place.

According to theories, this was the time when the first village communities in southeastern Turkey (and the world) became associated with intensive agriculture and plant and animal domestication.

Klenck states, "Some scholars see this transition period as cataclysmic with dramatic increases in sea-levels, flooding, animal extinctions, and decreases in human populations; others assert this phase was simply a cold, dry period evidenced by sparse vegetation."

"In the midst of this debate," he notes, "there is a large wooden structure and a cave with artifacts resembling an *Epipaleolithic* assemblage positioned at a high elevation on Mount Ararat."

Attack from Dr. Amy

At the same time as publishing his first press announcement, Dr. Klenck was personally attacked on a web page by *Dr. Amy L. Beam*. The reason for this severe attack was that in September 2011 Joel Klenck had participated in an expedition on Mt. Ararat with Amy L. Beam as a guide. Here, he disappeared from the group when they were resting at Base Camp 2, and he was gone for four hours. This led to the involvement of the authorities, and the result was that the group was ordered to cancel the climb.

Dr. Klenck himself says that he got lost. But Amy Beam claims that he instead went to see the secret site of the Chinese, which according to her can be seen from Base Camp 2.

Dr. Klenck had previously enquired about the possibility of either departing from the route or climbing the mountain on his own, but Dr. Amy categorically refused this as the authorities have prohibited departing from the tourist routes.

Amy L. Beam is a partner in Murat Camping - which is at war with Parasut's firm.

Apparently Klenck ran the risk, and while he was gone, Dr. Amy examined his notebook in which it appeared that he knew of the ark site and had met Parasut and Clara Wei. He has, however, kept this a secret and denied everything when questioned by Amy Beam, not knowing that he was being filmed by a hidden camera. Afterwards, she put all of the details on the Internet[6] as a personal attack, calling him a fraudster and stating negative personal details about his job situation, speed tickets, child support, and self-promotion of his own books. – It seems venomous.

Amy Beam invites viewers to "spread the word", and she even gives permission to publish her photos and video to "help fight fraud." In the pictures she writes "permission given two use with credits." We thus feel free to reproduce a few of her most interesting photos with reference to her website (www.mountainararattrek.com/ark/arkfraud3b.htm).

Pictures from Dr. Amy Beams website with her own text inserted. According to her this is the site where Parasut and NAMI found the "ark."

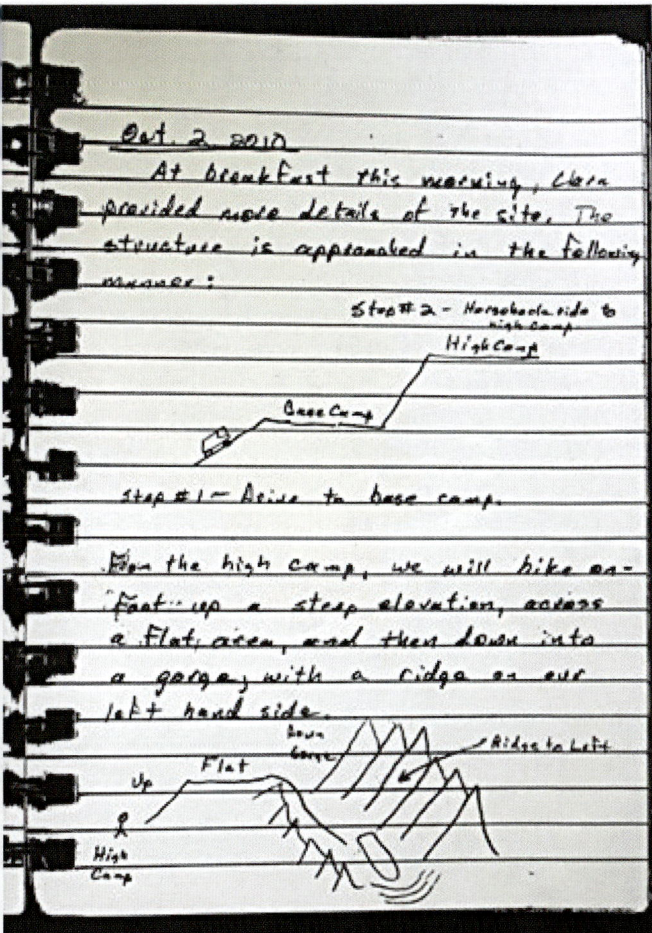

Oct. 2 2010
At breakfast this morning, Clara provided more details of the site. The structure is approached in the following manner:

Step #2 - Horseback ride to high camp
High Camp
Base Camp
Step #1 – Drive to base camp.

From the high camp, we will hike on foot up a steep elevation, across a flat area, and then down into a gorge, with a ridge on our left hand side.

Down Gorge
Ridge to Left
Flat
Up
High Camp

Amy Beam also publishes a few pages of Dr. Klencks notebook. Here he has drawn and described how to find the ark site. First, he'll be driven up to Base Camp 1. Then, he'll climb to Base Camp 2.
"From the high camp we will hike on foot ... up a steep elevation, across a flat area, and just down into the gorge, with a ridge on our left-hand side."

Rivalries between Parasut and Murat Camping

Klenck responded by questioning Amy L. Beam's motives. The fact is that she is a partner with *Murat Camping* which is at war with Parasut's firm.

In his third press announcement, Klenck writes, "Patton, Price and others pay a tourism company, Murat Camping, large sums of money each year to search for the ark. Murat Camping and their American partner have a financial motive to discredit anyone that supports research at the archaeological site because they continue to receive income from various ark search groups who mislead these teams. There are personal rivalries between Murat and Parasut Camping, so there are a lot of emotions associated with this discovery."

Replies to Critics from Creationist Circles

Concerning Price's allegation that Parasut and a small team built the structure on Mount Ararat, Klenck states, "That claim is incorrect." He continues, "The site is large, perhaps over one-hundred meters in length, at least two floors deep, and buried under as much as fifteen meters of stones and ice."

Klenck goes on, "Parasut and his team did not build the features; instead they removed ice and stones from previously excavated passages formed as late as the Bronze Age, as evidenced by a small bowl from this period, to access the site."

Not Modern Marks

Carl Wieland from *Creation Ministries International* reported that straight, cross-grain marks on wood planks, appearing in several photographs from the Ararat site, were produced by a modern industrial planer.

Klenck responds, "These same marks are found on other wood features in antiquity, particularly maritime constructions such as the Binissafuller from the sixth century AD in Minorca, the Fiumicino from the fifth century AD in Rome, the Kyrenia from the fourth century BC, and planks from the sixth century BC vessel found at Pabuç Burnu in Turkey. These marks were caused by stone and later, metal adzes and other tools used to create smooth surfaces and the construction of futtocks or cross timbers. The wood planks at the Ararat site are most certainly of ancient construction."

Wieland also claimed that a large, five-meter-high structure at the Ararat site does not comprise wood but a cave of columnar basalt.

"Again, Wieland is mistaken," states Klenck. "There are two loci in the large wood structure with heights around five meters that were constructed using a series of vertical wood planks, some showing severe states of decomposition."

He adds, "These two all-wood loci appear to have a different function than other areas of the edifice. Both loci have much botanical remains scattered on their floors."

The Spider's Webs

Others have claimed the excellent preservation and spider's webs at the Ararat site suggest photographs of a modern building or ship at a lower elevation.

Klenck remarks, "These claims are also incorrect. Different features in the large wood structure show different states of conservation, with the smaller loci in the interior of the large wood structure exhibiting the best preservation."

He continues, "The vegetal material demonstrates superior preservation because these remains are encased within structures in the interior of the larger wood edifice, which is itself buried under tons of ice and rocks."

Regarding the site's superior preservation, Klenck asserts, "Many people are familiar with the baby woolly mammoth found in 1977 in the Kolyma River, Siberia, or the hunter recovered in 1991 in the Schnalstal glacier in the Ötztal Alps. The Ararat archaeological features have better taphonomic factors since these loci are preserved in multiple layers of rock, ice, and wood, the archaeological equivalent of a Russian matryoshka doll."

With regard to the spiders' webs, Klenck states, "Insects are evident today at comparable elevations on Mount Ararat along with birds. Also, spiders are found at much higher elevations than Mount Ararat, at 6,700 meters above sea level. It is reasonable and expected that arachnids would enter this site during ancient periods."

Too Early for The Ark?

Andrew Snelling of *Answers in Genesis* claims the parameters of the initial calibrated radiocarbon dates from the Ararat structure, between 9,858 BC and recent times, suggest a hoax.

Klenck counters, "Additional archaeometry work needs to be completed to ascertain the dates the site was built and briefly occupied during later periods. However, the parameters of the initial calibrated radiocarbon dates are consistent with the archaeological data and observed phenomena at the site."

"Snelling and the other critics are trying to advocate flood geology creationism claims and assume the Noachian deluge formed most geological strata in one year. All archaeological remains represent post-flood artifacts deposited around 5,300 years ago, and the deluge destroyed any continuity between the pre- and post-flood earth."

An Argument Biting Its Own Tail

As it appears from the above, Dr. Klenck builds his theories on conventional dating. In his opinion, therefore, the artifacts found in the Ark show that it belongs to an older period around 10,000 BC and not to 3,300 BC as believed by Snelling and others to be the time of the great flood catastrophe.

As previously mentioned, the conventional geology is based on certain doubtful assumptions biting its own tail in this case. As it is, the fixing of time periods (the Late Epipaleolithic Period, the later Chalcolithic and Bronze Age etc. mentioned by Klenck) is actually built on assumptions and theories saying that there *hasn't been* any major flood catastrophe as mentioned in the Bible.

However, *if there has been a flood*, you cannot uncritically use the conventional fixing of time to determine the age of the find as practiced by Klenck.

But irrespective of the discussion of age, Klenck has restored the credibility of the find by making it clear that the site is real and not made-up and that it contains genuine artifacts from ancient periods.

Whether or not it is Noah's Ark is another issue on which Klenck doesn't take any position yet. But as he states, it is interesting to find such a big wooden structure on Mt. Ararat in connection with a discussion about there being a flood catastrophe or just a long, dry winter before the first village communities in southeastern Turkey became associated with intensive agriculture and plant and animal domestication.

Provisional Conclusion

So, unfortunately, we cannot here and now establish whether Noah's Ark has actually been found.

The new find on Mt. Ararat at the elevation of 4,200 meters is very promising, but due to the many different interests and prejudices among both scientists and Christians, many conflicting views are sure to be put forward in the years to come.

I contacted Klenck directly to ask him some additional questions about what convinced him of the credibility of the site.

He answered, "The sites are credible. The artifact assemblages support the factual nature of the archaeological sites. Many artifacts, such as the stone tools, were overlooked by NAMI since they had little archaeological experience."

I went on pumping and asked, "Could the artifacts examined by you at the site have been brought up to the site? Or was there anything indicating that they belonged to the place?"

He answered, "No, the value of several individual artifacts, the features and architectural methods of the wood structure, the records of the provenience of the artifacts, the consistent assemblage, and the preliminary radioisotope dates all support the efficacy of this site and its assemblage."

Despite Dr. Klenck's assurances, it still cannot be completely eliminated that we are dealing with a fraud. Not only the wood structure, but also the above mentioned artifacts from ancient ages could have, hypothetically, been taken to the site before Klenck's examination. It is hardly probable and actually very improbable, yet it is not quite unthinkable.

And not only is Parasut's integrity being questioned, but some are also questioning Dr. Klenck's integrity.

While waiting for more clarification, let us take the next chapters to look at the many facts and indications that all seem to show that there has actually been a flood catastrophe and an ark some 5,000 years ago – or more.

Endnotes

1 According to Patton's website www.Noahs-ark.tv

2 The *Epipaleolithic Age* was a period marked by more advanced stone blades and other tools than the earlier *Paleolithic Age* (or Stone Age), although still before the development of agriculture in the *Neolithic Age* (the newer, last part of the Stone Age).

3 Press release - www.sbwire.com/press-releases/sbwire-114562.htm

4 The *Chalcolithic* (greek for copper+stone) period or *Copper Age* is a phase of the *Bronze Age* in which the addition of tin to copper to form bronze during smelting remained yet unknown by the metallurgists of the times. The *Copper Age* was originally defined as a transition between the *Neolithic Age* (the last part of the *Stone Age*) and the *Bronze Age*.

5 *Pleistocene* (greek for most+new) and *Holocene* ("entirely recent") periods refers to the theory of an Ice Age ending c. 10,000 years ago when a warm period started the present (known) period with the growth and impact of humans world wide.

6 Amy L. Beam's website at www.mountainararattrek.com/ark/arkfraud3b.htm

PART 3
BACKGROUND

This is an old Sumerian "world map" in roasted clay. Sumer was probably the same region as the Shinar Plaine mentioned in the Bible as the first civilization after the Flood.

While the Flood report nowadays is often perceived as a sweet and funny story about the animals in the Ark, often with an ecological point, the Ark story in the past was perceived in a more serious perspective. As here on Gustave Doré's copperplate, where the drowned lie lifeless after the water has sunk down from the mountains ...

Chapter 29

Was There Actually A Flood?

A number of things indicate that it actually is Noah's Ark that has been found on Mt Ararat. Let's look at a couple of the clues:

1. **The "Ark" has the right age.**

The Carbon 14 tests that have been made so far show an average of 4,800 years. An age that fits extremely well with the time when the Ark was constructed according to the Biblical chronology. If one simply takes the genealogy used in the Bible in which the life span of each generation is noted, one arrives at the date of the Flood to be 2,349 BC (i.e. 4,360 years ago). However, as it shows in another chapter, one can calculate the date in another way, resulting in a date a thousand years older.

The Carbon 14 method isn't one hundred percent accurate; it can easily show dates several hundred years off the right date, depending on the condition of the wood. Therefore, 4,800 years of age for the wood is an incredibly strong indication that this is in fact the legendary ship. (It would have been more dubious if the tests showed only 1300-1700 years as was the case with Navarra's wood.

2. **The "Ark" was found at the historically correct place.**

The Bible says that the Ark was stranded on "The Ararat Mountains" (in the plural) so it could also have been a mountain in the ancient Ararat (Urartu) kingdom. And there was a time when I myself was inclined to believe that the site was on a smaller mountain on the other side of the valley, east of Mt. Ararat, where the "boat-like object" was found. However, if you consider the many non-biblical historical sources, most of them point to the largest mountain, Mt Ararat.

3. **The "Ark" has been found several times at the same place.**

The large wooden structure which has now been found frozen under the ice at the altitude of approximately 4,200 meters. Apparently, it has been partly exposed earlier. This fits with the accounts eye witnesses have given a number of times in history – for instance, the Turkish Relief Commission in 1883. According to these eyewitnesses, they saw parts of the ship very close to the top. When it from time to time was uncovered, it could have been due to earthquakes – as in 1883 – or mild winters with little snow and hot summers when the snow was melting. It is a known fact that there have been periods in time when the climate has grown warmer.

4. **The wooden structure is divided into rooms.**

The rooms are too large to be a little cabin if one in his wildest fantasy could imagine the existence of a cabin in such an uninhabitable place. (However, there is no historical evidence indicating that there ever has been human habitation at an altitude over 3,500 m.) Some rooms are very lofty, others are too small for humans and in some places the sides slope or round out. There are no signs of more recent construction by the use of nails, screws, or angle-iron. Everything is tenoned like it was done in ancient times. The wood is solid and dark. It has the same colour as described by the eyewitnesses.

Exciting Investigation Ahead

In the coming years much scientific investigation will be made, which will unveil more secrets of the find. If it is the ancient boat, the investigation can probably enlighten us concerning the living conditions of mankind 4,000-5,000 years ago. We know very little about this prehistoric time. The written sources and the finds become very scarce when we go back just 3,000-4,000 years. And if it is a large ship that became stranded on the top of Mt. Ararat, there had to have been a very vast and powerful flood, and this being the case, the ship will undoubtedly tell us something about the Pre-flood period. This Flood must have turned a lot of things upside down. According to the Bible, this catastrophe for example had a great impact on the lifespan of man.

Expect Contradiction

There is hardly any doubt that some – often in the name of science – will argue energetically and fanatically against the find being Noah's Ark, almost regardless of the probability and proof one may come up with. The Ark is not allowed to exist.

The reason for this is simply that the discovery of the Ark questions the fixed dogma and evolutionary theories on which the Western societies have based their world-view for the last 150 years.

Therefore, one can expect rather reasonable academics to argue that "this find is not Noah's Ark, for the Ark doesn't exist. It is a myth." This was how a professor of The Old Testament at the University of Copenhagen argued in a recent article in Kristeligt Dagblad (the major Christian newspaper).

However, this is a very unscientific way of viewing the matter. If one says that something CANNOT exist because one doesn't BELIEVE in its existence, then one is no longer dealing with science but belief or disbelief.

Just as belief can open one's eyes to new dimensions, belief can also close one's eyes to some facts, notwithstanding it being a religious belief or a belief in a theory.

To Think Freely

It is easy to fall into the trap where you close your eyes to new discoveries.

When I wrote my first book about Noah's ark in 2005, I was so convinced that the sources, who found evidence of the Durupinar find, told the truth.

By and by I thought that the remains of the Ark were to be found in the soil under the "boat-shaped object." And many things seemed to indicate that this was the case. Therefore, the Ark could, of course, not also be located on Mt. Ararat. The more I became interested in the Durupinar Formation and all the theories that relate to it, the more I assumed that stories about Noah´s Ark being found on Mt. Ararat must be wrong. In fact I thought they were lies or misunderstandings. It got so that I barely kept myself updated on what was claimed to have been found over on the other mountain because I thought I knew it was not possible! Furthermore, I was downright angry with people who kept claiming that they had seen something new over there on the other side of the valley.

This remarkable find had to be made before I was willing to revise my theories – my dogma. I just had to gape and wonder with open mouth while I tried to find my shaky legs under me and my understanding of reality again.

Most people in the modern world understand their reality through some theories put forward in the mid 1800s. Theories which most scientists and institutions of higher education assume are in keeping with reality. But the discovery of Noah's Ark puts a question mark by these entrenched theories – and for this we should be glad, because it opens up for new discoveries and new ways of thinking.

Only if one does not automatically exclude some possibilities, one can think freely and carry on unprejudiced research, free of bias.

When Reality Surpasses Theories

In the following chapters we will bring up some exciting new perspectives in light of the discovery of Noah's Ark.

First, there are many questions that the ancient report (the Bible, etc.) does not answer for us. It is much easier to call it all a myth, a legend from the old days. However, now it is obviously situated up there under the ice, the old boat. It is no longer a myth! It has materialized. There was a ship. A mighty ship! And it ended up there because the Earth was going through change of catastrophic dimensions back then. It may sound unbelievable, but when you read the next few chapters, you will experience what I experienced when I examined the body of evidence on which the chapters are based: There are ample clues in history, in myths, in the development of languages, in names of places and peoples, in the old maps of the world, in geology, and even in the Ark structure itself, which indicate that the ancient report concerning Noah was not just a myth. In fact, it was a historical event that took place only approximately 5000 years ago.

But before we get started with the exciting new perspectives, we need to take the bull by the horns regarding the established science community's deadlocked "faith" in the evolution theory. Most people think that this theory of everything developing over millions of years has long since been proven, but it is far from true. It is only a theory on which scientists base everything, just as researchers of the past based their conclusions on other theories and religions. But it is only a theory. Remember that!

Faith and Science

The explanation for these negative vibrations is simply that in the past centuries two theories about the world's development have arisen and since then won almost total acceptance in the scientific community. They have in fact become so integrated in modern practice and theory that it has almost forgotten that these are only working theories. At present they are dogma.

The first theory is Charles Darwin's well-known theory of evolution. As most of us know, this theory states, in a nutshell, that living things have developed from lower stages through a process over an unfathomable number of years. This theory is now taught in public schools everywhere. On half-scientific TV programs assumptions of this theory are tossed out without any further explanation with phrases like, "when our ancestors crawled down from the trees" and "millions of years ago when our ancestors were fish or one-celled animals." They don't even take the time to state that in spite of everything that has been said, this is only a theory – one that can and must continually be questioned.

The second theory is the so-called theory of uniformity that Charles Lyell developed in the same period. Since its introduction there have been new discoveries that speak against this theory, but it has been canonized as dogma, which discourages all independent research.

Simply put, the theory says that all changes in the universe have taken place at the same pace, as can be seen today. That is to say, the pace is incredibly slow, and therefore it is supposed that change takes place over many millions of years.

For example, it is popularly assumed that the geological layers have been created by millions of years of dust and other materials laying on top of each other. But anyone that lived in parts of the world other than Lyell's safe, comfortable England knows that the pace at which the landscape erodes will surpass the tremendously slow pace at which it is supposed the layers are formed or created. Such illogical relationships exist in the theory of uniformity, which, unfortunately, is quietly accepted. Why? Because we often get the impression that "science" really does have a good grip on all the millions of years being bounced around. However, this is far from the truth.

Charles Darwin's theory of evolution was first looked at with humor, but today it has become dogmatized in a way that makes it difficult to consider other possibilities.

Datings on Shaky Ground

The theory saying that it is possible to date fossils from the geological layer in which they are found is problematic because some fossils are found in several layers. They are called polystrata fossils.

For example, you find trees and plants having their roots down in the

Carboniferous layer (which means that they should be 360-286 millon years old), whereas their trunks stands in the Permian layer (and therefore should be 286-245 mill. years old) and their top is in the Triassic layer (i.e. between 245-208 million years old). It goes without saying that this can't be true. And yet this system of dating is used uncritically when you are so lucky as to find a fossil in a particular layer. This type of reasoning doesn't seem very serious.

Sometimes animals and plants are also found in the „wrong layers" – according to the theory of evolution. In fact, animals and plants supposedly extinct for millions of years, have been found in layers together with works of art from ancient Greece. But then they are just called „out of place" – and scientists continue using the theory confirming their preconceived notions. Does this seem reasonable?

Forbidden Archaeology

In the book „Forbidden Archaeology"[1] Michael A. Cremo and Richard L. Thompson speak among other things about the Nampa goddess, a small earthenware figurine found in 1889 about 100 meters underground between two sedimentary layers (Pliocene and Pleistocene) so that it should actually be dated 2 million years old even though it is, in all probability, only several thousand years old. Very deep in the coal seams (at least 286-360 mill. years ago according to the theory) several man-made objects were found in 1926 in Bear Creek, Montana, together with two human teeth.

In 1912 an iron pot was found in the coal seams near the town of Thomas, Oklahoma. An iron bell has also been found in a lump of coal in West Virginia.[2] A whole human skeleton was found deep down in a coal field in Italy in 1958 – even though this layer should correspond to an age of about 300 mill. years ago.

In 1891 a woman in Illinois dropped her coal scoop on the floor so that the coal broke. It turned up that a gold chain was enclosed in some of the coal – supposed to have been formed about 300 mill. years ago ...[3]

In Freiburg in Germany you can view a fossil of a human skull that has been found in the coal seams...[4] Also a spoon has been found enclosed in coal – and three wooden spears were found in a coal mine in Schöningen near Hannover in Germany. They are of fir and Institut für Denkmalpflege dates them to between 380,000 – 400,000 years – not because they can measure it, but because they think that man at that point in time had evolved to that stage.[5] But according to the theory of the geological layers upon which this understanding of evolution is built, these spears were actually lying in layers which were 300 mill. years old ... oops!

At the same place thousands of legs of animals have been found, with marks of cuts and stabbing – indicating that they have been killed by men. But unfortunately, they were lying in the devon-, the coal- or the tertiary-layers – and therefore they should be 408-66 mill. years old which does not at all fit in with the model of evolution saying that man evolved and first appeared only a few hundred thousand years ago.

Not Trustworthy

This whole system of dating is not to be trusted, and seems pretty ridiculous.

Today we also know from ecological research that nature has to be constantly in circulation and balance. So that the idea that a fish may have changed into a lizard is not as simple as Darwin thought.

The problem with these two outdated theories is that they have become so totally dominant that they prevent all open-minded research that doesn't fit into the theories already in place.

Room for a Creator?

You can't help but notice that these theories arose in a context in which there were religious undertones. There was a focus on getting rid of religion. But instead Darwin's and Lyell's theories became the new religious dogmas that you had to believe in – and they apparently still may not be questioned.

Ever since then, atheist school teachers have tried to knock child-like faith out of their tiny pupils by claiming that the Bible was wrong about the Flood. Yes, even theology (the study of God) has been affected because certain theologians have tried to conform to that which was "known to be fact." This is of course the easiest way, but is it true?

In previous centuries Lyell and his followers categorically precluded the possibility of a flood or any other form of colossal world catastrophe. Until then, the Flood was accepted within the scientific community. It was thought that geologic layers were created by a worldwide flood that occurred some 4,500 – 5.500 years ago. In other words the flood spoken of in the Bible during the life of Noah.

The Original Model of Explanation

The fact is that the geological layers in particular can also be interpreted as the best proof of a global flood.

For over 75% of the earth and 95% of the sea bed are covered by an enormous layer of sediments. This layer consists of minerals and organic material, and it may have arisen either due to a very slow process of crumbling (Lyell's theory) or due to – a gigantic flood!

The sedimentary layers are a huge burial place for all sorts of animals, fish, birds, reptiles, insects, plants, and human beings. Ninety-nine to one hundred percent of all the species that have ever lived on earth are, according to the paleontologists, buried here. And they are lying in fairly good order with the smallest animals at the bottom and the bigger and faster on top. The huge heavy dinosaurs are lying somewhat lower. The way they would be lying if they had been caught in a catastrophe.

Nowadays animals and plants rot and decompose rapidly when they die. Why they shouldn't have done so previously is difficult to know – unless they in fact were buried due to a catastrophe.

In the 1700's and 1800's mass graves were found with a wide variety of animals all thrown together in a pile, animals that didn't normally associate with each other. Some still had grass in their mouths. Everything seems to point to them having died in a catastrophe.

Experiments with having different materials slopping around in a reservoir also show that they gradually settle down in layers – like the geological layers. It is actually very simple as long as you make room for the Flood.

But science is still injuriously affected by the fact that in the 18th and 19th centuries all the religious ideas were disposed of – and the Flood was thrown out. Later however, archeologists and anthropologists realized that the Bible is not the only source that tells of a great flood. Almost all of the ancient civilized nations have accounts of it.

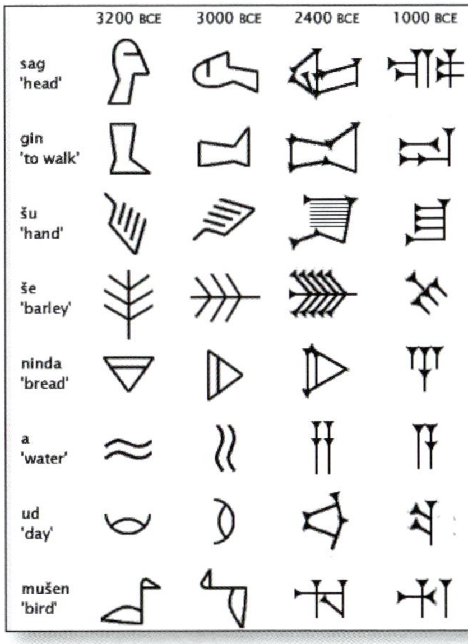

The Sumerian cuneiform consisted of a sign for each word. The signs were eventually simplified so they were faster to write or press into the soft clay tablet.

Discovery of the Sumerian Tablets

In 1872, a few decades after Lyell had established that there never had been a flood, a several-thousand-year-old account of it from a non-biblical source was found.

By 1849 an English attorney and employee of the embassy, Henry Austin Layard, had already retrieved approximately 10,000 clay tablets from the ancient city of Nineveh (Mosul) in Iraq. These came from an extensive library that the last great Assyrian king, Assurbanipal (668-626 BC) had collected shortly before Nineveh was destroyed in 612 BC (which, by the way, was prophesied by both Nahum[6] and Zephaniah[7] in the Old Testament).

The tablets were transferred to the British Museum in London, but it took decades to decipher the thousands of tablets with inscriptions pertaining to law, trade, religious laws, and things like food rations for political prisoners.

Noah – Utnapsihtim – Ziuzudra – Atrahasis

Then in 1872 the English Assyriologist, George Smith discovered an account of a hero named Gilgamesh. When he got to the 9th and 10th tablets, he read that Gilgamesh in his sorrow and searching for the meaning of life visited a wise old man named Utnapishtim (which means "he who found life") – a person that surprisingly resembled Noah!

The poem has since been translated into many languages.[8] And it is considered one of the great documents of world literature. The ancient clay tablets' speak of the lineage of kings both before and after the Flood, and in the tablets there were up to 10 kings before the Flood (just as in the Bible's ten patriarchs), and Gilgamesh was the 5th king after the Flood. He was king in the city-state Uruk, in southern Iraq – one of the oldest cities in the world, by the way. The archeologists also found an ancient Sumerian account of the

Agatha Christie was married to the archeologist Max Mallowan and wrote multiple novels connected to the excavations they experienced together. Among those works are Murder on the Orient Express and Murder in Mesopotamia whose excavation leaders are very similar to Woolley. The most autobiographical of these was They Came to Baghdad, which she wrote in Nimrod in 1951.

Noah's flood - The new scientific discoveries about the event that changed history by William Ryan & Walter Pitman. Simon & Schuste, New York.

Flood in which Noah is named Ziusudra, a Sumerian name for Utnapishtim (which also means, "he who found life"). Ziusudra was the king of Shuruppak before the Flood. According to the tablets, it was an ancient city that lay on the shores of the Euphrates. Ziusudra also built a ship and survived the Flood.

An earlier Babylonian account from approximately 1700 BC is about Atrahasis (which means the "extra wise") and is thought to come from the Sumerian period (some 1,000 years earlier) because it gives an account of the kings of Sumeria before the Flood where Atrahasis was the last king in Shuruppak. Atrahasis is also saved from the Flood by building a boat. So there is no doubt that this account, too, is about the Noah written of in the Bible.

To sum it up, all of these ancient tablets support the Bible's account.

Mesopotamia – the Birthplace of the World

It is not so strange that these ancient accounts of the Flood were found precisely here in Mesopotamia. The area between the Euphrates and the Tigris is the home of the first civilizations known to man.

According to the Bible, this was also the area where most people went after the Flood. Many of the cities in this region are mentioned; for example "The beginning of his (Nimrod's) kingdom was Babel, Erech, and Accad, all of them in the land of Shinar. From that land he went into Assyria, and built Nineveh, Rehoboth-ir, Calah, and Resen between Nineveh and Calah; that is the great city." [10]

The oldest lager culture found here is the Sumerian, but there are traces of earlier peoples (before the Flood perhaps).

Sumer is probably the same country known as Shinar in the Bible. Shinar was the great plain where those that wandered here from the landing place of the Ark built the Tower of Babel, according to the Bible. Most of what scientists know about Mesopotamia comes from the excavations performed in the 18th and 19th centuries, not least of all being the tablets in Nineveh and thousands of other tablets found in Aleppo in Syria.

Woolley's Dig in Ur

Another great source of knowledge came in 1922 when the English archeologist Sir Leonard Woolley excavated the ancient city of Ur in southern Iraq. The city dates back to c. 2100 BC, and many believe it to be the birthplace of Abraham. The British were deeply involved in the Mesopotamian excavations, and even the detective novelist Agatha Christie was present at a number of the digs in Ur, Nineveh, and Nimrod from 1930 until 1958.

Relevant to Ark research is the fact that under the potsherds in the ancient city of Ur, Leonard Woolley discovered another layer of clay several meters thick. There was nothing found in that layer, but under the thick layer of clay there were other layers where interesting finds again appeared. The deep layer of clay was from a great flood that covered at least the entire southern part of Mesopotamia. This can be confirmed because other similar flood layers have been found in the same region. It is only natural to wonder if this layer wasn't from the Flood.

The Flood in the Black Sea?

One of the most interesting findings in connection with the question of whether or not there has actually been a great flood came just a few years ago. In connection with these findings, the distinguished Danish geologist, Minik Rosing, wrote the following:

> "There is good reason to believe that the biblical flood, which we started considering a fantasy-filled myth, was actually a historical event. An event which loses none of its ability to fascinate in spite of our burgeoning understanding of the complex correlation between climate, geology, and cultural history from which it has been born."[11]

The Black Sea is a mighty inland sea situated between Europe and Asia. It is 721 miles long and up to 380 miles wide. The Black Sea is about 7,200 ft. deep. Through the Bosporus Strait, the Marmara Sea, and the Dardanelles, there is a route leading to the Mediterranean. The Black Sea was once a fresh water lake. Today it is salty, and large parts of it are dead because of a lack of oxygen.

He is only one of many geologists and archeologists that have been forced to adjust their perception of the world after new discoveries have been made in the Black Sea within the past few years by geophysicists William Ryan and Walter Pitman.[12]

Their discoveries show that around 7,200 years ago water gushed into the Black Sea with a force equal to 200 times that of Niagara Falls. On the bottom of the Black Sea they found a sand bar that couldn't keep up with the water flow. Both salt-water and fresh-water muscles have been found in the same place. This is a sign that the sea changed from being a fresh-water reservoir to a salt-water sea. Even a house has been found on the bottom of the sea...

The scientists' theory is that the flood is a result of the water from the Mediterranean breaking through the Straight of Bosporus. The area that has become the Black Sea was inundated with one cubic kilometer of water per hour after the break until there again was equilibrium.

With such enormous flooding, one can't help but think about the biblical flood connected with Noah's Ark – especially so when one finds out that it's dated around 7,200 years ago – not the usual millions of years ago as geologists often juggle with. According to the numbers in the Bible, the Flood should have happened around 4,500-5,500 years ago. This is not exactly the same time, but the difference could be that Ryan and Pitman established the age based on the muscle shells that were found, shells which could be older than the event itself. Furthermore, both events belong to the first civilizations of antiquity, to pre-history.

Local Or Worldwide?

Now, it's not normal for scientists to accept detailed biblical accounts as such. There is no talk of a worldwide flood, but rather the flooding of an immense valley measuring over 1,600 miles from north to south and east to west. Here, where the Black Sea is now located, they believe lay the known "world" of that time. They also think that the flood was a result of melting during the Ice Age in Northern Europe and has been put in the Bible (and other ancient sources) as a punishment sent from God. It is a very exciting theory that is built upon the conventional theories of an ice age. But these theories are not necessarily valid because Antarctica and Greenland were evidently ice-free 4,000-6,000 years ago. (More in another chapter about this.) Whatever the case, Ryan and Pitman have found evidence of a tremendous flood of huge proportion.

Ryan and Pitman have explored the bottom of the Black Sea together with scientists from Bulgaria and Turkey. With the help of ultrasound waves and samples taken of the soil, they have established that the Black Sea was once a fresh water lake that lay hundreds of meters under today's sea level.

Their hypothesis is that at that time the Straight of Bosperus was closed off and that the area where the Black Sea is located today was once a very fertile valley – a paradise one is tempted to call it – with a glorious fresh water lake at its center. Just behind that narrow isthmus that divided the Mediterranean from the Black Sea, the elevation dropped a sudden 150 meters, while the lake itself sank to a depth of 2,000 meters or 6,500 feet.

One could imagine that the valley was flooded with such terrible force that the entirety of the first civilization was completely wiped out with the exception of very few – possibly Noah and his family, who, because of the prevailing winds, drifted eastward landing on Ararat.

Evidence of a Flood Catastrophe?

Scientists have found an embankment of water-worn pebbles at a depth of almost 500 feet close to the Black Sea. This suggests that the coast had once been there. In deeper waters, sandbars have been found which can normally only be found at 10 feet or less.

If the water had risen slowly, the beach along with the sandbar would have followed. The fact that evidence of a beach has been found at such a depth suggests that the water had to suddenly rise more than 300 feet. There had to have been a water cataclysm of some kind.

From 500 feet below the surface and up to the present-day coastline, there are also layers that are otherwise only found on the side of dry valleys. A thin layer of mud now covers it.

On the beach at 500 feet below, clams and muscle shells have been found. These shells are from fresh water muscles. In contrast to this, the shells that have been retrieved further up the sea bottom are all of salt-water muscles.

Dating with the carbon-14 method, which should be taken with a grain of salt, shows that the youngest fresh water muscles and the oldest salt-water muscles are of the same age. Based on their ages, the "Flood" is thought to be dated around 7,200 years ago.

The egyptologist John Anthony West and other scolars believe that the Sphinx as well as the pyramids have been subjected to water erosion and therefore originate in an earlier civilasation when the desert was fertile land.

A House on the Bottom of the Black Sea

On the bottom of the Black Sea – though only 311 ft. deep (95 m.) – a house has been found. Robert Ballard was the first to catch a glimpse of it miles away from land while leading an archeological exploration of the depths of the Black Sea in 2000.

The house is about 40 x 13 feet and built out of twigs and clay. A nearby dung heap – still under water – contained pieces of wood, branches, and polished stones. A man-made container and some tools were found around the house. Ballard estimates the location to be from 5500 BC. Such an old domicile under water is almost unheard of. Wood is usually destroyed very quickly under water because of bacteria and worms but not in the Black Sea because the oxygen level is so low that these things cannot survive as told by marine biologist W.B. Ryan from Columbia University to the press.

The Flood – More Than a Local Event?

One could easily believe that the flood from the Bible and other ancient sources was actually just a local, but massive flood: the Black Sea Flood. There have been attempts to explain the Flood in the same way by citing an enormous flood that occurred in southern Iraq about 5,000 years ago, of which clear signs can be found in the layers of the earth in the ancient cities of Ur and Nineveh. But there is still new evidence appearing of a great Flood.

The Sphinx at the Giza Pyramids is the most famous sphinx statue - but there are sphinxes worldwide. The oldest, thought to be around 9,000 years old, is found in southern Turkey near Harran, where Abraham lived. It is in the upper part of Mesopotamia between the Tigris and Euphrates where the first humans also must have lived. A sphinx is a lion figure with a woman's face.

Geologists Jim Teller from the University of Manitoba in Canada, Nick Lancaster from the Institute of Desert Research in Reno, Nevada, and Ashok Singhi from the Laboratory for Physical Research in India have presented evidence that there was at one time a mighty flood in the Arabian Desert. And they think that the Gulf, which is only around 330 feet deep, was previously dry. They presented their findings for the American Geological Society's annual meeting in Reno in 2000.[13]

These geologists believe their flood to be the product of shed glacial water from the ending of the Ice Age. One is tempted to say, 'of course', given the fact that these scientists have to interpret their evidence based on the theories that already exist. But for people that are convinced that there once was a flood, The Flood, this is again evidence that a worldwide catastrophe did occur.

Were the Pyramids under Water?

There are also signs that the great Sphinx at The Giza Pyramids in Egypt have been under water. The Egyptologist John Anthony West[14] and several geologists have inspected the giant statue on the Nile's west bank. They consider it to be a fact that the Pyramids have been under water.

Nobody knows when the Sphinx was built. Tutmoses IV set a plate on it in 1400 BC, but there is a general agreement that the Sphinx was built much earlier. It is believed that it originates from the fourth dynasty (2723-2523), a period from which a smaller Sphinx portraying Queen Hetepheres II is known. Egyptologists usually believe that the pyramids were built at about this time and thereafter.

But people have always wondered how our "primitive ancestors" were able to build these masterpieces.

After more than ten years of research, John Anthony West says that they are much older than from the time of the Pharaohs and that there is evidence of a flood. He claims that Egypt once was a land of great fertility, but it turned into a desert over the last few thousand years.

The Sphinx and the pyramids bear signs of being eroded by a flood or large quantities of rainwater. Today, however, it hardly rains in this desert, and since the rain could leave such deep traces, John Anthony West believes that the Sphinx was built about 30,000 years ago!

The explanation could also be that – as the Bible and other ancient sources tell us – there was a great deluge, a flood, just before the famous Egyptian civilization flourished. So even though the huge structures often bear the names of later pharaohs, who used them as tombs, there are indications that they can be dated back to the time before the Flood.

This could also explain how the master builders possessed the technical skills to calculate and the capacity to build these marvels. According to our working hypothesis, people generally were more capable before the flood. They lived longer and they were larger, etc., as shown in other chapters.

Drowned Cities in the Pacific Ocean

On the Japanese island Okinawa, a strange legend has it that their ancestors lived at the bottom of the sea!

Some years ago a city was found at the bottom of the sea, which had been submerged once in the past. Professor Masaaki Kimura himself dived down to the bottom of the sea and unveiled buildings, yes, even a temple and a fortress. At the centre of the city there is a pyramid! There is a broad street and a square.[15]

Scientists believe that there is a deluged civilisation under the Pacific Ocean, greater than all of South America. It lay between Japan, Okinawa and Taiwan. But at some point in time, the waters came, and flooded it all.

Did anybody say – the Flood….?

Civilisation Wiped Out in China – by Flood

In China archaeologists have found a strange ancient city approximately 40 km from Chengdu. Since 1920 many highly refined objects have been found from the highly advanced Sanxingdui civilisation which probably existed 3,700-5,000 years ago.[16]

The strange thing is that the thousands of people, who lived there and occupied an area of over 12 square kilometers (app. 4,6 square miles) with palaces and brick houses who cultivated soil and graveyards, suddenly disappeared with out a trace.

Historians now believe that Sanxingdui was destroyed by a sudden flood due to sudden climatic changes.

Atlantis

Actually there are signs of deluged cities in many places around the world. The "myth" of Atlantis – the country that disappeared under the sea – has hardly developed just out of thin air and fantasy. If one emerges oneself in the old myths, it usually turns out that they are based on something that has actually happened, as was the case with Atlantis. The Greek Solon heard of the missing country from the Egyptians in Saïs, and 200 years later Platon expanded on this – thereby making the story into a myth. Since then, however, a number of examples of submerged cities have appeared around the world.

In 2004 Robert Samast found a submerged city between Cyprus and Syria.[17] And he argues that the lost Atlantis lay south and east of Cyprus, and that the entire Mediterranean was once not totally dry land but had a very low water level. He explains that the reason was because there must have been a closure of the Atlantic Ocean at the Straits of Gibraltar and that there was a break.

But what then of the other Atlantises? For instance the city of Okinawa? Here there are no broken straits like Gibraltar or Bosperus that can explain the floods. The most natural explanation of the world's Atlantises is in fact the Flood, which the Bible tells about, and with which scientists reckoned – until someone in the 1,700-1,800s got busy rejecting anything to do with religion.

So the Flood was kicked out and banned from science, but traces of it keep turning up all around the world.

Endnotes

1 Michael A. Cremo and Richard L. Thompson, *Forbidden Archeology: The Hidden History of the Human Race,* (BBT Science 1996), ISBN #: 0-89213-294-9.

2 Charles Sellier and Bryan Russell, *Ancient Secrets of the Bible.* (New York: Dell Publishing 1994), 243-247.

3 George Mulfinger, *The Flood and the Fossils*, (Greenville: Bob Jones University Press), 5.

4 Otto Stutzer, *Geology of Coal*, (University of Chicago Press, 1940), 271.

5 *Archaelogy* (May-June 1997), 25.

6 The Book of Nahum is about Nineveh. In 722 BC the Assyrians destroyed Samaria with atrocities as never before had been seen. But 80 years later Nahum prophesied that Nineveh, the capital of the Assyrian Kingdom, would be destroyed. In 612 BC this happened when The Babylonians and the Medes captured the city. The city, which was considered invincible, was penetrated by the Tigris River which made it possible for the enemy to come right in (see Nahum chapter 1:8 and 2:6).

7 Zephaniah imparted his message in the latter part of the 7th century BC – most likely before 621 BC Zephaniah 2:13-15 says, "And he will stretch out his hand against the north, and destroy Assyria; and he will make Nineveh a desolation, a dry waste like the desert. Herds shall lie down in it, every wild animal; the desert owl and the screech owl shall lodge on its capitals; the owl shall hoot at the window, the raven croak on the threshold; for its cedar work will be laid bare. Is this the exultant city that lived secure, that said to itself, 'I am, and there is no one else'? What a desolation it has become, a lair for wild animals! Everyone who passes by it hisses and shakes the fist." Today, scientists are the only ones who know of the beauty and majesty hiding under the fields of Mosul where the sheep graze.

8 Translations are very different. An English translation can be found at: ancienttexts.org/library/mesopotamian/gilgamesh/index.html

9 The Book of Jasher, however, may possibly have been rediscovered in the form of scrolls as we will later see.

10 Genesis 10:10-12.

11 Minik Rosing in an article from the otherwise characteristically atheistic newspaper, *Politiken*, under the scientific topic: Vid og Sans (Wit and Sense) (8/12/01)

12 William Ryan and Walter Pitman, (italicize the title with all words in caps except the. also put a : after Flood), (New York: Simon & Schuste, 2000).

13 "Manitoba geologist thinks he's found evidence of Noah's flood" Canadian Press, Monday, Jan. 15, 2001, WINNIPEG (CP)

14 www.jawest.net

15 Submarine Geology around the Southern Ryukyu Islands, with Special Reference to the Okinawa Trough. 1979

16 Sanxingdui – www.chinamuseums.com/sanxingduim.htm

17 "Discovery of Atlantis", www.discoveryatlantis.com

Chapter 30

The Ship Expert: A Sensible Construction

The engineer Hans Otto Kristensen Holmgaard has worked with almost all aspects of ship construction in the maritime industry and within international organizations. He is also a lecturer at the Danish Polytechnical University.

What did Noah's Ark look like? How good was it at sailing?

An expert on ships will tell us some surprising things about this in the following chapter. The dimensions of the Ark are not only well-proportioned, but in certain areas it actually fulfills and surpasses the standards established by the international Load Lines Convention drawn up by the United Nations' International Maritime Organization (IMO), which is also used today for ship building internationally. The 4,500-year-old proportions of height and width are equivalent to what will most likely become the European Union's newest rules for the transportation of animals...

Let's Ask an Expert

Hans Otto Kristensen is employed at DTU, (the Danish Polytechnical University) where he works on research, development, and the construction of different types of ships. Besides this, he teaches ship design and maritime environmental conditions at Copenhagen Business School. He is a technical expert in maritime safety and for many years has taken part in the development of future regulations and methods of calculating to estimate the stability of ships.

Hans Otto Kristensen is also the adviser for several official authorities and ministries on environmental conditions relating to shipping, including the future legislation for the reduction of the CO2 exhaust from shipping to minimize global warming.

Having many years of consulting experience for a number of Danish ferry companies, Hans Otto Kristensen has taken part in constructing many of the ferries that are sailing in Danish waters. Simply put – he is an expert.[1]

Are the Proportions Reasonable?

In Genesis chapter 6, verses 14-17, there aren't a lot of building instructions given.

> "Make for yourself an ark of gopher wood; you shall make the ark with rooms, and shall cover it inside and out with pitch. This is how you shall make it: the length of the ark three hundred cubits, its breadth fifty cubits, and its height thirty cubits. You shall make a window for the ark, and finish it to a cubit from the top; and set the door of the ark in the side of it; you shall make it with lower, second, and third decks."

"What does this information tell us?"

"Compared to the often very thick documents from which ships are constructed today, the description of Noah's Ark can be called an extremely short outline specification, in technical language," says Hans Otto Kristensen. "Its brevity doesn't make it of any less value in that the description contains some facts that, from a historical as well as a ship-technical perspective, are very exciting. Noah's Ark was most likely the first large ship built in the history of the world."

Divided Into Rooms

"The first thing we need to call attention to is the fact that the Ark was to be furnished with rooms. What's interesting here is that by far the majority of ships that have been built afterwards have been built without rooms.

"One only has to think of the Nordic Viking ships where the hull of the ship constitutes a long open room where the crew's quarters and the cargo room were one and the same.

"Of course, one could rightly say that Noah's Ark was to be built with rooms so that there was enough room for the many animals onboard.

"This is obvious, and because this account is more like supervisory blueprints, I will allow myself to interpret the description of dividing the boat into rooms as a preparation or pre-cursory measure to prevent the entire ship from being filled with water if water were to seep through a single hole. Such an anti-leakage provision is called securing the ship's aptitude to float. The mapping up of wooden ships into watertight rooms is an issue of debate in ship-building circles because it is very difficult to divide a wooden ship's hull into watertight crosssections using transverse bulkheads.

"Until modern times, (that is the 17th century), such division into rooms has only been seen in Chinese ships known as "junks." It wasn't until the 1800's that others started to subdivide the hull for practical reasons such as separating the engine room from the crew's quarters and the cargo. Another reason that room divisions became more popular was, as mentioned above, so that the entire hull wouldn't fill with water if there was a leak due to a collision or grounding," Says thc ship cxpcrt.

"The mapping of ships into watertight zones has nowadays turned into a very mathematic and technical science – something that Hans Otto Kristensen is very familiar with after many years of experience."

The Dimensions

"The most interesting aspect of the Ark's plans though, is the choice of principal dimensions," say Hans Otto Kristensen. "They are interesting because, on the one hand you get a feeling of the ship's size, and on the other hand, but just as interesting, because you can compare these principal dimensions' mutual relationship with the corresponding relationships that are used in modern ship building today.

"One cubit was about 18 inches long or ½ meter, which gives Noah's Ark

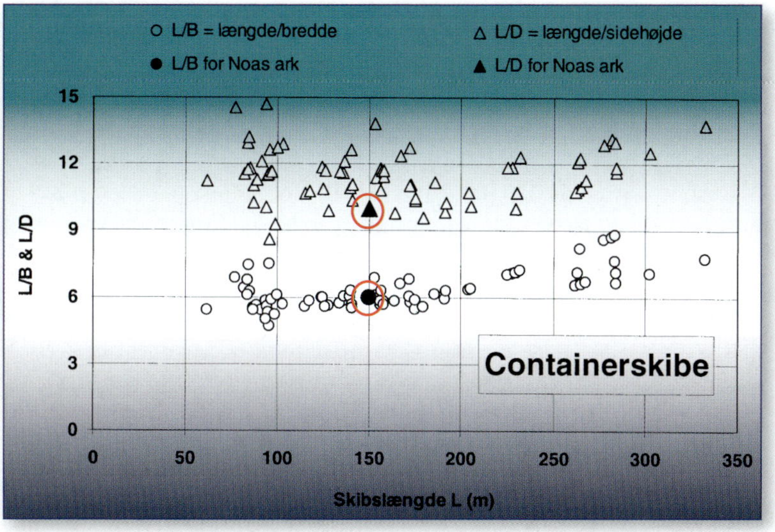

The illustration shows the length-width ratio that is used by modern container ships (shown with a round circle). Similarly, you can see which length to height ratio of the various container ships are built after (marked with a triangle). In both cases, the ark is placed in the center, i.e. a design which is very close to what we today regard as ideal ship construction - despite the fact that the archaeal dimensions date from several thousands of years ago.

the following approximate measurements:

Length = L = 150 m (492 ft.)
Width = W = 25 m (82 ft.)
Height = H = 15 m (49 ft.)

"These measurements give us a feeling of the Ark's size, which, by the way, is the same size as some of the world's largest animal transport ships that can carry about 40,000 head of sheep.

"In addition, it is very interesting to see that the relationship between the height and the length (H/L) of the ship and that of the length and width (L/W) of the ship are equivalent to the normal construction practice used today for modern containerships which is shown in the figure below.

Roofing Lives Up to International Requirements

"Another interesting thing about Noah's Ark, which for a person without knowledge of ship construction can seem meaningless, is the fact that the Ark's roof ridge was raised one cubit, that is 1/50 of the ship's width.

"The roof ridge of this boat is the deck, and the deck's camber (rising) causes any water that may come onto the deck to easily flow overboard again.

"When seen through the eyes of a ship builder, this little detail called a roof ridge is very notable because the same construction is also used today when building ships.

"Even more interesting is the fact that the measurements used here, 1/50 of the width of the ship, is the exact same standard that has been established by the United Nations' Maritime Organization, IMO, and used internationally when building ships.

The Stability of Animal Transport – by EU Standards

"One last comment on the Ark's principal dimensions is that these dimensions would give the ship such stability that it would be able to fulfill the requirements for stability that the European Union (EU) has worked out regarding animal transport ships," Hans Otto Kristensen explains.

Today, many of the different types of ships are so high so that animals in transport, when faced with bad weather, can be put in circumstances that surpass what an animal can take.

The new requirements that the EU has worked out (which Hans Otto Kristensen has also taken part in) will assure that animals under transport do not experience great accelerations. The Ark's principal dimensions have been chosen so well that they would fulfill all of the EU's new requirements for stability.

Hans Otto Kristensen would like to stress that his short explanation should not be understood as scientific evidence of the existence of Noah's Ark. The sole purpose is to show that from a technical point of view, there is nothing in the account from the Bible about the Ark that defies the knowledge and experience we have today about shipbuilding.

"From a technical point of view, one can't help but notice that the Bible's account amazingly agrees with modern shipbuilding principles in that the description contains details that were not incorporated into standards of shipbuilding until many years after the building of the Ark. Some of them have not even come as far yet, but most likely will within the coming years – apropos the coming rules of the European Union on ship stability in transporting animals animals," Hans Otto Kristensen concludes.

Endnotes

1 Master **Hans Otto Kristensen Holmgaard** is a trained engineer and is senior scientist in the "Ship Design" at the Danish Technical University in the Department of ships, shores and constructions, where he works on research and development to reduce ships' energy consumption (CO2 emissions). Beside these activities he teaches ship design and maritime environmental conditions at the Copenhagen Business School Maritime Master program.

He has worked at the research institution FORCE Technology, primarily with the testing of ship models for new marine projects in the laboratory's approx. 250 m long experimental pool. He is an expert in maritime safety and participates via the United Nations Maritime Organisation, IMO, in the development of future rules and methods for determining ship stability.

As a longstanding adviser Hans Otto Kristensen has helped to construct a very large number of the ferries that are currently sailing in Danish waters, and through his engagement with the Naval Material Command for more than five years he has supervised the development several of Denmark's most modern warships.

He is Secretary General of the Technical Shipping Society and sits in a number of professional committees of the English technical ship engineering organization Royal Institution of Naval Architects (RINA) and the American engineering organization Society of Naval Architects and Marine Engineers (SNAM).

Chapter 31

Meteor Showers before the Flood

The crater in Iraq which was discovered on an aerial photograph was caused by a meteor shower c. 2,000 B.C. or earlier. Around 2,345 B.C. a sudden decline occurred in the cultures of the world. According to the traditional understanding of the chronology of the Bible, the Flood took place in 2,349 B.C. (See the chapter about new chronology later in the book.)

The *Sunday Telegraph* in London printed a notable story on November 4, 2001.[1]

The article related that Dr. Sharad Master, a geologist at the University of Witwatersrand, Johannesburg, South Africa, had satellite photographs of an enormous crater measuring over 2 miles in diameter in southern Iraq.

He discovered this by accident when reading an article about Saddam Hussein's canals and saw a picture showing different formations – one of which was very circular. Studies of old satellite photos from the 1980's show that the depression previously held a small lake. But Saddam drained it in his campaign against the Marsh Arab Area, causing an elevated ring-shape, typical of craters, to become visible in the dried-out lake.

Some scientists have suggested that this crater was formed when a meteor destructively hit the earth about 4,000 years ago. The power of this meteor's collision with the Earth was equivalent to the power of hundreds of atom bombs put together. The crater is in the Al 'Amarah region, about 10 miles northwest of where the Tigris and Euphrates flow together into a delta.

The strike may have caused destructive fires and floods. Therefore, we must ask: Is this when the Flood started, or was it in connection with this event that the Tower of Babel came crashing down further north where fire and brimstone rained from the heavens causing the people to spread in every direction?

Here the First Civilizations Fall

The Sunday Telegraph states that this could possibly explain why many earlier cultures seemed to have disappeared around 2,300 BC. This is true of the Akkad culture of central Iraq (Babylonia) with its mysterious ruler, Sargon (was this the Bible's Nimrod?); it is also true concerning the sudden end of the 5th dynasty of the ancient Egyptian kingdom after having built the great pyramids as well as the sudden disappearance of hundreds of contemporary settlements in what is today modern Israel. Until now, archeologists have explained the fall of these early civilizations with such things as war or climatic change, while astronomers have suggested a meteor impact as being the possible cause.

Whatever the case, the crater is relatively new.

"The sediments in this region are very young, geologically speaking, so whatever caused this crater-like structure must have happened within the last

6,000 years," says Dr. Master, who has described his findings in the November 2001 issue of *Meteoritics & Planetary Science.* His discoveries have also been cited in other journals. Dr. Master is part of a scientific group, Impact Cratering Research Group, which researches craters caused by meteors from outer space.

Dr. Benny Peiser, who teaches on impact craters at John Moores University, Liverpool, England, calls the crater one of the most meaningful discoveries from this period which confirms his own and others' research in this area. He also mentions that a crater found in Argentina dates back to this same period, which suggests that the earth was hit by a shower of massive meteors at that time.

The discovery of this crater also casts new light on the legend of Gilgamesh, which talks about the "Seven Judges of Hell" who lifted their torches setting fire to the countryside and bringing about a storm that turned day into night and created a mighty flood.[2] (See the Gilgamesh chapter)

This epic poem normally dates back to around 3,000 BC.

Another source from the period in question is called *Akkad's curse* which speaks of flaming potsherds raining from the heavens.

Such Large Meteors Would Release a Flood

Shortly before the time of Christ, the Jewish astronomer, Rabi bar Nachmani, wrote in the so-called "Babylonian Talmud" that the Flood in the days of Noah was caused by two "stars" falling from the sky. "When the Holy One . . . wanted to bring a flood upon the world, He took two stars from *Khima* and brought a flood upon the world."[3]

Was he really referring to two great meteors that were known of in the Middle East, one of which being the meteor in question falling in Iraq?

Bill Napier, an astronomer at Armagh Observatory believes there was a meteor shower. He told *Science* Tuesday[4] that a comet named Encke, which was discovered in 1786, is the remnant of a larger comet that broke into thousands of pieces about 5,000 years ago spreading throughout the universe and possibly hitting the earth in the early Bronze Age where a cloud of meteor debris could have darkened the sun. Napier connects these events with a cooling of the climate, which is measured in tree rings over the period 2,354-2,345 BC.

According to Benny Peiser from Liverpool John Moores University, a dozen or so large impact craters have been found, and due to the Earth consisting of more sea than land, we can only expect that there are more than twice as many enormous meteor impacts in the ocean.

This would have caused great tidal waves, Tsunamis, of greater consequence than meteors hitting the land.

Do the Years Fit?

Once again, we see that the Biblical accounts and other "myths" such as

Gilgamesh are not merely carefully crafted stories as often claimed, but can very well refer to factual events. If we were to add up the genealogies from the Flood to the time of Christ, as Irish Archbishop and astronomer James Ussher did in1650, the equation dates the Flood to 2,349 BC.

Of course, these accounts should be taken with a grain of salt, because some generations may have been left out, and my personal opinion is that the Flood dates further back in time to around 3,500 BC. The reason this date doesn't fully agree with Ussher's calculations is due to a fault in the Hebrew (so-called Masoretic) translation and of an omission of "evil years." (See Barry Setterfield's chronology, www.setterfield.org/scriptchron.htm)

If the meteor showers must fit with the *Gilgamesh Epic*, then the meteor showers must have taken place before 3,000 BC – provided that the dating of Gilgamesh is correct.

Some scientists set the Flood around 4,950 years ago based on Carbon-14 dating.[5] From that periord of time, there was a large rise in the number of dead humans and animals found. Actually, there suddenly are over double the number of such examples at this time than from earlier periods, and oppositely, there is only 1/8 as many found in the five years following. This could suggest that the population was drastically minimized precisely 3,000 years before the time of Christ.

If this was caused by the Flood, then it happened about 5,000 years ago. And the meteor impact in Southern Iraq may have been connected with the nearby Tower of Babel. This could reasonably have happened around 600 years later, and if the people spread out after that point in time, then it would also lead to a temporary decline in the Babylonian civilization, as well as, other contemporary civilizations.

Whether the meteor impact in Iraq was connected with the Flood or the Tower, it remains absolutely certain that a meteor strike of such caliber didn't

Barringer Meteor Crater in Arizona is 3,900 ft.wide and 650 ft. deep. It is estimated to be 50,000 years old, but as is common knowledge, dating over a few thousand years is based upon theories that have not been proven. The diameter of the crater in Iraq is more than double this size – i.e. approx. 10,000 ft.

happen quietly! And it will be exciting to follow the story as scientists finally set a date as to when the meteor struck. This can be done by measuring radioactivity in any melted rocks or glass that would have been caused by the heat of such a collision. But those things have yet to be found.

Velikovsky Said It...

Russian-American scientist, Immanuel Velikovsky, postulated a theory that the earth was hit by a number of catastrophes following a meteor and the influence of other planets whose orbits had come too close to the earth. His theories were very popular during the decades just after World War II, but he was considered a heretic in the scientific community, which held on to Lyell's dogma that the earth has evolved at an immensely slow tempo (the theory of uniformity) without major changes (catastrophes).

Today, observations from space have confirmed some of Velikovsky's theories, and the discovery in Iraq might be just one more example.

In his books, Velikovsky dishes up hundreds of examples from nature that demonstrate the fact that at least one violent and worldwide catastrophe took place in the beginning of historical time.

Is the Comet Theory as Old as the Flood Itself?

Even before Velikovsky, astronomers and others throughout history have had similar thoughts. The best known is Englishman William Whiston, who in 1696 published the book *New Theory of the Earth*. In an appendix[6] to the book, he referred to Halley 's Comet, which had appeared in the sky just a few years prior in 1682 and had caused a lot of interest in astronomy. (It was Edmund Halley who received the honor for his theory that the comet returned every 70 years, but the same observation had already been made in the 2nd century by a Jewish astronomer.[7])

Whiston believed that the comet returned at an interval of 575 ½ years and had been here in 2,346 BC where it caused a massive flood. Whiston also found ancient sources that spoke of a year that only lasted 360 days around 700 BC.

Before Whiston, David Herlicius in 1619 had published a document about a comet that had shown itself in 1618. He cited Cicero that misfortune always followed comets and believed, as did his predecessors Abraham Rockenbach (16th cent.), Seth Calvisius (1556-1615), Henricus Ecstormius, Christopher Helvicus (1581-1617), and David Herlicius (1557-1636), that a comet had caused the Flood in the year 2,292 BC.

Abraham Rockenbach, almost as a matter of fact, relates that in the year 1656 after the creation of the world, three days before the death of Methuselah, "a comet appeared in the constellation Pisces and was seen by the entire world as it traversed the twelve signs of the zodiac in the space of a month; on the sixteenth of April, it again disappeared. After this the Deluge immediately followed..." [8] However, he doesn't quote any direct sources. He could have gotten his information from Rabbi Isaac ben Solomon (Rashi), the great Jewish expert of astronomical phenomena who lived in the South of France in the Middle Ages – the 11th century to be precise. His commentary on the Bible and the Talmud is still considered the authority among rabbis.

Khima?

Rabbi Rashi had commented on the stars written of in what is most likely the oldest book in the Bible, Job in both chapter 9, verse9[9] and in chapter 38, vers 31[10], as well as in the book of Amos 5:8[11]. The stars are called Aish, Kesil, and Khima in Hebrew. In English they are translated as Arcturus, Orion, and Pleiades.

He called *Khima*, translated as Pleiades (the seven sisters), "a star with a tail" – a comet. In the Jewish explanation, the Talmud, *Khima* is connected with the Flood.

Velikovsky demonstrates that translators of different ages have chosen different stars, and by comparing it with other quotes from the Talmud, he finds that this Khima must be Saturn. Therefore, Job 38:31 should actually read: "Canst thou bind the bonds of Saturn and loosen the reins of Mars?" And that makes sense because the "bonds" of Saturn can still be seen today with a telescope. There are, of course, rings around the planet. And Mar's "reins" are the two small moons in its orbit. They were already known of in Homer's time.

'Two Meteors from Saturn Caused the Deluge'

So what the Jewish rabbi in the 2nd century before Christ is saying is probably that "two meteors broke away from the planet Saturn and caused the Deluge." In ancient times Saturn was actually connected with water and catastrophes. The Chaldean astronomer Berosus tells in his account of the Flood that Saturn (Kronos in Greek) warns King Xisuthros (Noah) that a universal flood would begin on the 15th day in the month of Dasios.

Saturn was the most important star to the great civilizations of the past. Actually, Saturn was worshipped in the Chaldean, Greek, and Egyptian

A few miles from Mt. Ararat just before you cross the Turkish-Iranian border, there is a crater of a more recent date from the last century. It measures c. 80 ft. in diameter and on the inside you can see how the meteor has forced its way down through earth and stone.

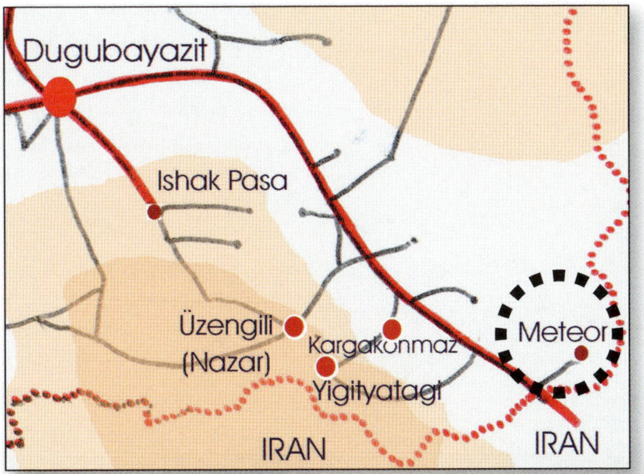

religions. In the Chaldean, Saturn was called the star of the god Tammuz, while the Greeks revered it as their greatest god, Kronos, later removed from the throne by Zeus (Jupiter). Likewise, in Egypt, Saturn was the strongest of the gods named *Osiris* who was the brother and husband of Isis (Jupiter). In India, Saturn was connected with Brahma and Siva with Jupiter. The same religious ideas ran throughout all of these early civilizations, and according to the Bible, the reason is that all people originally spread from Babel in Iraq to the various corners of the earth.

Whether you believe in the Tower of Babel or not, the evidence points to a common start. The story of the Tower of Babel can also be found in the most unexpected places and cultures long before the influence of missionaries or other biblically knowledgeable people was possible. Just like Noah's Ark, this is apparently a common heritage from the beginning of mankind.

But let us conclude this chapter by stating we have both historical sources and modern observations suggesting that two "stars" (meteors) fell to the earth just 4,000-5,000 years ago, bringing about a monstrous flood.

Endnotes

1 Robert Matthews, "Meteor Clue to End of Middle East Civilisations," Daily Telegraph, London, November 8, 2001.

2 ...and the seven judges of hell ... raised their torches, lighting the land with their livid flame. A stupor of despair went up to heaven when the god of the storm turned daylight into darkness, when he smashed the land like a cup." – An account of the Deluge from the Epic of Gilgamesh, circa 2200 BC.

3 Tractate Brakhot (Seder Zerafim) chapter IX, Fol. 59a, transl. by Maurice Simon, ed. by I. Epstein (London, 1948): "When the Holy One . . . wanted to bring a flood upon the world, He took two stars from Khima and brought a flood upon the world."

4 Science.com, November 13, 2001.

5 Whitelaw, "Time, Life, and History in the Light of 15,000 Radiocarbon Dates", Creation Resource Society Quarterly, 1970, 7,56-71,83.
"The Biblical Record of Creation, Flood, and History in Light of 30,0000 Radiocarbon Dates," 1979, 15th Anniversary Convention of the Bible Science Association, 197-202.

6 "The Cause of the Deluge De-monstrated" (Appendix to the 2nd edition of the New Theory of the Earth)" (London, 1708).

Is this what happened? One or several meteors hitting the Earth knocked a hole in the Earth's crust, thus catalyzing the greatest catastrophe the Earth has ever seen?

7 Rabbi Joshua: "There is a star which appears every 70 years and misleads the captains of boats." (Perhaps a reference to Halleys komet.) W. M. Feldman, Rabbini-cal Mathematics and Astronomy (New York, 1931), 11, 216.

8 "In the year of the creation of the world 1656, after Noah had attained the age of 600 years, three days before the death of Methusalem, a comet appeared in the constellation Pisces, was seen by the entire world as it traversed the twelve signs of the zodiac in the space of a month; on the sixteenth of April it again disappeared. After this the Deluge immediately followed, in which all creatures which live on earth and creep on the ground were drowned, with the exception of Noah and the rest of the creatures that had gone with him into the ark. About these things is written in Genesis, chapter 7." Velikovsky, *In The Beginning*.

9 "He is the Maker of the Bear and Orion, the Pleiades and the constellations of the south." Job 9:9.

10 "Can you bind the beautiful Pleiades? Can you loose the cords of Orion?" (Job 38:31)

11 "He who made the Pleiades and Orion, who turns blackness into dawn and darkens day into night, who calls for the waters of the sea and pours them out over the face of the land- the LORD is his name." (Amos 5:8)

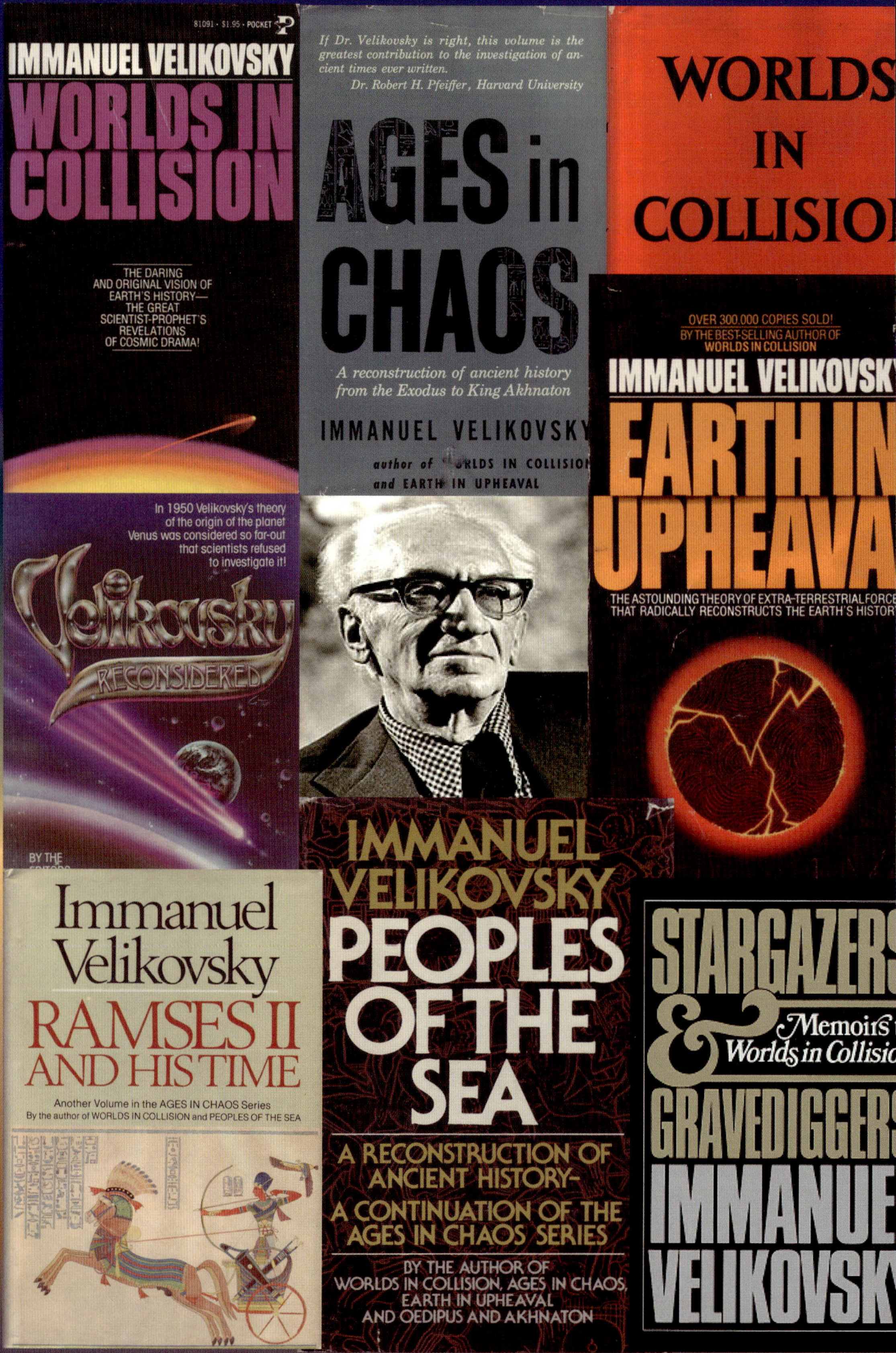
81091 · $1.95 · POCKET
IMMANUEL VELIKOVSKY
WORLDS IN COLLISION
THE DARING AND ORIGINAL VISION OF EARTH'S HISTORY— THE GREAT SCIENTIST-PROPHET'S REVELATIONS OF COSMIC DRAMA!
If Dr. Velikovsky is right, this volume is the greatest contribution to the investigation of ancient times ever written.
Dr. Robert H. Pfeiffer, Harvard University
AGES in CHAOS
A reconstruction of ancient history from the Exodus to King Akhnaton
IMMANUEL VELIKOVSKY
WORLDS
IN
COLLISIO
OVER 300,000 COPIES SOLD!
BY THE BEST-SELLING AUTHOR OF WORLDS IN COLLISION
IMMANUEL VELIKOVSK
EARTH IN
UPHEAVA
THE ASTOUNDING THEORY OF EXTRA-TERRESTRIAL FORCE
THAT RADICALLY RECONSTRUCTS THE EARTH'S HISTOR
In 1950 Velikovsky's theory of the origin of the planet Venus was considered so far-out that scientists refused to investigate it!
Velikovsky
RECONSIDERED
Immanuel Velikovsky
RAMSES II AND HIS TIME
Another Volume in the AGES IN CHAOS Series
By the author of WORLDS IN COLLISION and PEOPLES OF THE SEA
IMMANUEL VELIKOVSKY
PEOPLES OF THE SEA
A RECONSTRUCTION OF ANCIENT HISTORY-
A CONTINUATION OF THE AGES IN CHAOS SERIES
BY THE AUTHOR OF WORLDS IN COLLISION, AGES IN CHAOS, EARTH IN UPHEAVAL AND OEDIPUS AND AKHNATON
STARGAZER
&
Memoirs
Worlds in Collisio
GRAVEDIGGER
IMMANUE
VELIKOVSK

Chapter 32

Velikovsky's Theories

Russian-American scientist Immanuel Velikovsky (b. 1895 in Vitebsk, Russia, d. 1979 in New York, New York) reported in his books[1] innumerable examples of archeological findings and geologically notable facts suggesting that the earth has experienced mighty catastrophes in the historical past.

Genius Albert Einstein found the manuscript of Velikovsky's book *Worlds in Collision* very interesting, but despite his interest, it was difficult for Velikovsky to find a publisher willing to print his first book because its contents posed serious questions to established science. MacMillan, the publishing house that accepted the book, was pressured by the scientific community to release it under a subsidiary publisher called Doubleday, which ended up causing the book to become the year's best seller.

Encouraged by the success, the publisher printed the first part of *Ages in Chaos* in 1952, which was Velikovsky's reconstruction of the historical events from 1450-840 BC. The continuation that was to cover successive years up to 33 BC grew into two large books *Ramses II and His Time* and *Peoples of the Sea*.

After these books came *Earth in Upheaval* in 1955, which is the most relevant book for us in connection with the Flood due to page after page of geological and paleontological evidence suggesting the veracity of the Flood. The book questions the established theories of geology that say everything we see has changed over millions of years of uniform evolution – with no dramatic disasters such as the Flood. Velikovsky was convinced that multiple cataclysms have taken place in the historical past.

After his book *Oedipus and Akhnathon* was released in 1960, Velikovsky started a manuscript that was never published. It was written about what he saw as the "common memory lapse" our culture suffers from due to our trying – seen from a Freudian point of view – to suppress the knowledge of the past.

An Exciting Heretic

An independent thinker is required to challenge established science on many levels, and Velikovsky was so independent he was unwanted at

Immanuel Velikovsky published a number of scientific books in the 50s and 60s, presenting a different view of the past from the conventional. Despite the complex nature of the substance, the books became bestsellers and were read diligently, as evidenced by these worn jackets.

Who Was He?

As a child in Russia, Immanuel Velikovsky spoke multiple languages and was exceptionally gifted in Russian and mathematics as seen by his grades at Medvednikov College in Moscow where he was given a gold medal in 1913. He then traveled to Europe as well as the Middle East. For a period he studied medicine in Montpelier, France, and studied pre-med at the University of Edinburgh in Scotland. Just before World War I he made it back to Russia where he finished his medicinal studies in 1921 at the University of Moscow.

Therafter he journeyed to Berlin where he edited the journal Scripta Universitatis, which employed Albert Einstein as the editor of the mathematics and physics section. He married violinist Elisheva Kramer and lived in what was then Palestine for 15 years where he practiced medicine and researched the newest findings of the time, Freud's psychoanalysis, and wrote articles for Freud's journal *Imago*.

In 1930 he published a thesis that introduced pathological encephalograms (x-rays of the brain) to detect epilepsy, now routine practice in the diagnosis of this sickness.

(cont.)

(Who Was He?)
In 1939, just a few weeks before the start of World War II, Velikovsky took his family and traveled to New York. While the world was at war, he researched Freud's Oedipus theories and later published a book *Oedipus and Akhnathon*, in which he argues that Akhnathon was the legendary Oedipus.

It was here in April of 1940 that he worked with his first ingenious idea about disasters. He was first taken by the references in Jewish history. There was also an Egyptian story of the plagues in the almost unknown Ipuwer-papyrus housed in Leiden, The Netherlands. In this document an Egyptian wise man, Ipuwer, grouches about an event that caused the so-called Middle Kingdom to fall.

Velikovsky was convinced that Ipuwer was referring to the same situation as the Bible. Based on this, he synchronized Egyptian and Israeli history in his book, *Ages in Chaos.*

After ten years of research in the US, *Worlds in Collision* as well as the other books supporting the theories of catastrophes based on astronomical happenings was published.

universities for a number of years. But after some of his theories seemed to be confirmed by the first vessels sent to Venus, Mars, and Jupiter, he was asked to give visiting lectures for large groups at so many universities that he could not honor all of the invitations. In 1972 the Canadian Broadcasting Corporation, CBC, aired a one-hour special about Velikovsky and his research, and the BBC (British Broadcasting Corporation) followed their lead in 1973. Again, he found acceptance. He encouraged and mentored younger scientists following up on his theories until his death in 1979.

Creation scientists that believe in some type of creation have demonstrated a lack of logic in the ruling Theory of Evolution both before and after Velikovsky. One must wonder why their arguments have been ignored; however, the explanation is simple; their "proofs" were thought to be based on religious motives. What is refreshing about Velikovsky is that he cannot be suspected of being on a religious mission. He was an atheist, a Freudian, and believed in a type of evolution – not over millions of years, but an adaptation over a short period of time, which has partially been confirmed.[22]

Even so, Velikovsky considered the ancient myths and stories – especially those from the Bible – as trustworthy and took them as a sign that some type of catastrophe really did happen in the historical past. He claims that the last astronomic calamity took place about 1500-700 BC, and his theory is an attempt to give a non-religious explanation for phenomena such as the crossing of the Red Sea and Joshua's "long day" where "the sun stood still" and "waited almost an entire day."[33] For example, he points out that before "the long day" there was a destructive rain, which Velikovsky understood to be a meteor shower. "As they fled before Israel, while they were going down the slope of Beth-horon, the Lord threw down huge stones from heaven on them as far as Azekah, and they died; there were more who died because of the hailstones than the Israelites killed with the sword." (Joshua 10:11)

When God Is Not *Allowed* to Exist...

From the 50's to the 70's when Velikovsky's works were first released, there was little understanding within the scientific world of other dimensions of reality than the purely material. Therefore, all things had to be explained based on the rules of positivistic science for time, space, and location – that is, things exist only if we can prove them based on what we already know.

Today, where there is more acceptance of supernatural phenomena, it is almost funny to think that rather than accepting the existence of a supernatural power (God), people would rather accept Velikovsky's almost free-floating astronomical explanations of Biblical events. For example, Velikovsky claims that the ten plagues in Egypt and the division of he Red Sea happened due to Jupiter releasing Venus as a massive super comet that nicked the Earth about 1500 BC. The 10 plagues spoken of in Exodus supposedly took place either directly or indirectly as a result of this encounter. Dust from the comet colored the water of the Nile blood red; the vermin that ravaged

Egypt came from the comet; flies and possibly scarabs fell out of the comet, while the heat the comet brought caused the native frogs to develop with haste; and the earthquakes caused by the comet demolished the lodgings of the Egyptians, but not those of the Hebrews.

"The only thing that doesn't seem to fall from the comet is cholesterol levels to harden Pharaoh's heart," Dr. Carl Sagan sarcastically observes in a review.

"All of this apparently falls from the comet's coma because at the exact moment Moses extends his staff over the Red Sea, it parts – either due to tidal changes caused by the gravitational force of the comet, or due to electrical or magnetic interplay between the comet and the Red Sea which is not discussed any closer. When the Hebrews reach safety on the other bank, the comet had obviously distanced itself so much that the parted Red Sea comes gushing back to drown Pharaoh's army," writes Sagan.[4]

What Sagan disregards is that a person using the same argumentation could argue against what is statistically seen is even more unlikely – a big bang leading to an immeasurably complex and magnificent swarm of species with complicated cell structures and DNA profiles that exist on our planet while all other planets seem to be lifeless. No explosion has ever caused life, nevertheless it is considered to be good Latin in our day to believe the Big Bang Theory.

When the supernatural and God are not *allowed* to exist and facts prove that something supernatural has apparently occurred, the explanations brought forth with toil based on a limited understanding are quite incredible.

But Still, He Was Right...

Even though Velikovsky's theories were at times speculative and doubtful, he did manage to have his focus set on two important areas:

1) We can't just write off old "myths" based on our present, limited understanding, but we need to examine these myths for their historical content with a greater respect for what they are actually saying.

2) He called attention to the massive amount of evidence suggesting that worldwide catastrophes have taken place throughout our history, as the ancient myths almost with one voice are saying to us.

It would take too long to delve into all of these impressive facts that suggest disasters, but at the end of his book *Earth in Upheaval*,[5] he summarizes all these facts in condensed form. They give an impression of how extensive the evidence is that points to catastrophic upheavals.[66]

Evidence Everywhere

"Wherever we investigate the geological and paleontological records of this Earth, we find signs of catastrophes and upheavals, old and recent. Mountains sprang from plains, and other mountains were leveled; strata of the terrestrial crust were folded and pressed together and overturned and moved and put on top of other formations; igneous rock melted and flooded enormous areas of land with miles-thick sheets; the ocean bed flowed with molten rock; ashes showered down and built layers many yards thick on the ground and on the bottom of the oceans in their vast expanse; shores of ancient lakes were tilted and are no longer horizontal; seacoasts show subsidence or emergence, in some places over one thousand feet," writes Velikovsky.

Remains From the Flood?

Velikovsky continues and describes the "graveyard" of geological layers after a mighty disaster. It is difficult not to think of the Flood and it's enormous upheavals.

"Rocks of the earth are filled with remains of life extinguished in a state of agony; sedimentary rocks are one vast graveyard, and the granite and basalt, too, have embedded in them numberless living organisms; and shells have closed valves as they do in a living state, so unexpectedly came the entombment; and vast forests were burned and washed away and covered with the waters of the seas and with sand and turned to coal; and animals were swept to the far north and thrown into heaps and were soaked by bituminous outpourings; and broken bones and torn ligaments and the skins of animals of living and extinct species were smashed together with splintered forests into huge piles; and whales were cast out of the oceans onto mountains.

"Rocks from disintegrating mountain ridges were carried over vast stretches of land, from Norway to the Carpathians, and into the Harz Mountains, and into Scotland, and from Mount Blanc to the Juras, and from Labrador to the Poconos; and the Rocky Mountains moved many leagues from their place, and the Alps traveled a hundred miles northward, and the Himalayas and the Andes climbed ever higher; and the mountain lakes emptied themselves over barriers, and continents were torn by rifts, and the sea bottom by canyons; and land disappeared under the sea, and the sea pushed new islands from its bottom, and sea beds were turned into high mountains bearing sea shells, and shoals of fish were poisoned and boiled in the seas, and numberless rivers lost their channels, were dammed by lava and turned upstream, and the climate suddenly changed; tillable land and meadows turned into vast deserts.

"Reindeer from Lapland and polar fox and arctic bears from the snowy tundras and rhinoceroses and hippopotami from the African jungles, and lions from the desert and ostriches, and seals, were thrown into piles and covered with gravel, clay, and tuff, and the fissures of multitudes of rocks are filled with broken bones; regions where the palm grew were moved into the Arctic, and oceans steamed, and the evaporated seas condensed under clouds of dust and built mountainous covers of ice over great stretches of continents, and the ice melted on heated ground and cast icebergs into the oceans in enormous fleets; and all volcanoes erupted.

"All human dwellings were shattered and burned, and animals tame and fierce and human beings with them ran for refuge to mountain caves, and mountains swallowed and entombed those that reached the refuge, and many species and genera and families of the animal kingdom were annihilated down to the very last one; and the earth and the sea and the sky again united their elements in one great work of destruction."

It Happened in the Recent Past

"Following the trail of geology, we were led by the merciless logic of facts and figures to the conclusion that the earth was more than once a stage on which acts of a great drama took place, and no place on earth was free of its effects," Velikovsky concludes.

"In the face of the evidence we were also compelled to concede that the most recent paroxysms of nature happened in historical times, only a few thousand years ago, when in some parts of the world civilization was already entering the Iron Age, but in other parts still lingering in the Neolithic or even, in the Paleolithic, or rude Stone Age.

"The laminations of lakes, the salt content of those without outflow, the retreat of waterfalls, the elevation of mountains, pollen analysis, and archaeological finds, as well as the recent drop of the ocean level, all show how close to our time the more recent paroxysms of nature must have occurred."

Changes in the Earth's Axis

Velikovsky continues, "The evidence is also overwhelming that the great global catastrophes were either accompanied or caused by shifting of the terrestrial axis or by a disturbance in the diurnal and annual motions of the earth. The shifting of the axis could not have been brought about by internal causes, as the proponents of the Ice Age theory in the nineteenth century assumed it was; it must have occurred, and repeatedly, under the impact of external forces. The state of lavas with reversed magnetization, hundreds of times more intensive than the inverted terrestrial magnetic field could impart, reveals the nature of the forces that were in action.

"Thus from the geological evidence we came to the conclusion to which we had also arrived traveling the road of the historical and literary traditions of the peoples of the world – that the earth repeatedly went through cataclysmic events on a global scale, that the cause of these events was an extraterrestrial agent, and that some of these cosmic catastrophes took place only a few thousand years ago, in historical times.

"Many world-wide phenomena, for each of which the cause is vainly sought, are explained by a single cause e.g.the sudden changes of climate, transgression of the sea, vast volcanic and seismic activities, formation of ice cover, pluvial crises, emergence of mountains and their dislocation, rising and subsidence of coasts, tilting of lakes, sedimentation, fossilization, the provenience of tropical animals and plants in polar regions, conglomerates of fossils of animals of various latitudes and habitats, the extinction of species and genera, the appearance of new species, the reversal of the earth's magnetic field, and a score of other world-wide phenomena."

Velikovsky sees all of these signs as the result of astronomical phenomena which have affected the earth. This view is arguable. Those that believe in God would say it was God that did it. Other than that, the two explanations don't exclude each other. If it was God who stood behind these events, He could easily have used astronomical mechanisms.

All of the evidence Velikovsky has compiled concerning a worldwide disaster should speak unequivocally to anyone and everyone that a Flood really did take place.

Endnotes

1 Dr. **Immanuel Velikovsky** wrote *Worlds in Collision*, *Earth in Upheaval*, *Ages in Chaos*, *Peoples of the Sea*, *Ramses II and His Times*, *Mankind in Amnesia*, *Stargazers*, and *Gravediggers*. He wrote other works as well, and many of his books can be found on the Internet. Specifically note www.varchive.org/itb/index.htm

2 For example, certain birds have been known to change feather color under varying environmental circumstances. And this is not over a period of millions of years, but rather only a few hundred.

3 Joshua 10:13-14: "And the sun stood still, and the moon stopped, until the nation took vengeance on their enemies. Is this not written in the Book of Jashar? The sun stopped in midheaven, and did not hurry to set for about a whole day. There has been no day like it before or since, when the Lord heeded a human voice; for the Lord fought for Israel."

4 An analysis of *Cosmic Collisions* by Dr. Carl Sagan, Cornell University. Translated from a quote in Danish on www.skeptica.dk

5 Immanuel Velikovsky, *Earth in Upheaval,* (Doubleday and Company Inc., 1995).

6 Velikovsky's work is written in a stream-of-consciousness style. He uses almost nothing but commas to give the reader a chance to breathe. Therefore, some of the sentences have been changed so they are more readable.

Chapter 33

From Where Did the Water Come?

Even if it now seems that the remains of the Ark of Noah have been found on Mount Ararat, many open questions obviously remain without any immediate explanation. How could the Ark contain all the animals? Did Noah catch them, or did they come, drawn by instinct, sensing oncoming disaster? Was there only one pair of each species? Etc.

A Feasibility Study

As a matter of fact, many intelligent people have methodically investigated these issues. For example, John Woodmorappe[1], a reputable geologist, has described all the conceivable "impossibilities" in his book *Noah's Ark: A Feasibility Study*, published in 1999.[2] The results of his and other's studies can also be found on several websites[3].

It is very interesting reading, and we might want to examine many of these calculations more thoroughly. However, when one gets into details, you can easily lose track of the bigger picture, and it is not the purpose of this book to "prove" that every detail of the biblical account of Noah is correct or possible. We want to stick to the big picture and leave it to others to deal with the details.

For me, the big picture seems to indicate that some thousand years ago a very extensive water catastrophe actually happened on the earth. Whether it was 4,000-5,000 years ago or more is not the most important thing. And whether the catastrophe only included parts of the earth or whether it was global is also up for discussion. But obviously there are signs all over the earth indicating that this catastrophe really happened, and if these really are the remains of Noah's Ark we've found at a height of some 14,000 ft., then we are dealing with more than local flooding around the Euphrates or the Black Sea. Irrespective of details, however, the big question to be considered more closely is: Where did the water come from?

From Both Above – and Below

In popular versions it just started to rain and rain, but Moses is more specific in his account.

We are told that "...in the second month, on the seventeenth day of the month, on the same day *all the fountains of the great deep burst open*, and *the floodgates of the sky were opened.* The rain fell upon the earth for forty days and forty nights." (Genesis 7:11-12)

As we are told, it didn't just rain – water also came from "fountains of the great deep." As a matter of fact, these fountains, or springs are mentioned before "floodgates of the sky" indicating, possibly, that they at least are of no less importance. The Hebrew word for fountain is Mayan. It means fountain,

John Wood Rappe has tried to calculate on the "impossibilities" in his book Noah's Ark - A Feasibility Study.

well, and spring. It could also be referring to the seas as the expression "the great deep" is used elsewhere in the Hebrew text about the seas. Therefore, it is quite plausible that huge amounts of water were put into motion, thus creating floods. Like the way we experienced the vast tsunami that killed 250,000 people on the 26th of August 2004. We just have to multiply that by 10 or 100 to imagine the results of a giant meteor crashing into the ocean.[4]

One could therefore imagine that it was the ocean's vast quantities of water that came in motion and caused flooding. Such as we saw with the powerful tsunami that killed 231,000 people, December 26, 2004. Only we have to multiply by 10 or 100, if the reason was a huge meteor...

The abyss or "the great deep" may also be referring to subterranean sources.[5] When the text says that these fountains were "breaking through" or "breaking up," some people believe this to be referring to the theory that large water reservoirs once existed below the surface of the earth. (In the story of Creation, we are told that the waters gathered in one place).

As a matter of fact, there is evidence of such hidden reservoirs below the surface. It is interesting to note that due to underground pressure up to 70 percent or more of that which comes out of a volcano during an eruption is water, often in the form of steam.

40 Days of Rain

Most of the professional researchers investigating whether the world was actually deluged or not believe that if this was the case, the water must have come from below and that the rain was caused by the bad weather following the dramatic upheaval.

In Genesis 7:11-12 Moses writes, "and the floodgates of the sky were opened. The rain fell upon the earth for forty days and forty nights." If the earth had been struck by a catastrophe, maybe caused by a meteoric impact or movements of other planets, this could easily lead to storms and rainfall for 40 days. But normally rain comes from vapor rising from the earth – condensation. Therefore, some scientists believe that the rain mentioned was some kind of extraordinary rain. And as a matter of fact, there is a rather interesting detail in Moses' Creation account that certainly stirs the imagination.

The Firmament Above

We are told in Genesis 1:6-8 that on the second day of creation God said, "Let there be an expanse in the midst of the waters, and let it separate the waters from the waters. God made the expanse, and separated the waters which were below the expanse from the waters which were above the expanse; and it was so. God called the expanse sky."

The account continues telling how the waters below the firmament, or the expanse, gathered in one place making the dry land appear.

The word "firmament" is the same as the Hebrew word *raqiya* meaning expanse. Later, we are told that the birds fly in this expanse implying that the expanse is the atmosphere.

The question is whether the waters *above* this firmament was simply a poetic way of telling us *the sky is as blue as the sea* or maybe a bit more technical indicating the fact that the atmosphere contains water – or was there really *a blanket of vapor and mist*?

Like Saturn still has rings of gas around it, as seen from the diagram above, the earth could have been surrounded by rings before the Flood catastrophe, and thus shielded the population from the cosmic radiation, which makes us age.

Primitive Men or Men of Genius?

Modern theologians seem to regard the words about "the expanse above" as primitive people's poetic description of the blue sky. But much seems to indicate that pre-historic people were not primitive at all and that they had greater knowledge in many fields than later generations – especially people living before the Flood, who allegedly grew extremely old.

Instead of considering the Bible and descriptions left behind from various cultures as primitive, we will attempt to look at them as indications of facts – although they are often surrounded by fairytale stories.

An example of this could be the "underworld" in the Greek myths which is looked upon as pure superstition; it may, however, be considered a remnant of times when prehistoric people in rush boats set out on journeys around the world exploring the "underworld" – down under as the Australians say – "where the sun shines at night and the moon during the day." (This was also true of the Americas (Atlantis?) where the Sumerians and Phoenicians possibly found their copper 3,000-4,000 years ago.)

So let's not underestimate the civilizations of prehistory.

Warmth and Coldness Blanketing the Earth

But is it at all possible that there could have been a blanket of water vapor surrounding the earth? Yes, it is possible. As we know, Saturn has rings around it and similar rings might have been around the earth.

The fact is the Earth has different layers in its atmosphere[6] being respectively very hot and very cold. Therefore, these layers may have stored both ice and vapor.

The troposphere being closest to the earth (0-10 km) gets between 10-15 degrees colder than the earth's surface temperature for each kilometer we move away from it. At a height of 45 miles (in the mesosphere) the temperature gets as low as 65 below (-54 C). But then it turns around.

The outermost layers of the thermosphere (beginning approximately 100 km or 62 miles out) are drastically heated up by UV and other rays from the sun. Around 1,000 km (621 miles) from the earth the temperature reaches as much as 1,300 degrees! That is why space rockets have to be equipped with a heat shield when moving through the thermosphere.

The higher the temperature, the more vapor can be stored in the layers.

The Water Vapor Canopy

Dr. Joseph Dillow[7] has done extensive research on the idea of such a water vapor canopy. The theory developed by Dillow was later modified by Dr. Larry Vardiman who believed that much of the waters engulfing the world at the time of the Flood could have been stored in small ice particles distributed in equatorial rings around the earth similar to those around Saturn.[8]

This water vapor canopy could have collapsed, falling as rain. Or volcanic eruptions associated with the breaking up of the fountains of the great deep could have thrown dust into the water vapor canopy causing the vapor to nucleate on the dust particles thus forming rain.

The canopy, however, couldn't have been too thick as this would have caused the earth's surface to be intolerably hot. And actually, researchers at Texas A&M University have demonstrated that the atmospheric pressure at sea level was once twice as much as it presently is (760 mm).[9]

Vardiman and Rush concluded that a maximum of 2 meters (6.5 ft.) of rain could be held in such a vapor canopy.[10] Even though it is quite a lot of rain, it is not enough to cover the earth completely including the mountains. Therefore, most creation scientists believe that the major source of the Flood waters did not come from above, but from the fountains and springs of the earth by the lifting up or tearing apart of the tectonic plates causing a series of volcanic eruptions.

You can almost imagine the massive amounts of water from the ocean being thrown up into the air like boiling water from mighty geysers, just to fall to the ground again over a period of 40 days. Maybe we will even one day hear of an "inner ocean" in the depths of the earth because evidence is mounting that there is still a huge amount of water stored deep in the earth in crystal lattices of minerals due to the immense pressure.[11]

The Ocean Floor Rose

A group of scientists[12] with geophysicist John Baumgardner in the lead has been working with the possibility that the earth's tectonic plates have at one point been lifted causing great amounts of seawater to be washed over the continents. The "starting point" for this theory is that the sea floor is very "young" geologically speaking. They even think that it was formed after the Flood.

The model is as follows: a piece of the earth's originally hard mantle is released under the sea. Part of the floor starts to sink into the warmer, softer parts of the mantle. Fiery heat follows, especially around the edges, which soften and sink in a wild, accelerating tempo. This causes the plates to move even more and rips a nearly 6,000-mile-long crevice in the earth's mantle. Through the crack, new hot material floods out of the inner earth to fill the void.

The glowing material creates enormous vertical geysers (maybe the same "fountains of the great deep" spoken of in Genesis 7:11 and 8:2).

The geysers spray boiling steam far into the atmosphere where it is cooled down and later falls as rain over 40 days.

The new sea floor that quickly replaced the old, hard mantle is warmer and therefore not quite solidified. Thus, the ocean bottom rises 3,000-6,000 feet. This sprays seawater unto the continents and even engulfs the mountains (the Flood). By the new movements of the tectonic plates, new mountain ranges are created throughout the earth: the Himalayas, the Andes, the Rockies, and the Ararat Mountains – right where three of the earth's tectonic plates meet.

(In current, widespread geological timelines, these mountain ranges are said to be much older. But these are not facts that can be measured, but again, the ruling theory of uniformity raises its head telling us that all things have evolved over millions of years without any catastrophes taking place. Baumgardner and many others reject this theory as out-dated and scientifically untenable.)

Greenhouse Climate – and Paradise?

But let's go a bit further. With a ring of water or a bubble encompassing the earth, the result would nearly be a paradise, at least climatically speaking. The earth would have had a more uniform "greenhouse" climate being pleasantly sub-tropical to temperate all around the globe, even at the poles where there is ice today, which is confirmed by Vadiman and Dillow.

This would have caused the growth of lush, succulent vegetation all around the planet. This theory is supported by discoveries in Antarctica of coal containing vegetation that obviously belongs to a totally different climate. The climate at the poles must have been warmer at that time[13]. Scientists have coincidentally discovered that the arctic Ellesmere Island in the North Western Territory of Canada, now covered by ice, shows clear evidence that "the climate in this area used to be swampy and temperate." (*New York Times*, September 24, 1976).

Their actual purpose was to research a theory that Europe at one time might have been connected with North America.

Last century in the arctic Spitzbergen, which is almost always covered in snow and ice, scientist Oswald Heer found 136 different types of fossilized plants. Among these were silver fir, common spruce, cypress, elm, hazel, and waterlillies. There is also clear evidence that there once were palm trees with dates in this arctic area.

Similar discoveries have been made in other places indicating that the climate in the not-too-remote past might have been quite different from what it is today, possibly due to a protective vapor or ice canopy surrounding the earth.

The wind and cloud conditions would be quite different in such a climate, and the

According to the Bible, the first human beings lived in heavenly surroundings. Illustration by José Pérez Montero.

mountains were possibly not as high as they are today (because the mountain chains are a result of the movement of the tectonic plates). This again would have an effect on the formation of rain clouds, so it is feasible that it didn't rain at all. (According to the Bible, the pre-Flood earth was only watered by a fountain that flowed into four rivers and by the mist or dew.)

If the greenhouse theory is correct – until the water catastrophe changed it – this may explain the missing annual rings in some of the wood-like stones (petrified wood?) found near the Ark-formation and in other places around the world. (The reason for this is that there were no seasons.)

Dinosaurs – and People with More Brains

A result of this greenhouse theory would be that plant and animal life was much more vigorous than today – developing into dinosaurs, mammoths, and sea monsters?

Another factor is that without the direct cosmic radiation of the universe making us grow old, both human beings and animals would live much longer and grow much larger. Analysis of fossils where flies and air are captured inside amber, point to the fact that the earth once had an atmosphere with an oxygen content of 30% compared to 21% today.

In such a climate, cuts would heal more quickly and people and animals would live longer. We would even have more brains. . .ha! We have around 200 billion brain cells when we are born, but within the first 6 weeks of our lives, we lose around half of them, probably due to lack of oxygen and lack of atmospheric pressure.

So this might be the reason why the Bible and old tales from almost all cultures tell about giants and gods with extremely long life spans...? One feels that we're onto something that could possibly solve many of the great riddles.

Endnotes

[1] John Woodmorappe is a noted Creation Scientist who has published extensively in creation journals. His book *Studies in Flood Geology* is a collection of papers that describe different aspects of the global flood. In particular, the paper "A Diluviological Treatise on the Stratigraphic Separation of Fossils" (Dec 1983) describes his TAB model (Tectonically-Associated Biological Provinces) for how the flood has produced the fossil record as it is found today. The Woodmorappe website (www.rae.org/johnw.htm) contains a study guide to his book *Noah's Ark: A Feasibility Study*, and a rebuttal against published objections to points made in the book.

[2] John Woodmorappe, *Noah's Ark: A Feasibility Study,* (Institute for Creation Research, 1-(619), 1999), 628-7640.

[3] For example, there is a power point presentation on http://emporium.turnpike.net/C/cs/ark/

[4] As in Genesis 1:2; Job 38:30, 41:32; Psalms 42:7, 104:6; Isaiah 51:10, 63:13; Ezekiel 26:19; Jonah 2:3.

[5] Ezekiel 31:4, 15.

[6] The Earth's atmosphere is split into the troposphere (<10 km), the stratosphere (10-50 km), the mesosphere (50-80 km), the thermosphere (>100 km), and the ionosphere, which is the ionized part of the upper atmosphere. It is divided into layers: D-layer (75-90 km), E-layer (95-150 km), and F-layer (>150 km).

[7] J.C. Dillow, *The Waters Above,* (Chicago, IL: Moody Press, 1981).
[8] L. Vardiman, *The Sky Has Fallen, Proc. First ICC*, 1986, 1:113-119.
[9] Russell, Ancient Secrets of the Bible, (New York: Dell Publishing, 1994), 99-101, 236-239.
[10] D.E. Rush and L. Vardiman, "Pre-flood Vapor Canopy Radiative Temperature Profiles," *Proc. Fourth ICC*, Pittsburgh, PA, 1990, 2:231-245 – L. Vardiman and K. Bousselot, "Sensitivity Studies on Vapor Canopy Temperature Profiles," *Proc. Fourth ICC*, 1998, pp. 607-618.
[11] See L. Bergeron, "Deep waters," *New Scientist*, 1997, 155(2097):22-26:"You have oceans and oceans of water stored in the transition zone. It's sopping wet."
[12] S.A. Austin, J.R. Baumgardner, D.R. Humphreys, A.A. Snelling, L. Vardiman and K.P. Wise, "Catastrophic Plate Tectonics: A Global Flood Model of Earth History" Proc. Third ICC.
[13] However, this coal could also originate from the motion in the tectonic plates of the earth – i.e. the theory that the continents used to be connected as they fit into each other.

The tsunami of December 26 2004 killed at least 231,000 people and showed us that we can not control nature's enormous powers when they come in disarray. This tsunami was caused by an underground earthquake - which pales in comparison with the tsunami that would ensue if a meteor struck a hole in the earth's crust.

The world map Ptolomaios's "Geography" was designed around 150 A.D. It is the first known map that shows the world as a sphere, but the size of the world's circumference was known long before. This copy is from 1290 and kept in Rome. (Codex Vaticanus Urbinas)

Chapter 34

Old Maps of the Pre Ice Age

Charles H. Hapgoods book Maps of Ancient Sea Kings, Evidence of Advanced Civilisation in the Ice Age.

In school children learn that the landscape in the northern part of the world has been formed during the Ice Ages. Simultaneously they are told that the Ice Age took place many thousands of years ago. Yes, indeed, some Ice Ages even took place a couple of millions of years ago. The latest allegedly ended 15,000 BC.

Danish ice scientists from the Niels Bohr Institute now believe that the Ice Age ended 11,700 years ago.[1] They base their theory on a change in the ice core which they obtained by drilling through the three-kilometer ice sheet in Greenland. They based this assumption on another theory stating that the ice sheet in Greenland is 60,000 years old.

However, in a radio program about the project, a scientist involuntarily happened to mention that only approximately 3,000-4,000 growth rings can actually be counted. The reason for this is supposedly that the nethermost layers have melted so that scientists end up with the astronomical dates that fit the theory... This, however, they don't tell the public. In the media the theories are presented as facts.

Plane Buried under 240 Feet of Snow in 50 Years.

A simple observation from real life ought to help us move through the frozen theories:

During a flight from England in 1942, a group of P-38F fighters ditched on the Greenland ice sheet. The crew was rescued but the 6 fighters were left.

In 1992 an American-German team succeeded in digging down to one of the planes, which to their surprise had been buried under approximately 75 meters (240 feet) of snow and ice in just 50 years. This means that the ice cover had increased 1.5 meters/year. Therefore, even though the Greenland ice sheet is up to 3 km deep, it wouldn't have taken the ice more than 2,000 years to reach that depth.

However, one must remember that the lower layers of the ice are actually layers that are more tightly pressed together, the farther we get down. By the way, in the upper layers one can also study the historical volcanic eruptions, and even by being generous one cannot count more than 8000 years. So allegations that one can actually count one's way to an age of 60,000 years – or more – are only based on theories, not on facts.[2]

And finally it has not been proven that the individual layers are really annual layers. They may be seasonal layers or may be storm-made.

The ice sheet may not actually be as old as the prevailing theories have it. Old maps namely show Greenland and Antarctica – without ice!

Old Maps Suggest a Different World

Charles H. Hapgood has collected some of these old maps in his book *Maps of Ancient Sea Kings: Evidence of Advanced Civilisation in the Ice Age.*[3]

These maps show that Antarctica, the South Pole as a continent was actually known of in the very old Greek legends. However, in more modern times this knowledge was rejected. On his two journeys in 1768-1775, James Cook established that the Greek accounts of a large continent around Antarctica were false. He could only see ice. But under that ice is the fifth largest continent in the world – that's what was shown by seismologic research performed in 1958.

The amazing thing is that the areas of land were drawn on Oronteus Finaeus' map of the world in 1531 – which was presumably based on ancient maps.

Phillippe Buaches' map of 1754 also shows Antarctica without ice and with a great fjord running through the middle of the continent between the seas of Ross, Weddel, and Bellinghausen. Buaches could only have had this knowledge from ancient maps. Modern measuring of the underground proved that these maps were accurate.

How could the old cartographer know what lay beneath a layer of 2-mile thick ice?

The explanation is simply that Antarctica must have been free of ice 4,000- 6,000 years ago. W. D. Urry and Dr. Jack Hough, atomic physicists at the University of Illinois, confirmed this after Hough had taken some sediment tests at a depth of 2,990-3,292 meters (9,809-10,800 ft.) under the ice during the Byrd Expedition in 1949.

This information disputes the teaching that the evolution of the earth has happened at a constant rate. If Antarctica and Greenland were free of ice 4,000-6,000 years ago – at the time of Noah – then the world at that time looked very different than it should according to conventional theories. The climate would have been much milder but quickly changed. (The fact that the hairy mammoths of Siberia were quickly frozen would also support this theory.) The question is: what made the poles freeze? And is it coincidental that they apparently froze immediately after the point in time that the Bible says the Flood took place?

An Old Map in the Sultan's Palace

During one of my Noah's Ark travels, I visited the old Sultan Palace in Istanbul, which has been made into an enormous museum. Here I bought a map that is a precise reproduction of the old Piri Re'is map of the world found here in 1929. The map can also be found in Charles H. Hapgood's

Old maps seem to indicate that only a few thousand years ago the world looked different - and that the theories about the development of the earth don't quite fit. Here is a map by Philippe Buaches from 1754 showing an ice-free Antarctia and with a large fiord between the Ross Sea, the Weddel Sea, and the Bellinghausen Sea. Later measurements through the ice have shown that it is true, but Buaches couldn't have known that in 1754 where Antarctia like today was covered by ice - unless his information built on ancient maps, but if so Antarctia would have been ice-free in historical times.

sea map collection.

Even if the map was allegedly drawn by the Turkish admiral Piri Re'is on parchment, something was wrong. The map showed the coasts of South America and Africa with the right degree of longitudes – something that was not mastered until centuries later…!

However, there was no doubt that Piri Re'is did draw the map in 1513. And he even stated that he had drawn the map based on 20 even older maps. Some of them allegedly dating back to the time of Alexander The Great (approximately 356-323 BC).

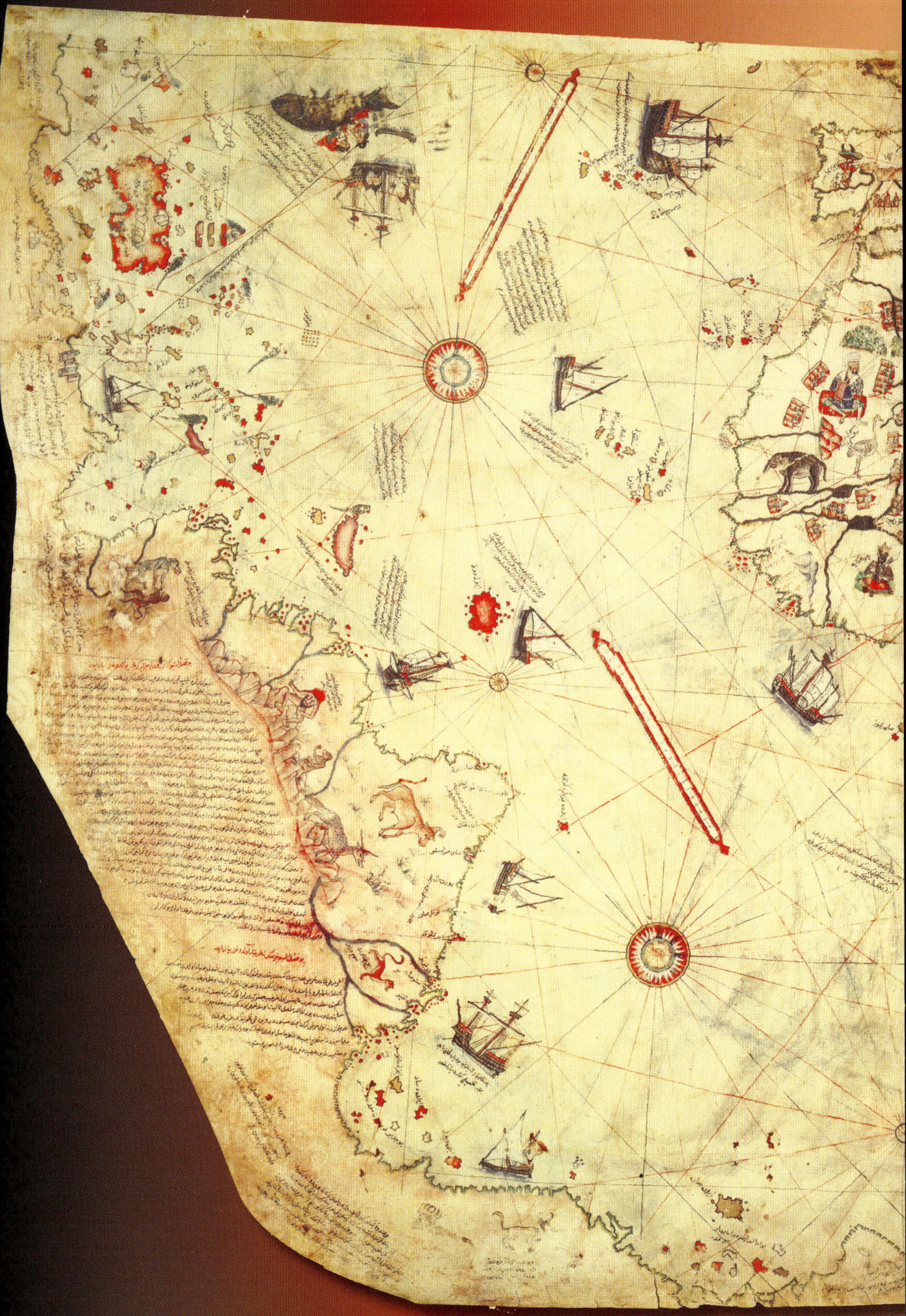

Something seemed to indicate that these maps had come to Constantinople from Alexandria where Ptolemaios founded his extensive and renowned library in approximately 300 BC. His goal was to collect the entire world's extant wisdom going back thousands of years.

Lost Knowledge

Could it be that our forefathers from ages ago had a much more detailed knowledge of the earth's degrees of longitude and latitude that by far surpassed the knowledge of the Middle Ages? An advanced knowledge that was lost millennia ago?

This idea was presented by captain Arlington H. Mallory, who had dedicated several years to the study of old sea maps, especially Viking maps of Greenland and North America after an outstanding career as engineer, navigator, archaeologist, and author.

The Iceless South Pole

After having studied the map, he became convinced that the southernmost part of Piri Re'is map also showed fjords and islands on the now frozen continent of Antarctica.

This idea was even wilder. For if the map could show what Antarctica looked like before the ice came, then those maps must have been drawn at a time when Antarctica was at least partly ice-free. However, according to the widely accepted evolutionary theories, the continent allegedly became covered in ice at least 100,000 years ago. And it was quite unlikely that the maps on which Piri Re'is based his map could be that old. More likely they were 2,000-4,000 years old. If this is the case, the ice of Antarctica isn't any older.

Advanced Maps

The experts, of course, rejected this theory off hand, because it would have made their own theories irrelevant. However, they couldn't come up with any better explanation. Conversely, professor Charles Hapgood could! With his students at Keene State College, he used several years to go through Piri Re'is' map and several other very old sea and land maps.

Even if the old maps looked somewhat distorted, it turned out that they

Piri Re'is was a famous captain in the Ottoman Empire fleet. His uncle was Admiral Kemal Re'is, and together they participated in many battles on the Mediterranean. Piri Re'is, however, produced a complete map of the world in Gelibolu in 1513, which he showed to Sultan Selim I in Cairo in 1517. On this last remaining part of the original map, the precise accounted coasts of both West Africa and Central and South American are shown - and even parts of Antarctica. Despite the fact that all this was first "discovered" much later, the map was found in the old Sultan's palace Topcapi - now a museum in Istanbul.

just used another system.

Hapgood and his students succeded in finding a pattern according to which these maps were drawn, enabling them to transfer them to the degrees of longitude and latitude of our days. As it turned out these ancient maps proved to be surprisingly accurate.

Already in 1966 Professor Hapgood collected the maps and went through them in his book *Maps of the Ancient Sea Kings*, which was later published in many editions and was republished only a few years ago.

The Same Knowledge Everywhere

Having intensely studied a Chinese map that corresponds to the other maps, Hapgood among other things concluded that this advanced knowledge of degrees of latitude that our forefathers possessed was the same in the whole of the ancient world.

"Evidence on this map indicates that a worldwide civilization existed in ancient times whose cartographers actually drew the entire globe using uniform technological methods, having the same knowledge of mathematics and probably the same instruments." [4]

So the knowledge of the division of the earth's surface into 360 degrees, which wasn't attained in Europe till after the Middle Ages, the Babylonians had already 1,000-2,000 BC and the Phoenicians of present- day Lebanon maybe as early as 1,000-3,000 BC. The ancient Phoenician port Byblos is believed to date back to 3,000 BC.

An Earlier Civilisation?

"But the science of the Babylonians was possibly inherited from a much older civilisation," says Hapgood.[5]

Professor Hapgood doesn't say *which* civilization this might be. However, the first chapters of the Bible describe this highly advanced pre-Flood civilisation when people lived longer and might also have been more intelligent.

The Norwegian author Aril Edvardsen reveals in his four volume work *Solgudens autostrada* with an abundance of sources and examples, that already before the Flood (in the Copper Age approximately 4500-3300 BC) and in the Bronze Age (approximately 3300-1200 BC) there was extensive sailing on the oceans, and that both America and Africa had been discovered and robbed of precious metals at that time – thousands of years before Columbus (re)discovered America in 1492. The same religious imagery, names, writings, and pyramids appear on the other side of the Atlantic, as found in Sumer and Egypt. Hence there must have been extensive traffic between the continents thousands of years before Columbus! [6]

Greenland without Ice

Hapgood also tells us about the Venetian Zeno brothers' map of the North

Atlantic Sea. He concludes that people of the Middle Ages could not have drawn these maps as there was a lack of knowledge of degrees of latitude. They copied their maps from much older maps because they at that time lacked knowledge about latitude. And we actually know that some of the maps of the Alexandrian library ended up in Venice. The Zeno Map shows that Greenland is not a single island but several islands. And there are mountains on this map, even though the common evolutionary theories have it that Greenland has been allegedly covered with ice for about 80,000 years. But here we have a map from the Middle Ages showing Greenland without the ice sheet. And later seismological measurements have also shown that Greenland in fact consists of several islands -like the South Pole under the ice is divided by a fjord!

Even if the medieval maps have been drawn after even older maps, the oldest maps are probably no more than 6,000 years old; Hapgood estimates.

Robert Gielow has constructed a model of the Flood outbreak which supposedly originated through collisions of the earth's rings of ice crystals. It also led to glaciation, which covered the poles and large parts of the northern hemisphere in ice and then caused a relatively rapid meltdown, which was reflected in the form of deep canyons like the Grand Canyon.

Outdated Theories Totter

Established science still holds on to its theories. Simultaneously via Hapgood's book and via "forbidden" archaeology's finds that don't fit with the prevalent theories, an alternative image of our past emerges.

Our forefathers weren't stupid club-swinging apes. There existed a highly advanced civilization 4,000-8,000 years ago that was destroyed by a flood-catastrophe mentioned in almost all the old myths of the world, and inexplicable traces of it are found in our day. The old maps seem to indicate that the world's geological and climatic "evolution" doesn't cover millions of years at all, but only a few thousand. (This doesn't mean that the universe might not be billions of years. Or eternal.

But the past of planet Earth seems closer and a lot more exciting than we thought.

A Model for Flood and Ice Age

Since official research is often hooked on a blind, almost religious belief in Evolution, it is hard for scientists having other views on the develpment of the world to get resources and possibilities to carry on research "outside the box." However some independent minds have worked with models using alternative schemes of the Ice Age history on their own initiative.

One of them is Robert L. Gielow, who has been connected to the American NASA space research for the Apollo project that succeeded in landing men on the moon. He has a Master of Science in Aeronautical and Astronautical Engineering and has created an enterprise specializing in calculating the movement and heat development of liquids via computer simulation. He used this knowledge to calculate how the ice of the Poles could have been created in

Several rings of ice crystals surrounded the earth at a distance of 400-13,250 km.

connection with the upheavals of the so-called Flood only 4,000-5,000 years ago. In fact, he believes that Noah's Flood was the beginning of the latest Ice Age.

In his book *Noah's Flood. Birth of the Ice Age*[7] (which he, by the way, dedicates to the scientists and professors who lost their jobs because they disagreed with the fixed dogma of Evolution), Robert L. Giehe outlines a calculated scheme of how the Flood came to be.

He doesn't believe that such vast quantities of water could have emerged through rain alone. Only ice crystals would make this possible as he explains in a correspondence in connection with his book. Here he also rejects the theory that water could cover the highest mountains. He doesn't believe (as some other scientists) that such vast quantities of water could have emerged through rain. Giehe believes that the water must come from enormous quantities of sleet covering the earth.

Here we have his model in simple terms:

1. Rings of ice: Earth in the prehistoric age was surrounded by rings ("the vault of heaven"[8]) in the exterior atmosphere. The rings consisted of frozen water (-150 degrees C) and were at a distance from Earth of approximately 400 – 13,250 km. The earth's rings consisted of snowballs like the rings of Saturn, but they were much smaller. These snowballs and ice crystals moved with a speed of 16,000 – 27,350 km/hour. So it took the inner rings ½ hour to circle around Earth whereas it took the outer rings approximately 7.6 hours. Due to friction the ring daily lost about1250 cubic meters of water. However, at the outbreak of the Flood there were still 625 millions cubic meters of water in the ring according to Gielow's model calculations.

2. Thick Ozon Layer protects: The rings around Earth caused a homogeneous hothouse climate in both the northern and southern hemispheres. A thick ozone layer in the stratosphere was caused by the rings of ice and acted as a filter for the uv radiation from the sun and other harmful radiation. That is why the first human beings were not susceptible to aging to such a degree as today. This explains why they, according to the Bible, lived up to ten times longer than we do. It also took them five times longer than us to reach puberty according to the genealogical tables. The diffused sunlight caused a very luxuriant flora and possibly also vibrant animal growth.

3. The Colliding Rings: 4,500 years ago a meteor disturbed the Earth's rings. The snowballs collided in great numbers over the poles, quickly freezing while sleet and rain grew to a depth of 1,200 meters everywhere on Earth. It took 40 days before the atmosphere had freed itself from sleet because the water had fallen down to Earth. At first the enormous quantity of water covered even the mountains, but gradually the water ran down into the hollows of Earth that now make up the oceans. Gielow sees the biblical expression "the sources of the primordial deep" as a name of the water stream coming down from the dark deep in space and not a name of sources in the depths of the Earth.

The instant freezing of the mammoths with grass in their mouth is a sign of the speed in which the catastrophe happened.

4. Flash Frost: The so-called Berezovka Mammoth – found in Siberia, still standing and with fresh grass in its stomach – is proof of the speed of the icy sleet which surprised the animals living in the proximity of the poles, where the temperature fell to -115 degrees C when the "rain" consisting of -185 degrees C ice crystals hit the surface of Earth. The mammoth shows signs of having been strangled and its foreleg was broken because of the heavy weight of ice suddenly descending upon the poles of the earth. Only a sudden quick frost made it possible for the mammoth's flesh to have been kept fresh in the normal frost of the next millennia.

5. Ice Age and Melt-water: The poles were now covered with ice, and the ice reached far down the continents. The vast cleft, the Grand Canyon, in the USA was formed by the melting of the ice and by enormous quantities of melt-water coming down from the glaciers. According to Gielow's calculations, it only took 40 years for the ice to melt, and in his opinion this happened immediately after the Flood approximately 4,000-5,000 years ago and not slowly through hundreds of thousands years. For the whole world shows signs of ice melting and drainage. A constant drying up of the earth has been taking place since the ice age that arose after the catastrophe of the Flood. Water and ice are disappearing year by year.

Atlantis and Paradise at the Bottom of the Mediterranean

Robert Gielow refers to examinations showing that the Mediterranean was once dry land and the Black Sea was a valley without salt water, but there was a sweet water lake at the bottom until the coming of the great Flood.[9] On the basis of the discoveries of the scientist Robert Sarmast,[10] Gielow suggests that the legendary lost Atlantis lay on the then dry land between Cyprus and Syria. And from the biblical description of the four rivers about the Garden of Eden, he concludes that Atlantis and Paradise are one and the same place. And that the first humans of our civilisation – Adam and Eve – did indeed originally live here.

In addition, Robert Gielow believes that the universe can very well be many

Robert L. Gielow believes that the Flood consisted of ice crystals of rings around the earth.

millions of years old, even if the earth is not that old. According to him the universe was created from a sort of opposite Big Bang – namely in a "white hole" in the universe – as opposed to the commonly known "black holes."

Endnotes

1 The NordGrip-Drilling in Greenland by Jørgen Peder Steffensen, lecturer, Ph. D. in ice physics at the Centre for Ice and Climate of the Niels Bohr Institute.

2 The scientist Larry Vardiman, Ph.D., expounds upon this in detail in an article on www.icr.org/index.php?module=articles&action=view&ID=355

3 Charles H. Hapgood, *Maps of Ancient Sea Kings; Evidence of Advanced Civilization in the Ice Age.* (Kempton, Illinois: Adventures Unlimited press, 1996).

4 Charles H. Hapgood, *Maps of Ancient Sea Kings,* 145

5 Charles H. Hapgood, *Maps of Ancient Sea King,* 185.

6 Arild Edvardsen, *Solgudens Autostrada* (Norwegian) consist of: Vol. 1: *Herakles Gylne Epler,* vol 2: *Ofirgullets makt*, vol 3: *Pyramiden og Orionmysteriet* og vol 4: *Atlantis & Globusenes hemmelighet*. Hermon forlag, 2002-2005.

7 Gielow, Noah's Flood: Birth of the Ice Age, (Axiom Press, 2009).

8 Here we refer to the "expanse" mentioned in Genesis, 1:6-8 where it states: "And God said, Let there be an expanse between the waters to separate water from water. So God made the expanse and separated the water under the expanse from the water above it. And it was so God called the expanse sky. And there was evening, and there was morning- the second day."

9 William Ryan and Walter Pitman's investigations with Glomar Challenger.

10 Robert Sarmast, *Discovery of Atlantis*, 2004.

Chapter 35

Why Did They Grow So Old?

The Bible, the royal genealogies of Mesopotamian, and several other prehistoric accounts declare that pre-Flood people lived for hundreds of years. The Mesopotamian tablets mention so many thousands of years that they are most likely referring to weeks, while the biblical accounts don't exceed 1000 years. Could these be mere exaggeration?

Methuselah

It is a matter of common knowledge that Methuselah is the oldest human being to have lived. "Methuselah lived 969 years and then he died." Furthermore, he died the same year in which the Flood occurred. Actually, his name means "when he dies, it will occur." Likewise, the other people mention from the pre-Flood time had very long life spans – Noah, for example, was already 600 years of age before the Flood; and, "after the flood Noah lived three hundred fifty years. All the days of Noah were nine hundred and fifty years; and he died." (Genesis 9:28-29)

Not surprisingly Bible critics have called these references to long life spans mythical and evidence that the Bible is unreliable, since we all know that people do not normally live more than 80 years or so, though we have had very rare accounts of people who have lived for as much as 120 years. The improved conditions of living and access to new medicines may have lengthened the average lifespan by some decades in some countries. Despite intense research over the past century, however, we have not been able to significantly increase the maximum age of mankind.

Maybe the old stories have secrets hidden within. As a matter of fact, the historian Moses himself mentions that something happened just around the time of the Flood. Moses, whom we must assume based his facts on ancient traditions, says in Genesis 6:3, "Then the Lord said, 'My Spirit shall not abide in mortals forever, for they are flesh; their days shall be one hundred twenty years.'" After that the genealogical tables show the lifespan of the succeeding generations to be shortened after the Flood. Moses himself, by the way, lived to be a perfect 120 years old.

We Do Not Die from Hard Work

To people who do not believe in an almighty God, it is, of course, just a myth that man's lifespan was suddenly shortened in the course of only a few generations. But now new research has proved that it only takes slight changes in one's biochemistry and the amount of cosmic radiation to obtain longer life spans, and scientists have even discovered a *Methuselah gene* that, when mutated, is able to prolong one's lifespan.

A supernova called Vela that exploded 20,000-30.000 years ago is the main source of cosmic radiation that decomposes the body causing us to age.

The reason is not that the human body is incapable of enduring more than 80 years. We do not die due to hard work, but rather because we are being exposed to some kind of poisoning from the chemistry of the body itself and from cosmic radiation which means that the cells of the body are being destroyed – thus causing us to grow old and die. If we were not exposed to this poisoning and radiation, we might be able to live for 900 years as in prehistory!

Dying by Supernova

There are several astronomical phenomena that might have affected human life span then and now. Cosmic radiation from the universe is, indeed, one of the main factors that limit human life expectancy. According to scientists, a star known as Vela exploded about 20,000-30,000 years ago and is the largest factor for the deadly cosmic radiation that silently bombards the earth today.[1]

A supernova is a rare celestial phenomenon, the explosion of most of the material in a star. And had it not been for this supernova Vela, long life spans *would* actually have been possible. Therefore, some people think that the Flood occurred at the same time the radiation from the supernova reached earth. This implies, however, that the Flood took place farther back in prehistoric time. But even if we don't juggle around with the placement of the Flood on our timelines, supernova Vela could still have played a significant role.

As mentioned in the chapter "Where did the Water come From?," some Flood scientists believe that there was once a layer of vapor or ice around the earth, which dissolved in connection with the catastrophe. If there were such a layer around the earth, it would have functioned as an effective shield against this cosmic radiation!

In other words, the people living in the "greenhouse" before the catastrophe were therefore not exposed to this age-limiting cosmic radiation. After the layer of vapor disappeared their radiation exposure started, but apparently it took a few generations for the harmful effects to have a lasting influence.

In the same way other astronomical phenomena that are not yet fully known might have had an effect on their life spans. As previously mentioned the myths seem to indicate a meteor shower – maybe from an explosion on Saturn. But there are other possible explanations for our aging.

Biochemical Explanations

In their efforts to procure longer life expectancy, scientists have discovered that biochemical mechanisms may in some cases increase life expectancy by nearly 50%.[2] Experiments with fruit flies and worms have proved that. Therefore, some scientists believe that in the near future it will be possible

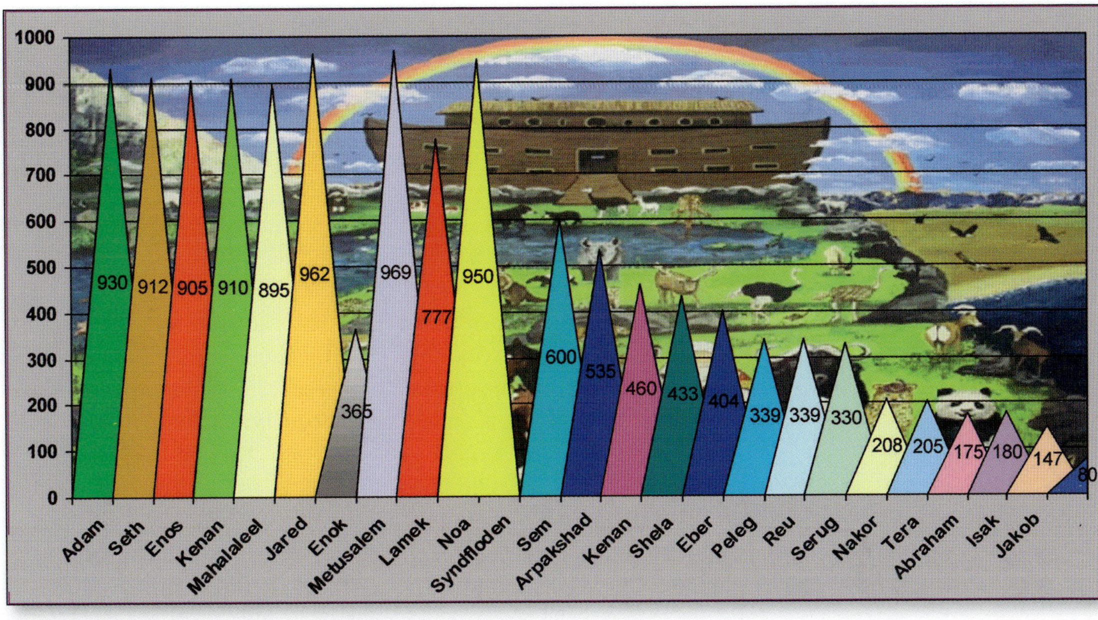

Before the Flood people apparently lived for hundreds of years. After the upheavals our lifespan has steadily gone downhill, but the fact that the first generations lived comparatively longer seems to indicate an accumulated influence. The survey is based on the genealogical tables according to the Greek Septuagint translation which also mentions Arpakshad's son Kenan. He is not mentioned in the later Masoretic text upon which most Bible translations are based. But Luke also mentions Kenan (Luke 3:36) which seems to indicate that Jesus and his contemporaries used the texts which formed the basis of the Septuagint in c. 300 B.C.

to manipulate genes or even remove those that cause us to age, in effect extending our life span as a species. Whether they are being too optimistic or not, only time will tell. But with their discoveries they have "incidentally" revealed a number of plausible explanations as to how human life expectancy could drop from 900 to 120 years relatively quickly.

Life Span Extended by 44%

The free radical theory[3] of aging is one of the leading explanations for senescence.

The free radicals damage the cells causing us to age. A team of pharmacologists recently demonstrated that the aging effects caused by the reactive oxygen can be largely subverted by augmenting the cell's native antioxidant defenses by using enzyme mimetics. So it has now been proven that a great part of aging can be prevented by reinforcing the defense mechanisms of the body with enzymes. Lab worms' life spans have thereby been prolonged by 44%.[4]

Researchers have also been able to extend the life span of fruit flies by about 40%. Instead of using enzyme mimetics, they manipulated the fruit flies' genes causing them to produce more SOD and catalase for their defense mechanisms.[5]

If humanity had a decrease in the level of SOD and catalase in connection with the water disaster and the change of environmental conditions, then this may explain our reduced life span.

ECs Contribute to Our Aging

Researchers have also discovered that by selectively reducing food intake (calories) by 30-70%, life span can be extended by up to 40% for a wide range of creatures from yeast to mammals.[6] (Therefore, a vegetarian diet may give longer life because consumption of vegetables yields fewer calories and prevents the intake of toxins that accumulate in animal flesh.)

Sometimes the chromosomes expell some genes with the code rRNA. That produces the so-called extra chromosomal DNA circles (ECs) that also damage our cells and reduce life expectancy.[7]

As it turns out, a team of researchers from the Massachusetts Institute of Technology has now found that the enzyme Sir2 plays a significant role in reducing the accumulation of the toxic ECs in yeast, thereby extending its life span.[8]

As Sir2 is not only found in yeast but also throughout the biological realm, including humans, Sir2 is possibly one of the substances that could prevent us from aging.

The Methuselah Gene

Researchers at the University of Connecticut have identified a mutation in fruit flies that disables a gene. The loss of this gene's activity means that the organism cannot extract energy from food very efficiently. This limits the energy available but, similar to caloric restriction, leads to longer life spans. Fruit fly life spans *doubled* as a result of this mutation.[9]

Oppositely, a mutation of a single gene in connection with the Flood may have led to shorter life spans. Actually, researchers have recently discovered another gene appropriately called the Methuselah gene. Again, experiments were carried out on fruit flies. Interestingly, many organisms seem to be genetically programmed to hasten mortality. When it comes to fruit flies, life expectancy is extremely short. But recently scientists have discovered a gene mutation that leads to longer life spans. The full function of this Methuselah gene has not yet been discovered, but when mutated it has been shown to extend life spans.[10]

Chromosome Disorders

Our shortened life expectancy since the Flood could also be due to a chromosome disorder. Humans have 23 pairs of chromosomes; one member of each chromosome pair comes from the mother and the other from the father.

Prior to cell division each chromosome duplicates, and after cell division the parent and daughter chromosomes separate from one another.

In connection with cell division and DNA replication, telomerase has a function.

Researchers have been able to extend life spans by introducing telomerase into cultured human cells that lack telomerase activity.[11] This leads one to wonder if the human body didn't cease telomerase activity in connection with the Flood, thus expediting the process of ageing.

Large Genome Size - But Few Genes

Scientists from Glasgow University in Great Britain[12] have recently uncovered a significant relationship between genome size and longevity. The term genome refers to the entire DNA makeup of an organism.

The Glasgow team surveyed 67 bird species and found that larger genomes lead to longer life. Humans have a large genome – three billion base pairs (genetic letters) but only 28,000 to 120,000 genes. This means that non-coding DNA makes up roughly 97% of the human genome. We have, in other words, wider prospects than we are currently using, and one may wonder whether it was different in prehistoric times.

Besides, researchers are on the threshold of additional breakthroughs in understanding the endocrinology and hormonal control of aging as well as deciphering Werner's syndrome (a disorder leading to premature aging). Also, as mentioned in chapter 9, increased amounts of oxygen in our atmosphere could have prevented humans from losing half of their brain cells within the first six weeks after birth. So there can be many reasons as to why the first humans lived longer and were larger (and smarter) than we are today.

Endnotes

1 B. Aschenback et al., "Discovery of Explosion Fragments Outside the Vela Supernova Remnant Shock-Wave Boundary," *Nature* 373 (1995), 588. – A. G. Lyne et al., "Very Low Braking Index for the Vela Pulsar," *Nature* 381 (1996), 497-589.

2 Simon Melov et al., "Extension of Life Span with Superoxide Dismutase/Catalase Mimetics," *Science* 289 (2000), 1567-69. – Judith Campisi, "Aging, Chromatin, and Food Restriction—Connecting the Dots," Science 289 (2000), 2062-63.

3 Toren Finkel and Nikki J. Holbrook, "Oxidants, Oxidative Stress and the Biology of Aging," *Nature* 408 (2000), 239-47.

4 Melov et al., 1567-69.

5 Sandeep Raha and Brian H. Robinson, "Mitochondria, Oxygen Free-Radicals, Disease and Ageing," *Trends in Biochemistry* 25 (2000), 502-08.

6 Leonard Guarente and Cynthia Kenyon, "Genetic Pathways that Regulate Ageing in Model Organisms," *Nature* 408 (2000), 255-62.

7 David A. Sinclair and Leonard Guarente, "Extrachromosomal rDNA Circles – A Cause of Aging in Yeast," *Cell* 91 (1997), 1033-42.

8 Su-Ju Lin et al., "Requirement of NAD and SIR2 for Life Span Extension by Calorie Restriction in Saccharomyces cerevisiae," *Science* 289 (2000), 2126-28.

9 Elizabeth Pennisi, "Old Flies May Hold Secrets of Aging," *Science* 290 (2000), 2048. – Blanka Rogina et al., "Extended Life Span Conferred by Contransporter Gene Mutations in Drosophila," *Science* 290 (2000), 2137-40.

10 Yi-Jyun Lin et al., "Extended Life Span and Stress Resistance in Drosophila Mutant methuselah," *Science* 282 (1998), 943-46.

11 Andrea G. Bodnar et al., "Extension of Life-Span by Production of Telomerase into Normal Human Cells," *Science* 279 (1998), 349-52.

12 Pat Monaghan and Neil B. Metcalfe, "Genome Size and Longevity," Trends in Genetics 16 (2000), 331-32.

Chapter 36

When Did It Happen?

James Ussher, Irish archbishop (1580-1656), was also a competent astronomer. In 1650 he drew up a chronology of historic events from pre-history but overlooked some of the "years of evil" not mentioned.

When trying to establish when Noah lived and when the Flood took place, it is natural to backtrack with the help of the chronologies we find in Genesis 5 and 11. But most theologians and other Bible experts would prefer to skip these chronologies covering long lifespans and recapitulate the statements of other scholars.

Actually, most of the numbers are still based on a formula the Irish archbishop and astronomer *James Ussher* (1580-1656) made back in 1650. According to these chronologies, the Flood occurred 2,349 years before Christ, and there is no doubt that Ussher did a serious and qualified job with his calculations. The problem, however, is that he assumed all generations were included. But *father* can also relate to a grandfather or ancestor. So some generations may have been omitted. Another mistake he made was that he did not account for holes from the "years of evil" under foreign rulers that could have simply been left out, as was a common practice in other Middle Eastern countries.

When considering the pre-Flood period, Ussher determined that it lasted 1,656 years because he based his calculations on the *Masoretic* version of the Old Testament in which more numerical mistakes have apparently been found when compared with the older Greek Septuagint. Quotes from the New Testament show that the Greek version was closer to the scriptures Jesus and his disciples referred to.

Please note that it is not our purpose to question or discuss the infallibility of the Bible,[1] but rather we are looking at a rewritten, faulty Hebrew version of the Bible that arose around 100 years after the death of Christ. This translation was in part a protest against the first Christian church.

In addition to the chronological mistakes, the Hebrew edition had built-in mistakes because of the new lettering system which consisted of letters that were more quadratic, and later in the 800's more mistakes apparently snuck their way in with the addition of dots and dashes, which equip the Hebraic consonants with vowel sounds. However, this translation has been used – a little too uncritically – by the Church in the western world since the 4th century because it was assumed that the Hebraic was the most correct. But actually, we should rely more on the Greek version, which the Egyptian king, Ptolemy, allowed 72 Jewish scribes to work on 250 years before Christ for the royal library in Alexandria, the so-called Septuagint or LXX.

Not 2,349 but 3,537 before Christ

In 1999 the Australian Barry Setterfield worked out a new "Creation and Catastrophe Chronology," on which the following argumentation is based.[2]

There are many numbers to keep track of so if you prefer to skip the many calculations, the conclusion is this:

The Flood did not take place in 2349 BC as bishop Ussher deduced, but in 2657 BC even if we use the usual Hebrew (Masoretic) Version as the basis for the Old Testament.

And if we use the older Greek Septuagint version, the Flood needs to be moved as far back as 3537 BC.

Now you can jump down to the last paragraph – unless you want to know why.

The Calculation

We will take the destruction of the temple in Jerusalem by King Nebuchadnezzar in **586** BC as a fixed point. This event is well documented and there is widespread agreement on this date, plus or minus only 1 year.

The prophet *Ezekiel*, who was a captive in Babylon, reports in his book (Ezekiel 4, verses 1-5) that Israel's worshiping of idols had taken place for 390 years, from the split of judges in Judah and Israel until the fall of Jerusalem. That means that the kingdom was split up in **976** B.C when Solomon died. (This can be verified by comparing with the lists of Chronicles.)

Solomon reigned for 40 years, and the building of the temple started in the fourth year of his reign, that is in **1012 BC.**

The period from the crowning of the first king of Israel, Saul, until the temple was destroyed was 40 + 40 + 4 + 426 = 510 years. So Saul became king in 1096. This can be verified by comparing the 2nd Book of Chronicles 36:21 and Jeremiah 25:11. They state that the captivity in Babylon lasted 70 years. This would correspond with the fact that the Jews were to have a sabbatical year every seven years. The Jews failed to do this, and the 70 years of captivity was their punishment. That is, the Jews had not kept sabbatical years for 7 x 70 years = 490 years.

The Book of Haggai 2:16 states that the captivity ended in the second year of King Darius' rule. That is 520 BC. If the 490 years ended in 520, the temple was built in 1010 BC which is very close to 1012 BC – the year we reached initially.

The Exclusion of the Years of Evil

Throughout history Kings have been known to periodically remove years from their annals in which foreign rulers had taken control (the exclusion principle).

King Solomon apparently did the same thing when he spoke in 1 Kings 6:1 of 480 years from the exodus of the Israelites from Egypt to the beginning of the building of the temple, because Luke in Acts suggests that there were 573 years!

Namely 40 years in the desert (Acts 13:18), 450 years of judges (Acts 13:20), 40 years under Saul (Acts 13:21), 40 years under David (1 Kings 2:11), and 3 years under Solomon before the temple was started (1 Kings 6:1).

Altogether 573 years – 93 more than Solomon mentions in 1 Kings 6:1.

Does that mean that Solomon was a bad mathematician? No, he just removed the years of evil.

If we look closely, Israel was under foreign rule for exactly 93 years: 8 years under the King of Mesopotamia (Judges 3:8); 18 years under the King of Moab (Judges 3:14); 20 years under the King of Canaan (Judges 4:2-3); 7 years under the Midianites (Judges 6:1); and 40 years under the Philistines (Judges 13:1). When added up, these numbers give 93 years – the exact same number of years removed from the lists in 1 Kings 6:1.

The chronologies worked out by the first Church Fathers indirectly confirm this.[3]

Since Solomon was able to remove the years under foreign rule that easily, it shows that the exclusion principle could possibly have been used in the Bible. Years of evil could have been removed. This does not mean that the Old Testament is not credible; it just means that we need to understand its oriental counting methods. This principle of exclusion is actually used in all of the ancient cultures. Egypt and ancient Babylon have experienced later rulers removing their predecessors from lists and monuments.

The Exodus Took Place Earlier than Assumed

We can now continue even further back in time. The temple was built in 1012 and the period from the Exodus out of Egypt to the temple's building was 573 years. So the Exodus occurred in **1583** BC plus or minus 6 years.

About 40 years after the Exodus, the Hebrews began the fight for Canaan (Israel) under the leadership of Joshua. The date was about **1545** BC.

Typically, the Hebrews were thought to have left Egypt around 1400 or 1200 BC at the end of the late Bronze Age in this area. But certain facts confirm our earlier dates.

According to the Bible, Joshua conquered the fortified cities in Canaan, like Jericho for example. Archeologists have often pointed out that there were no cities to conquer around 1400 because the cities of Canaan were already destroyed at that time based on digs.

The archeological journal, *Biblical Archaeology Review*,[4] claims that the cities of Jericho, Gibeon, Hebron, Hormah/Zephath, Ai, and Arad (Tel Arad and Tel Malhata) did not exist at the end of the Late Bronze Age. But all of these cities, as well as Debir, Lachish, Hazor, and Bethel, did exist at the end of the Middle Bronze Age, normally dated to 1550. According to our calculation the Hebrews actually immigrated in 1545...!

In fact, most of the cities were surrounded by walls as mentioned in the Bible. And they were all destroyed at the end of the Middle Bronze Age (II-C).

(The only exception is Ai, which may not be the true Ai. On the other hand, Khirbet Nisya fulfills both the biblical and archeological requirements. Gibeon was also abandoned at this time. Its destruction is mentioned in Joshua 9:27.)

The archeological evidence confirms that Joshua would not have had any cities to defeat if he didn't come until 1400, but all of the cities were there –

Barry Setterfield has also written about astronomy and the varying speed of light in: *The Atomic Constants, Light, and Time*. His conversion of atomic light years to normal years among other things means that the geological layers from the Flood ca. 3,536 BC correspondsto the geological period called pre-cambrian time 600 million years ago. Even though he is a creationist, he has faced a lot of opposition from the creationalist environment in the USA, due to his un-orthodox ideas. Among other things Institute for Creation Research has published a report (Has the Speed of Light decayed? - *IMPACT* No. 179, May 1988 by Gerald A. Aardsma), challenging his ideas.

Read more in his book *Creation and Catastrophe*. Setterfield, Box 318, Blackwood SA 5051, Australia.

and were defeated – when Joshua invaded them, according to our corrected chronology.

Plus 430 Years in Egypt

Now we are going to attempt another step back to the *immigration* of the Hebrews into Egypt. In Exodus 12:40-41 Moses writes that the Exodus occurred on "the very same day" as Jacob and his family came to Egypt, just 430 years later. As an Egyptian prince, Moses would have known the exact date based on the royal registry.

This agrees with Genesis 15:13 according to which God predicted to Abram (Abraham) that his descendents would "be oppressed for four hundred years." This is also spoken of in Acts 7:6. So both the New and the Old Testament agree. The first church fathers also confirm that the Hebrews spent a full 430 years in Egypt.

We know that the Hebrews were accepted at first when Joseph was in power, but after this they were used as slaves. This could have happened when Joseph lost power as the next pharaoh took the throne. Based on other sources, Barry Setterfield states that the massive change took place 39 years after Joseph was named an official and 41 years before his death at 110.

(Others have attempted to limit the period to 200 years because they were unable to make the generations fit. Barry Setterfield, however, believes that the Hebrews in the lists of their ancestors regularly omit generations born in Egypt during the slavery. They only mention the first and the last generations, thus omitting the intermediary ones according to the principle of exclusion as mentioned before. This fits better with the 430 years.)

Abraham Born Already in 2305

Now we have gone back 1585 plus 430 years – altogether **2015** years BC (+/-6 yrs.). We even know that it was probably April, because the exodus happened during the Jewish Passover, which is celebrated in spring. And the same goes for the immigration.

At the time (2015 BC) Jacob and his sons traveled into Egypt, Jacob was 130 years old.[5]

Since Isaac was 60 when he had Jacob, and Abraham was 100 when he had Isaac, we can go back 160 years before Jacob was born in **2145** and set Abraham's birth at **2305** BC (2145+160).

This is confirmed by the first church fathers, who most likely had their information from the Apostles, who had it from the Master himself. According to Theophilus of Antioch, Abraham was born 760 years before Moses died.[6]

It is interesting that both the Qur'an and Arabic tradition set Abraham's birth at 2300 BC.

The 17,000 so-called Ebla tablets (found in 1975-76 in northern Syria) are from that exact period (2400 – 2250 BC). They include writings about cities in Canaan (Israel) which were previously thought to have come from a later period: Salim, possibly Melchizedek's city,[7] Hazor, Lachish, Megiddo, Gaza, Dor, Sinai, Ashtaroth, Joppa, and Damascus. Urusalima (Jerusalem) is mentioned here for the first time in history.

Professor of Archeology D. N. Freedman from the University of Michigan is convinced that the account of Abraham's meeting with Mekchizedek (found in Genesis 14) and the stories about Abraham that follow come from the Ebla Period, not from a later millennium as was once believed.[8]

Inconsistent Translations

Abraham's birth being fixed at 2305 BC (+/- 6 years) is not dependent on the Old Testament (OT) translation used, but the chronology *before* Abraham is very much affected by our using the Masoretic or the Greek Septuagint. Which text is the most original? For example, we can look at the OT quotes Jesus and his disciples used. Sometimes they don't quite match the Masoretic OT, which is the basis for modern translations. They are, however, more in accord with the Greek Septuagint, which is over 300 years older.[9] We can see that one of Paul's important quotes from the Pentateuch is not even found in the Masoretic version.[10]

Ezra and Nehemiah's Compilation

The prophet Ezra[11] and governor Nehemiah[12] are thought to have collected the books of the Old Testament, which were recognized shortly afterwards by the so-called Great Synagogue (ca. 440 BC). The source written in ancient Hebrew is called the Vorlage. In time this text served as the source for three different versions.

1) The first was the *Samaritan Pentateuch,* SP (the 5 first books of the Bible written by Moses) also written in old Hebraic from 408 BC. Tobias the Ammonite took a copy of this when he was thrown out of Nehemiah's temple (see Neh. 13:4-9 and Ezra 4:1-4). This makes up the Holy Scriptures for Samaritan Israelites today.

2) The other version was the *Septuagint (LXX)*, which was translated from the original in 250 BC by 72 Jews trained in Alexandria. This version was necessary due to the growing number of Greek-speaking Jews who lived in Egypt under the Greek Ptolemaic Dynasty. Most authorities agree that the LXX translation of the Pentateuch and the Book of Joshua were very precise because of the revered position they held in the canonical scriptures. The Eastern part of the Christian Church still considers the Septuagint translation to be the official OT text.

3) Much later, around 100 AD, the ancient Hebrew text was re-written to the so-called *Masoretic version* with the quadratic "modern" Hebrew signs, and then around 900 AD vowel signs were added. Unfortunately, this version

is the basis for many versions of the Old Testament. In *Our Bible and the Ancient Manuscripts*,[13] Sir Frederick Kenyon wrote that this double procedure could easily be "a significant source of fallacy."

The Dead Sea Scrolls Reveal the Change

The Dead Sea Scrolls, found after World War II, contain scriptures written over a period from approximately 300 years before Christ to 100 years after.

The texts before year 70 are the same as the Septuagint as well as the OT quotes used by Josephus, Jesus, and the apostles in the New Testament.[14]

The scrolls written after the year 100, however, fit the Masoretic text.[15]

Professor Sigried Horn writes that he is "sure that Mathew quotes from a Hebrew text that agreed with the source the Greek translator (of the LXX) used."

These Hebrew and Greek texts existed and were quoted from before the destruction of Jerusalem in 70 AD by Titus. They were, with Professor Horn's words, "the Hebrew Bible, which circulated while Jesus and the Apostles worked."

Why Was the Text Changed?

Horn writes that at the end of the 1st century, a compilation was standardized after the Synod in Jamnia, which took place around 100 AD Not even one single copy of a divergent text survived (except for the Dead Sea Scrolls which had already been hidden).

Rabbi Akiba ben Joseph was the incontestable head of the Synod. In his old age, Akiba supported *Bar Kokba*'s rebellion against the Romans with all that he owned. He was even celebrated as the Messiah. Akiba was eventually captured and sent to Rome where he was executed in 137 AD at the age of 82.

The Synod in Jamnia rejected the original Hebrew versions and the LXX version which was based on the Hebrew. According to Professor Horn, it was because "...it had become the Christians' Bible." Horn, Sir Frederick Kenyon, and other experts agree the Masoretic text (MT) was a 'rivalised version' in relation to the Christians. But even so, the Masoretic text has, with few exceptions, been used as the basis for most of the OT translations since the 4th century.

Unfortunate Compilation Becomes Standard

Around 200 AD the Christian Copt, *Origen of Alexandria*, collected a sixfold version of the Old Testament. It was based on the three Greek versions, built on the Masoretic version as well as the MT (Masoretic text) in Hebrew, the MT in Greek and LXX revised by Origen. Since 5 out of the 6 versions were built on the Masoretic version, the compilation was full of mistakes.

Sir Frederick notes, "...Origen's work was not to find the *original* version of the Septuagint LXX, but to bring it in harmony with the Masoretic Hebrew text which was used at that time, and for that purpose, he made changes in the text with great freedom." Luckily, Bishop Taulus of Tella in Mesopotamia produced a *Syrian* translation in 617 AD which gave a detailed look at Origin's changes. As a result, the LXX was kept in its original version and still exists today. In most cases the differences between the texts are relatively minor, but the *chronologies* have some very significant differences.

Genesis 5 delineates the patriarchs from Adam to Noah (and the Flood), while Genesis 11 covers the period from the Flood (and Shem) up to Abraham. How many years have we got here?

Septuagint's Chronology Is Correct

Here is, in fact, a difference of 1,300 years between the Masoretic version and Septuagint. So which one is the correct one?

If you compare the Septuagint, the Samaritan Pentateuch, and *Josephus*' historical writings, you reach the conclusion that the LXX list of patriarchs in Genesis 5 is confirmed by Josephus while the list in Genesis 11 is confirmed by the Samaritan Pentateuch.

And there is a greater probability that the *Hebrew* translation does not agree with the original source as quoted by Christ and the Apostles.

Also the church fathers' chronologies follow the LXX. Actually, the Gospel of Luke includes Kenan in its list of patriarchs from the period after the Flood, just as the LXX does.

This strongly supports the LXX chronology.

In chapter 5, the difference between Septuagint and MT is 600 years. In chapter 11, the difference is more than 700 years.

It looks like a figure for 100 has disappeared or been systematically omitted in the copying from the Paleo-Hebraic (Old Hebrew) to the Masoretic version (MT) in these important chapters.

Multiple archeological discoveries confirm the credibility of the Septuagint too. When Joshua died he was buried "at Timnath-serah, which is in the hill country of Ephraim, north of Mount Gaash" (Joshua 24:30). The LXX adds an important remark: "*In that grave where they buried him they placed there the stone knives with which he circumcised the sons of Israel in Gilgal.*"

Professor Werner Keller tells on page 163 in *The Bible as History* that stone graves can actually be found in a cliff face near Joshua's village Kef'r Ishu'a. In 1870 a large number of stone knives were found in one of the graves on the north side of the mountain.

Year of the Flood: 3537 BC.

Using the ages of the patriarchs when their specific sons were born according to the Septuagint LXX version, the Flood consequently occurred 1,232 years before Abraham's birth, that is in **3537** BC. And the creation of Adam was then 2,256 years earlier, or 5793 BC.

This is very much in agreement with the understanding of the Ancient Church. Theofilus of Antioch (115-181 AD) dates Creation to 5537 BC, Hippolit mentions 5500 BC, and Julius Africanus (who died in 240 AD) sets it at 5537

BC. The Annals of Axum establish it to be 5500 BC, while the Talmudist (Petrus Alliacens) offers a date around 5344 BC. Arabic documents say 6174 BC.

Unnecessary Conflict with Archeology

The Masoretic text cannot set the date earlier than 2657 BC for the Flood. And here is where the biblical digits come – unnecessarily – in conflict with various archeological finds.

For example, in the USA there are bristlecone pines of approximately 4,600 years; one of the trees is even as old as 4,900 years. The oldest of these trees started growing around 2900 BC. This disagrees with the Masoretic chronology but agrees nicely with the new one.[16]

The new revised date for the Flood fits much better with the archeological finds[17] and our knowledge of the Egyptian and Sumerian civilizations, which we can clearly see were AFTER the Deluge and not as previously believed BEFORE.

If we mix the biblical and the archeological information, the result is the following time-table (with all possible reservations, of course).

Endnotes

1 Because of the liberal Bible criticism, it is important for some Christians to focus on the infallibility of the Bible. 2 Timothy 3:16-17 says, "All scripture is inspired by God and is useful for teaching, for reproof, for correction, and for training in righteousness, so that everyone who belongs to God may be proficient, equipped for every good work."
Whether you agree with the one or the other, the Bible is still the best possible source for the original and true Judaism and Christianity.

2 Updated on www.setterfield.org/scriptchron.htm
Setterfield has also written an exciting work about astronomy and the varying speed of light entitled The Atomic Constants, Light, and Time. His conversions of atomic light years into earth years mean that the geological layers from the Flood ca. 3,536 BC fit into the infra-Cambrian period, which is set at 600 million years ago. Even though he is really a Creationist, he has encountered a great deal of opposition from Creationists in the US due to his unorthodox ideas. Among these smites is a report from The Institute for Creation Research in which his ideas are refuted. This report is entitled "Has the speed of light decayed?" printed in IMPACT No. 179, May 1988 by Gerald A. Aardsma.

3 "Theophilus to Autolycus" in The Ante-Nicene Fathers, Book III, Chs. 23-30, A. Roberts and J. Donaldson, eds. Eerdmans Publishing Company.

4 Biblical Archaeology Review for September/October 1987, pg. 53.

5 Genesis 47:9

6 Theophilus of Antioch pointed out that there were 660 years from the birth of Isaac to the end of the wilderness wanderings and death of Moses. This comprised Isaac's 60 years to the birth of Jacob; then Jacob's 130 years at his entry into Egypt; then the 430-year sojourn in Egypt; and finally the 40 years in the wilderness – a total of 660 years. As Abraham was 100 when Isaac was born, this inevitably means that Abram himself was born [660 + 100 = 760] years before Moses' death and Israel's entry into the Promised Land. This information from Theophilus indicates that both Abram's birth date of 2305 BC ± 5 years, and the 430-year Egyptian sojourn is in complete accord with the teaching of the church fathers. (Barry Setterfield)

New time-table of pre-historic times

Adam and Eve's creation according to the Bible	c. 5,793 B.C.
Metsamor-culture in Armenia – metalwork, etc.	c. 5,000 B.C.
Signs of the first people in Mesopotamia (now Turkey-Iraq)	c. 5,000 B.C.
Noah's birth according to Gilgamesh in Shuruppak on the Euphrates	c. 4,137 B.C.
Ubaid culture in Mesopotamia (potsherds, temples, knowledge of iron)	c. 3,900 B.C.
Warka culture in Mesopotamia (proliterate period)	c. 3,600 B.C.
The Flood destroys all ancient cultures (3,537-36)	c. 3,537 B.C.
The Tower of Babel and dispersion	c. 3,302 B.C.
Noah dies – he most likely lived in the Ararat Mountains	c. 3,187 B.C.
The earth (continents?) is "separated" (in Peleg's time)	c. 3,006 B.C.
Decreased population to 1/8 (based on 30,000 C-14 measurements)	c. 2,950-2,450
Sumerian city-states arise in southern Mesopotamia/Iraq	c. 2,900 B.C.
The first **Ur Dynasty** in southern Mesopotamia	c. 2,750 B.C.
Egypt's 1st dynasty and the beginning of the Egyptian Sothis calendar	c. 2,770 B.C.
Indus civilization blooms in Pakistan and western India	c. 2,500 B.C.
Cooling of the climate measured in three tree rings	c. 2354-45 B.C.
Sargon I (Nimrod?) starts the Acadian kingdom in Mesopotamia	c. 2,340 B.C.
Fall of the Acadian and Egyptian cultures, probably around	c. 2,300 B.C.
The birth of **Abraham**	c. 2,305 B.C.
Abraham flees from Ur to Karan (after his clash with Nimrod?)	c. 2,250 B.C.
Abraham leaves Karan (Turkey) and travels to Canaan and Egypt	c. 2,230 B.C.
3rd Ur Dynasty in Mesopotamia	c. 2,100 B.C.
Jacob enters Egypt	c. 2,015 B.C.
Moses is born, discovered by princess Meris and raised as a prince	c. 1,665 B.C.
Moses collects materials and writes of the Creation and the Flood	c. 1,600 B.C.
Exodus - Moses leads the Hebrews away from slavery in Egypt	c. 1,585 B.C.
The Hyksos People invade (or the Hebrews leave) a weak and chaotic Egypt	c. 15-1600 B.C.
Joshua leads the Israelites into Canaan – wins cities	c. 1,545 B.C.
In the end of the Bronze Age II, the cities of Canaan are destroyed	c. 1,550 B.C.

Endnotes (cont.)

7 Genesis 14:18.

8 D. N. Freedman: Archaeology and Biblical Religion 1978:
"It is now my belief that the story in Genesis 14 not only corresponds in content to the Ebla Tablet, but that the Genesis account derives from the same period. ... Briefly put, the account in Genesis 14, and also in Chapters 18-19, does not belong to the second millennium BC, still less to the first millennium BC, but rather to the third millennium BC." (quoted in Ebla Tablets – Secrets of a Forgotten City by Dr. Clifford Wilson, p.126-127, Master Books, 1979).

9 Examples: Jesus' quote from Psalm 8:3 in Matthew 21:16 or the Apostle Paul's quote of Hosea 13:14 in 1 Corinthians 15:55, or his quote from Isaiah 64:4 in 1 Corinthians 2:9. Based on such a comparison it is obvious that quotes from the New Testament follow the LXX almost exactly. If, on the other hand, we were to compare NT quotes with the more modern OT, we would find a discrepancy in our OT version. It is quite obvious that our modern OT was translated based on the Masoretic version.

10 In Hebrews 1:6 Paul quotes Deuteronomy 32:43. He writes, "And again, when he brings the firstborn into the world, he says, "Let all God's angels worship him." If we look at the passage in Deuteronomy, we see that Paul's important quote about the Messiah's divinity is not there! It is left out of the Masoretic text but can be found in the Greek, just as Paul quotes. Actually, the Masoretic leaves out another important part of the verse, but the Greek continues: "And let all of the son's of God be strengthened in him."

11 Ezra was a Jewish priest, the author of the Book of Ezra, and possibly 1st and 2nd Chronicles. He tells of the events toward the end of the Jewish exile in Babylon, the period from the release of the Jews in 538 BC by King Kyros of Persia, and Ezra's reformation in Israel in 458 BC.

12 Nehemiah wrote the Book of Nehemiah (c. 430 BC) and was a high Jewish official under King Artaxerxes of Persia. In 445 BC, as the Persian king's governor, he was given permission to rebuild Jerusalem. He completed his work over the following 13 years and then returned to the royal court in Persia. Nehemiah returned two years later to fight corruption and decline.

13 *Our Bible and the Ancient Manuscripts*, (London: Eyre and Spottiswoode), 49.

14 Sigfried H. Horn, emeritus professor of archeology at Andrews University, Berrien Springs, Michigan, in "Ministry", November 1987: "The Old Testament texts in Antiquity."

15 Frank Cross in 1953 in The Bulletin of American Schools of Oriental Research, No. 132, pp. 15-26.

16 Peleg (which means scattered) was called such "for in his days the earth was divided." Some believe that this refers to the separation of the continents.

17 But there are still unsolved mysteries. A few archeological finds of humans are set to periods thousands of years before Adam and Eve were created. Here are two possibilities: the dating can be faulty, or another civilization could have existed previously starting with Adam. There are some people that consider the story of Creation in the Bible to be a "re-creation" after a previous period of chaos. (We are ignoring the dating that is not based on carbon-14 tests and are only looking at theories of the age of geological layers or other million-year-theories, which are not proven either.)

Chapter 37

The Valley of the Eight

The flat part of the valley that twists around the west side of Mt. Ararat is called "The Valley of the Eight."

The name "The Valley of the Eight" or "The Region of the Eight" of course refers to the eight that, according to the Bible, survived the Flood by taking refuge in the Ark. Many ancient civilizations and religions speak of eight forefather-gods. This is a study in itself, and here we will only mention its existence rather than get lost in all of its details.[1]

The special thing about this valley is the multiple anchor stones with holes in their tops that have been found here. *Ron Wyatt* was the first to stumble across these large stones. He supposedly found a total of 13 anchor stones together with his employees. Two of the stones have later disappeared. According to *Dr. Salih Bayraktutan*, there is supposedly one more anchor stone in the present Armenia. (Wyatt is famous for his re-discovery of the so-called "boat-shaped object" approximately 20 km away. It is a curious protuberance in a ravine that has exactly the length of the Ark and that has attracted Ark-interest for decades.)

Wyatt called the place by its Armenian name *Kazan*, probably to confuse grave robbers. The little village here is now called *Arzep* and to add to the confusion it is also called *Sagliksuyu* or Sa Lik Suxu (acid water) in Turkish. And there is also a Kazan a few more kilometers up the mountain.

Mrs. Birthe Nissen and the author by one of the famous anchor stones that have been found in "The Valley of the Eight" just 13 miles from Mt. Ararat in the background.

Armenian Cemetery

Many of these strange stones are found in Arzep, and some call it "The Village of the Eight."

There is also an Armenian graveyard here, partially destroyed, which probably contains the remains of crusaders and pilgrims. It is located east of the village and is no longer a beautiful sight. Many headstones have already been removed and used as building materials, while other graves are more or less open where bones are up for grabs. As we walk around the cemetery, Kurdish children ran around playing with skeleton arm and leg bones.

This cemetery is worth studying more closely. It probably contains not only bodies of the Armenians who lived here until they were driven away, but possibly also crusaders who came here in search of the Ark. During the times of the crusaders, they had their own little kingdom in the south of Turkey around Harran, the town of Abraham.

Mighty Anchors of Stone

In another area north of the village, huge headstones that look like anchors have been found. They have – or rather had in some cases – a hole in the top. Some of the stones are still intact where we can see these holes.

We also saw a house in this town where the two halves of one of these very old engraved stones were used as building material.

Other places in the world, like on the Nile, this method of tying a boat to a

"The Valley of the Eight" is approx. 13 miles away from Mt. Ararat, and due to the big anchor stones found here many Ark hunters are convinced that Noah and Na'ama settled here. Feizal, the head of the village, is showing the stone that Wyatt believed to have been Noah's altar.

large stone with a hole in it is practiced. Normally these anchor stones are no longer than a meter, usually one half.

But here in this village and throughout the hills surrounding The Region of the Eight, eleven such stones have been found, and they are not one meter long, but 2 and even 3 meters!

The holes in these stones are special; they slope inwards. Therefore, they are fit to tie a rope to so that the knot slides into the hole and stays put.

According to Professor *Robert Michelson*, Georgia Tech, the purpose of the anchor stones is "to create a drag in the water." He says, "If these devices are attached to the end of a boat, the drag produced as a wind driven boat pulls it along through the water will cause the boat's hydrodynamic pointed bow or stern to face into the wind and the oncoming wind-blown waves.

Without such a device, a wave can hit the boat and turn it sideways to the wind and waves. The next wind impacting the side of the boat will then have a greater likelihood of rolling the boat over. Sea anchors and drogue stones effectively prevent this." [2]

We found this Russian 2 Kopek coin from1916 in Arzap - The Village of the Eight. It was probably from the first World War when a part of the Armenian area was under Russian hegemony for a short period.

Anchors of Stone at 1500 Meters above Sea Level?

Some of the anchor stones were found on the hillsides of this valley southwest of Mt. Ararat. What could be the reason that these anchor stones ended up in the hills 1500 meters above sea level? There doesn't seem to be a logical explanation. We are far from a sea or a lake. And why are the anchor stones so over-dimensioned? It doesn't seem logical – unless there once was a mighty boat up here.

The name of the village, Arzap or Arzep, possibly comes from the Turkish Arz zapt which means "to capture the earth" or possibly further back from Semitic in eretz tsap, which can be translated as "to cling to the earth." [3]

At least one of the stones is on top of a hill. Maybe this was the first time the anchor stones had contact with a peak as the water began to sink. They had connected with the earth – arz zapt – Arzap.

The purpose of Noah's Ark was not to sail around the world but only to protect people and animals until the Flood was over. Therefore, it would have been sensible to equip it with drogue anchors that could stabilize the boat.

Armenian Crosses

Most of the stones have crosses on them. They look like Byzantine/Armenian crosses that curve outwards at the tips, but the vertical beam is not always longer than the horizontal.

Ron Wyatt also found anchor stones with holes that stuck out of the ground in which no crosses were engraved. This could suggest that the crosses were made after the stones were re-discovered, probably by crusaders or by the Armenians to symbolize and memorialize the eight from the Ark.

Some critics have tried to explain these anchor stones away with the suggestion that they were merely stones used for mystical rituals by locals where the holes were used to hold candles or the like. But if this were the case, then it would be impractical that the holes narrow as they reach the center. And besides, there is no other evidence that such religious practices have existed in this area.

The *Yezidi* sect that can be found in parts of southeast Turkey is the closest we come to a fire-religion. But they have no such ritual. One offshoot of this sect worships the sun by lifting up sick children at sunrise, for example, while another group worships fire. But this is performed in dances around a bonfire.

There are neither signs of candles or fire in the holes nor signs of blackening on the stones themselves.

Astronomic Calendar

If one was to look for another explanation for the anchor stones, I would rather suggest that they were stones used as a *calendar* for the seasons – as probably was the case with the big stones in *Stonehenge*, England – or in *Metsamor*, just on the other side of the frontier in Armenia.

This explanation is also suggested by a team of researchers, among others Ark researcher Rex Geisler. The team presented their study of archaeological finds in the area in a report in 2008.[4]

Stone Reference in Gilgamesh

The Bible does not mention anchor stones. When considering the Ark in the Qur'an, anchors are mentioned in Houd Sura 11: "In the name of Allah it will cast Anchor."

In the Sumerian epic poem Gilgamesh, strange articles of stone are named which could possibly be the mighty anchor stones. This happens when Gilgamesh has to sail across a body of water in order to reach Utnapishtim (Noah). In the English version, which is based on the standard Acadian version with additions from the ancient Babylonian, where words are missing in the Acadian, the ferry keeper, Urshanabi, says the following to Gilgamesh: [5]

Urshanabi spoke to Gilgamesh, saying,

> It is your hands, Gilgamesh, that prevent the crossing! You have smashed the stone things, you have pulled out their retaining ropes (?). 'The stone things' have been smashed, their retaining ropes (!) pulled out!

It sounds as if a number of anchor stones have been destroyed and that the ropes that bind the stones to the boat have been pulled out.

The Crow Who Wouldn't Land...

It was primarily the ark hunter and the treasure hunter David Fasold who argued that the stones were anchor stones. Besides, he was very interested in place names and also found his way to the village Kargaconmaz. The name means "the raven (or the crow) will not land," which rings a bell to those who know the Biblical account: "After forty days Noah opened the window he had made in the ark, and sent out a raven, and it kept flying back and forth until the water had dried up from the earth." Genesis 8: 6-7

So Kargaconmaz has a name that reminds us of the Ark story, just like other places in the Ararat Mountains.

These particular names were given to the places long before anybody searched for the Ark here. In fact, the then inhabitants were victims of ethnic cleansing approximately one hundred years ago and replaced by another people in connection with the clash between Kurds, Turks, and Armenians. And the names originate in a long-forgotten past.

Kargaconmaz lies at the altitude of ca. 2000 meters on the mountains between Mt. Ararat and the Iranian border. Not far from the "boat-shaped object." The village is behind a characteristic crest called Yigityatagi, where Turkish frontier-guards are always present. Yigityatagi supposedly means "the heroes' bed or hearth." Maybe it is a reference to the eight of the Ark, who were later regarded as both heroes and gods. From ancient times the locals have also named the crest "The Wall of Heaven."

Endnotes

1. See Aril Edvardsen's *Solgudens Autostrada* (Hermon Publishing House, Norway).
2. Robert Michelson http://avdil.gtri.gatech.edu/RCM/RCM/5RCMArkeology/6Durupinar.html
3. In Turkish, arzap means to take possession of the earth or land. Arz meaning earth or land, and Zapt means seize or take possession. (Langenscheidt Universal Turkish). While in Semetic (Hebrew in this case) eretz means earth, or land and zab means "to cling to, as a lizard clings to a rock." (Strong's Exhaustive Concordance of the Bible)
4. *Bible and Spade*, Vol. 21, No. 3, 2008, 70-96. "Mount Ararat Archaeological Survey" by Professor Dr. Cevat Baaran, Assistant Professor Dr. Vedat Kele, and Rex Geissler.
5. www.ancienttexts.org/library/mesopotamian/gilgamesh/index.html by Timothy R. Carnahan.

Climbing Mt. Ararat requires strong legs (Photo: Frede Donskov)

Chapter 38

The Book of Jasher

The Book of Jasher is named twice in the Old Testament.[1] Sephir Ha Yasher means "the book of the upright." Around 1500 the book disappeared, but in the Middle Ages a scroll with the same name showed up once again. It was printed in Hebrew in 1625 in Venice (possibly 1613) and was later translated and published in sections in Krakow, Prague, Frankfurt, Constantinople (Istanbul), Amsterdam, and Calcutta.[2] It was finally published in English in 1839 in the USA.

That translation was given by a well-known American-Jewish politician, Mordecai M. Noah.[3] Moses Samuel, a professor in Hebrew from Liverpool, England, started the translation, but when a fake book of Jasher came out, he gave up his work and sold the translation for £150 to M. M. Noah. The 19th of November 1828 he wrote in a letter to the editor in the *London Courier* that he had been given the Hebrew text by a Jew from North Africa. This English version has been reprinted many times and is also accessible via the internet.[4]

An Amazing Work

A number of false copies of the Book of Jasher have shown up, but they have all been easy to detect. The Book of Jasher we will be looking at is different from the others.

The book speaks of the same people the Bible refers to – from Adam, all the way to Joshua – and for the most part it agrees with the Bible. It also includes some interesting details about people, places, and dates. The dates given here actually clear up 60 missing years around the time of Abraham's birth, a mistake brought in by the Irish archbishop James Ussher (1580-1656) when he tried to create a chronology of the Bible. (Though there are parts that are thought to be added from other time periods and could even be taken from Greek mythology, unless of course Greek mythology is developed using a common past.)

The book is so inclusive and detailed that it would be almost impossible to recreate. And according to translators it is written in a very pure and ancient Hebrew in such a beautiful style that it should be read as a great literary work, even though it cannot be proven that this is the same Book of Jasher that existed 3,000-3,500 years ago.

Where Does It Come from?

Josephus, the famous Jewish historian who cooperated with the Romans at the time of Christ, also knew about the Book of Jasher. He says that "by this book are to be understood certain records kept in some safe place on purpose, giving an account of what happened among the Hebrews from year to year, and called Jasher or the upright, on account of the fidelity of the annals." It can also be translated as "the correct record."

According to the Hebrew version's preface, the scrolls were found during the destruction of Jerusalem in the year 70 under Emperor Titus. While sacking and plundering a house, an officer named Sidrus found a false wall behind which a room full of Jewish books was found. In the middle of it all sat an old man hoping to escape the plundering of the Romans. The officer took the old man and all of the books along with him from city to city until they ended up in Seville, Spain, where he built a spacious house for himself, the old man, and the books.

When Seville was attacked by "the kings of Edom" (the Muslims?), 12 identical copies of the book were taken to Napuli (Naples) and later printed.

Possibly from the Library in Alexandria

Even if this story isn't true, the manuscript could be real. It could come from the Great Library that *King Ptolemy II of Egypt* built in Alexandria 280 BC. He gathered all of the world's works of wisdom and holy books, but in 391 AD the library was destroyed and the manuscripts spread throughout North Africa.

We know that many Jews sought refuge in Morocco and Spain. They also brought a large number of their holy scrolls. Many of these were placed in their school in Cordoba in southern Spain in the 11th century.

Doubtful Paragraph

A French professor *Jacqueline-Lise Genot-Bismuth*, who has researched the Book of Jasher in connection with a reprinting of the Hebrew Venice version from 1625 at the *Université de la Sorbonne Nouvelle* in 1986,[5] believes the work to be written in the Middle Ages by a learned Jew. She bases this theory on the fact that European words are seen in the text, words that should come from a newer period.

Others believe that these European sections could be newer additions, a kind of updating, but that the work itself is much older. Besides this, Genot-Bismuth proves the likelihood of the book being brought to the Venetian publisher from Morocco by *Jacob Son of Atya,* whom she believes to be the same person as *Jacob the Scribe*, a famous man from the Portuguese association with Morocco in the 16th century.

When the Rabbi Council of Venice took it upon itself to publish the Book of Jasher, it was done with great difficulty. The members had to decipher the ancient Hebrew text from a tattered scroll where at times it was almost illegible. This fact is told to us by the translator, *Joseph Haqatan* from Venice, in the printed Hebrew version of 1625.

What Can We Use It For?

We do not know if the Book of Jasher is the same as the book mentioned in the Bible 3,500 years ago, but even if it came later, it contains information the Jews – either orally or in writing – passed down since ancient times.[6] For example, it says that Noah's wife was the daughter of Enoch and was named Naamah, that the people were given 120 years to turn from their ways, and that it took five years to build the Ark.

Unfortunately, we cannot be sure of this information, just as we cannot be 100% sure of other sources. Therefore, we must accept reading the Book of Jasher as an interesting book that may well contain reliable information. That is why we have taken it into consideration here.

For the believing Christian, it is important that the book has not been canonized by the church as being inspired by God, and as one critic of the authenticity of The Book of Jasher remarks, "I can only conclude that while Jasher is an interesting book to read, the reader must be very discerning as to the truth of all or any of the writings in Jasher."[7]

Mordecai Manuel Noah (1785-1851) journalist, playwright, diplomat, attorney, and politician in New York. In 1825 he planned on gathering all of the world's persecuted Jews to create a state in the western part of New York State – together with the Indians. He became the consul in Tunis in 1813. Owner and editor of the New York newspaper, the 'National Advocate', which supported state independence and slavery. From 1820-1828 he was elected New York City sheriff and in 1829 director of the Port Authority. In 1826 he founded The New York Enquirer, which merged with the 'New York Morning Courier' in 1828. In 1833 he started he 'Evening Star', which went down in 1842. He continued as a journalist and politician until his death in 1851. At this point he was the most well-known Jew in America.

The Book of Jasher

We shall now read chapters 4-6, which deal specifically with Noah and the Ark. Footnotes refer to the equivalent biblical text.

Remarks to Chapter 4:

- Chapter 4 is more or less the same as the biblical story, but the evil of man is defined more precisely here. In the Bible, Genesis 6:5 states, "Then the Lord saw that the wickedness of man was great on the earth, and that every intent of the thoughts of his heart was only evil continually" and in 6:13, "...for the earth is filled with violence because of them."
- In verse 20 it is mentioned that the righteous died out before the flood came. This is reiterated in chapter 5, verse 5.

Remarks to Chapter 5:

- In verses 8-11 mankind is given a 120-year warning. In the Bible (Genesis 6:3) 120 years is also mentioned, but this is normally translated as a limit on the age of man being 120 years.
- In verses 15-18 Noah marries Naamah, who is 91 years older than he is and is the daughter of Enoch. We are also told that Japheth was born first and then Shem (the father of the Jews and the Arabs) and Ham. In Genesis 6:10 they are named as Shem, Ham, and Japheth. We are not told who is the oldest.
- In verses 22-24 we are told that Noah and Methuselah tried to warn the "sons of men", but when that did not work, God decided to fulfill his threat. In the Bible we do not hear about this.
- In verse 28 Noah is to „finish above a cubit." That is, add one more cubit "above." In Genesis 6:16 the text is a bit shaky. Some Bible

translations are in agreement with the Book of Jasher, while others understand it to mean a row of windows.

- In verse 32 Noah chooses wives for his sons, while the Bible just says they took their wives with them on the Ark. In verse 35 we are told that they were siblings and Methuselah's daughters.
- In verse 34 we are told that the Ark took 5 years to build.

Remarks to Chapter 6:

- Here we are given a vivid description of how the animals got into the Ark (verses 1-10). The Bible only mentions that "...they went into the ark to Noah, by twos of all flesh in which was the breath of life." Genesis 7:15.
- In verse 11 the way the Flood came is revealed: "...the Lord caused the whole earth to shake, and the sun darkened, and the foundations of the world raged, and the whole earth was moved violently, and the lightning flashed, and the thunder roared, and all the fountains in the earth were broken up, such as was not known to the inhabitants before." This leads one the think of the theory that the Flood was caused by a mighty meteor or that another planet came too close to the earth causing violent upheaval.
- Both the Bible and Jasher speak of "the fountains of the deep" that were broken up (a volcanic eruption?) so that water (came spraying?) up.
- In verses 16-25 we are shown a picture of people that wanted to get into the Ark – even by force.
- Verses 28-31 reveals that the Ark did not just float around but was tossed violently, and all were afraid.
- Verse 35: The resting place is the same: the mountains of Ararat.
- Verse 36: tells us that they were tired of being closed up in the Ark.
- In verse 38, Jasher tells us that Noah and the others were in the Ark an entire year. The Bible names two specific dates: the 17th day in the second month where the fountains of the great deep burst open and the floodgates of the sky were opened (Genesis 7:11). On the 27th day in the second month (the following year), the earth was dry (Genesis 8:14). One year and ten days.

Book of Jasher

CHAPTER 4

1 And all the days that Enoch lived upon earth, were three hundred and sixty-five years.

2 And when Enoch had ascended into heaven, all the kings of the earth rose and took Methuselah his son and anointed him, and they caused him to reign over them in the place of his father.

3 And Methuselah acted uprightly in the sight of God, as his father Enoch had

taught him, and he likewise during the whole of his life taught the sons of men wisdom, knowledge and the fear of God, and he did not turn from the good way either to the right or to the left.

4 But in the latter days of Methuselah, the sons of men turned from the Lord, they corrupted the earth, they robbed and plundered each other, and they rebelled against God and they transgressed, and they corrupted their ways, and would not hearken to the voice of Methuselah, but rebelled against him.

5 And the Lord was exceedingly wroth against them, and the Lord continued to destroy the seed in those days, so that there was neither sowing nor reaping in the earth.

6 For when they sowed the ground in order that they might obtain food for their support, behold, thorns and thistles were produced which they did not sow.

7 And still the sons of men did not turn from their evil ways, and their hands were still extended to do evil in the sight of God, and they provoked the Lord with their evil ways, and the Lord was very wroth, and repented that he had made man.[8]

8 And he thought to destroy and annihilate them and he did so.

9 In those days when Lamech the son of Methuselah was one hundred and sixty years old, Seth the son of Adam died.

10 And all the days that Seth lived, were nine hundred and twelve years, and he died. 9

11 And Lamech was one hundred and eighty years old when he took Ashmua, the daughter of Elisha the son of Enoch his uncle, and she conceived.

12 And at that time the sons of men sowed the ground, and a little food was produced, yet the sons of men did not turn from their evil ways, and they trespassed and rebelled against God.

13 And the wife of Lamech conceived and bore him a son at that time, at the revolution (the end) of the year.

14 And Methuselah called his name Noah, saying, "The earth was in his days at rest and free from corruption," and Lamech his father called his name Menachem, saying, "This one shall comfort us in our works and miserable toil in the earth, which God had cursed."[10]

15 And the child grew up and was weaned, and he went in the ways of his father Methuselah, perfect and upright with God.

16 And all the sons of men departed from the ways of the Lord in those days as they multiplied upon the face of the earth with sons and daughters, and they taught one another their evil practices and they continued sinning against the Lord.

17 And every man made unto himself a god, and they robbed and plundered every man his neighbor as well as his relative, and they corrupted the earth, and the earth was filled with violence.

18 And their judges and rulers went to the daughters of men and took their wives by force from their husbands according to their choice, and the sons of men in those days took from the cattle of the earth, the beasts of the field and the fowls of the air, and taught the mixture of animals of one species with the other, in order therewith to provoke the Lord; and God saw the whole earth and it was

corrupt, for all flesh had corrupted its ways upon earth, all men and all animals.11

19 And the Lord said, "I will blot out man that I created from the face of the earth, yea from man to the birds of the air, together with cattle and beasts that are in the field for I repent that I made them."

20 And all men who walked in the ways of the Lord, died in those days, before the Lord brought the evil upon man which he had declared, for this was from the Lord, that they should not see the evil which the Lord spoke of concerning the sons of men.

21 And Noah found grace in the sight of the Lord, and the Lord chose him and his children to raise up seed from them upon the face of the whole earth.

CHAPTER 5

1 And it was in the eighty-fourth year of the life of **Noah**, that Enoch the son of Seth died, he was nine hundred and five years old at his death.

2 And in the one hundred and seventy ninth year of the life of Noah, Cainan the son of Enosh died, and all the days of Cainan were nine hundred and ten years, and he died. [12]

3 And in the two hundred and thirty fourth year of the life of Noah, Mahlallel the son of Cainan died, and the days of Mahlallel were eight hundred and ninety-five years, and he died.

4 And Jared the son of Mahlallel died in those days, in the three hundred and thirty-sixth year of the life of Noah; and all the days of Jared were nine hundred and sixty-two years, and he died.

5 And all who followed the Lord died in those days, before they saw the evil which God declared to do upon earth.

6 And after the lapse of many years, in the four hundred and eightieth year of the life of Noah, when all those men, who followed the Lord had died away from amongst the sons of men, and only Methuselah was then left, God said unto Noah and Methuselah, saying,

7 "Speak ye, and proclaim to the sons of men, saying, 'Thus saith the Lord, return from your evil ways and forsake your works, and the Lord will repent of the evil that he declared to do to you, so that it shall not come to pass.'"

8 "For thus saith the Lord, 'Behold I give you a period of one hundred and twenty years; if you will turn to me and forsake your evil ways, then will I also turn away from the evil which I told you, and it shall not exist,' saith the Lord."

9 And Noah and Methuselah spoke all the words of the Lord to the sons of men, day after day, constantly speaking to them.

10 But the sons of men would not hearken to them, nor incline their ears to their words, and they were stiff-necked.

11 And the Lord granted them a period of one hundred and twenty years, saying, "If they will return, then will God repent of the evil, so as not to destroy the earth."

12 Noah the son of Lamech refrained from taking a wife in those days, to beget children, for he said, "Surely now God will destroy the earth, wherefore then shall I beget children?"

13 And Noah was a just man, he was perfect in his generation, and the Lord
chose him to raise up seed from his seed upon the face of the earth.13
14 And the Lord said unto Noah, "Take unto thee a wife, and beget children,
for I have seen thee righteous before me in this generation.
15 "And thou shalt raise up seed, and thy children with thee, in the midst of
the earth"; and Noah went and took a wife, and he chose Naamah the daughter
of Enoch, and she was five hundred and eighty years old.
16 And Noah was four hundred and ninety-eight years old, when he took
Naamah for a wife.
17 And Naamah conceived and bare a son, and he called his name Japheth,
saying, "God has enlarged me in the earth"; and she conceived again and bare
a son, and he called his name Shem, saying, "God has made me a remnant, to
raise up seed in the midst of the earth."[14]
18 And Noah was five hundred and two years old when Naamah bore Shem,
and the boys grew up and went in the ways of the Lord, in all that Methuselah
and Noah their father taught them.
19 And Lamech the father of Noah, died in those days; yet verily he did not
go with all his heart in the ways of his father, and he died in the hundred and
ninety-fifth year of the life of Noah.
20 And all the days of Lamech were seven hundred and seventy years, and
he died.[15]
21 And all the sons of men who knew the Lord, died in that year before the
Lord brought evil upon them; for the Lord willed them to die, so as not to behold
the evil that God would bring upon their brothers and relatives, as he had so
declared to do.
22 In that time, the Lord said to Noah and Methuselah, "Stand forth and
proclaim to the sons of men all the words that I spoke to you in those days,
peradventure they may turn from their evil ways, and I will then repent of the
evil and will not bring it."
23 And Noah and Methuselah stood forth, and said in the ears of the sons of
men, all that God had spoken concerning them.
24 But the sons of men would not hearken, neither would they incline their
ears to all their declarations.
25 And it was after this that the Lord said to Noah, "The end of all flesh is come
before me, on account of their evil deeds, and behold I will destroy the earth.16
26 "And do thou take unto thee gopher wood, and go to a certain place and
make a large ark, and place it in that spot.
27 "And thus shalt thou make it; three hundred cubits its length, fifty cubits
broad and thirty cubits high.
28 "And thou shalt make unto thee a door, open at its side, and to a cubit thou
shalt finish above, and cover it within and without with pitch.
29 "And behold I will bring the flood of waters upon the earth, and all flesh be
destroyed, from under the heavens all that is upon earth shall perish.
30 "And thou and thy household shall go and gather two couple of all living

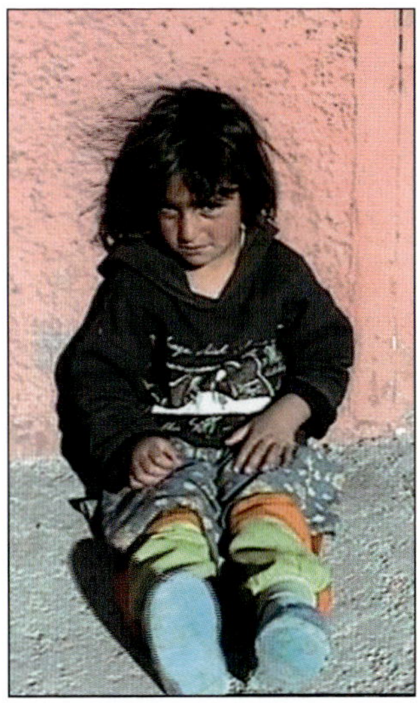

One shouldn't trust strangers, this little Kurdish girl from the village Üzengili seems to think...

things, male and female, and shall bring them to the ark, to raise up seed from them upon earth.

31 "And gather unto thee all food that is eaten by all the animals, that there may be food for thee and for them.

32 "And thou shalt choose for thy sons three maidens, from the daughters of men, and they shall be wives to thy sons."

33 And Noah rose up, and he made the ark, in the place where God had commanded him, and Noah did as God had ordered him.

34 In his five hundred and ninety-fifth year, Noah commenced to make the ark, and he made the ark in five years, as the Lord had commanded.

35 Then Noah took the three daughters of Eliakim, son of Methuselah, for wives for his sons, as the Lord had commanded Noah.

36 And it was at that time Methuselah the son of Enoch died, nine hundred and sixty years old was he, at his death.[17]

CHAPTER 6

1 At that time, after the death of Methuselah, the Lord said to Noah, "Go thou with thy household into the ark; behold I will gather to thee all the animals of the earth, the beasts of the field and the fowls of the air, and they shall all come and surround the ark.[18]

2 "And thou shalt go and seat thyself by the doors of the ark, and all the beasts, the animals, and the fowls, shall assemble and place themselves before thee, and such of them as shall come and crouch before thee, shalt thou take and deliver into the hands of thy sons, who shall bring them to the ark, and all that will stand before thee thou shalt leave."

3 And the Lord brought this about on the next day, and animals, beasts and fowls came in great multitudes and surrounded the ark.

4 And Noah went and seated himself by the door of the ark, and of all flesh that crouched before him, he brought into the ark, and all that stood before him he left upon earth.

5 And a lioness came, with her two whelps, male and female, and the three crouched before Noah, and the two whelps rose up against the lioness and smote her, and made her flee from her place, and she went away, and they returned to their places, and crouched upon the earth before Noah.

6 And the lioness ran away, and stood in the place of the lions.

7 And Noah saw this, and wondered greatly, and he rose and took the two whelps, and brought them into the ark.

8 And Noah brought into the ark from all living creatures that were upon earth, so that there was none left but which Noah brought into the ark.

9 Two and two came to Noah into the ark, but from the clean animals, and clean fowls, he brought seven couples, as God had commanded him.

10 And all the animals, and beasts, and fowls, were still there, and they surrounded the ark at every place, and the rain had not descended till seven days after.

11 And on that day, the Lord caused the whole earth to shake, and the sun

darkened, and the foundations of the world raged, and the whole earth was moved violently, and the lightning flashed, and the thunder roared, and all the fountains in the earth were broken up, such as was not known to the inhabitants before; and God did this mighty act, in order to terrify the sons of men, that there might be no more evil upon earth.

12 And still the sons of men would not return from their evil ways, and they increased the anger of the Lord at that time, and did not even direct their hearts to all this.

13 And at the end of seven days, in the six hundredth year of the life of Noah, the waters of the flood were upon the earth.

14 And all the fountains of the deep were broken up, and the windows of heaven were opened, and the rain was upon the earth forty days and forty nights.

15 And Noah and his household, and all the living creatures that were with him, came into the ark on account of the waters of the flood, and the Lord shut him in.

16 And all the sons of men that were left upon the earth, became exhausted through evil on account of the rain, for the waters were coming more violently upon the earth, and the animals and beasts were still surrounding the ark.

17 And the sons of men assembled together, about seven hundred thousand men and women, and they came unto Noah to the ark.

18 And they called to Noah, saying, "Open for us that we may come to thee in the ark—and wherefore shall we die?"

19 And Noah, with a loud voice, answered them from the ark, saying, "Have you not all rebelled against the Lord, and said that he does not exist? and therefore the Lord brought upon you this evil, to destroy and cut you off from the face of the earth.

20 "Is not this the thing that I spoke to you of one hundred and twenty years back, and you would not hearken to the voice of the Lord, and now do you desire to live upon earth?"

21 And they said to Noah, "We are ready to return to the Lord; only open for us that we may live and not die."

22 And Noah answered them, saying, "Behold now that you see the trouble of your souls, you wish to return to the Lord; why did you not return during these hundred and twenty years, which the Lord granted you as the determined period?

23 "But now you come and tell me this on account of the troubles of your souls, now also the Lord will not listen to you, neither will he give ear to you on this day, so that you will not now succeed in your wishes."

24 And the sons of men approached in order to break into the ark, to come in on account of the rain, for they could not bear the rain upon them.

25 And the Lord sent all the beasts and animals that stood round the ark. And the beasts overpowered them and drove them from that place, and every man went his way and they again scattered themselves upon the face of the earth.

26 And the rain was still descending upon the earth, and it descended forty days and forty nights, and the waters prevailed greatly upon the earth; and all flesh that was upon the earth or in the waters died, whether men, animals, beasts,

creeping things or birds of the air, and there only remained Noah and those that were with him in the ark.

27 And the waters prevailed and they greatly increased upon the earth, and they lifted up the ark and it was raised from the earth.

28 And the ark floated upon the face of the waters, and it was tossed upon the waters so that all the living creatures within were turned about like pottage in a cauldron.

29 And great anxiety seized all the living creatures that were in the ark, and the ark was like to be broken.

30 And all the living creatures that were in the ark were terrified, and the lions roared, and the oxen lowed, and the wolves howled, and every living creature in the ark spoke and lamented in its own language, so that their voices reached to a great distance, and Noah and his sons cried and wept in their troubles; they were greatly afraid that they had reached the gates of death.

31 And Noah prayed unto the Lord, and cried unto him on account of this, and he said, "O Lord help us, for we have no strength to bear this evil that has encompassed us, for the waves of the waters have surrounded us, mischievous torrents have terrified us, the snares of death have come before us; answer us, O Lord, answer us, light up thy countenance toward us and be gracious to us, redeem us and deliver us."

32 And the Lord hearkened to the voice of Noah, and the Lord remembered him.19

33 And a wind passed over the earth, and the waters were still and the ark rested.

34 And the fountains of the deep and the windows of heaven were stopped, and the rain from heaven was restrained.

35 And the waters decreased in those days, and the ark rested upon the mountains of Ararat.

36 And Noah then opened the windows of the ark, and Noah still called out to the Lord at that time and he said, "O Lord, who didst form the earth and the heavens and all that are therein, bring forth our souls from this confinement, and from the prison wherein thou hast placed us, for I am much wearied with sighing."

37 And the Lord hearkened to the voice of Noah, and said to him, "When thou shalt have completed a full year thou shalt then go forth."

38 And at the revolution of the year, when a full year was completed of Noah's dwelling in the ark, the waters were dried from off the earth, and Noah put off the covering of the ark.

39 At that time, on the twenty-seventh day of the second month, the earth was dry, but Noah and his sons, and those that were with him, did not go out from the ark until the Lord told them.

40 And the day came that the Lord told them to go out, and they all went out from the ark.

41 And they went and returned every one to his way and to his place, and Noah and his sons dwelt in the land that God had told them, and they served the Lord all their days, and the Lord blessed Noah and his sons on their going

out from the ark.

42 And he said to them, "Be fruitful and fill all the earth; become strong and increase abundantly in the earth and multiply therein."

The World Is Split into Three

After all of this, in chapter 7, the names of the children of Japheth, Ham, and Shem are given. The interesting thing is that the names of the children and grandchildren become the names of the new peoples and their regions. Based on this information, Wayne Simpson[20] has created a list in which he identifies the nations that emerged. It is too comprehensive to get into now, but it is very interesting. The most important thing is that the sons of Japheth spread towards the West and got Europe, Shem's descendants got what later became the Arabic lands and the East, and Ham's descendents got Egypt and Africa.

But there are a number of modifications.

There are indications that Indo-Europeans (who spoke Sanskrit) settled in the Indus Valley. In other words some of Japheth's descendents built the first great civilization in the East.

Ham's grandson took a portion of Shem's area (i.e. later Israel, which was called the land of Canaan, one of Ham's sons). And Ham's grandson Nimrod was the first ruler of Mesopotamia where the world's first great civilization arose. The Semites and Indo-Europeans later fought valiantly to gain control of the same area.

The third great civilization, Egypt, which flourished on the Nile around the same time as the other two was most likely founded by Ham's descendents but later taken by the Greeks, who were among Japheth's seed, the kings of Egypt.

Adam and Eve's Clothes in the Ark?

In chapter 7 we see the story about Nimrod, the first ruler in the new world. He was the son of Cush, the son of Ham. He became a tyrant that later built the Tower of Babel. We can read about this in Jasher 7:24-34:

24 And the garments of skin which God made for Adam and his wife, when they went out of the garden, were given to Cush.

25 For after the death of Adam and his wife, the garments were given to Enoch, the son of Jared, and when Enoch was taken up to God, he gave them to Methuselah, his son.

26 And at the death of Methuselah, Noah took them and brought them to the ark, and they were with him until he went out of the ark.

27 And in their going out, Ham stole those garments from Noah, his father, and he took them and hid them from his brothers.

28 And when Ham begat his first born Cush, he gave him the garments in secret, and they were with Cush many days.

29 And Cush also concealed them from his sons and brothers, and when Cush had begotten Nimrod, he gave him those garments through his love for him, and

Endnotes

1 In Joshua 10:13 and 2 Samuel 1:17.

2 The book is translated into Ladino, Latin, Spanish, and English. A number of these translations can be found in the British Library's catalog (1893-1960 catalog, Vol. II). A Jewish German edition and a Hebrew edition for youth printed in Warsaw in 1923 exists, as well as, a Greek translation called "Lo Libris de los divitiis."

3 Mordecai Manuel Noah (1785-1851) journalist, playwright, diplomat, attorney, and politician in New York. (See more under picture pg. 277)

4 See http://www.ccel.org/a/anonymous/jasher.

5 Seminaire sur le Sefer Hayashar de le Centre des Recherches sur la Culture Rabbinique, Ginzberg, The Legends of the Jews (Philadelphia: Jewish Publication Society of America, 1912) includes Jasher 3:2-38 (vol. 1, pp. 127-30) and the end note (vol. 5, pp. 157-8) assumes that The Book of Jasher is a collection of older sources. Jasher is considered an authentic source in The Jewish Encyclopedia (NY: Funk and Wagnall, 1905), XII:588-9 and The Universal Jewish Encyclopedia (NY: Universal Jewish Encyclopedia Co., 1942), 6:41.

Nimrod grew up, and when he was twenty years old he put on those garments.

30 And Nimrod became strong when he put on the garments, and God gave him might and strength, and he was a mighty hunter in the earth, yea, he was a mighty hunter in the field, and he hunted the animals and he built altars, and he offered upon them the animals before the Lord.

31 And Nimrod strengthened himself, and he rose up from amongst his brethren, and he fought the battles of his brethren against all their enemies round about.

32 And the Lord delivered all the enemies of his brethren in his hands, and God prospered him from time to time in his battles, and he reigned upon earth.

33 Therefore it became current in those days, when a man ushered forth those that he had trained up for battle, he would say to them, "Like God did to Nimrod, who was a mighty hunter in the earth, and who succeeded in the battles that prevailed against his brethren, that he delivered them from the hands of their enemies, so may God strengthen us and deliver us this day."

34 And when Nimrod was forty years old, at that time there was a war between his brethren and the children of Japheth, so that they were in the power of their enemies.

Sumer Is Founded

We also hear that Nimrod goes to war with Japheth's descendents and increases his power. He builds his first city, Shinar – probably the same word as Sumer, the name of the oldest known civilization in Mesopotamia:

43. And they found a large valley opposite to the east,[21] and they built him a large and extensive city, and Nimrod called the name of the city that he built Shinar, for the Lord had vehemently shaken his enemies and destroyed them.

44. And Nimrod dwelt in Shinar, and he reigned securely, and he fought with his enemies and he subdued them, and he prospered in all his battles, and his kingdom became very great.

Abraham and Noah

But Nimrod falls to evil and haughtiness, and later in the Book of Jasher we hear that Abraham, the son of Nimrod's general, Terah, has to flee and seeks refuge with Noah where he stays for 39 years learning all the wisdom Noah and Shem can give him. In this period he stops worshiping the sun, moon, and stars (the astrology of the Chaldeans) and begins to worship the Creator himself – God. Later he stops his father from worshiping the trees, and after a long bout with Nimrod, Terah and Abraham leave Ur. They end up in Haran – just as it is told in the Bible.

Endnotes

6 Hugh Nibley writes the following concerning Jasher 3:5-10, "Passages such as this which closely follow both the Hebrew and the Slavonic Enoch show that the book of Jasher used very ancient sources and was far more than a medieval novel."
Collected Works of Hugh Nibley, Vol. 2, p. 301, fn. 380.

7 Deane Schaub, Logos Resource Pages, logosresourcepages.org/jasher.htm

8 Jasher 4:7-8 - Genesis 6:6-7.

9 Jasher 4:10 - Genesis 5:8.

10 Jasher 4:13-14 - Genesis 5:29.

11 Jasher 4:18b-19.21 - Genesis 6:5-8.

12 Jasher 5:1-4 - Genesis 5:11-20.

13 Jasher 5:13 - Genesis 6:9-10.

14 Jasher 5:17-18 - Genesis 5:32, 6:10.

15 Jasher 5:20 - Genesis 5:31.

16 Jasher 5:25-33 - Genesis 6:13-22.

17 Jasher 5:36 - Genesis 5:27.

18 Jasher 6:1-31 - Genesis 7:1-24.

19 Jasher 6:32-42 - Genesis 8,1-22-9:1.

20 Found as an appendix to Wayne Simpson's version of The Book of Jasher: The Authentic Annals of the Early Hebrews. Morris Publishing, 1995.

21 Here it says, "opposite to the east." The Bible formulates this phrase as, "journeyed east" (Genesis 11:2).

Chapter 39

The Graves of Noah and Naamah

Feizal at the finest anchor stone in the village of Arzap. It is now covered with crosses, but may have been a part of a Megalite observatory - or an astrological cult.

Each time I have been in Eastern Turkey, I have gone to "The Valley of The Eight" about 20 km from Dogubayazit. The village Arzep,[1] where the large anchor stones are, was destroyed by an earthquake in 2004. Many people died. We were lucky to visit the village just before the earthquake. We went to tea with the village leader Feizal and had the opportunity to explore the whole area.

Besides the large anchor stones, there are other stones with engravings. On one of the stones there is a so-called Zigurrat, a pyramidal temple tower, which makes us think of the Tower of Babel, mentioned shortly after the Flood. There is also an ancient symbol that reminds us of the Hurrians.

On one of the stones some ancient writing is engraved that has not yet been deciphered. Maybe it was here Noah and his wife Naamah lived after the Flood. According to the ancient Book of Jasher, Noah's wife was called *Naamah* and was a daughter of Enoch, who also was the father of Methuselah according to Genesis 5:18-20.[2]

Tea at Feizal's

Hot springs pop up all around the volcanic area like this one, a dammed pool in the vicinity of Arzep.

In the beginning, the villagers in Arzep were hostile towards foreigners; they even threw stones at them. Maybe this is due to the Armenian and Christian origins of this village whose ancestors were persecuted over a hundred years ago. The Armenians were not completely without blame in that they sought help from Russia, but that is another very complicated story. War and strife have left a dark shadow of hate and hostility towards outsiders – or maybe it's because of a feeling of guilt. Whatever the case, being on guard against foreigners is a part of Eastern culture. Outsiders are the enemy until proven otherwise. But once deemed a friend, the hospitality of the East is at one's feet. This is made obvious by, among other things, eating together.

When we came here in 2004, we were even invited into Feizal's house, which was equipped with a satellite dish on the roof and woven carpets on the floors.

We put our shoes outside and sat on pillows on the floor as Feizal and his wife and children welcomed us with tea served in glasses. Pictures from earlier visits were happily shown and then given to those who were in them.

A group of children popped their heads in the open door in order to see the strangers. After tea and talk we went out to the stones together.

The Tower of Babel and the Writing on the Stone

We studied and took pictures of the stones and poured water on them to see the shades more clearly. We found the stone with the "Tower of Babel." It had been made in a more primitive way than the crosses.

On another stone were engraved some characters which nobody had been able to decipher so far and which we therefore assumed was to be very old. And below them, again we could see some crosses and a beautifully engraved tree or flower.

In May 2004, I sent the picture to Michael Westh, a theologian who has been living in Armenia and is considered to be an expert in the field. He was able to tell me that it was Armenian.

The first line goes: "Put up cross." Then a line follows that makes no sense: "jare khav sjusi." The third line begins with: "aj. Ira (or Illa)."

It is written in West Armenian, the dialect where the orthography up to this day is closest to Old Armenian.

In the line "Put up cross" (3rd person singularis, aorist) the "writer" has used the second 'v' and not the first 'v' in the Armenian alphabet which usually characterizes 3rd person singular aorist. In other words, he used the 'v' that a modern Armenian would use in East Armenian or which a non-academic would use.

"The Armenian alphabet came into existence shortly after Byzantium and Persia divided the Armenian kingdom in 387 A.C., which meant that it stopped existing," Westh tells.

In Armenia, as in Iran/Babylon, they formerly used cuneiform, Syrian or Greek alphabets, and it was to preserve Armenian identity, language and culture that the Armenian alphabet was created only a few years later.

Above: A stone with a cross and a very old Hurrian or Hittite symbol.

Below: A close-up of the upper portion of the stone with an inscription written with letters that were at the time yet to be deciphered. We later found out that it was either West Armenian or Old Armenian…

However, Michael Westh doesn't think that the writing on the stone is more than 250 years old, and compared to Armenian standard writing, it is more like graffiti. But the exact meaning of the text is still unknown.

"You find a similar poor style in the dreadful years from the middle of the seventeen hundreds in Armenia, i.e. toward the end of the Iranian period," Westh says, who thinks that the cross and the ornamentation, on the other hand, are very old. "You find the ornamentation *under* the big cross in the middle used in the same way in Armenia as part of a cross where the cross may appear as a tree of life. But here you find an extra "bar" under the cross which might indicate that the cross and the bar with the ball have been made at different times."

Hot Springs

After having seen the stones in the village, we began, together with Feizal, on a long trek through the surrounding area to find the other stones.

The Region of the Eight is filled with natural hot springs and natural soda water. A Turkish family is having their family washing day at one of the springs that forces water up through the ground forming a little pond. Of course, it is the women that do the hard work while the men and boys swim in the pond. They invite me in, and after having walked so much in the blistering sun, I'm ready. So I pull up my pants and wade in the cool soda water together with them.

We're running around with cameras, so we are naturally asked to take pictures of these lovely people, and we promise to send them copies. When they find out that we are here because of Nuhun Gemisi – Noah's Ark – they point to Mt. Ararat, which rises impressively against the blue sky.

Noah and Naamah's Graves Plundered?

The Valley of the Eight has its namesake in the eight that survived the Flood. Maybe that number had already increased by the time they left the Ark, and non-biblical accounts tell of others. Whatever the case, the numbers grew quickly because after just a few centuries we can read about the existence of thousands of people, even nations.

The stone with the Tower of Babel or at least an engraved zigurrat. - Close-up is below.

We assume that the survivors gathered quickly and grew to a number too large to live in this valley, so the sons and their descendants spread out. They followed the rivers – for example, the Euphrates – down from the mountains and into the open plains.[4] They called the plains Shinar. Even today Shinar is the name of a large plain in southern Turkey that can be found by following the Euphrates down through the mountains and then turning east. But most Bible experts think that Shinar refers to an area further south in Iraq.

That is where they set down roots, and that is where they built the Tower of Babel. And there in Mesopotamia between the two great rivers – the Euphrates and the Tigris – the first known civilizations developed.

But Noah and Naamah probably stayed up here in the Valley of the Eight in the Ararat Mountains. At least we are not told that they followed the others.

In 1977 Ron Wyatt's two sons, Danny and Ronny, actually found two very interesting gravestones. Both markers had eight crosses engraved on top of an older engraving (a so-called petroglyph, a drawing in stone) that suggested the death of Noah on the one and his wife on the other. The stones were found in front of a very old stone house in a flat, open field just below some small mountains.

The site was videotaped, and Mrs. Mary Nell Wyatt later drew a sketch of the engravings.

In it we can see a rainbow over eight people. Half of them have long hair (women), and half have long beards (men). Six of the people are smaller than the other two, who most likely represent Noah and Naamah. On the drawing Naamah is looking down with closed eyes, which could show that she died first, while both have closed eyes and bowed heads on the second stone. This might suggest that Noah, too, had died.

Feizal helping us to find "Naamah's grave"...

...and Elin immediately sees how much room is in the grave by crawling down into the dark hole, lit up on this photograph to show the size.

There is also a boat on top of a wave, which is quite a sight up here in the mountains where there are neither lakes nor seas. There can be no doubt that this engraving is a reference to the story of the Ark.

Besides all of this, the story of the Flood was found described on one of the walls of the house. This is documented on a video recording in the possession of the Wyatt's who have, for the time being, not made the tape available in its entirety. On a video sold by the Wyatt Archaeological Museum, the two gravestones can be seen but the engravings cannot due to the lighting which causes the headstones to appear black. These stones and the wall were probably engraved long after Noah and Naamah, but we don't know because the stones were removed by local thieves shortly after, and the house was destroyed by the villagers who used the stones from the building in constructing their own houses. However, the video proves that this is not just a good story. The stones and the house were there, and to this day remains of the house are still there. If one looks closely, the plundered graves can be found as well.

Where Are They Now?

Today, where the graves were claimed to have been, we find only a big hole in the ground where the house stood. There are also two new holes on the right side of the house where Mary Nell Wyatt's drawings show that the gravestones were. Gold fever has infected the locals and not without merit! A large treasure of gold and jewelry has supposedly been removed from Naamah's grave along with everything else that may have been there.

A strong local rumor says that a large sarcophagus, 18 feet (5½ meters) in length, was dug up from under Naamah's headstone. The sarcophagus disappeared; it was taken during the night.

Who Were the Grave Robbers?

Jonathan Gray, an Australian Ark hunter, claims in his book *The Ark Conspiracy* [5] that the graves were plundered by an ark hunter in collusion with the village chief, Mehmet, and taken on a truck in the middle of the night.

While we were there, I heard a different explanation though. Rumors now say that a prominent official stood behind the looting, and the villagers don't claim responsibility for the theft. Feizal explained to Bill Fry that he and his wife heard a truck in the middle of the night and saw it drive off with its lights turned off, and the next day the grave was empty.

Both Bill Fry and Jonathan Gray have asked the authorities about the stone coffin that was removed, but no one seems to know anything about it.

We observe an "anchor stone" - or is it one of the stones that were used to calculate the seasons? It also has crosses engraved but is partially destroyed at the end where the hole exists. It doesn't lie with the other stones in Arzap but high upon a hilltop - and one may wonder how it ended up here ...

Not a Coffin, But a Tomb

A few days later, I was talking with Dr. Bayraktutan, who has been involved in research in this area for over 20 years. He is skeptical of all of these stories. He doesn't lend any credence to the account of an oversized skull either, which we will talk about later on.

"But," he says, "on the other side of the border, in Iran, there is a place where the Muslim pilgrims go; it is called 'Noah's wife's grave'. There is a grave there too that is 5-6 meters long. It is also a type of sarcophagus, but the body – if there is one – is not lying in a stone coffin. The walls of the grave are made of stone. It is very normal in Eastern Anatolia to find old graves that are 5-6 meters long. The body doesn't fill the entire grave. It is just the grave chamber that is so large. As far as I know, that is also the way it was out here in the Region of the Eight. The stones made a grave chamber that was 18 feet long. They have since been removed, just as the local people take everything else they can use," sneers Salih. "They have no understanding of the archeological worth. What they see is stone – and gold."

Among the special attractions to which the boys in the Valley of the Eight led us were also "Noah's footsteps" - and there is actually a "footprint" in the rocks beside what some consider to be Noah's altar. One may wonder how it came to be there...

Noah's Altar?

We walked around looking for the place that Wyatt and others suspected of being Noah's altar. It is supposed to be found a short distance up in the small mountains towards the west. We were just a handful of people, and we had Feizal from the village with us when we got to the supposed altar. We were not very convinced. There may have been a groove carved in the large rock for the blood to run out, but it didn't look like an altar. Using "sign language," we asked Feizal if this was Noah's altar. "No," he answered and pointed further up the mountain. We followed him and together found some large stones with crevices chiseled in them so the blood from offered animals could run out. It would also be more likely to build an altar here, further up the mountain.

Encouraged by Feizal's guidance, we also asked about the

grave of Noah's wife. He pointed in the opposite direction of the house, and again we followed him over rocky terrain. After a longer hike, he showed us a large hole with flat walls. This was clearly a grave chamber. It was, however, most definitely not 18 feet long anymore.

Feizal claimed that three people lay in this grave. We needed to get this cleared up, once and for all. We found a local guide and translator, Zafer Önay, and asked him to explain what Feizal had shown us. When he started translating, it suddenly turned into a very complicated story. We asked again and Zafer told us a different story...

Ron Wyatt (right) with the "too long" thumb bone found in "The Valley of the Eight." The bone is on display at the Wyatt Archaeological Museum.

Larger People?

We made it up to an area where there is an entire cemetery of ancient Urartu graves from the first kingdom in this area – Urartu; a word that is later changed to Ararat in the Bible. Urartu was a great kingdom that ended around 700 BC but whose beginnings are unknown. Maybe it went back to the days of Noah. The only other nation that may have been in this area before them is the Hurrian. The name means the ancient or the noble. No one really knows if they were an independent people or if this was a term for the first, probably *larger* people that lived up here after the Flood.

Larger people...?

1. In connection with the Flood, the Bible tells that *before* it (the Flood) "but also since" there have been giants.

2. Both the Bible and the Sumerian tablets tell of ten kings that lived before the Flood and who lived much longer than those that came after it. The Sumerian is the oldest known kingdom in Mesopotamia – and the world. The ages of their kings are much higher than those of the Bible, which are under 1,000 years, while the Sumerians' speak of ages as high as tens of thousands of years. The reason for this is probably a mistranslation where weeks became years in the ancient scriptures.

3. Ron Wyatt found a human bone here, specifically the top joint of a thumb, which was almost twice as big as ours are today; almost four inches. A picture taken of the bone can be seen below.

We find a number of stones from the Hurrian or Urartu Period. Here is one with a sword.

But being the skeptics we are, we wanted to see proof ourselves.

Suddenly, something happened. Vivian Broughton, a young Norwegian nurse, hopped down from one of the tombs the grave robbers have recently emptied in their search for treasure. And here she found some human bones. Together, we moved some of the stones lying on

In a closed courtyard in Kazan Arzap, we found this ram, presumably made by Hurians or Urarturians 3,000-4,000 years ago.
The second stone ram among other things had a curved sword engraved - which residents had highlighted in green paint ...

The rescue party reaches the earth-quake-stricken villages; 18 have already been lost.
(Photo: Zafer Onay, 2004)

Feizal, who had welcomed us heartily the week before, on this picture is seen in his bed outdoors. An earthquake had hit The Valley of the Eight and destroyed his house. (Photo: Zafer Onay)

the bottom, and more bones came forth. Some of the bones seemed to come from a child. But one bone surprised us. Again, it was a finger joint, and Vivien said it was probably longer than a normal finger joint.

I found a grave that not only contains the remains of a ram's head with its curly horns, which suggests that this is an Urartian grave, but also contains a curved sword! It is not just buried. No, the sword is prominent because part of the stone around it has been removed.

Again, we had to settle with photography and film and then leave this fantastic memory of prehistory to grave robbers and treasure hunters. It's very frustrating, but at the same time it's impossible to protect an entire valley 24 hours a day.

After a long day of trekking dusty trails with the harsh rays of the sun beating down on us, we returned to the hotel in Dogubayazit. I found the Book of Jasher, which has previously been mentioned and read again the story of Noah and Naamah hoping to discover something new.

Endnotes

1 According to the Book of Jasher 5:16-18, Noah's wife Naamah was the little sister of Methuselah, whose name means "when he dies, it will come." And the same year he died, the Flood came. Interestingly enough, it does not say that Noah's father-in-law, Enoch, died, but rather, "Thus all the days of Enoch were three hundred sixty-five years. Enoch walked with God; then he was no more, because God took him." Genesis 5:23-24

2 This village has previously been mistakenly called Kazan. But Kazan is a few miles up in the mountains and does not have any headstones (not anymore at least). This is the village we visited in the valley, Arzep, which has the many headstones connected to the name "The Region of the Eight."

4 "And as they migrated from the east, they came upon a plain in the land of Shinar and settled there." Genesis 11:2

5 *The Ark Conspiracy* was released in 1993 for Australian Seminar Services, P.O. Box 3370, Greenfield Street, Adelaide 5000, South Australia, Australia.

Chapter 40

Gilgamesh Visits Noah

One of the Sumerian clay tablets containing part of the story about Gilgamesh written in cuneiform.

Back to the days of Noah.

Five generations after Noah, a man by the name of Gilgamesh lived in Iraq.

Thousands of clay tablets have been found in the ancient city of Nineveh by the Tigris River that tell a long and fascinating story about Gilgamesh. Gilgamesh was a king in the city Uruk in Sumer in southern Iraq. At one point he visited a sage named Utnapishtim up in the mountains. This wise man was probably old Noah.

That's why the story of Gilgamesh is an exciting piece in our search for the actual existence of Noah's Ark.

We have here a very, very old source, maybe older than the Bible, that also tells us about the Flood and a man that survived it. Even more so, the hero visits this man and hears his story.

The tablets from Nineveh (as well as tablets found other places) have texts written in Sumerian, Akkadian, Babylonian, Assyrian, Hittite, and Hurrian. The account that is normally translated regarding Gilgamesh is the Akkadian account from 700 BC with some additions from the other versions in order to fill in some of the holes.

There is a lot of variation in how the account is told, but there is no doubt that the reference is to the same event.

Before and After the Flood

"The Flood was even more deeply rooted in the Babylonian historical consciousness than ours. They split up their past into 'before the Flood' and 'after the Flood' and everything that lay 'before the Flood' was mysterious prehistory," wrote the two Danish experts, Ulla and Aage Westenholz in the preface to their new 1995 translation of Gilgamesh.[1]

The Sumerian tablets tell about a line of up to 10 kings that reigned before the Flood and a line of kings that reigned afterwards. The Bible also mentions precisely 10 forefathers that were before the Flood.

King in One of the First City-States

In order to place Gilgamesh in a historical context, we are again going to look at both archeological views and biblical accounts. Archeologists are roughly in agreement that around 3,000 BC and thereafter, a number of small city-kingdoms arose in ancient Sumer. At this point there was no unified kingdom, but some of these cities had created a cooperative union.

One of these city-states was Uruk. According to the ancient tablets, the fifth king of Uruk after the Flood was Gilgamesh. Even though archeologists and historians of ancient history date Gilgamesh to be around 2900 BC, Gilgamesh could have lived later or earlier than this, because Gilgamesh is first spoken of as the king of Uruk in a source written in 1820 BC, and the Akkadian version, the source most translated, is from the 7th century BC.

When scientists want to establish a date, they are often walking on shaky ground and have to set their dates based on assumptions of fixed points in time which can later be moved based on new findings. For example, a seal cylinder has been found which is confirmed to be from around 2120 BC. This cylinder apparently has a scene from Gilgamesh on it of a man fighting with a bull. We can thus conclude that Gilgamesh lived before this time. In the story, Gilgamesh takes a warning, and we know (or think) that portending was practiced between 2000 and 1850 BC. He could have lived at this point, but because it is believed that he lived earlier, this portending is assumed to be an addition at this point.

But as mentioned above, archeologists and ancient historians assume that Gilgamesh lived around 2900 BC. According to the old Septuagint version of the Old Testament, the Flood can be fixed at around 3537 BC. According to this chronology, Noah died in approximately 3187 BC. Gilgamesh visited Noah (called Utnapishtim) while he was still a young hunter with much strength and before he became king in Uruk, so he was probably not more than 40 years old. But Gilgamesh's description of Noah as a man who has gained eternal life could lead to the assumption that this happened in Noah's old age. My guess is that Gilgamesh came to see him around 3185 BC and that Gilgamesh himself lived from 3225 BC and that the city states in Sumer arose a bit earlier than normally assumed. Some historians actually believe that the cities began to appear already around 3300 BC, so here are no major differences of opinion.

Gilgamesh can very possibly have lived at the time when descendants of Noah's sons and daughters had populated Mesopotamia. He might even have been one of Kam's great-great-grandchildren.[2]

Gilgamesh conquerors with his friend Enkidu the mysterious "Sky Bull" shown on this old picture seal from Iraq.

Thousands of Clay Tablets

The clay tablets that tell, among other things, about Gilgamesh were first brought to light in the 19th century through a number of digs completed further north in Nineveh on the Tigris in northern Iraq. Nineveh was the strongest city in the Middle East when the Assyrians ruled in the last millennium before Christ.

At that time the Assyrian King Sargon II (722-

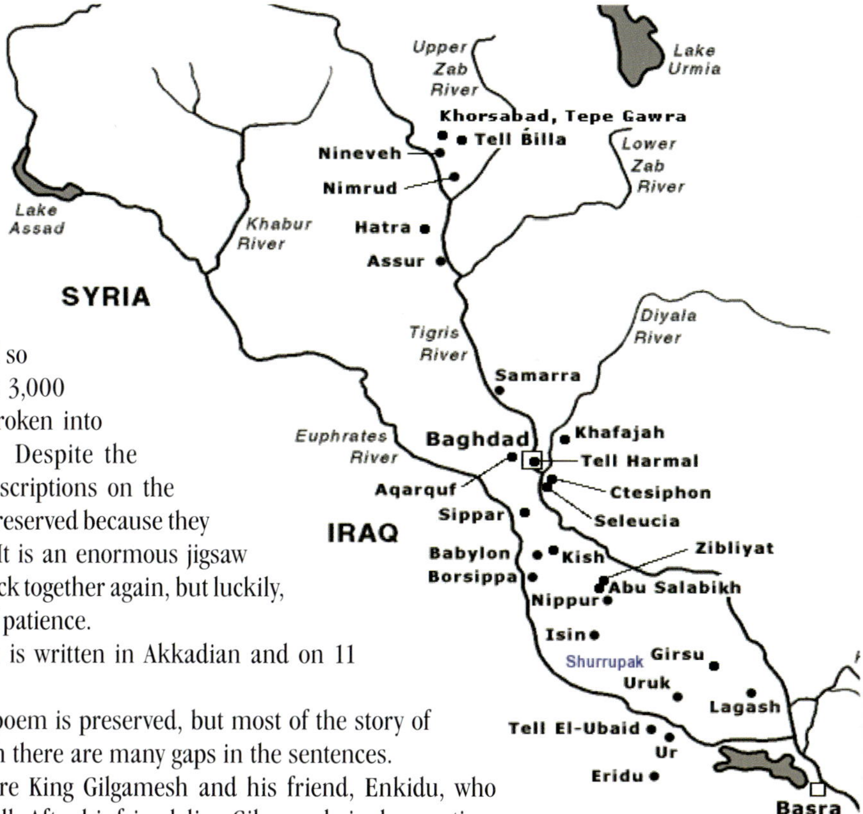

Noah is called Utnapishtim in the Gilgamesh story and came from Shurrupak. His father was Ubara-Tutu. This name is actually found in the list of kings from the ancient city of Shurrupak, known as Fara today, which lies northwest of Uruk. All of this evidence indicates that the Gilgamesh poem is more than just a story ....

705 BC) established a library in Nineveh made up of burned clay tablets. Under his successor, King Assurbanipal (669-627 BC), the library was expanded so that it contained at least 3,000 tablets, which are now broken into 24,000 bits and pieces. Despite the 2,500-3,500 years, the inscriptions on the tablets are relatively well preserved because they have lain underground. It is an enormous jigsaw puzzle to put the pieces back together again, but luckily, archeologists have a lot of patience.

The story of Gilgamesh is written in Akkadian and on 11 clay tablets.

Only about half of the poem is preserved, but most of the story of Noah can be found though there are many gaps in the sentences.

The main characters are King Gilgamesh and his friend, Enkidu, who conquer a supernatural bull. After his friend dies, Gilgamesh, in desperation, seeks out his forefather, Utnapishtim, in order to find the meaning of life. Utnapishtim is described as immortal after having survived a great flood, which very much resembles the biblical Flood. That Noah is considered immortal is not difficult to understand. He came from the generation before the Flood – a generation which lived many more years than later generations [3] – and Noah lived through many of the following generations, those of his descendants.

What Does Gilgamesh Tell Us?

The story about Gilgamesh's meeting with Noah (Utnapishtim) starts on tablet IX and continues on tablets X and XI.

Besides being a magnificent story from a literary point of view, the story of Gilgamesh may give us some relevant information, though wrapped in rhetoric and poetic wording. Here we'll cite only a few lines from this very extensive poem.

There are three factors that lead me to believe that the poem is based upon a true story.

1. Gilgamesh was a real person – he can be found named on the list of kings of Uruk as the fifth king in the city Uruk that did exist and is located in southern Iraq.

2. Gilgamesh travels through geographical surroundings that could reflect the journey from Sumer to the mountains of Ararat. The entire Anatolian plateau is full of mountains he had to pass.

3. Gilgamesh is surprised by the fact that Utnapishtim is a normal person. Even though the poem is later turned into a fairy-tale-like story, the original ingredients can still be found.

Our working theory, therefore, is that Gilgamesh existed, and due to his search for the meaning of life or immortality, he went on a journey to find ancient Noah (Utnapishtim). On the way he comes to the Twin Peaks (Mashu); he sails over a lake (possibly Turkey's largest lake, Lake Van); he sees some mighty anchor stones, and he speaks to Noah. When he comes back again, he tells his story, which is later retold from generation to generation and at some point is written down by a poet as a dramatic and mythological poem based on the successive and somewhat unrealistic account.

Having visited the area it is very easy to imagine Gilgamesh's journey.

Tablet IX starts as such in lines 1-8: [4]

Over his friend, Enkidu, Gilgamesh cried bit-
terly, roaming the wilderness.
"I am going to die!—am I not like Enkidu?!
Deep sadness penetrates my core,
I fear death, and now roam the wilderness -
I will set out to the region of Utnapishtim, son of Ubartutu,
and will go with utmost dispatch!
When I arrived at mountain passes at nightfall,'
I saw lions, and I was terrified!

After this a fight with a pride of lions follows.

Our knowing that Utnapishtim is not just an imaginary figure is based on the naming of his father. And this Ubara-Tutu can be found on the lists of kings from Shurrupak, modern Fara, northwest of Uruk. He is the only king of Kish besides Utnapishtim that is named in the list of kings before the Great Flood! So Noah and his father originated from Iraq, from a place that is now called Fara and which is situated north-west of Uruk.

In line 37 Gilgamesh is by Mashu, the "Twin Peaks":

The mountain is called Mashu.
Then he reached Mount Mashu,
which daily guards the rising and setting of the Sun,
above which only the dome of the heavens reaches,
and whose flank reaches as far as the Netherworld below,

there were Scorpion-beings watching over its gate.
Trembling terror they inspire, the sight of them is death,
their frightening aura sweeps over the mountains.
At the rising and setting they watch over the Sun.

These "Twin Peaks" lead one to think of the mountain with two connected crests, namely Big and Little Ararat.

Naturally, Gilgamesh didn't wander through the mountains as there were no tunnels but rather between them. Instead of walking around the 12-mile wide mountain, he scaled it. And that could have taken a number of days and nights, which coincides with the poem, which tells us that he can see nothing in the dark as he journeys. According to the geologist Dr. Bayraktutan, there were at least three volcanic eruptions from Mount Ararat, so it may have been possible to walk between the mountains instead of going many miles around them.

As already mentioned some English translations use the original name of Mashu instead of Twin Peaks. The old Armenian name for the mountain is Marris. According to some researchers, Mashu refers to the names of Mashur and Masher situated near the so-called boat-shaped object found on the other side of the valley in 1948 after an earthquake.[5]

Masher means Judgment Day. Mashur means Risen.

The Valley of Paradise – Or of the Eight

Finally, Gilgamesh reaches a lush garden full of gemstones. In Sumerian mythology the Noah figure found himself to be in a paradisiacal location known as Dilmun (a location that has later been determined to be some island in the Gulf, which is a misunderstanding).

I believe Gilgamesh has been telling about the "Valley of the Eight" where, according to local tradition, Noah lived and grew his grapes after the flood. The beautiful valley must have been like an oasis for Gilgamesh after a challenging trek through the mountains, and in the early morning after the terrible night, the valley may have shined like crystals to the exhausted Gilgamesh. Here he meets a female innkeeper, Siduri, who after first being frightened by Gilgamesh's jaded appearance, has a conversation with him.

The Valley of the Eight
- The valley of Paradise?

The Stone Things?

He asks for directions, and she leads him to Urshanabi, Utnapishtim's ferry keeper. He has "the stone things" (line 88). This is possibly a reference to the anchor stones Gilgamesh told of.

Shortly thereafter, Gilgamesh gets into a fight with the ferryman and ends up breaking the stone things. From line 156:

Urshanabi spoke to Gilgamesh, saying:
"It is your hands, Gilgamesh, that prevent the crossing!
You have smashed the stone things,' you have pulled out their retaining ropes (?).
'The stone things' have been smashed, their retaining ropes (!) pulled out!

As it appears from the chapter about "The Valley of the Eight," 13 such anchor stones have been found here, all with a hole at the top through which you tie a rope and use them for maneuvering the ship. If these are not the anchor stones referred to by the ferryman, what else could he be referring to? Instead, Gilgamesh is now sent into the forest to remove the bark from 300 tree trunks to make 300 poles.

Which Sea?

The question is where did this "sea" lie? Could it be Lake Van, south of Mt. Ararat, which is the biggest lake in Turkey. Gilgamesh had probably reached this lake on his way from Sumer to Ararat. It is, of course, before the Twin Peaks, but the poet may have reversed the order of events for dramatic purposes. In the poem we hear about the "Dead Sea," and Van Lake is actually a salt-water lake without outlet – a dead sea.

Another explanation would be that the valley between the mountains was not drained as now is the case. Dr. Bayraktutan believes that he has found geological signs showing that the water level was at some point in time as high as 1500 metres in the area around Dogubayazit and the Ark. Today, only a river flows through the valley, but the strata of earth show signs that there formerly has been much more water in the area.

Through Pathless Mountains

Gilgamesh tells of his grief and search for eternal life repeating that he went through trackless mountains – quite different from the flat Sumer he knows. From line 249:

Gilgamesh spoke to Utanapishtim, saying:
"That is why (?) I must go on,
to see Utanapishtim whom they call 'The Faraway.'"
I went circling through all the mountains,

When Gilgamesh visited Noah (called Utnapishtim), he passed The Twin Mountains. It is probably Mt. Ararat to which the poem refers. (Here seen from the west. Little Ararat left.) Photo: Fut-

I traversed treacherous mountains, and crossed all the seas—
that is why (!) sweet sleep has not mellowed my face,
through sleepless striving I am strained,
my muscles are filled with pain.

Afterwards, Utnapishtim tells him not to worry himself for all shall die and no one knows when. From line 298:

You have toiled without cease, and what have you got!
Through toil you wear yourself out,
you fill your body with grief,
your long lifetime you are bringing near
(to a premature end)!
Mankind, whose offshoot is snapped off like a reed in a cane break,
the fine youth and lovely girl ... death.

Just a Man

On tablet XI the conversation continues. From line 1:

Gilgamesh spoke to Utanapishtim, the Faraway:
"I have been looking at you,
but your appearance is not strange—you are like me!
You yourself are not different—you are like me!
My mind was resolved to fight with you,
(but instead?) my arm lies useless over you.
Tell me, how is it that you stand in the Assembly of the Gods,
and have found life!"

Utnapishtim Tells the Story of the Flood

Utanapishtim spoke to Gilgamesh, saying:

I will reveal to you, Gilgamesh, a thing that is hidden,
a secret of the gods I will tell you!
Shuruppak, a city that you surely know,
situated on the banks of the Euphrates,
that city was very old, and there were gods inside it.
The hearts of the Great Gods moved them to inflict the Flood.
Their Father Anu uttered the oath (of secrecy),
Valiant Enlil was their Adviser,
Ninurta was their Chamberlain,
Ennugi was their Minister of Canals.
Ea, the Clever Prince(?), was under oath with them
so he repeated their talk to the reed house:
'Reed house, reed house! Wall, wall!

O man of Shuruppak, son of Ubartutu:
Tear down the house and build a boat!
Abandon wealth and seek living beings!
Spurn possessions and keep alive living beings!
Make all living beings go up into the boat.
The boat which you are to build,
its dimensions must measure equal to each other:
its length must correspond to its width.
Roof it over like the Apsu.

From this explanation one would think that the boat should be as broad as it is long, but what is said is that the sides should correspond to each other. And that is something quite different. The sailor and Ark hunter David Fasold read this as an instruction to build the boat according to the universal rules for boat building.[6]

I understood and spoke to my lord, Ea:
'My lord, thus is the command which you have uttered
I will heed and will do it.
But what shall I answer the city, the populace, and the Elders!'
Ea spoke, commanding me, his servant:
'You, well then, this is what you must say to them:
"It appears that Enlil is rejecting me
so I cannot reside in your city (?),
nor set foot on Enlil's earth.
I will go down to the Apsu to live with my lord, Ea,
and upon you he will rain down abundance,
a profusion of fowl, myriad(!) fishes.
He will bring to you a harvest of wealth,
in the morning he will let loaves of bread shower down,
and in the evening a rain of wheat!"'
Just as dawn began to glow
the land assembled around me-
the carpenter carried his hatchet,
the reed worker carried his (flattening) stone,
... the men ...
The child carried the pitch,
the weak brought whatever else was needed.
On the fifth day I laid out her exterior.
It was a field in area,
its walls were each 10 times 12 cubits in height,
the sides of its top were of equal length,
10 times 12 cubits each.

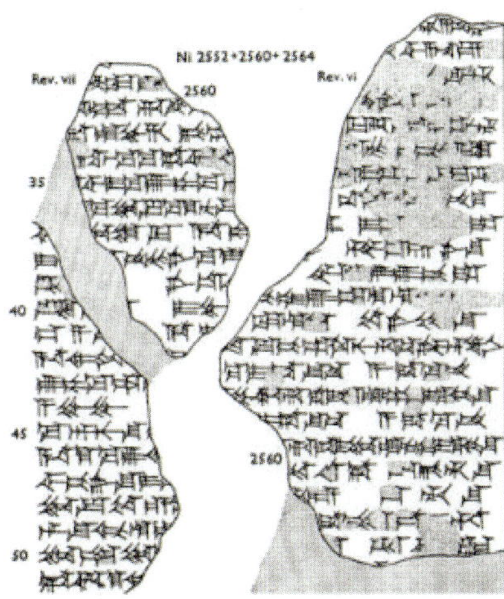

The epic of Gilgamesh is found on several cuneiform tablets on which cuneiform was pressed into wet clay tablets and then dried and roasted. Because of breakage of the tablets, the scholars often have to guess the meaning of words.

The “field in area mentioned” refers to the size of the deck and is one IKU – the old Babylonian area unit, equaling the English acre (4046 square meters). This is double the size mentioned in the Bible.

I laid out its (interior) structure and drew a picture of it (?).
I provided it with six decks,
thus dividing it into seven (levels).
The inside of it I divided into nine (compartments).

In the Bible only three decks are mentioned. Interestingly these decks are also said to have been divided into several rooms. As we have mentioned before, it was quite unique to build a ship with rooms as on Noah’s Ark. This wasn’t done again until much later.

Noah / Utnapishtim continues:

I drove plugs (to keep out) water in its middle part.
I saw to the punting poles and laid in what was necessary.
Three times 3,600 (units) of raw bitumen I poured into the bitumen kiln,
three times 3,600 (units of) pitch ...into it,
there were three times 3,600 porters of
casks who carried (vegetable) oil,
apart from the 3,600 (units of) oil which they consumed (!)
and two times 3,600 (units of) oil which
the boatman stored away.

Also in this Sumerian poem, it is mentioned that the Ark was smeared with bitumen and asphalt just as does the information in the Bible.

I butchered ox for meat(!),
and day after day I slaughtered sheep.
I gave the workmen(?) ale, beer, oil, and wine, as if it were river water,
so they could make a party like the New Year’s Festival.
... and I set my hand to the oiling(!).
The boat was finished by sunset.
The launching was very difficult.
They had to keep carrying a runway of poles front to back,
until two-thirds of it had gone into the water(?).
Whatever I had I loaded on it:
whatever silver I had I loaded on it,
whatever gold I had I loaded on it.
All the living beings that I had I loaded on it,

I had all my kith and kin go up into the boat,
all the beasts and animals of the field
and the craftsmen I had go up.

Shamash had set a stated time:
'In the morning I will let loaves of bread shower down,
and in the evening a rain of wheat!
Go inside the boat, seal the entry!'
That stated time had arrived.
In the morning he let loaves of bread shower down,
and in the evening a rain of wheat.
I watched the appearance of the weather—
the weather was frightful to behold!
I went into the boat and sealed the entry.
For the caulking of the boat, to Puzuramurri, the boatman,
I gave the palace together with its contents.
Just as dawn began to glow
there arose from the horizon a black cloud.
Adad rumbled inside of it,
before him went Shullat and Hanish,
heralds going over mountain and land.
Erragal pulled out the mooring poles,
forth went Ninurta and made the dikes overflow.
The Anunnaki lifted up the torches,
setting the land ablaze with their flare.
Stunned shock over Adad's deeds overtook the heavens,
and turned to blackness all that had been light.
The... land shattered like a... pot.

A sample of the approximately 3700 year-old Atrahasis Plate, which has been found in Sippar southwest of Baghdad. It tells of a man who survived a mighty flood because he built a ship. The plate is now in the British Museum in London.

The South Wind

All day long the South Wind blew ...,
blowing fast, submerging the mountain in water,
overwhelming the people like an attack.

Again a special point worth noticing is in the first line it reads: "All day long the South Wind blew..." – and if Noah's boat was to drift from Shuruppak in Iraq to the Mountains of Ararat in the north, it had to blow from the south. Utnapishtim continues:

No one could see his fellow,
they could not recognize each other in the torrent.
The gods were frightened by the Flood,
and retreated, ascending to the heaven of Anu.
The gods were cowering like dogs,

crouching by the outer wall.
Ishtar shrieked like a woman in childbirth,
the sweet-voiced Mistress of the Gods wailed:
'The olden days have alas turned to clay,
because I said evil things in the Assembly of the Gods!
How could I say evil things in the Assembly of the Gods,
ordering a catastrophe to destroy my people!!
No sooner have I given birth to my dear people
than they fill the sea like so many fish!'
The gods—those of the Anunnaki—were weeping with her,
the gods humbly sat weeping, sobbing with grief(?),
their lips burning, parched with thirst.
Six days and seven nights
came the wind and flood, the storm flattening the land.
When the seventh day arrived, the storm was pounding,
the flood was at war—struggling with itself like a woman writhing (in labor).

The sea calmed, fell still,
the whirlwind (and) flood stopped up.
I looked around all day long—quiet had set in
and all the human beings had turned to clay!
The terrain was as flat as a roof.

The Boat Grounds on Nisir

I opened a vent and fresh air (daylight!)
fell upon the side of my nose.
I fell to my knees and sat weeping,
tears streaming down the side of my nose.
I looked around for coastlines in the expanse of the sea,
and at twelve leagues there emerged a region (of land).
On Mt. Nimush the boat lodged firm,
Mt. Nimush held the boat, allowing no sway.
One day and a second Mt. Nimush held the boat,
allowing no sway.
A third day, a fourth, Mt. Nimush held the boat,
allowing no sway.
A fifth day, a sixth, Mt. Nimush held the boat,
allowing no sway.

Has Nisir Been Found?

Utnapishtim tells Gilgamesh that the Ark grounded on Nimush. Previously this has been read as Nisir or Mount Nisir; now it is translated as Nimush.[7] But the word KUR, meaning mountain, in line 140 in tablet XI, "a-na KUR ni-ir i-te-mid GIŠ eleppu" doesn't mean mountain in Sumerian but rather hill or countryside or area.

Robert M. Best, who wrote a book in which he claims the story of the Ark to be nothing more than a localized flood of the Euphrates River,[8] translates this line to read "in country Nisir grounded wooden boat."

And he goes even further to argue that the Ark landed on a sandbank or an elevated surface! This however, seems to do injustice to the text in order to make it fit one's own hypothesis.

A Mesopotamian illustrated seal shows The Tree of Life which gives eternal life. The Tree of Life is known from the Bible as Paradise.

The Dove and the Raven

Utnaphisthim continues:

When a seventh day arrived
I sent forth a dove and released it.
The dove went off, but came back to me;
no perch was visible so it circled back to me.
I sent forth a swallow and released it.
The swallow went off, but came back to me;
no perch was visible so it circled back to me.
I sent forth a raven and released it.
The raven went off, and saw the waters slither back.
It eats, it scratches, it bobs, but does not circle back to me.
Then I sent out everything in all directions and sacrificed (a sheep).
I offered incense in front of the mountain-ziggurat.
Seven and seven cult vessels I put in place,
and (into the fire) underneath (or: into their bowls)
I poured reeds, cedar, and myrtle.
The gods smelled the savor,
the gods smelled the sweet savor,
and collected like flies over a (sheep) sacrifice.

After this, a discussion breaks out among the gods, whereupon Enlil is requested never to send a flood of such magnitude again.

Enlil blesses Utnapishtim and turns him into a half-god.

Tree of Life

Utnapishtim then gives Gilgamesh a test. He is not to sleep for 7 days and 6 nights. He fails. The epic ends with Gilgamesh taking a bath and being sent home. He is given *a plant* that will give him *eternal life*, but a snake eats it on the journey home – a clear parallel to the serpent in the Garden of Eden.

At long last he comes to his hometown Uruk, which, it is noted, was established by the "Seven Sages," and he himself has reinforced the walls.[9] Uruk, or Erek as it is called in the Bible, may very well be a rebuilt town from before the flood. According to Berosus the first generations after the flood went back to the towns in Iraq that had been buried in order to rebuild them.

The Same Event

Despite the religious context, in Utnapishtim's account we find the same events as those in the biblical narrative of Noah.

1. The gods are/ God is angered by evil.
2. Both Utnapishtim and Noah are warned of impending disaster.
3. Both Utnapishtim and Noah are to build a boat to save life on earth.
4. The boat consists of numerous levels and is caulked with pitch.
5. The boat is lodged on a mountain.
6. Both Utnapishtim and Noah open a hatch.
7. Both Utnapishtim and Noah send out a dove and a raven.
8. Both make sacrifices to God/the gods.

Regardless of the differences, there can be no doubt that these stories are referring to the same incident.

Are Atrahasis and Ziusudra Older?

Even older accounts can be found. In Akkadian, the main character is named Atrahasis (the extra wise). Even further back, we find the Sumerian narrative of Ziusudra. The original version has been lost, but copies that were written down later still exist.

It is up for debate whether the Bible's or the Sumerian-Akkadian account is older. As far as we know, Genesis was written after the first clay tablets were; this, however, is not decisive since both are preceded by long *oral* traditions.

The story Moses tells, though, is more objective and precise. It doesn't give a picture of the supernatural in detail but only mentions God as the one behind it all. Moses, as an Egyptian prince, most likely had access to the libraries of Pharaoh and the wise men as well as Hebraic oral tradition.

What's important is not which was written down first but rather that they *confirm* each other. Various phrases are so identical that there can be no doubt that they are talking about the same flood. When this story is found in the first Mesopotamian civilizations – and most other ancient civilizations, for that matter – it suggests that we're dealing with the same great universal catastrophe.

The story of the Flood is an inheritance the various ethnic groups took with them when they spread out from the Mountains of Ararat and the plain of Sinear throughout all the Earth by land and sea.

The Bible is not the only source that speaks about this kind of ethnic population spreading (in connection with the Tower of Babel). William Ryan & Walter Pitman points in their book that all Indo-European languages can be traced back to one single proto-indoeuropean language that came out of this region.[10]

The linguists Thomas V. Gamkrelidze and V.V. Ivanovs had traced all the Indo-European languages back to their starting point in Armenia – i.e. back to the Mountains of Urartu, the Ararat Mountains – to the place where Gilgamesh probably found Utnapishtim and the purpose of his life.[11]

Endnotes

[1] *Gilgamesh – Enuma Elish. Guder og mennesker i oldtidens Babylon*. (Gods and huimans in Ancient Babylonia) By Ulla and Aage Westenholz, Carsten Niebuhr Institute at the University of Copenhagen. Spektrum Publishers, 1995.

[2] In Mesopotamia there is also evidence of earlier habitations – the Ubaid culture (potsherds, temples, knowledge of iron) c. 3900 BC and the Warka culture (the so-called Proliterate period) c. 3600 BC. If these datings are correct and if the time of the Flood is correct, they have consequently belonged to the culture BEFORE the flooding. Utnapishtim (Noah) actually mentions in the Gilgamesh poem that before the flooding he used to live by Euphrates in the town of Shuruppak. According to the Bible civilization before the flooding dates back to c. 7793 BC.

3 Some believe the "firmament in the midst of the waters" spoken of in Genesis 1:6-8 to be a layer of steam in the thermosphere which filtered cosmic radiation out causing humans to age more slowly than after the Flood. Inside of this „bubble" the Earth would be like a greenhouse where people, plants, and animals would have lived longer and grown larger. This theory may also explain the monsters of the past like the dinosaurs and mammoths, which were only found in prehistory.

[4] We will be quoting from an online translation, which can be found at the following address http://www.ancienttexts.org/library/mesopotamian/gilgamesh/

A parenthesis ( ) shows that part of the tablet is missing, while a (word) in parenthesis shows that the translator has inserted a word that is known from another version.

[5] According to Fasold, Ark-Update May – June 1991.

[6] David Fasold: *The Ark of Noah*, chapter 5.

[7] An other translation reads: "To the country of Nizir, went the ship; the mountain of Nizir stopped the ship, and to pass over it, it was not able. The first day and the second day, the mountain of Nizir the same. The third day and the fourth day, the mountain of Nizir the same. The fifth and sixth, the mountain of Nizir the same." (The Chaldean Account of the Deluge by George Smith.)

[8] Robert M. Best, *Noah's Ark and the Ziusudra Epic, Sumerian Origins of the Flood Myth*. (Enlil Press).

[9] According to David Fasold's theory these "Seven Sages" may be the seven ancestors in Kain's tribe who were exterminated together with the Flood. As is well known Cain was the first murderer – he killed his brother Abel and was exiled to the country called Nod – east of Eden.

[10] Noah's flood – The new scientific discoveries about the event that changed history by William Ryan & Walter Pitman. Simon & Schuste, New York.

[11] Published in Scientific American – see: rbedrosian.com/Classic/sciam1.htm eller Indo-European and the Indo-Europeans: A Reconstruction and Historical Typological Analysis of a Protolanguage and Proto-Culture. Parts I and II. Thomas V. Gamkrelidze and Vjacheslav V. Ivanov. Tbilisi State University, 1984.

The author with the Dutchman Johan Huibers aboard his Noah's Ark I.

Chapter 41

The Man Who Built an Ark in the Netherlands

In 1992 Johan Huibers took a walk along the beach with his son Roy. The following night he dreamed that The Netherlands would be flooded.

Next morning he shared this dream with his wife Bianca. When she went to pick up the kids from school, a cousin told her that he had dreamed that The Netherlands would be flooded too.

When Johan on the same day was restoring a shop called Noah's Ark, he saw a book titled *Honor Who Deserves Honor.* The book contains pictures of animals from Noah's Ark. That night Johan was convinced that he should build an ark.

Became a Christian as a Young Man

Johan Huibers is an engineer and lives in The Netherlands, but for many years he has worked on development projects. For example, he drilled for water for the peoples of Ethiopia. Already as a 21-year-old, he felt a calling to help people in developing countries.

"As a youngster I was not a Christian," he says, while we sit on the upper deck in his version of Noah's ark. The big boat is at the dock in Kampen, 100 km north of Amsterdam.

"I sometimes talked with some people who were Christians, and I was very interested in what they said. When they would tell me something, I said, 'We can talk about it next week.' Then I went home and researched it in the Bible. And eventually I became convinced that it was the truth. One day I saw a poster for a documentary about the organization called Dorcas Aid in Africa. I went to see the movie, but there was no one except me."

"Should we cancel it, or do you want to see the movie?" the organizers asked me.

"I'd like to see it," I answered, and they showed the movie just for me. The movie made such a big impression on me that I joined as a volunteer.

Prophecy of a Deluge

Later Johan married Bianca, and they had three children. They lived abroad regularly, and the children had an international upbringing. As a construction manager, Johan himself got involved in building some of the major dikes off the coast of The Netherlands. Most of The Netherlands is below sea level, so without the dikes most of the country would be flooded.

"Do you think that your dream was a vision of something that is going to happen?" I ask Johan.

"I'm sure," he says without hesitation and begins to draw on my paper. "And I know exactly how it will happen. See here between the big dike and the countryside, builders have built a dike of metal plates on a six kilometer stretch. But there is nothing behind the plates to resist if the water goes through the dikes. I've seen when there are storm surges. The sea may hammer and throw huge boulders ashore during a storm. They are such enormous forces that it is hard to imagine. The iron plates will collapse. And if it just happens at one place, everything will fall down, and the water will flow in and flood the whole of northern The Netherlands where we live."

"Was this what you saw in the dream?" I asked.

"Yes," he answers seriously. "And when I thought about it, it was obvious.

Johan Huiber's second edition of Noah's Ark in full-size (bottom) is able to sail around the world - in contrast to the first ship half the size, which was built as an exhibition ship. Half a million visitors have already been aboard the Ark where the Bible story's highlights are told.

I am a builder, and I've even worked on the dam. Of course it will happen."

14 Years of Preparation

Now, Johan isn't a dreamer but a serious builder. After the dream in 1992, he spent 14 years preparing to obtain permits and save money before he began building the ark in 2006. In 20 weeks he was busy sawing wood; 1200 trees from Belgium, Germany, and The Netherlands were required. The outer hull is made of cedar and the inner hull of soft pine. Johan spent 1 ½ years building the ark, mostly alone, sometimes with help from his son Roy. Later, volunteers joined him. In April 2007, the boat was finished and opened to the public. For the first three months, it was placed in Schagen (North The Netherlands), the place where it had been built. While in Schagen, it was visited by 50,000 visitors. After a short period, the number of visitors reached more than half a million, explains Johan's daughter, Deborah, who heads the volunteer guides onboard.

Guided Tour in the World of the Bible

Deborah takes me on an exciting tour. First, we pass some large artificial animals:

"Dad and I were in Hollywood to see how they build scenery, laughs Deborah, who is equally committed to Noah's Ark as her father.

"The animals aboard are made of polyester. We've got them from the Philippines. Most of them are in full body size, as you can see. There are also many stuffed animals, some of which have been donated to us, and others we have purchased ourselves."

"It must have cost a lot of money to build the ark?"

"Yes, about one million dollars in materials. But now we've got the money back because of the many visitors. And now the money is being spent to build a new version of the Ark in the right size. This ark is only in half size. It is 70 meters long, 9.5 meters wide and nearly 14 meters tall. And it has an iron hook in the wood, she explains, and knocks on the hull. If we had not built it like this, we would only be allowed to have approximately 100 visitors on board – but now we can have 700.

Follow the Elephant Tracks!

"When the new ark will be ready, it will be able to sail around the world and get people to think of God," says Johan's daughter, pointing to some painted elephant footprints on the floor.

"These elephant footprints lead visitors through the Ark exhibitions. First you will be lead down to the lower deck where there is a cinema with space for approximately 150 people. The film runs continuously, telling the story of the Flood."

The "new ark" to which Deborah refers was finished in June 2010 but was delayed due to the lack of a sailing permit. Huiber's first ark was built as an exposition ship that wasn't intended for or approved for sailing. The new ark will be approved as a coaster and was invited to the Olympic Games in London in 2012, as it is also going to sail as an exhibition ship in other European harbors. It has been built in full size of approximately 135 meters long in Dordrecht in the Netherlands. (Some believe that the ark should actually be 157 meters as the Egyptian cubits were longer than the English ones.) The millions of dollars for the new large ark have partly been acquired by ticket sales from the first ark and from gifts and loans.[1]

Experience the Flood!

Having visited the cinema, we pass an imitation of the Deluge, whichwas designed especially for children. Here they can test what happens when the water gushes out. On the walls above it there are paintings by the Dutch artist Peter Spier. They show the chronology of what happened during the Flood. The last one is a beautiful picture that illustrates hope and new beginnings. Here is a fishing boat which is to remind us of the day when Jesus made the storm subside on the Sea of Galilee.

We go into the next room where we find Abraham, Isaac, and Jacob's tent. It is meant to show the way people lived in the Middle East in biblical times. Here is also Gideon's sheepskin, which children can touch.

"Gideon asked God for a sign as an answer to his question about whether he was the chosen one to lead Israel out of Midian captivity or not. The first time he prayed, the grass was dry and the wool was wet; next time it was the opposite. He knew then for certain that God had called him for this task. God can use people who are not leaning against their own strength. He does not ask if we are fit; only if we are available, explains Deborah, while moving on to Joseph's cave.

The Ark of the Covenant

The Ark of the Covenant with the Ten Commandments has been made by Johan Huibers himself according to drawings of how the box is believed to have looked like with two cherubs. The Ark of the Covenant is now gone. Many adventurers are looking for it.

We proceed to an imitation of Jesus' tomb from Gordon's Garden Tomb in Jerusalem. Inside is a production of the Nativity in Bethlehem. Then there is also a wooden cottage that could belong to the tax collector Zacchaeus. And an "eye of a needle" – i.e. a small narrow door in the wall which a camel cannot go through.

Here are the water troughs from Cana where Jesus turned water into wine. And a scarlet rope tells the story of the prostitute Rahab, who hid the two Jewish spies in the city of Jericho. The last Bible story in this room tells of Paul's escape over the wall in a basket. After walking up the stairs you pass a lamb along with some lions, which refers to an era of peace and to Jesus, called "The Lion of Judah" and "The

Shipbuilder Johan Huibers and his daughter Deborah study the book "Noah's Ark Uncovered" at the upper deck.

Lamb" which was sacrificed for our sins .

Science and the Biblical Story

On the next deck there is a scientific presentation of the Flood and Creation. The Biblical story is compared to evolutionary theory, and Deborah shakes her head a little about what she was conned to believe in school about the apes, etc.

In Noah's cabin one gets some idea of the time that Noah and his family spent on the Ark: A total of 372 days! Across from the cabin is an informative DVD presentation, where Rod Walsh from Australia tells of facts, figures, and size of the real Ark, etc.

There are many other DVD presentations – for all age groups. Here one can learn more about the facts connected to the Flood and Creation of Earth.

"We also had The Netherland's first presentation of the new funny movie about Noah's Ark, *Evan Almighty* aboard the ship, says Deborah.

The film Evan Almighty is a modern ecological Noahs Ark story.

An Intelligent Designer

At the other side of the bridge, a film titled *Life's Story* reveals a lot about DNA and the patterns seen in Creation. All together it is something that suggests an intelligent design rather than coincidence. And an intelligent creator as well. Here one also sees fossils with an explanation of how they were buried under the Deluge and how they prove that we live on a "young earth", the opposite theory of evolution claiming ages of millions of years, yes, even billions of years. The fossils result from particular pressure under particular conditions. Another DVD shows a tour of the Ark led by the developer Johan Huibers. We meet him again on the upper deck where a cafeteria has been established. There are also stuffed birds, and on the wall one sees "The Biblical Chronology of History" with the entire lineage from Adam to Jesus Christ. It also displays a Dead Sea scroll. Children can draw and paint here and there is a reading corner where grandparents can tell Bible stories for children. Standing on the top deck, you get an idea of how big the ark is. It was necessary to have open windows to get fresh air for animals and personnel. The exterior water barrel was used to collect fresh water. There are many more practical things that we normally don't give a thought but which were necessary to keep people and animals alive.

"Like the Days of Noah…"

"Why did you build the ark?" we ask the captain Johan on the upper deck.

"Not to literally rescue animals and people from the coming Flood, but to get people of today to just think about life. Many children and young people do not know the Bible story, but here it is brought to life for both children and adults," says Johan, smiling at the thought of the positive feedback he has received.

"The Bible says[2] that a time like Noah's time will come when people think they can live without God. This leads to chaos, injustice and war. God wants us to live in harmony and peace with each other and with hope for the future. He has a plan for us that we may spend eternity with Him where there will be no death, disease or suffering.

"We do not know how much time we have left to decide upon God by faith in Jesus Christ. We hope that the ark will help someone to realize that they should not wait too long, says Johan.

Endnotes

1 The Dutch Noah project's homepage is: www.arkvannoach.com

2 In Matthew 24:37-41 Jesus says: "For the coming of the Son of Man will be just like the days of Noah. For as in those days before the flood they were eating and drinking, marrying and giving in marriage, until the day that Noah entered the ark, and they did not understand until the flood came and took them all away; so will the coming of the Son of Man be.
Then there will be two men in the field; one will be taken and one will be left. Two women (will be) grinding at the mill; one will be taken and one will be left."

Postscript

Has The Ark Been Found?

Has The Ark finally been found?

Well, judge for yourself from the information you have just received and then follow up on the exploration of the fantastic discovery on Mount Ararat that will be carried out in the years to come.

I hope that this book has led to a new and more exiting understanding of our common past than the one we are incessantly indoctrinated with via the obsolete theories of the evolution of the species and the endlessly slow change of everything through billions of years.

Theories that will hopefully soon fall, so that research will finally be free from having to view everything through the cloudy optics of this outdated theory that attempts to reduce all alternative theories to stupidity.

I hope my book will, in some small way, help to make this the case.

There Was a Deluge...

Whether you are now convinced that Noah's Ark has really been found or not, I hope to have made plausible the idea, that there actually was a worldwide catastrophe at least once in history, namely the Deluge. As we have seen, it isn't only the Bible that speaks about it, but almost all the ancient civilisations of the world. It is mutual heritage. We all originate from the highland of the Ararat.

And our ancestors weren't primitive apes swinging their clubs – but they created highly developed civilisations that were in some respects superior to ours.

Can We Trust the Bible?

I hope that it has become clear that the Bible is, in fact, *surprisingly trustworthy* when compared to other sources. And as the archaeological expert *Dr. Nelson Glueck* put it, "No archaeological discovery has ever questioned a biblical reference. Scores of archaeological finds have been made that confirm the broad outline and the exact detailed historical information of the Bible. And for the same reason, thorough examinations of biblical descriptions have often led to astonishing discoveries."[1]

In spite of all criticism of the Bible, experience shows that we can believe in its historical information as well as its eternally valid truths about the human condition - before, now, and in the future.

Endnotes

1 **Dr. Nelson Glueck** excavated some archeological sites in Jordan and 500 in the desert of Negev. He located Solomon's copper mines, the place near the Red Sea where Solomon met the Queen of Sheba, and much more by comparing the facts found in the Bible with archeological knowledge. In 1963 he was pictured on the cover of Time Magazine.

Thanks

Finally I would like to thank you who have read the whole book and attempted to accompany me through its 40 chapters. It is for you, after all, that I have written the book.

You are very welcome to write to me, the author, if you have information or questions that I may be able to answer. Write to henri@nissen.mail.dk

There are also a great number of people to whom I owe thanks for their co-operation on my first Noah book – *Noah's Ark Uncovered* – which, due to the Kurdish-Chinese discovery is now republished in a totally revised edition.

This applies to the artist *Elfred Lee*, who gave an interview and his permission to use the photos from his search for Noah's Ark and the beautiful paintings he made from eyewitnesses' accounts.

Bill Fry for permission to use photos from his homepage and historical photos for which he obtained the copyright from the late Ron Wyatt.

Elin Berglund for co-operation on travels and for materials of Ron Wyatt.

Dr. John Baumgardner and *Dr. Salih Bayraktutan* for interviews, photos, and illustrations from their scientific research of the boat-shaped object.

Dr. Robert Michelson for his benevolence in giving me information, photos, and illustrations from his personal research.

David A. Deal for photos and illustrations from his research.

Viveka Ponten for information and photos.

Prof. Hans Otto Kristensen for the interview and cooperation.

Dr. Lennart Möller for photos from his book *Exodus*.

In connection with this new book I especially want to thank *Panda Lee, Wing Cheung Yeung, Clara Wei, and Ricky and Gerrit Aalten* for interviews, information, and photos. Unfortunately, I didn't succeed in obtaining an interview with *Parasut*, neither in The Netherlands, Dogubayazit or Istanbul, but thanks for your kind text messages.

Thanks to the mountaineers *Erik Futtrup* og *Frede Donskov* for photos from Mt. Ararat. Thanks also to *Tracy Skondin, Dorthe Orbesen, Irene Kjædegaard, and Anne Clark* for great assistance with editing and translation.

Thanks to publisher *Jørgen Vium Olesen* for his enthusiastic support and understanding, in spite of deadlines that had to be changed more than once.

Thanks to my sons *Henrik*, who accompanied me to Turkey to make video recordings and *John*, who accompanied me and recorded the video in the Netherlands. Thanks to my daughter *Maj-Britt*, who has always encouraged me, and my dear wife *Birthe*, who was patient and understanding even when I worked for 10-18 hours a day for several months.

I think it was worth it.

Henri Nissen
Christiansfeld, Denmark. April 2012.